EARLY CHILDHOOD EDUCATION 97/98

Eighteenth Edition

Editors

Karen Menke Paciorek
Eastern Michigan University

Karen Menke Paciorek is an associate professor of Early Childhood Education at Eastern Michigan University in Ypsilanti. She has degrees in early childhood education from the University of Pittsburgh, George Washington University, and Peabody College of Vanderbilt University. She is past president of the 4,500-member Michigan Association for the Education of Young Children. Dr. Paciorek presents at local and national conferences on a variety of topics, including curriculum planning, establishing a quality learning environment, and guiding young children's behavior

Joyce Huth ▮

Joyce Huth Munro does consulting and editorial wo▮ ▮ the
Professional Development Advisory Panel of the Natic▮ ▮ Young
Children. She has been an administrator and professc ▮▮▮, ▮outh Carolina,
and New Jersey. Currently, she is an editor for a teaching cases series and coeditor (with Karen Menke Paciorek) of another Dushkin/McGraw-Hill publication, *Sources: Notable Selections in Early Childhood Education*. At regional and national conferences, she presents seminars on innovative methods of teacher education and curriculum design. Dr. Munro holds an M.Ed. from the University of South Carolina and a Ph.D. from Peabody College at Vanderbilt University.

Annual Editions
A Library of Information from the Public Press
Dushkin/McGraw·Hill
Sluice Dock, Guilford, Connecticut 06437

The Annual Editions Series

ANNUAL EDITIONS is a series of over 65 volumes designed to provide the reader with convenient, low-cost access to a wide range of current, carefully selected articles from some of the most important magazines, newspapers, and journals published today. ANNUAL EDITIONS are updated on an annual basis through a continuous monitoring of over 300 periodical sources. All ANNUAL EDITIONS have a number of features that are designed to make them particularly useful, including topic guides, annotated tables of contents, unit overviews, and indexes. For the teacher using ANNUAL EDITIONS in the classroom, an Instructor's Resource Guide with test questions is available for each volume.

VOLUMES AVAILABLE

Abnormal Psychology
Adolescent Psychology
Africa
Aging
American Foreign Policy
American Government
American History, Pre-Civil War
American History, Post-Civil War
American Public Policy
Anthropology
Archaeology
Biopsychology
Business Ethics
Child Growth and Development
China
Comparative Politics
Computers in Education
Computers in Society
Criminal Justice
Criminology
Developing World
Deviant Behavior
Drugs, Society, and Behavior
Dying, Death, and Bereavement

Early Childhood Education
Economics
Educating Exceptional Children
Education
Educational Psychology
Environment
Geography
Global Issues
Health
Human Development
Human Resources
Human Sexuality
India and South Asia
International Business
Japan and the Pacific Rim
Latin America
Life Management
Macroeconomics
Management
Marketing
Marriage and Family
Mass Media
Microeconomics

Middle East and the
  Islamic World
Multicultural Education
Nutrition
Personal Growth and Behavior
Physical Anthropology
Psychology
Public Administration
Race and Ethnic Relations
Russia, the Eurasian Republics,
  and Central/Eastern Europe
Social Problems
Social Psychology
Sociology
State and Local Government
Urban Society
Western Civilization,
  Pre-Reformation
Western Civilization,
  Post-Reformation
Western Europe
World History, Pre-Modern
World History, Modern
World Politics

Cataloging in Publication Data
Main entry under title: Annual editions: Early Childhood Education. 1997/98.
       1. Education, Preschool—Periodicals. 2. Child development—Periodicals. 3. Child rearing—United States—Periodicals. I. Paciorek, Karen Menke, *comp.;* Munro, Joyce Huth, *comp.* II. Title: Early Childhood Education.
       ISBN 0–697–37251–0   372.21′05   77–640114

© 1997 by Dushkin/McGraw·Hill, Guilford, CT 06437, A Division of The McGraw·Hill Companies.

Eighteenth Edition

Cover image © 1996 PhotoDisc, Inc.

Printed in the United States of America

Printed on Recycled Paper

Editors/Advisory Board

Members of the Advisory Board are instrumental in the final selection of articles for each edition of ANNUAL EDITIONS. Their review of articles for content, level, currentness, and appropriateness provides critical direction to the editor and staff. We think that you will find their careful consideration well reflected in this volume.

EDITORS

Karen Menke Paciorek
Eastern Michigan University

Joyce Huth Munro

ADVISORY BOARD

Staff

To the Reader

In publishing ANNUAL EDITIONS we recognize the enormous role played by the magazines, newspapers, and journals of the *public press* in providing current, first-rate educational information in a broad spectrum of interest areas. Many of these articles are appropriate for students, researchers, and professionals seeking accurate, current material to help bridge the gap between principles and theories and the real world. These articles, however, become more useful for study when those of lasting value are carefully *collected, organized, indexed,* and *reproduced* in a *low-cost format,* which provides easy and permanent access when the material is needed. That is the role played by ANNUAL EDITIONS. Under the direction of each volume's *academic editor,* who is an expert in the subject area, and with the guidance of an *Advisory Board,* each year we seek to provide in each ANNUAL EDITION a current, well-balanced, carefully selected collection of the best of the public press for your study and enjoyment. We think that you will find this volume useful, and we hope that you will take a moment to let us know what you think.

Early childhood education is an interdisciplinary field that includes child development, family issues, educational practices, behavior guidance, and curriculum. *Annual Editions: Early Childhood Education 97/98* brings you the latest information on the field from a wide variety of recent journals, newspapers, and magazines. In making the selections of articles, we were careful to provide the reader with a well-balanced look at the issues and concerns facing teachers, families, society, and children. This edition begins with a historical look at the American family and how changes in family life have brought changes for the early childhood profession.

The three themes found in readings chosen for this eighteenth edition of *Annual Editions: Early Childhood Education* are (1) the changes occurring in America's families, (2) collaborative efforts between families and schools on a variety of issues, and (3) curriculum planning that is a joint effort between children and teachers, leading to many opportunities for exploration and discovery.

The lead articles in units 1 and 6 both address the American family. Unit 6 begins with Stephanie Coontz's article "Where Are the Good Old Days?" It is based on her award-winning book *The Way We Never Were: American Families and the Nostalgia Trap* (Basic Books, 1992).

In the same unit, we are pleased to bring you the articles "Movers and Shapers of Early Childhood Education" and "Child Advocacy Directory," both from *Child Care Information Exchange.* It is important to be familiar with those who have gone before us and are continuing to make major contributions to our profession. Next time you are in the library, seek out more information on these outstanding individuals and organizations. Many of the leaders have touched our lives and continue to serve as inspiration to work even harder. The staff at the listed agencies are always willing to provide information for the interested educator or parent.

Given the wide range of topics it includes, *Annual Editions: Early Childhood Education 97/98* may be used with several groups: undergraduate or graduate students studying early childhood education, profession-als pursuing further development, or parents seeking to improve their skills.

The selection of readings for this edition has been a cooperative effort between the two editors. We meet each year with members of our advisory board, who share with us in the selection process. The production and editorial staff of Dushkin/ McGraw-Hill ably support and coordinate our efforts.

To the instructor or reader interested in the history of early childhood care and education programs throughout the years, we invite you to review our latest book, also published by Dushkin/McGraw-Hill. *Sources: Notable Selections in Early Childhood Education* (1996) is a collection of numerous writings of enduring historical value by influential people in the field. All of the selections are primary sources and therefore allow the reader to experience firsthand the thoughts and views of these important educators. The instructor interested in using both *Sources* and *Annual Editions* may contact the editors for a list of compatible articles from the two books.

We are grateful to readers who have corresponded with us about the selection and organization of previous editions. Your comments and articles for consideration are welcomed and will serve to modify future volumes. Please take the time to fill out and return the postage-paid *article rating form* on the last page. You may also contact either one of us on-line at: **ted_paciorek@online.emich.edu** or **jhmunro@aol.com**

We look forward to hearing from you.

Karen Menke Paciorek

Joyce Huth Munro
Editors

Contents

UNIT 1

Perspectives

Six selections consider both the national and international development of early childhood education.

The concepts in bold italics are developed in the article. For further expansion please refer to the Topic Guide and the Index.

UNIT 2

Child Development and Families

Seven selections consider the effects of family life on the growing child and the importance of parent education.

The concepts in bold italics are developed in the article. For further expansion please refer to the Topic Guide and the Index.

UNIT 3

Educational Practices

Eight selections examine various educational programs, assess the effectiveness of some teaching methods, and consider some of the problems faced by students with special needs.

The concepts in bold italics are developed in the article. For further expansion please refer to the Topic Guide and the Index.

UNIT 4

Guiding and Supporting Young Children

Seven selections examine the importance of establishing self-esteem in the child and consider the effects of stressors and stress reduction on behavior.

The concepts in bold italics are developed in the article. For further expansion please refer to the Topic Guide and the Index.

UNIT 5

Curricular Issues

Ten selections consider various curricular choices. The areas covered include creating, inventing, emergent literacy, motor development, and conceptualizing curriculum.

UNIT 6

Reflections

Six selections consider the
present and future of early
childhood education.

Selected World Wide Web Sites for Early Childhood Education

(This is just a small sampling of the many World Wide Web sites that are timely and informative to students and professionals involved in early childhood education. Some Web sites are continually changing their structure and content, so the information listed here may not always be available.)

American Academy of Pediatrics

http://www.aap.org/ This organization provides data for optimal physical, mental, and social health for all children.

Child Care Resource Center, Inc. (CCRC)

http://dialin1.wing.net/~ccrc.aol.html CCRC is a private not-for-profit agency that provides referral information throughout the United States to ensure that all families have access to quality, affordable child care.

Child Welfare League of America (CWLA)

http://www.handsnet.org/cwla/ Providing a wide range of services to support and strengthen families for children, CWLA is the nation's oldest and largest organization devoted to the well-being of children.

Children's Defense Fund (CDF)

http://www.childrensdefense.org CDF provides data on key children's issues involving child care and Head Start. It also monitors the implementation and development of federal and state policies.

Classroom Connect

http://www.classroom.net/classroom/ This site provides data on K–12 educational resources as well as online discussions with educators.

Education Resources Information Center (ERIC)

http://ericir.syr.edu/ ERIC provides a variety of services and products on a broad range of education-related issues. Data on research information, lesson plans, digests, and journal articles are available.

Macomb Projects

http://www.mprojects.win/edu/ This research and development unit, located in the College of Education and Human Services at West Illinois University in Macomb, IL, is directed toward improving educational opportunities for children ages birth through eight, with mild and severe disabilities, their families, and staff.

National Association for the Education of Young Children (NAEYC)

http://www.america.tomorrow.com/naeyc/ NAEYC promotes improvements in professional practice and working conditions in all family child care homes, early childhood programs, and centers.

National Child Care Information Center

http://ericps.ed.uiuc.edu/nccic/nccichome.html/ The Child Care Bureau, one of several divisions of this group, was established to administer federal child care programs for low-income children and families.

U.S. Department of Education

http://www.ed.gov/ Hosted by the National Library of Education (NLE), this Web site provides information about offices and programs of the U.S. Department of Education, education initiatives, reports, and publications, as well as federal grand money. A teacher's guide is also available.

We highly recommend that you check out our Web site for expanded information and our other product lines. We are continually updating and adding links to our Web site in order to offer you the most usable and useful information that will support and expand the value of your *Annual Edition.* You can reach us at *http://www.dushkin.com.*

The concepts in bold italics are developed in the article. For further expansion please refer to the Topic Guide and the Index.

Topic Guide

This topic guide suggests how the selections in this book relate to topics of traditional concern to students and professionals involved with early childhood education. It is useful for locating articles that relate to each other for reading and research. The guide is arranged alphabetically according to topic. Articles may, of course, treat topics that do not appear in the topic guide. In turn, entries in the topic guide do not necessarily constitute a comprehensive listing of all the contents of each selection.

TOPIC AREA	TREATED IN	TOPIC AREA	TREATED IN
Abuse	24. Breaking the Cycle of Violence	Developmentally Appropriate Practice	6. NAEYC Position Statement: Technology and Young Children
Advocacy	11. Families and Schools		15. Bringing the DAP Message to Kindergarten and Primary Teachers
	42. Child Advocacy Directory		16. Fourth-Grade Slump
Assessment	19. Seven Ways of Being Smart		17. Strategies for Teaching Children in Multiage Classrooms
	20. Profile of Every Child		19. Seven Ways of Being Smart
	21. Your Learning Environment		34. Worksheet Dilemma
	38. How Good Is Your Early Childhood Science, Mathematics, and Technology Program?		35. Framework for Literacy
		Discipline	23. Encouraging Positive Social Development
Child Care: Full Day/Half Day	1. Changing Demographics		25. Taking Positive Steps toward Classroom Management in Preschool
	5. It's Hard to Do Day Care Right—and Survive		27. Misbehavior or Mistaken Behavior?
Child Development	3. "Fly Till I Die"	Diversity	1. Changing Demographics
	6. NAEYC Position Statement: Technology and Young Children		9. Labeled for Life?
	7. Educational Implications of Developmental Transitions		30. Project Work with Diverse Students
	10. Creativity and the Child's Social Development		44. It Takes a School
	14. Understanding through Play	Divorce	1. Changing Demographics
	43. Mrs. Paley's Lessons		2. Next Baby Boom
			12. Life without Father
Collaboration	11. Families and Schools	Emergent Literacy	35. Framework for Literacy
	28. Building Successful Home/School Partnerships		37. Interactive Writing in a Primary Classroom
	42. Child Advocacy Directory		
	44. It Takes a School	Families	1. Changing Demographics
			2. Next Baby Boom
Creativity	10. Creativity and the Child's Social Development		3. "Fly Till I Die"
	30. Project Work with Diverse Students		6. NAEYC Position Statement: Technology and Young Children
			11. Families and Schools
Curriculum	14. Understanding through Play		12. Life without Father
	29. Voice of Inquiry		13. Bridging Home and School through Multiple Intelligences
	30. Project Work with Diverse Students		22. Helping Children Become More Prosocial
	31. To Build a House		28. Building Successful Home/School Partnerships
	32. Teachers and Children Together		39. Where Are the Good Old Days?
	34. Worksheet Dilemma		
	35. Framework for Literacy	Guiding Behavior	22. Helping Children Become More Prosocial
	36. Read Me a Story		23. Encouraging Positive Social Development
	38. How Good Is Your Early Childhood Science, Mathematics, and Technology Program?		25. Taking Positive Steps toward Classroom Management in Preschool
			26. Caring Classroom's Academic Edge
			27. Misbehavior or Mistaken Behavior?
		History	39. Where Are the Good Old Days?
			40. Sisterhood and Sentimentality
			41. Movers and Shapers of Early Childhood Education

Perspectives

Early childhood care and education continues to be a field that is and will be in great demand, but one that very few individuals or policy makers are committed to investing time or resources to support. The first two readings in this unit address the changes occurring in families. These changes, such as an increase in diverse family and living situations, nontraditional employment and the resulting need for extended hours of child care, and increasing economic inequality among families, will require innovative solutions.

If we are to prosper as a society, we must find ways to improve the lives of children and their families. As Cornell University Professor Urie Bronfenbrenner stated in 1970, "A society that does well by its children and parents is basically sound." When we have over 16 million children living in poverty and denied access to medical care, proper nutrition, shelter, and educational opportunities, we are not a sound society. How has the face of the American child changed over the years? Why is the poverty of today deeper and more irreversible than it was 35 years ago? We have a new generation of young children, the babies of the post–World War II baby boomers. These 72 million children are living in a world vastly different from that of their parents. One in 35 is multiracial, 27 percent live with a single parent, 5 percent live in a grandparent's home, and 46 percent of black children live in poverty. These are just some of the statistics that describe the children of the baby boomers.

With many political leaders talking of welfare reform, the key message to remember is this: Welfare reform will work only if child care works. Most people on welfare are children, and most of the adults on welfare are the mothers of those children. The current push to reform welfare and return mothers to the workforce will only be successful if the mothers have affordable, quality, and regulated or licensed child care for their children. Families who receive reimbursements so small that they can pay only for low-quality, unstimulating care will not be contributing members of the workforce. In California, parents were twice as likely to drop out of a welfare-to-work program during the first year if their children were in unlicensed and poor-quality care. Many welfare reform proponents want to skimp on the funding available for quality child care to make their reforms work. This is unwise. Quality early care and education should be the cornerstone of successful welfare reform.

Becoming a parent means making wise decisions that affect not only oneself but also young children who are unable to make effective decisions. The nationwide attention that surrounded the April 18, 1996, airplane crash that killed Jessica Dubroff, her father, Lloyd, and flight instructor Joe Reid prompted many to ask, "What kind of parent would encourage a child of seven to pilot a plane across the country? Was this something Jessica really wanted to do, or was she being pushed by adults in her life to accomplish a task that would bring her, and them, much fame and glory?" Many interesting questions are raised in the essay "Fly Till I Die." Is there a point when parents who are not making sound decisions for the safety

and well-being of their children should receive intervention? Just how far can a society go to protect children? Parents who do not seek timely and proper medical care for their children are charged with neglect. What about parents who continuously make poor child-rearing decisions?

Effective parenting and teaching require the adult to monitor a wide variety of the experiences that children encounter. This has become increasingly true today as television, video, and computer games occupy a great deal of children's time. The amount of violence a young child witnesses on a screen does affect his or her behavior. The key finding and recommendations presented in "The National Television Violence Study: Key Findings and Recommendations" lead one to conclude that television violence has increased at an alarming rate. Children do not see perpetrators of violence punished in 73 percent of violent scenes. In real life, our behavior has consequences. Children do not see those consequences on television, and are, thus, not learning the true effects of violent behavior from this medium. As violence increases in our communities, teachers, parents, and public leaders must work together to develop ways to use the media and technology we have established to entertain and educate in appropriate ways. Indeed, many teachers are beginning to see themselves not only as educators but also as strong advocates for children.

Looking Ahead: Challenge Questions

How can quality preschool programs benefit children?

What changes occurring in families will affect the care and education available in a community?

Are parents pressuring young children into adulthood?

As technology becomes more and more a part of our lives, how can it effectively be used to benefit all people?

What separates the haves from the have-nots in this new generation of baby boomers?

Changing Demographics: Past and Future Demands for Early Childhood Programs

Donald J. Hernandez

Donald J. Hernandez, Ph.D., is chief of the Marriage and Family Statistics Branch of the U.S. Bureau of the Census.

Abstract

This article provides a historical analysis of how demographic changes in the organization of American family life from the mid-1800s to the present have shaped the demand for programs to complement the efforts of families to educate and care for their children. The author asserts that the United States is in the midst of a second child care revolution. The first occurred in the late 1800s, when families left farming to enable fathers to take jobs in urban areas and when compulsory free public schooling was established for children age six and above. The second has developed over the past 55 years as the proportion of children under six living in families with two wage earners or a single working parent has escalated and propelled more and more young children into the early childhood care and education programs discussed throughout this journal issue.

Looking to the future, the author sees indications that the demand for early childhood care and education programs will continue to grow while the needs of the children to be served will become increasingly diverse. To meet these dual pressures, the author argues that public funding for early childhood programs—like funding for public schools—is justified by the value such programs have for the broader society.

Today's children are the adults—the parents, workers, and citizens—of tomorrow. Yet while they learn and develop the abilities they will need later in life, children depend almost entirely upon adults to meet their needs and to make decisions on their behalf. Key among those are decisions about the roles parents and children will take on both inside and outside the home. This article takes a historical look at how changing patterns of employment among parents have been linked to changes in children's attendance at school and out-of-home child care programs like those discussed throughout this issue.

During the past 150 years, the family economy was revolutionized twice, as fathers and then mothers left the home to spend much of the day away at jobs as family breadwinners. With these changes, with instability in fathers' work, and with increasing divorce and out-of-wedlock childbearing, never during the past half century were a majority of children born into "Ozzie and Harriet" families in which the father worked full time year round, the mother was a full-time homemaker, and all of the children were born after the parents' only marriage. Corresponding revolutions in child care occurred, as children age six and over, and then younger children, began to spend increasing amounts of time in school or in the care of someone other than their parents.

This article reviews each of these revolutions to clarify the factors that lie behind the growing demand for out-of-home programs to serve preschool-age children, drawing on census and survey data charting a wide array of family and economic changes from the mid-1800s to the present.[1] It addresses the following questions:

1. To what extent have young children experienced a decline in parental time potentially available for their care?

2. How have increasing employment among mothers and the rise in one-parent families contributed to the decline in parental availability to care for children at home?

3. What major demographic and family trends are responsible for increasing employment of mothers and for one-parent family living?

4. How may demographic trends influence the demand for child care during the coming decades?

5. What lessons from the first child care revolution—compulsory public schooling—can guide child care policy today?

The focus on historical changes as experienced by children provides a unique vantage point for understanding the child care revolution young children are now experiencing and for speculating about what the future may hold.

The Decline in Parental Availability for Child Care

The daily experiences young children have at home, in school, or in child care depend in important ways on the composition of their families. In the middle of the twentieth century, most children under the age of six lived in breadwinner-homemaker families, that is, in two-parent families where the father worked outside the home to support the family, and the mother could care for the children at home because she was not in the paid labor force. In 1940, 87% of young children (throughout this article, the term "young children" refers to children under the age of six) had a nonemployed parent who could provide full-time care. By 1989, however, the same could be said of only 48% of children under six.

This dramatic decline resulted from the growing prevalence of dual-earner families and one-parent families with an employed head. As Figure 1 shows, between 1940 and 1989, the percentage of young children living in dual-earner families (that is, two-parent families with both parents in the labor force) increased sevenfold, from 5% to 38%. During the same period, the proportion of children living with a lone parent who worked increased fivefold, from 2% to 13%. In about half the families, the parents worked full time; in the others, one or both parents worked part time. Together, the trends toward dual-earner households and one-parent families increased by 43 percent-

Figure 1

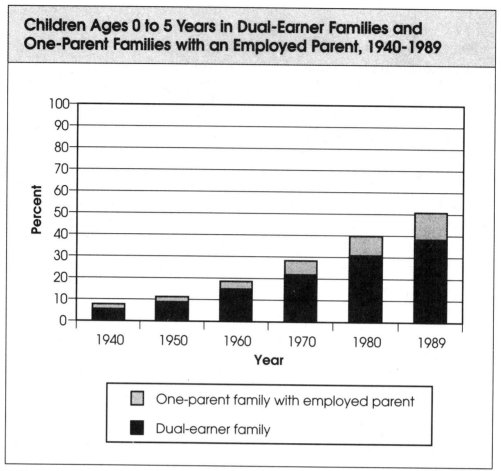

Children Ages 0 to 5 Years in Dual-Earner Families and One-Parent Families with an Employed Parent, 1940-1989

☐ One-parent family with employed parent

■ Dual-earner family

Source: Hernandez, D. J. *America's Children: Resources from family, government, and the economy.* New York: Russell Sage Foundation, 1993, Table 5.2. Reprinted by permission of the Russell Sage Foundation.

age points the proportion of young children who did not have a parent at home who could provide full-time care. From 1940 to 1989, the percentage of children under six who needed alternative child care arrangements rose from 8% to 51%.

About three-fourths of the increased demand for child care was accounted for by dual-earner families, and the remaining one-fourth stemmed from one-parent families with working parents. Because the growing demand for child care for preschool-age children is rooted in the new prevalence of dual-earner families and one-parent employed families, an understanding of what the future may hold must rest upon an examination of the earlier historical changes that led to these transformations in the family lives of children.

The Revolutionary Increase in Mothers' Employment

The proportion of young children with employed mothers jumped from about 7%

in 1940 to 43% in 1980. Since then it increased again to 51% in 1990, but no further change had occurred as of 1993.[2] The explanation for much of this increase in mothers' employment after 1940 can be found in earlier historic changes that occurred in fathers' work and family residence, in family size, and in children's school attendance and educational attainment. Each of those factors paved the way for the growing participation of mothers in the paid labor force.

Fathers' Increasing Nonfarm Work

For hundreds of years, agriculture and the two-parent farm family were the primary forms of economic production and family organization in Western countries. On the family farm, economic production, parenting, and child care were combined as parents and children worked together to support themselves. This life pattern changed with the Industrial Revolution, however. Families moved to urban areas, and

Figure 2

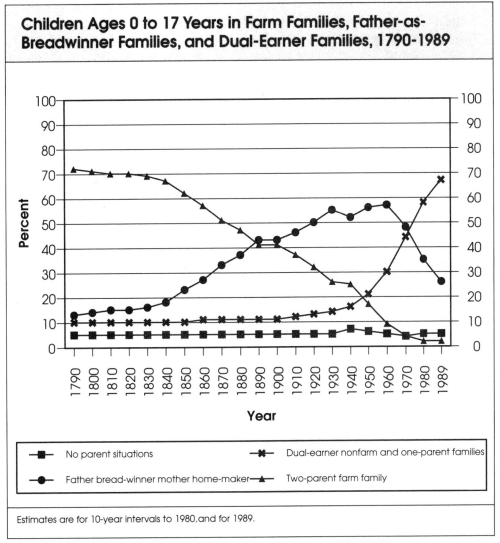

Children Ages 0 to 17 Years in Farm Families, Father-as-Breadwinner Families, and Dual-Earner Families, 1790-1989

Legend:
- No parent situations
- Dual-earner nonfarm and one-parent families
- Father bread-winner mother home-maker
- Two-parent farm family

Estimates are for 10-year intervals to 1980, and for 1989.

Source: Hernandez, D. J. *America's Children: Resources from family, government, and the economy.* New York: Russell Sage Foundation, 1993, p. 103. Reprinted by permission of the Russell Sage Foundation.

childhood was transformed in unprecedented ways. Fathers in urban families spent much of the day away from home working at jobs to earn the income required to support their families, while mothers remained at home to care for their children and to perform other household chores.

The shift away from farming, when it occurred, was very rapid. Figure 2 provides a historical view of the likelihood that children would live in each of four basic family types between 1790 and the present. Between 1830 and 1930, the proportion of children living in two-parent farm families dropped from about 70% to only 30%, while the proportion living in nonfarm families with breadwinner fathers and homemaker mothers jumped from 15% to 55%.

The shift from farming to urban occupations enabled many families to improve their relative economic status because comparatively favorable economic opportunities existed in urban areas. Urban jobs generated incomes higher than many people could earn through farming, and, given the precarious economic situations faced by many rural families, even poorly paid or dangerous jobs in urban areas were attractive.

Falling Family Size

The massive migration to urban areas was accompanied by a dramatic decline in family size. Figure 3 depicts the number of siblings in typical families from 1865 to the present. Among children born in 1865, 82% lived in families with five or more children, but only 30% of those born in 1930 had such

Figure 3

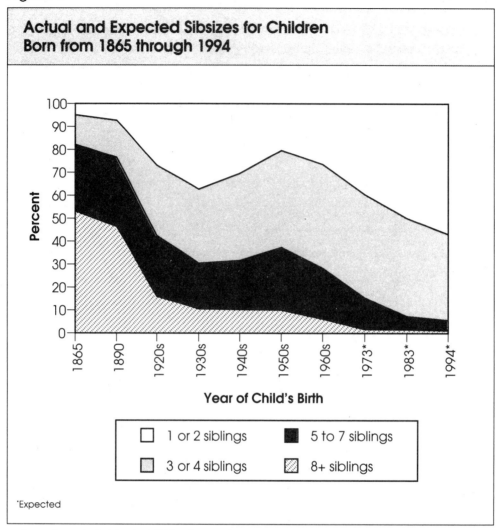

Actual and Expected Sibsizes for Children Born from 1865 through 1994

Year of Child's Birth

| ☐ 1 or 2 siblings | ■ 5 to 7 siblings |
| ☐ 3 or 4 siblings | ▨ 8+ siblings |

*Expected

Source: Hernandez, D. J. *America's Children: Resources from family, government, and the economy.* New York: Russell Sage Foundation, 1993, p. 34. Reprinted by permission of the Russell Sage Foundation.

large families. The median number of siblings in a typical family dropped from more than seven siblings to only two or three.

Parents may have restricted themselves to a small number of children for reasons of household economics. Moving from the farm to urban areas meant that housing, food, clothing, and other necessities had to be paid for with cash, so the costs of supporting additional children became increasingly apparent. Also, as economic growth led to increases in the quality and quantity of available consumer products and services, expected consumption standards rose. Individuals had to spend more money simply to maintain the standard of living they considered normal, and their rising expectations also increased the costs of supporting each additional child at a "normal" level.

Meanwhile, the economic contribution that children could make to their parents and families was sharply reduced by the passage of laws restricting child labor. More and more parents limited their families to a comparatively small number of children, ensuring that available family income could be spread less thinly and that the family's expected standard of living could be maintained.

Increasing Schooling and Educational Attainments

A third revolutionary change in children's lives resulted from the enormous increase in school enrollment and educational attainments that took place between 1870 and 1940. As farming was overshadowed by an industrial economy in which fathers worked for pay at jobs located away from home, the

Figure 4

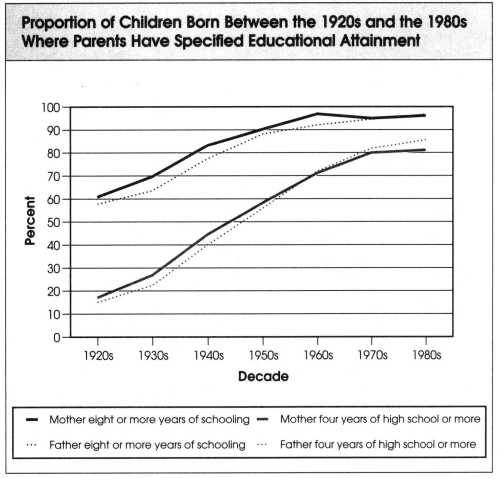

Proportion of Children Born Between the 1920s and the 1980s Where Parents Have Specified Educational Attainment

Legend:
— Mother eight or more years of schooling ▬ Mother four years of high school or more
··· Father eight or more years of schooling ··· Father four years of high school or more

Source: Hernandez, D. J. *America's Children: Resources from family, government, and the economy.* New York: Russell Sage Foundation, 1993, p. 197. Reprinted by permission of the Russell Sage Foundation.

economic role of children also changed with the enactment of compulsory school attendance and child labor laws. School enrollment rates jumped sharply. In 1870, about 50% of children 5 through 19 years old were enrolled in school. By 1940, 95% of children 7 through 13 years old were enrolled, as were 79% of children 14 through 17. The length of the school year also increased over that period. The number of days that enrolled students spent in school doubled from 21% to 42% of the total days in the year, or 59% of the nonweekend days. This represented a dramatic change in how children who were six or over spent much of their waking time.

Why did parents send their children to school in greater numbers and for longer periods? There are several plausible explanations. School enrollments increased during the period when laws limiting child labor were passed. Labor unions sought these laws

to ensure that jobs would be available for adults (mainly fathers), while the child welfare movement sought them to protect children from unsafe and unfair working conditions. Compulsory education laws supported by the same movements led to universal schooling that was mandated and paid for by local governments.

In addition, as time passed, higher educational attainments were needed to obtain jobs with higher incomes and greater prestige. Hence, parents encouraged their children's educational attainments as a path to achieving economic success in adulthood. Because the children of today are the parents of tomorrow, this enormous increase in schooling led to significant later increases in the education levels of parents. For example, as Figure 4 shows, only 15% of children born in 1920 had fathers who had completed four years of high school, compared with 39% of those born in 1940. Levels of education among mothers increased as well. By 1940, fully 44% of young children had mothers with four years of high school education. Today, more than 80% of adolescents have parents who completed at least four years of high school.

Explaining the Increasing Employment of Mothers

How did the historic shifts toward nonfarm work, urban residence, smaller families, and increased educational attainments that took place between the Industrial Revolution and about 1940 lead to increased employment by mothers? One explanation focuses on efforts parents made to maintain, improve, or regain their economic standing relative to other families.

Until about 1940, three major avenues were open to parents who wanted to improve their economic standing. First, they could move off the farm to allow the husband to work in a better-paid job in the growing urban-industrial economy. Second, they could limit themselves to a smaller number of children so that available family income could be spread less thinly. Third, they could increase their educational attainments so as to be qualified to enter well-paid occupations. By 1940, however, most families had already taken these steps. Only 23% of Americans still lived on farms; 70% of parents had only one or two dependent children in the home; and adults beyond age 25 often found it difficult or impractical to pursue additional schooling. Consequently, for many parents, these historical avenues for improving their economic standing had run their course.

A fourth major avenue to increasing family income emerged between 1940 and 1960, namely, paid work by wives and mothers. The traditional supply of female nonfarm labor—unmarried women—was limited, while the war effort and the economic boom created an escalating demand for additional female workers.[3] Meanwhile, mothers also were becoming more available and qualified for work outside the home. By 1940, the enrollment of children over six in school had released mothers with school-age children from child care responsibilities for about two-thirds of a full-time workday, and for about two-thirds

of a full-time work year. In addition, many women were highly educated because compulsory, free schooling applied to girls as well as boys and the educational attainments of women had increased along with those of men. By 1940, young women were more likely than young men to graduate from high school, and they were about two-thirds as likely to graduate from college.

Paid work for mothers was becoming increasingly attractive both as an economic advantage in a competitive, consumption-oriented society and as a hedge against possible economic disaster. Families with two earners could jump ahead economically of many families with only a single earner.[4] Moreover, a woman of 24 could look forward to about 40 years during which she could work for pay to help support her family. Additional motivations that drew many wives and mothers into the labor force included the personal nonfinancial rewards of working, the opportunity to be productively involved with other

By 1993, about 24% of young children lived in mother-child families; in about half those families, the parent worked.

adults, and career satisfactions for those who entered a high-prestige occupation. In addition, the historic rise in divorce (discussed below) made paid work attractive to mothers who feared they might lose most or all of their husband's income through divorce.

Economic insecurity among families in which the fathers faced low wages or joblessness made mothers' work virtually essential. Many families experienced economic insecurity and need when widespread unemployment prevailed during the Great Depression. In 1940, 40% of children lived with fathers who did not work full time year round. While this proportion declined after the Great Depression, it has continued at high levels. Throughout the past 50 years, at least one-fifth of children have lived with fathers who, during any given year, experienced part-time work or joblessness. This has been a powerful incentive for many mothers to work for pay.

Figure 5

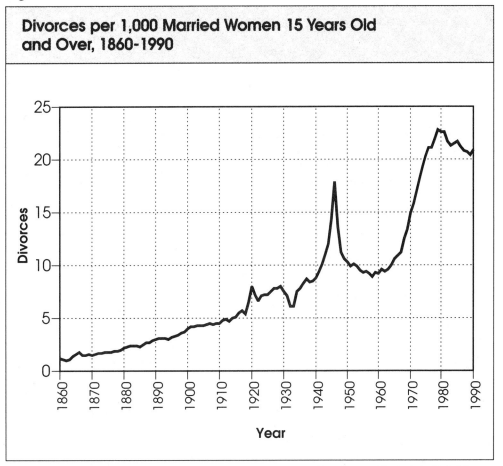

Divorces per 1,000 Married Women 15 Years Old and Over, 1860-1990

Source: Jacobson, P. H. *American Marraige and Divorce*. New York: Rinehart, 1950; U. S. National Center for Health Statistics. *Advance report of final divorce statistics, 1988*. vol. 39, no. 12, supplement 2. Washington, DC: USNCHS, 1991.

The Rising Number of Mother-Only Families

In addition to increasing employment among mothers, a second reason for the decline in parental availability to provide full-time child care lies in the new prevalence of one-parent, working-parent families that became evident after 1960, 20 years after the rise in dual-earner families began. Most one-parent families are mother-child families, created through separation, divorce, or out-of-wedlock childbearing. By 1993, about 24% of young children lived in mother-child families (another 4% lived with their fathers only). In about half those families, the parent worked: 12% of young children lived with a lone working mother; and an added 3% lived with a lone working father. A number of earlier changes in family life help explain these revolutionary changes in family structure.

High Rates of Divorce

As Figure 5 shows, a remarkably steady rise in rates of divorce is evident between the 1860s and the 1960s, resulting in an eight-fold increase during the century. (See also the Spring 1994 issue of *The Future of Children*, which focused on Children and Divorce).[5] One way of explaining this long-term increase focuses on the role the family plays as an economic unit. On preindustrial farms, fathers and mothers had to work together to sustain the family, but with a nonfarm job, the father could depend on his own work alone for his income. He could leave his family but keep his income. And, at the same time as urban employment weakened the economic interdependence of husbands and wives, by moving to urban areas families also left behind the rural small-town social controls that once censured divorce.

In addition, recent research suggests that the economic insecurity and need that result from erratic or limited employment prospects for men can also increase hostility between husbands and wives, decrease marital quality, and increase the risk of divorce.[6-8] In fact, during each of the three economic recessions that occurred between 1970 and 1982, the proportion of mother-only families increased substantially more than during the preceding nonrecessionary period. Those recessions can account for about 30% of the overall increase in mother-child families between 1968 and 1988 or for about 50% of the increase in families headed by separated or divorced mothers.[1]

Stresses on Black Families

Between 1940 and 1960, black children experienced much larger increases than white children in the proportion who lived in a mother-child family with a divorced or separated mother. The factors that led to increased separation and divorce were similar among whites and among blacks—movement off the farm and exposure to economic insecurity. Those forces affected black families with special intensity, however. The proportion of blacks living on farms dropped precipitously during the 20-year period between 1940 and 1960. In 1940, 44% of black children lived on farms, while by 1960, this figure had plummeted to only 11%. This startling drop and the extraordinary economic pressures and hardships faced by black families may account for the fact that a much higher proportion of black children than white children came to live in mother-child families.[1]

In addition, especially since 1970, black children have experienced extremely large increases in the proportion who live with a never-married mother. One explanation for this difference is offered by William Julius Wilson, who points out that unemployment among young males makes marriage less likely and so contributes to the rate of births that occur out of wedlock.[9] Calculations using survey data show that in 1955 there was little difference in rates of joblessness for young black and young white men. However, by 1976–1989, white men 16 to 24 years old were 15 to 25 percentage points more likely to be employed than were black men of the same ages.[1] The large and rapid drop in the ability of black men in the main family-building ages to secure employment and provide significant support to a family appears to have depressed marriage rates. Many young black women may be reluctant to initiate a

marriage that would likely be temporary and unrewarding, instead choosing to bear children out of wedlock.

Summary

In short, the growing reliance of American families on nonparental child care is rooted in several historical changes. First was the revolutionary increase in mothers' labor force participation that occurred during the past half-century. By 1940, many mothers were potentially available for work, and mothers' work had become the only major avenue available to most couples over age 25 who sought to improve their relative social and economic status. Parents had earlier limited themselves to smaller families and moved off the farm so that fathers could work at better-paid jobs in urban areas. Increasing rates of school attendance by children six years old and over freed many mothers from the need to stay home, and, over time, public schooling increased the educational attainments of young women and made them better qualified as employees. After 1940, not only was there an increasing economic demand for married women to enter the labor force, they also faced the need to work and experienced the attractions of work.

By 1989 about 40% of preschoolers spent considerable time in the care of someone other than their parents while the parents worked.

In addition, the proportion of young children living in one-parent, working-parent families has increased substantially since 1960. Underlying this increase are sharply rising rates of divorce and out-of-wedlock childbearing. The incomes of working women helped to weaken the economic interdependence between husbands and wives, setting the stage for a historic rise in rates of separation and divorce. The experience of economic insecurity associated with fathers' part-time work, joblessness, or difficulties finding employment also made marriage less attractive and less sustainable for many families.

The consequence of all these trends is the fact that today most children live either in dual-earner families in which both parents work at jobs away from home or in one-parent families. As a result, a growing proportion of children under six need care by people other than their parents for a significant portion of the day.

Demographic Trends: Implications for Child Care

The family and economic circumstances in which children live have important implications for the development of early childhood programs. By 1989, although about 12% of children lived in dual-earner families in which the parents worked different hours or days and could personally care for their children, about 40% of preschoolers spent considerable time in the care of someone other than their parents while the parents worked. If mothers' labor force participation continues to rise, the demand for nonparental child care will rise with it.

Continued Growth in the Demand for Child Care

The revolutionary increase in mothers' labor force participation during the past half-century led to enormous increases in nonparental care of young children. Looking to the future, between 1992 and 2005, the labor force participation rate for women between the ages of 25 and 54 is projected to increase from 75% to 83%.[10] Continued increases in rates of employment among women are likely to lead to a further decline in the availability of mothers who can be home to provide full-time care for their children.

The rising prevalence of one-parent families also is likely to continue. The divorce rate reached a peak in 1979 and declined slightly thereafter, but the graph in Figure 5 shows that the divorce rate remains extremely high by historical standards. Meanwhile, the proportion of births occurring out of wedlock continues to increase at a steady pace. If this trend persists, the proportion of children in one-parent families with working parents will rise even further.

Some families headed by single mothers with limited labor force participation have been able to rely financially on public assistance through the Aid to Families with Dependent Children (AFDC) program.

Most current welfare reform proposals, however, aim to increase labor force participation among AFDC recipients. If such reforms are enacted and if they successfully increase employment rates, there will be a corresponding increase in the need for nonparental child care for children of these mothers.[11]

As a result of all these demographic and policy changes, the need for nonparental child care for children in one-parent, working-parent families is likely to continue to rise.

Characteristics of the Children Who Will Need Child Care

This article has focused thus far on how family and economic change is increasing the demand for nonparental child care. But the changing family life of children can also influence the nature and content of the care that children will need. Ongoing demographic trends suggest that, in the coming decades, early childhood programs will be serving a population of children which is increasingly diverse in economic resources, racial and ethnic background, and family structure.

Increasing Economic Inequality

Economic well-being can be viewed in terms of absolute levels of family income or in terms of relative economic standing compared with other families. Economists from Adam Smith to John Kenneth Galbraith have argued that poverty must be defined in

The proportion of children under age 18 who are white is projected to decline steadily and rapidly, from 69% in 1990 to only 50% in 2030.

terms of contemporary standards of living.[12] In Galbraith's words, ". . . people are poverty-stricken when their income, even if adequate for survival, falls markedly behind that of the community."

In an absolute sense, real income levels and living standards rose dramatically between 1940 and 1973, as median family income more than doubled, although it has changed comparatively little since then. Since 1959, however, economic expansion

Figure 6

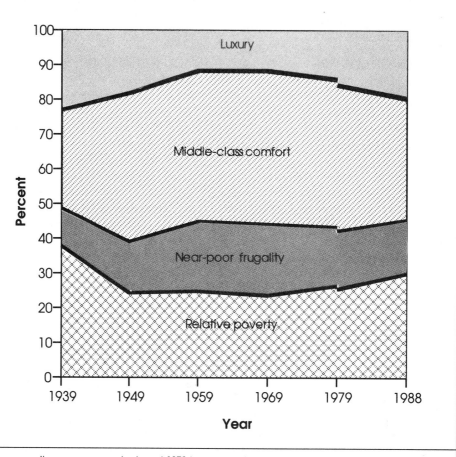

Distribution of Children Ages 0 to 5 Years by Relative Income Levels, 1939-1988

Lines separating areas appear broken at 1979 to account for the change from using Decennial Census poverty data to Current Population Survey poverty data.

Source: Hernandez, D. J. *America's Children: Resources from family, government, and the economy.* New York: Russell Sage Foundation, 1993, p. 260. Reprinted by permission of the Russell Sage Foundation.

has done little to reduce the uneven distribution of income across families, and since 1969, economic inequality has increased. To examine the income distribution, families can be classified as living in relative poverty, near-poor frugality, middle-class comfort, or luxury, based on income thresholds set at 50%, 75%, and 150% of median family income in specific years and adjusted for family size.[1]

Figure 6 is a graph showing the distribution of children into these income categories from 1939 to 1988. This measure shows that the proportion of young children from birth to five years living in relative poverty dropped from a high of 38% after the Great Depression to remain at less than 25% from 1949 through 1979, before it jumped to 30% in 1988 and 33% in 1993. Another 15% of children in 1988 and 1993 lived in near-poor frugality. At the opposite extreme, the proportion of young children in families with luxury level incomes declined from 23% in 1939 to about 12% in the 1950s, before increasing to 20% in 1988 and to 23% in 1993. The years from 1969 to 1993 saw a significant decline in middle-class comfort, as more and more children lived at the extremes of luxury and poverty.

In other words, the past 25 years—when the demand for nonparental child care was growing fastest—also brought a substantial expansion in economic inequality among families. As a result, the quantitative increases in the total need for nonparental care during the past quarter-century have been accompanied by increased qualitative differences in the educational needs of the children who enter child care.

In families with higher incomes, parents can usually afford to provide resources and educational experiences that foster the development of their children, while children from poor homes rely more on child care and preschool programs to provide those experiences.[13] As a result, children from families at different income levels may enter child care situations with different needs. In recognition of the unmet developmental needs of many children who live in poverty, for example, the Head Start program adds to its preschool educational activities a comprehensive set of nutritional, health, and social services that are not typically offered to children from more advantaged families.[14] Research, policies, and programs that explicitly address these differences are sorely needed.

Growing Racial and Ethnic Diversity
Race and ethnic origin define another dimension along which it seems likely that educational needs of young children may differ.[15] American children were already quite racially and ethnically diverse as of 1990, when 69% of children under age 18 were white (and not of Hispanic origin), 15% were black, 12% were Hispanic, and 4% were from another racial or ethnic group.

Immigration and differential birthrates across ethnic groups will likely increase that diversity in the coming years. Looking to the future, Figure 7 shows that the proportion of children under age 18 who are white is projected to decline steadily and rapidly, from 69% in 1990 to only 50% in 2030. Conversely, the proportion of all children who are Hispanic or who are black or of another nonwhite race is expected to climb from 31% to 50%.

Poverty, language barriers, and cultural isolation are important factors that influence many nonwhite or Hispanic children, who may have educational needs (and related social needs) that differ from those of white children. As a result, these projections highlight an increasing need to understand these differences through research and to plan

new child care policies and programs appropriate to a diverse population of children.[16]

Diverse Family Living Arrangements
Children also vary greatly in their family living arrangements, and this is true separately for children within specific racial and ethnic groups. Even among children under age one, historical data show that, in 1940, 7% of white infants and 25% of black infants lived in a one-parent family or were separated from their parents. By 1980, these rates had doubled to 13% for whites and 54% for blacks. In 1993, the proportion of children under age six with one parent in the home was 21% for whites, 66% for blacks, and 34% for Hispanics.

Recent evidence indicates that, compared with children in two-parent families, children in one-parent families have higher risks of dropping out of high school, bearing children as teenagers, and not being employed by their early twenties. The low incomes and sudden declines in income experienced by children in these families are the most important reason for

The United States is in the midst of a child care revolution, as more and more young children under the age of six are cared for by someone other than their parents.

their disadvantaged outcomes, although research suggests that other differences in family life also play a significant role.[17] Children in one-parent families are therefore likely to have educational needs that differ from children in two-parent families and that should be understood and addressed.

Summary
In short, the United States is in the midst of a child care revolution, as more and more young children under the age of six are cared for by someone other than their parents. Broad demographic trends as well as efforts to reform the welfare system are likely to increase rates of labor force participation by mothers with young children, further expanding the demand for nonparental child care. At the same time, the diversity in the characteristics and needs of the nation's

Figure 7

Percentage of Children Who Are Non-Hispanic White, Black, and Hispanic, 1980, 1990, and Projected Through 2050

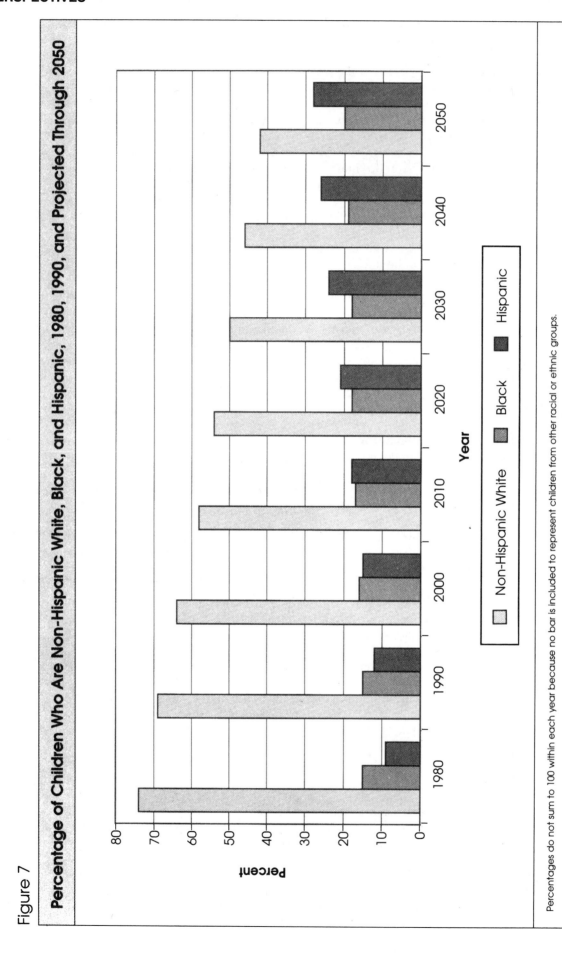

Percentages do not sum to 100 within each year because no bar is included to represent children from other racial or ethnic groups.

Source: U.S. Bureau of the Census. *U.S. Population Estimates by Age, Sex, and Hispanic Origin: 1980-1991*. Current Population Reports, Series P-25, No. 1095. Washington, DC: U.S. Government Printing Office, 1993; U.S. Bureau of the Census. *Population Projections of the United States, by Age, Sex, Race, and Hispanic Origin: 1993-2050*. Current Population Reports, Series P-25, No. 1104. Washington, DC: U.S. Government Printing Office, 1993.

children has also increased, particularly in terms of their economic circumstances, their racial and ethnic backgrounds, and their family living arrangements. Child care policies and programs must be designed to respond to the differing needs of the many children who use them.

Lessons to Guide Child Care Policy

The first child care revolution began more than 100 years ago, and it affected children over age five. Through compulsory education laws, government both mandated and paid for universal schooling for all children age six and over. As time passed, the upper age limit for compulsory schooling was raised, and public funding for schooling increased. This led to enormous improvements in the skills and knowledge of the labor force, thereby contributing to economic development and rising real incomes.

Today, as global economic competition becomes an increasing concern, the United States is in the midst of a second child care revolution, one affecting children under age six whose parent or parents work. From this perspective, one can see child care as valuable or essential to society at large. It facilitates the work of mothers and their contribution both to their family income and to the economy. The quality of child care may also influence the future international competitiveness of the U.S. economy by fostering the development of productive workers who will support the baby boom generation as it reaches retirement.

When high-quality child care, like the preschool programs that are the subject of this journal issue, leads to improved educational and developmental outcomes for children, it has value not only for the child and the parents, but also for the broader society. Child care is expensive, however. Overall, families with a preschool child who pay for child care devote about 10% of their incomes to child care, but this figure ranges from only 6% for families with annual incomes of $50,000 or more to 23% for families with annual incomes under $15,000.[18] The relative cost of child care as an expense associated with having a job is quite high for low-income families. The question then

arises: Should the cost of that care be borne mainly or solely by parents?

The first child care revolution was mandated and paid for by government as a social good in the public interest. Today, evolving economic conditions effectively require that an increasing proportion of mothers work, and proposed welfare reforms will mandate that other mothers of young children find employment to support their families. In this context, it is important that new research inform the public policy debate about the kinds, the costs, and the quality of child care available to the youngest members of American society. Research about the value of child care to children, parents, and society at large may also help inform policy debate about the appropriate role of government in fostering and funding quality care for American children.

The author is indebted to Arthur J. Norton for institutional leadership, scholarly counsel, and personal enthusiasm and encouragement which created an indispensable and nurturing home in the U. S. Bureau of the Census for writing the book which provides the foundation for this article. Thanks are due also to Edith Reeves and Catherine O'Brien for statistical support, and to Stephanie Kennedy for secretarial support. The author bears sole responsibility for the results and opinions presented here.

NOTES

1. This article draws especially on research reported in the author's recent book which used census and survey data for 1940, 1950, 1960, 1970, 1980, and 1989 to develop the first-ever statistics using children as the unit of analysis. These data chart a wide array of family and economic changes that affected children from the Great Depression through the 1980s. Additional analyses of previously published data extend the investigation back an additional 150 years. Hernandez, D. J. *America's children: Resources from government, family, and the economy.* New York: Russell Sage Foundation, 1993. This research was also reported in Hernandez, D. J. Children's changing access to resources: A historical perspective. *Social Policy Report* (1993) 8,1:1–23.

2. The precise estimate of 6% to 8% is obtained from note no. 1, Hernandez, *America's chil-*

dren, Table 5.2. The estimates for 1980, 1990, and 1993 were provided by the U.S. Bureau of Labor Statistics, Howard Hayghe.

3. Oppenheimer, V. K. *The female labor force in the United States.* Population Monograph Series, No. 5. Berkeley, CA: Institute of International Studies, University of California Press, 1970.

4. Oppenheimer, V. K. *Work and family.* New York: Academic Press, 1982.

5. *The Future of Children* (Spring 1994) 5,1.

6. Conger, R. D., Elder, G. H., Jr., Lorenz, F. O., et al. Linking economic hardship to marital quality and instability. *Journal of Marriage and the Family* (1990) 52:643–56.

7. Conger, R. D., Elder, G. H., Jr., with Lorenz, F. O., Simons, R. L., and Whitbeck, L. B. *Families in troubled times: Adapting to change in rural America.* New York: Aldine de Gruyter, 1994.

8. Liker, J. K., and Elder, G. H., Jr. Economic hardship and marital relations in the 1930s. *American Sociological Review* (1983)48:343–59.

9. Wilson, W. J. *The truly disadvantaged: The inner city, the underclass, and public policy.* Chicago: University of Chicago Press, 1987.

10. U.S. Department of Labor, Bureau of Labor Statistics. Bulletin 2452. Washington, DC: U.S. Government Printing Office, April 1994, Table A-1.

11. Another important goal of many welfare reform proposals is to reduce out-of-wedlock childbearing, but available evidence suggests that the effect of welfare on out-of-wedlock childbearing is small. For a discussion of the extent to which welfare programs have contributed to the increase in mother-only families, see note no. 1, Hernandez, *America's children* pp. 291–300.

12. Adam Smith was cited in U.S. Congress. *Alternative measures of poverty.* Staff study prepared for the Joint Economic Committee. Washington, DC, October 18, 1994, p. 10. The quote from Galbraith can be found in Galbraith, J. K. *The affluent society.* Boston: Houghton, Mifflin, 1958, pp. 323–24.

13. For recent studies on the effects for children of poverty and economic inequality, see papers from the Consequences of Growing Up Poor conference, held February 2–3, 1995, at the National Academy of Sciences, organized by the National Institute of Child Health and Development (NICHD) Family and Child Well-Being Network, the Russell Sage Foundation, and the National Academy of Sciences Board on Children and Families.

14. U.S. General Accounting Office. *Early childhood centers: services to prepare children for school often limited.* GAO/HEHS-95–21. Washington, DC: U.S. GAO, March 1995.

15. For additional discussions of child indicators pertaining to race, ethnicity, and educational needs, see Lewit, E. M. and Baker, L. G. Race and ethnicity—changes for children. *The Future of Children* (Winter 1994) 4,3:134–44.

16. Phillips, D., and Crowell, N. A., eds. *Cultural diversity and early education.* Washington, DC: National Academy Press, 1994.

17. McLanahan, S., and Sandefur, G. *Growing up with a single parent: What hurts, what helps.* Cambridge, MA: Harvard University Press, 1994.

18. Hofferth, S. L., Brayfield, A., Deich, S., and Holcomb, P. *National Child Care Survey,* 1990. Washington, DC: Urban Institute Press, 1991.

The Next Baby Boom

┌─ SUMMARY

The 72 million children of baby boomers form a huge generation that will come of age in the next five years. They will be the first generation to accept mixed races, "nontraditional" families, and gender-bending sex roles as mainstream. Unlike the original baby boomers, most will think their parents are cool. They will also cope with stark economic divisions based on high-tech skills.

Su∫an Mitchell

Susan Mitchell is the author of The Official Guide to the Generations *(New Strategist, 1995) and a contributing editor of* American Demographics.

Two-year-old Julie couldn't wait for Halloween.

"What are you going to be, Julie?"

"Geen powie anja! Geen powie anja!"

If you need a translator, you aren't a parent. Julie, like millions of her playmates, went trick-or-treating as the green Power Ranger.

The youngest Americans are opinionated consumers before they even learn to speak. Teenage Mutant Ninja Turtles, Barney the purple dinosaur, and now a multiracial fivesome of teenage boys and girls—the Mighty Morphin' Power Rangers—capture the imagination of young children and a huge quantity of their parents' dollars. Their teenage brothers and sisters already exert a heavy influence on music, sports, computers, video games, and dozens of other consumer markets. Yet the consumer power of today's children is just the first ripple of a huge wave.

Americans aged 18 and younger will form a generation as big as the original baby boom. Like the baby boom before them, their huge numbers will profoundly influence markets, attitudes, and society. Their true power will become apparent in the next five years as the oldest members come of age. Their habits will shape America for most of the 21st century.

A HUGE GENERATION

Our country wasn't always on a demographic roller coaster. In the first half of the 20th century, the annual number of births in the U.S. remained fairly steady,

1. PERSPECTIVES

at 2.7 million to 3 million a year. Then, about nine months after the end of World War II, the number of births began a quick, steep climb. It rose from 2.9 million in 1945 to 3.4 million in 1946 to 3.8 million in 1947. The boom continued for 19 years, with 4.3 million babies born in the peak year of 1957. Births remained above 4 million until 1965, when they dropped to 3.8 million. When it was all over, a grand total of nearly 76 million baby boomers had arrived.

Through the late 1960s and early 1970s, births remained well below 4 million a year, dipping to only 3.1 million in 1973. But in 1977, the beginning of the next baby boom, annual births began climbing again. Births topped 4 million in 1989 and continued at that high level through 1993. In 1994, however, the next baby boom finally came to a close. Last year's births dipped just below 4 million, to 3,979,000.

The next baby boom is 72 million Americans, and their proportion of the total U.S. population rivals that of the original boom. Children and teens aged 18 or younger are 28 percent of the total population; the original baby boom, now aged 31 to 49, is 30 percent.

This new generation differs from the baby boom in significant ways. While the boomer generation was a relatively uniform group, the children of the next boom

In 1994, fewer than two-thirds of newborns were non-Hispanic white.

differ radically from each other in race, living arrangements, and socioeconomic class. The children of this generation also face much more serious problems than the boomers did when they were children. AIDS, crime, violence, and divorce cast long shadows over their world. As the children of working parents, they often have to assume adult responsibilities at an early age.

Members of the next baby boom may be more competent, confident, and wary

---

THE NEXT BOOMERS ARE

Self-Confident Leaders

Today's entering college students are the leading edge of the next baby boom. They are more confident and ambitious than baby boomers were as freshmen.

(attitudes of college freshmen, 1971 and 1993)

REASONS NOTED AS VERY IMPORTANT IN DECIDING TO GO TO COLLEGE:	1993	1971
parents wanted me to go	34.6%	22.9%
get a better job	82.1	73.8
gain general education	65.3	59.5
make more money	75.1	49.9
learn more about things	75.2	68.8
prepare for graduate/professional school	61.1	34.5
OBJECTIVES CONSIDERED TO BE ESSENTIAL OR VERY IMPORTANT:		
raise a family	70.6	60.2
be very well off financially	74.5	40.1
help others in difficulty	63.3	62.7
be successful in own business	42.6	41.9
participate in community action	25.6	25.9
STUDENT RATED SELF ABOVE AVERAGE OR TOP 10 PERCENT IN:		
academic ability	56.2	50.6
leadership ability	55.9	34.9
mathematical ability	43.0	32.0
popularity	45.6	29.2
self-confidence (intellectual)	59.6	34.8
self-confidence (social)	51.3	27.4

Source: The American Freshman, Higher Education Research Institute University of California-Los Angeles

---

than the original baby boom. If you could sum them up in one word, the word would be diverse.

ACCEPT MIXED RACES

In the 20th century, international migration and differing fertility rates have made each generation of Americans more racially and ethnically diverse than its predecessor. The original baby boomers are 75 percent non-Hispanic white, according to Census Bureau estimates. Eleven percent are black, 9 percent are Hispanic, and 4 percent are Asian or American Indian, Eskimo, or Aleut. The next baby boomers are only 67 percent non-Hispanic white; 15 percent are black, 14 percent are Hispanic, and 5 percent are Asian or American Indian, Eskimo or

Aleut. Within this generation, younger cohorts are even more racially diverse. Only 64 percent of infants born in 1994 are non-Hispanic white. Sixteen percent of infants are Hispanic, 15 percent are black, and 5 percent are Asian or American Indian, Eskimo, or Aleut.

The Census Bureau's broad racial and ethnic categories tell only part of the diversity story. The next baby boom will be the first generation to seriously question all traditional racial categories. The reason is that many of today's children and teens are of mixed races. In 1990, there were nearly 2 million children under age 18 who were reported as being "of a different race than one or both of their parents," according to the Census Bureau. The largest group is children of black and

How Times Have Changed

Compared with their parents, the next baby boomers are growing up in a more dangerous and complex world.

(10 cultural attributes of the original baby boom and the next baby boom)

original baby boom	next baby boom
cold war	regional wars
nuclear threat	terrorist threats
mother's care	day care
"Father Knows Best"	father isn't home
TV dinners	low-fat fast food
network TV	cable TV
45s and "American Bandstand"	CDs and MTV
Ma Bell	Internet
VW buses	minivans
free love	condoms

Source: American Demographics

12 to 17 believe members of minority racial and ethnic groups receive too little respect. And reflecting their greater tol-

One in 35 members of the next baby boom is multiracial.

erance for diversity in all forms, 57 percent believe gays are also too little respected, according to the Gallup Institute.

While increased diversity might lead to greater racial tolerance, other signs point to further polarization among the races. Schools were successfully integrated decades ago, but many neighborhoods are as firmly segregated as ever. Race-related violence and organized racial "hate groups" are increasingly visible, and schools around the country report increased racial tensions among students.

For the original baby boom, racial issues were explosive and defining. Race will be just as important to the next baby boom, but in a different way. More of today's kids have first-hand experiences with integration, prejudice, and other race issues.

"NONTRADITIONAL" FAMILIES

When the original boomers were children, new friends would often ask each other, "What does your father do for a living?" But for the children of the next baby boom, the question is more likely to be, "Does your dad live with you?" The next boomers' family arrangements are widely varied, and increasingly, they do not include a father.

In 1970, 85 percent of children under age 18 lived with two parents and 12 percent lived with one parent. By 1993, this had changed significantly. Only 71 percent of children have two parents present, and 27 percent live with a single parent, according to the Census Bureau.

Striking racial differences in family composition are driving the diversity of this new generation. In 1993, 77 percent of white children and 65 percent of Hispanic children live in two-parent families.

white parents, but close behind are children of white and Asian parents. That translates into about 1 mixed-race child for every 35 members of the next baby boom, or about one in every school classroom.

The larger share of minorities in the next baby boom means that there is far more interaction between people of different races than there was for most of the baby-boom generation. The oldest half of the original boomers was born into a fully segregated society, with separate schools, neighborhoods, and public facilities for whites and blacks. The next baby boom is the product of a more integrated society.

Today, white kids have nonwhite playmates, a casual appreciation for "ethnic foods," and heroes of every race. Teens of all races listen to rap, hip hop, and Tejano music. "Minority teen culture has an incredible influence on white teens," according to Peter Zollo of Teenage Research Unlimited. "Everything from music to fashion to language seems to be adopted by a large number of suburban white teens."

One reflection of racial and ethnic diversity among children can be seen in the toy market. Mattel, Tyco Toys, and Playskool are just some of the big players that are responding to ethnic and racial diversity. "We have Dream Doll House families that are African American, Hispanic, Asian, and Caucasian," says Laurie Strong of Fisher-Price, a subsidiary of Mattel.

Zollo says the key is inclusion. "Advertisements, even those for large mainstream brands should be very inclusive," he says. That's why some marketers now shoot different versions of the same ad using rap, alternative rock, and even country music to reach all the different groups of teens and children.

Teens know their world is multicultural, even if grownups don't. Almost three-fourths of 12-to-17-year-olds say they receive too little information at school about Muslims, according to a 1991 poll by the George H. Gallup International Institute. About two-thirds say they receive too little information about "Africans before they came to this country" and about nonwhite women. Well over half feel that Asian Americans and Hispanics are given short shrift in school.

In addition, the majority of people aged

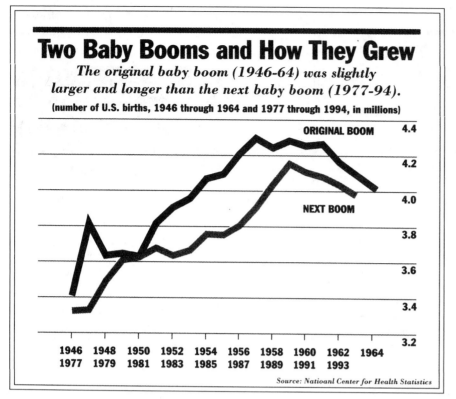

Two Baby Booms and How They Grew

The original baby boom (1946-64) was slightly
larger and longer than the next baby boom (1977-94).

(number of U.S. births, 1946 through 1964 and 1977 through 1994, in millions)

ORIGINAL BOOM

NEXT BOOM

4.4
4.2
4.0
3.8
3.6
3.4
3.2

| 1946 | 1948 | 1950 | 1952 | 1954 | 1956 | 1958 | 1960 | 1962 | 1964 |
| 1977 | 1979 | 1981 | 1983 | 1985 | 1987 | 1989 | 1991 | 1993 | |

Source: Natioanl Center for Health Statistics

Yet only 36 percent of black children have two parents present.

Since the 1970s, more children (and their families) have had to move into grandparents' homes for economic reasons. In 1991, 5 percent of all children lived in grandparents' homes, including 12 percent of black children, 6 percent of Hispanic children, and 4 percent of white children, according to the Population Reference Bureau. In about half of these cases, the mother also lives there. Both parents live with grandparents in 17 percent of these cases. In 28 percent of these households, neither parent is present and grandparents are solely responsible for their grandchildren. Even children in "intact" families may have an absent parent. Among children of the next baby boom who live with two parents, 16 percent live with a stepparent, according to the Census Bureau.

Children today are also far more likely to live with a never-married mother than boomers were. Among children living with one parent, 7 percent in 1970 and 31 percent in 1990 were living with a parent who had never married. Among single-mother families in 1993, 21 percent of white mothers, 35 percent of Hispanic mothers, and 55 percent of black mothers have never been married.

As the children of divorce, the next baby boomers will grow up determined to have strong marriages for themselves. Three-fourths of children aged 13 to 17 believe it's too easy to get divorced, and 71 percent believe people who have divorced did not try hard enough to save their marriages, according to a 1992 survey by the Gallup Institute. This could mean divorce rates will plunge in the next decade, as the next boomers work harder to save their new marriages. Or it could bring further delays in marriage, as the next boomers wait longer to take their vows.

PARENTS ARE COOL

When the original baby boom came of age, America was rocked by a huge clash of values between young adults and their parents. Much of that generation gap persists today, as attitude surveys show a solid demarcation between people under and over the age of 50. The major reason for the gap is higher educational attainment, which pits the boomer generation against their less-educated parents.

Today, there is little evidence of a comparable gap between the original boomers and their next-generation children. While many of the boomers' parents never finished high school, nearly nine in ten boomers did. This achievement should be realized again with the new generation. One-fourth of boomers completed college, and about the same percentage of their children are also expected to obtain college degrees, according to the Census Bureau.

Nearly half of children think their parents are "up to date" on the music they like, according to a 1993 study by *Good Housekeeping* and Roper Starch Worldwide. Few boomers could make the same claim of their parents when they were teenagers. The children surveyed also say their parents' opinions matter most to them when it comes to drinking, spending money, and questions about sex and AIDS. They even listen more to their parents than their friends about which snack foods to eat.

The next baby boom will not attach a stigma to young men and women who still live with their parents. On the contrary, they will seek close bonds with parents and other relatives as a way to find security in an uncertain world.

GENDER-BENDING

The next baby boom may also reject advertising that sells a product or service specifically to men or women. Calvin Klein has seen the future in "cK one," a unisex fragrance. Tomorrow's young men will be more likely to try hair color and jewelry, while women will be more likely to visit the hardware store.

The next baby boom is growing up in an era when the shifting sex roles of the 1970s and 1980s have become the new social norms of the 1990s. Young women already outnumber men at college, and they are making substantial headway in professions traditionally dominated by men, such as law and medicine. The women of the next baby boom will take these gains even further. Fifty-eight percent of young women and 44 percent of young men believe the women's movement has done a good job. Twenty-five percent of

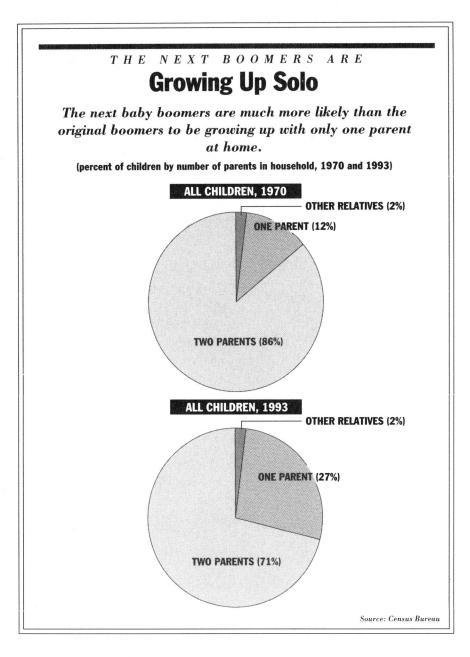

THE NEXT BOOMERS ARE

Growing Up Solo

The next baby boomers are much more likely than the original boomers to be growing up with only one parent at home.

(percent of children by number of parents in household, 1970 and 1993)

ALL CHILDREN, 1970

OTHER RELATIVES (2%)
ONE PARENT (12%)
TWO PARENTS (86%)

ALL CHILDREN, 1993

OTHER RELATIVES (2%)
ONE PARENT (27%)
TWO PARENTS (71%)

Source: Census Bureau

young men, but only 5 percent of young women, believe it has "gone too far," according to a 1991 Gallup Institute poll.

In fact, the young women of the next baby boom are taking the women's movement into new arenas such as sports and entertainment. Title 9, a federal law prohibiting sex discrimination at colleges, including college athletics, "has done a lot to make girls more prepared to take their place in new areas," says Irma Zandl, president of the Zandl Group in New York City. While they are gaining as athletes, young women are also gaining greater attention and status as musicians and entertainers.

But the battle between the sexes is still far from over. Young women are more likely than young men to believe that men do not understand the issues that concern women the most—62 percent of teenage girls believe this, compared with 56 percent of teenage boys. Yet 67 percent of teenage boys and girls believe that the gains women have made have not come at the expense of men, according to the Gallup Institute.

Most social scientists expect the daughters of employed women to have a positive view of having a career. But Peter Zollo of Teenage Research Unlimited found that teenage girls with stay-at-home moms expect to work for a slightly differ-

ent reason. "What's driving young women to want to have their own careers is that divorce rates are so high they don't want to rely on any man," he says. Even their fathers are pushing them to make sure they can be self-reliant and not dependent on a husband.

STARK ECONOMIC DIVISIONS

In 1959, at the peak of the first baby boom, 27 percent of children lived in poverty. In 1993, a smaller percentage—23 percent—of children under age 18 were poor. But the finances of the next baby boom are far from secure. In fact, their situation is getting worse.

From 1950 until 1969 the average family's economic situation was improving. The poverty rate for children dropped from 27 percent to 14 percent. During the 1970s, the proportion of children in poverty fluctuated between 14 and 17 percent. For the next baby boom, however, the years of their birth have coincided with steadily increasing poverty among children, with rates rising from 16 percent in 1977 to 23 percent in 1993.

Even more significant for this generation is the racial difference in poverty rates. While 18 percent of white children are poor, 46 percent of black children live in poverty. For black children, the proportion of poor children has not been lower than 40 percent since 1959, when the Census Bureau first measured childhood poverty rates.

The rapidly changing nature of the workplace makes it more difficult for some people to escape poverty. Even the lowest-paid jobs are increasingly dependent on high-tech equipment, such as computerized cash registers and inventory systems. Children who have little or no experience with technology early in life may have little comfort or facility with it as adults. Unfortunately, the next boomers are divided into haves and have-nots according to their access to technology and the ability to build important skills early in life.

This technology gap worsens the existing socioeconomic divisions among children and teens. The poorest members of

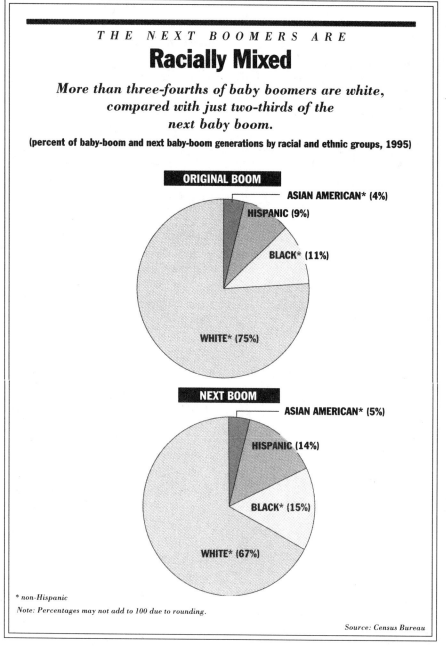

THE NEXT BOOMERS ARE

Racially Mixed

*More than three-fourths of baby boomers are white,
compared with just two-thirds of the
next baby boom.*

(percent of baby-boom and next baby-boom generations by racial and ethnic groups, 1995)

ORIGINAL BOOM

ASIAN AMERICAN* (4%)
HISPANIC (9%)
BLACK* (11%)
WHITE* (75%)

NEXT BOOM

ASIAN AMERICAN* (5%)
HISPANIC (14%)
BLACK* (15%)
WHITE* (67%)

* non-Hispanic

Note: Percentages may not add to 100 due to rounding.

Source: Census Bureau

Education is still the ticket out of poverty, and members of the next baby boom value education even more than their parents did. In 1971, 60 percent of college-bound boomers were motivated by a desire to gain a general education and 69 percent wanted to "learn more about things that interest me." In 1993, 65 percent were interested in education in general and 75 percent wanted to learn more about things of interest, according to the Higher Education Research Institute at the University of California, Los Angeles.

The freshman class of 1993 sees a dual role for education: it is a worthy goal in itself, and also the key to financial success. In 1971, 74 percent of boomers indicated they decided to go to college to get a better job and 50 percent cited the desire to make more money. Among 1993 freshmen, 82 percent said they were going to college to get a better job and 75 percent wanted to increase their earning power.

Twenty-four years ago, baby boomers were noted for their self-confidence. Yet the freshmen of 1993 are even more confident of their abilities than were the freshmen of 1971. One-third of baby-boomer freshmen rated themselves above average in leadership, mathematics, popularity, and intellectual and social self-confidence. In 1993, 43 percent of entering students rated themselves above average in these areas.

The next baby boom will need all the confidence it can get. Their parents, the original boomers, experienced social turmoil during their childhood and young adulthood. But many of the issues facing today's young adults are far more frightening. They live in a world where violence and infectious diseases compete for attention with savage economic competition and rapid technological change.

As a new century begins, the next baby boom will enter the adult world and begin struggling with these problems. But their place in the record books is already secure. They may one day surpass their parents to become the largest and most influential generation in U.S. history.

the next baby boom are the least likely to have access to up-to-date technology. Two-thirds of households with personal computers in the home are headed by college graduates earning over $50,000, according to a 1994 survey by The Times Mirror Center for The People & The Press. But computers are present in only 15 percent of homes where the householder did not graduate from college and has earnings of less than $30,000. Half of college-educated parents say their children use PCs at home, compared with only 17 percent of parents with a high school diploma or less.

Changes in the computer market may eventually narrow this gap. "A lot of kids say they only have an old computer or access through a friend or someone else," says Zollo. "The gap in access may decrease as technology becomes more affordable and kids have more opportunities to use up-to-date technology at school."

Regardless of access, the next baby boom is convinced that computers are cool. Sixty-two percent of those aged 12 to 19 say online computing is 'in,' but only about 13 percent have been online in the past month," says Zollo. "That gap represents a huge opportunity."

"FLY TILL I DIE"

A little girl had a crush on planes. Her dad set his sights on sudden fame. Who had the sense to stop them?

RICHARD STENGEL

DAEDALUS WARNED HIS SON ICARUS not to fly too high, or the sun would melt his waxen wings. But the boy, intoxicated with flight, soared above his cautious father. In the clear blue sky, the warmth of the sun dissolved his delicate wings, causing him to plunge to his death in the green sea below. The myth of Icarus is used to illustrate the ancient Greek word Hubris, a term for the overweening human pride and vanity that often result in tragedy.

Jessica Dubroff's wings may have been frosted with ice, and she had no joy of flight on her last ride. She took off in a cold rain and died when her single-engine Cessna 177B nosedived onto the black tar of a suburban roadway. But her senseless death last week could also be attributed to a modern kind of hubris. For Jessica was urged on by overzealous parents, by a media drawn to a natural human-interest story and by a willfully blind Federal Aviation Administration, which permitted a 4-ft. 2-in., 55-lb. seven-year-old whose feet did not reach the rudder pedals to fly an airplane across the country in a misbegotten publicity stunt—as long as a licensed pilot was beside her. At week's end a federal investigator suggested that Jessica's Cessna was overloaded for the thin Rocky Mountain air and wind shear may have induced the flight instructor to take over the controls in the plane's last few moments.

The brief flight and violent fall of Jessica, her father Lloyd and flight instructor Joe Reid was seized upon and transformed into a kind of modern morality tale of parents looking for meaning and morning shows searching for novelty. On talk raid and in coffee shops, her soaring spirit and tragic plunge were the subjects of outrage and debate. Overnight she became the poster child of parental and media exploitation, of an ethos that granted children too much freedom rather than too little, of a parental drive not content to let children be children. Many wondered whether the freedom to pursue personal identity had been pushed too far.

Reared by separated parents whose fuzzy New Age philosophy was that children should follow their bliss, Jessica was encouraged to pursue an adult ambition that ill fitted her. After her death so many of the bright words that preceded the trip take on a grimly poetic quality. Her father, in Cheyenne after the first leg: "This started off as a father-daughter adventure, and its' gotten wonderfully out of hand." Jessica, to the *Times* of London: "I'm going to fly till I die." Her father: "I think I finally got my job description in order as a parent. I used to think being a parent meant teaching things. Now I feel my job is to help them learn by exposing them to new experience."

The hype of the whole enterprise, in retrospect, seems reckless. Let us tick off the deceptions that everyone involved pretended were true: the trip was Jessica's idea; she was doing it for the joy of flying; she was truly piloting the plane; it was safe; she wasn't scared. For the most part, the public played along with this game, for it is easier not to question the received platitudes. Yet, looking at her taped interviews after the fact, it is clear that the dutiful little girl who didn't want to disappoint her father, who insisted, "I fly for joy," looked anything but joyful.

Instead of a bogus record that inevitably would have been challenged by a still younger child (the *Guiness Book of Records* officially discontinued its Youngest Pilot categories in 1989, fearing accidents), Americans have a macabre photo album of little Jessica. A mini–Amelia Earhart, in a leather bomber jacket and riding pants. A plucky, pug-nosed girl in a baseball cap who seemed more at home on one of her beloved ponies than in a plane.

JESSICA'S QUEST TO BECOME THE YOUNGEST person to fly across the continent began last Wednesday in Half Moon Bay, California. She was to fly east in three legs, laying over in Cheyenne, Wyoming, and Fort Wayne, Indiana, before finally reaching Falmouth, Massachusetts, the town

where she was born. She had bumped down in Cheyenne on Wednesday night in a heavy crosswind. "The wind was pushing us out," she told reporters. "You just have to give the plane more power." According to her father, she had been assisted in the landing by Reid, her flight instructor, a veteran pilot and the president of the Half Moon Bay Pilots Association who had given her 35 hours of flying lessons. "We're trying to set a record," her father said, "But we're not trying to be stupid about it."

At the Cheyenne airport, the publicity machine went into action. The arrival was recorded by camera crews and a clutch of reporters, notebooks in hand. An exhausted Jessica seemed to understand that she always had to appear perky. "I enjoyed it," she said, forcing a smile, sounding, as always, like she was imitating adult speech. "I had two hours sleep last night." She was due to take off at 8:20 the next morning.

Cheyenne is a high-altitude airport, 6,156 ft. above sea level. The thinner air requires longer takeoff runs, and the pilot must factor this into the flight plan. "You may ask whether a seven-year-old did the figuring, and I don't know," says Charles Porter of Sky Harbor Air Service in Cheyenne. "A lot of pilots whose time is limited to sea level have forgotten and ended up in the golf course." The weather was ugly. A thunderstorm was moving in from the northwest, winds were 25 to 30 m.p.h. Thunderstorms are a potent cocktail for pilots, a possible mixture of updrafts, downdrafts, turbulence, icing and hail all at once. "I would have taxied up the runway and headed back," says "Red" Kelso of Cheyenne, a retired pilot with 52 years of flying experience. "There's no way I would have gone up in weather like that."

"The pilot is the person responsible for evaluating the weather conditions and determining whether to go," says airport manager Jerry Olson. The weather conditions were VFR—visual-flight rules—meaning instruments were not required, although another plane warned the control tower of wind shear. Jessica spoke to her mother on a cellphone as the plane was taxiing. "Mom, do you hear the rain?"

It was a sluggish, shaky takeoff. The four-seat Cessna seemed to shudder from the moment it lifted off Runway 30, and investigators have suggested it was too heavy for the conditions at that altitude. Everyone on board must have instantly realized something was wrong. Jessica's plane was equipped with dual controls, so that Reid could immediately take over in an emergency, and presumably he did—his arms were fractured more severely than hers, suggesting he had his hands on the yoke. In such a situation, an experienced pilot might have landed the plane on the golf course at the end of the runway or the four-lane road near the crash site. Instead, the Cessna was attempting a 180° turn to make its way back to the runway when it appeared to stall. For a moment, it seemed to stop in midair before it plunged vertically near the driveway of a single-story brick house about a mile north of the airport. It crumpled like a giant child's toy. Tom Johnson, a former pilot and claims adjuster for State Farm, was driving nearby and witnessed the crash. "It was struggling. You could tell it was overloaded," he said. "It fell like a lawn dart, straight down." According to the authorities, everyone on board was killed on impact.

Within half an hour, the plane was covered with a tarpaulin, like a shroud. Only its red-white-and-blue tail peeked out from beneath the covering. Soon the people of Cheyenne began to visit the crash site, leaving poems, flowers and stuffed animals. Two investigators for the National Transportation Safety Board were at the scene within a few hours. The plane did not have a flight recorder, nor was it required to have one. Steve McCreary, an NTSB investigator, could not say whether Reid had declared some sort of emergency before the crash.

Experienced pilots were left to wonder what happened. Perhaps Jessica would not have been able to maneuver out of the storm, but Reid certainly would have. Warren Morningstar of the Aircraft Owners and Pilots Association, said, with dual controls "the pilot in command can easily control the aircraft from either seat. There is never a situation in which the nonpilot can put the plane into such immediate peril that there is no recovery." Only after an analysis and "probable cause" finding in about six months will the FAA review its regulations covering young pilots.

JESSICA'S PARENTS SEEMED DETERMINED TO give their daughter independence from the start: she was delivered in a birthing tub without benefit of doctor or midwife. Her mother Lisa Blair Hathaway says she wanted her daughter to have a feeling of "floating." Her parents seemed to embrace a philosophy that was a mishmash of '60s idealism, Emersonian self-reliance and New Age cliché. Hathaway describes herself as an artist and a spiritual healer. While Jessica was mostly raised in Massachusetts,

> ## "This started off as a father-daughter adventure and it's gotten wonderfully out of hand."— Jessica's father

she lived in Pescadero, California, a tiny onetime fishing village where old dogs lazily patrol the streets because there is no traffic. It was 25 miles to Jessica's father's home in suburban San Mateo County, where he worked as a corporate consultant and lived with his current wife. Jessica and her mother lived in a house without television, which explains why Jessica's mother did not know who Jane Pauley was when the NBC star came to call after Jessica's death.

Real life was the best tutor, experience the best preparation for life. That was the attitude of Jessica's parents, and as a result, they kept Jessica, her brother Joshua, 9, and sister Jasmine, 3, at home—without filing a home-schooling plan with the local authorities. Hathaway seemed to have a reflexive distrust for institutions and convention and a fear of stifling her children. Jessica did not have dolls but tools. Instead of studying grammar, the children did chores and sought what their mother called "mastery." Boundaries seemed to be off limits, and parenting seemed to consist of cheerleading. "They're getting a tremendous education from having their lives be in the real world," Hathaway had said. "What it takes to get this flight scheduled and done is much better than sitting in a math classroom." Whether or not her children could do long division, they were seen by the townspeople who knew them as bright, curious and confident. "You get the feeling that everyone in the family was at peace," says Zona O'Neill, a Massachusetts friend. "My children enjoyed being around them because they were so loving and happy."

Jessica became interested in flying after her parents gave her an airplane ride for her sixth birthday, which was only 23 months ago. She began taking flying lessons twice a week with Reid, who said she was an able pilot, though what that means for a seven-year-old is open to question. Her father footed the bill for the flying lessons—about $50 an hour—and also shelled out about $15,000 for the cross-country odyssey.

"That's less than I'd pay for private school," Dubroff told the San Francisco Examiner.

He also admitted that "the trip was my idea but was presented to Jessica for her choice." No one disputes the girl was gung-ho, and her father became her press agent, courting all the usual engines of modern publicity: TV, radio, print. For all their New Age patter, Jessica's mother and father seemed to be stage parents of the old school, pushing their daughter in front of the curtain, hoping she would become a star, Macaulay Culkin in a cockpit. The week before the flight Jessica handed out signed photographs to members of the Half Moon city council. Dubroff spent $1,300 on custom-made baseball caps to distribute to friends and the media. They read, JESSICA WHITNEY DUBROFF, SEA TO SHINING SEA, APRIL 1996. He also primed her to write a letter to President Clinton, inviting him along for a ride. "To visit you at the White House would be wonderful," she wrote in her simple, child's hand, "and clearly to pilot an airplane that you would be in would bring me even greater joy." (The White House did not accept.)

But Jessica's flight plan found a receptive audience at the television networks. It was an ideal human-interest story. Upbeat. A natural narrative. Good visuals. A telegenic little girl with a dusting of freckles on her nose. A challenge. A record. Triumph. End with slo-mo of Jessica throwing her baseball cap in the air. Music from Chariots of Fire.

NBC's Today show did an interview with Jessica, her father and her flight instructor. CBS's overnight broadcast did a five-minute interview with Jessica and her dad in Cheyenne the morning before her last flight. The day before the flight, ABC gave Lloyd a Hi8 video camera, so he could "document the flight," an ABC spokeswoman said.

But even while they were covering the event, some at the networks were chary. This was not a child prodigy playing the violin at Carnegie Hall but a first-grader flying across the country. There was something queasy about the whole thing, a little girl going too far in pretending to be an adult. On Good Morning America, Forrest Sawyer asked Lloyd Dubroff, "[The flight] does raise the question. . . . I mean, when we hear this, we're kind of shocked. Is it illegal or dangerous or anything like that?"

To its credit, ABC confronted the issue of whether television was complicit in the

> ## "I just like to fly. It's like floating."— Jessica Dubroff

tragedy. On *Nightline*, Ted Koppel spoke for the network when he said, "We need to begin by acknowledging our own contribution. . . . We feed one another: those of you looking for publicity and those of us looking for stories." Then he posed the question of "whether we in the media . . . by our ravenous attention contribute to this phenomenon," and answered it himself: "We did."

J. Mac McClellan, editor in chief of *Flying* magazine, agrees. "Jessica's flight is the kind of thing that, absent media coverage, would never have happened," he says. So-called flying records by youngsters, he maintains, are a bogus concept. "We've intentionally ignored attempts like this here at *Flying* because we didn't want to promote the activity. It has no validity from an aviation sense; the pilot in reality is the certified pilot." The FAA regulations that allow children "to fly" with a certified pilot at the other controls are intended to facilitate teaching, not to encourage stunts. In what seems a semantic distinction, the FAA says Jessica was technically a passenger; a pilot must be at least 16 and have a license.

The gruesome irony is that the crash proved to be the best television story of all. Jessica completing her journey would have been the spirit-lifting final story on the evening news, the tale of human triumph over which anchors could smile winsomely and then say good-night, leaving the viewer with the feeling that all was right with the world. But Jessica's plane crash led all three network news broadcasts and headlined the front pages of newspapers across the country.

That night and the next morning, TV viewers were treated to a spectacle almost as disturbing as the accident itself: Jessica's eerily composed mother saying that if she had to do it over again, she would have done nothing differently. In Falmouth, where she got the news while waiting for her daughter's arrival, she declared, "I would want all my children to die in a state of joy. I would prefer it was not at the age of seven." The next morning she appeared on the *Today* show and told Katie Couric, "I'd have her do it again in a second. You have no idea what this meant to Jess." She even vowed to make sure the FAA doesn't revise its rules: "I can't bear the thought of them changing anything. Talk about setting people back!" Even at the crash site in Cheyenne, where she arrived with flowers in the afternoon, she continued to explain her philosophy of life. When a small boy tried to give her a teddy bear, she refused it, explaining that her children do not play with toys.

In Cheyenne on Friday evening, in an interview with TIME, she defended her own response to her daughter's death. Clutching a plastic bag of Jessica's clothes, she said defiantly, "I know what people want. Tears. But I will not do that. Emotion is unnatural. There is something untruthful about it." When she and her son Josh received the news of Jessica's death, Hathaway said, "Josh started to cry." Then she rephrased the sentence, as if the verb were somehow incorrect. "No, I would rather say he was in tears. He said he didn't want to fly anymore. I begged him to re-choose based on what he wanted instead of reacting to someone else's choice."

Jessica's mother even attached a patriotic gloss to Jessica's death, putting it in the context of the Declaration's rights to "life, liberty and the pursuit of happiness." "I did everything so this child could have freedom and choice," she told *Today*, "and have what America stands for. Liberty comes from being in that space of just living your life." But the Founding Fathers made a distinction between liberty and license, the latter being freedom that is used irresponsibly. License may have been precisely the freedom Jessica's parents gave her.

One of the notes placed at the crash site says simply, "God's newest little angel." But angels, of course, have wings to fly. —*Reported by Kerry A. Drake and Elaine Lafferty/Cheyenne, Sharon Epperson/Falmouth, Jerry Hannifin/Washington and William Tynan/New York*

Editor's note: In March 1997, the National Safety Board said that the weather and the pilot-instructor's fatigue and poor judgment in allowing Jessica Dubroff to take off during a storm were responsible for the plane crash. Evidence from the wreck indicated that Joe Reid, not Jessica, was most likely in command of the plane when it went down.

The National Television Violence Study: Key Findings and Recommendations

Editor's note: *The National Television Violence Study is a three-year effort to assess violence on television. Underwritten by the National Cable Television Association, the independent analysis is coordinated by an autonomous nonprofit organization, Mediascope. Oversight is provided by a council whose members reflect national leadership in education, medicine, violence prevention, the creative community, law, psychology, and communication, with one-third of the council representing the entertainment industry. Four universities are involved in three study components. The Universities of California at Santa Barbara and Texas at Austin are doing a content analysis to assess the amount and context of television violence. The University of Wisconsin at Madison is researching how children respond to viewer advisories and ratings, and the University of North Carolina at Chapel Hill is examining adolescents' responses to antiviolence messages on television. This report is excerpted from the* National Television Violence Study 1994–95 Executive Summary, *the first in a series of three annual reports. Here we present a summary of key findings related to the content analysis and the study's recommendations.*

Preventing violence involves identifying the combination of factors that contribute to it, from biological and psychological causes to broader social and cultural ones. Among these, television violence has been recognized as a significant factor contributing to violent and aggressive antisocial behavior by an overwhelming majority of the scientific community.

However, it is also recognized that televised violence does not have a uniform effect on viewers. The outcome of media violence depends both on the nature of the depiction and the sociological and psychological makeup of the audience. In some cases, the same portrayal of violence may have different effects on different audiences. For example, graphically portrayed violence may elicit fear in some viewers and aggression in others. Family role models, social and economic status, educational level, peer influences, and the availability of weapons can each significantly alter the likelihood of a particular reaction to viewing televised violence.

The context in which violence is portrayed may modify the contributions to viewer behaviors and attitudes. Violence may be performed by heroic characters or villains. It may be rewarded or it may be punished. Violence may occur without much victim pain and suffering or it may cause tremendous physical anguish. It may be shown close-up on the screen or at a distance.

This study is the most comprehensive scientific assessment yet conducted of the context in which violence is depicted on television, based on some 2,500 hours of programming randomly selected from 23 television channels between 6 A.M. to 11 P.M. over a 20-week period. Television content was analyzed at three distinct levels: (1) how characters interact with one another when violence occurs (violent interaction); (2) how violent interactions are grouped together (violent scene); and (3) how violence is presented in the context of the overall program.

Violence is defined as any overt depiction of the use of physical force—or the credible threat of such force—intended to physically harm an animate being or group of beings. Violence also includes certain depictions of physically harmful consequences against an animate being or group that occur as a result of unseen violent means.

Key findings

• *The context in which most violence is presented on television poses risks for viewers.* The majority of programs analyzed in this study contain some violence. But more important than the prevalence of violence is the contextual pattern in which most of it is shown. The risks of viewing the most common depictions of televised violence include learning to behave violently, becoming more desensitized to the harmful consequences of violence, and becoming more fearful of being attacked. The contextual patterns noted below are found consistently across most channels, program types, and times of day. Thus, there are substantial risks of harmful effects of viewing violence throughout the television environment.

• *Perpetrators go unpunished in 73% of all violent scenes.* This pattern is highly consistent across different types of programs and channels. The portrayal of rewards and punishments is probably the most important of all contextual factors for viewers as they interpret the meaning of what they see on television. When violence is presented without punishment, viewers are more likely to learn the lesson that violence is successful.

• *The negative consequences of violence are not often portrayed in violent programming.* Most violent portrayals do not show the victim experiencing any serious physical harm or pain at the time the violence occurs. For example, 47% of all violent interactions show no harm to victims and 58% show no pain. Even less frequent is the depiction of any long-term consequences of violence. In fact, only 16% of all programs portray the long-term negative repercussions of violence, such as psychological, financial, or emotional harm.

• *One out of four violent interactions on television (25%) involves the use of a handgun.* Depictions of violence with guns and other conventional weapons can instigate or trigger aggressive thoughts and behaviors.

• *Only 4% of violent programs emphasize an antiviolence theme.* Very few violent programs place emphasis on condemning the use of violence or on presenting alternatives to using violence to solve problems. This pattern is consistent across different types of programs and channels.

• *On the positive side, television violence is usually not explicit or graphic.* Most violence is presented without any close-up focus on aggressive behaviors and without showing any blood and gore. In particular, less than 3% of violent scenes feature close-ups on the violence and only 15% of scenes contain blood and gore. Explicit or graphic violence contributes to desensitization and can enhance fear.

• *There are some notable differences in the presentation of violence across television channels.* Public broadcasting presents violent programs least often (18%) and those violent depictions that appear pose the least risk of harmful effects. Premium cable channels present the highest percentage of violent programs (85%) and those depictions often pose a greater risk of harm than do most violent portrayals. Broadcast networks present violent programs less frequently (44%) than the industry norm (57%), but when violence is included its contextual features are just as problematic as those on most other channels.

• *There are also some important differences in the presentation of violence across types of television programs.* Movies are more likely to present violence in realistic settings (85%) and to include blood and gore in violent scenes (28%) than other program types. The contextual pattern of violence in children's programming also poses concern. Children's programs are the least likely of all genres to show the long-term negative consequences of violence (5%), and they frequently portray violence in a humorous context (67%).

Recommendations

These recommendations are based both on the findings of this study and extensive research upon which this study is based.

For the television community

• Produce more programs that avoid violence. When violence does occur, keep the number of incidents low, show more negative consequences, provide nonviolent alternatives to solving problems, and consider emphasizing antiviolence themes.

• Increase portrayals of powerful nonviolent heroes and attractive characters.

Although violence in society has many causes, the effect of thousands of messages conveyed through the most powerful medium of mass communication cannot be ignored.

• Programs with high levels of violence, including reality programs, should be scheduled in late-evening hours when children are less likely to be watching.

• Increase the number of program advisories and content codes. In doing so, however, use caution in language so that such messages do not serve as magnets to children.

• Provide information about advisories and the nature of violent content to viewers in programming guides.

• Limit the time devoted to sponsor, station, or network identification during public service announcements (PSAs) so that it does not compete with the message.

For policy and public interest leaders

• Recognize that context is an essential aspect of television violence and that the basis of any policy proposal should consider the types of violent depictions that pose the greatest concern.

• Consider the feasibility of technology that would allow parents to restrict access to inappropriate content.

• Test antiviolence PSAs, including the credibility of spokespersons, with target audiences prior to production. Provide target audiences with specific and realistic actions for resolving conflicts peacefully.

• When possible, link antiviolence PSAs to school-based or community efforts and target young audiences, 8 to 13 years old, who may be more responsive to such messages.

For parents

• Watch television with your child. In this study, children whose parents were routinely involved with their child's viewing were more likely to avoid inappropriate programming.

• Encourage critical evaluation of television content.

• Consider a child's developmental level when making viewing decisions.

• Be aware of the potential risks associated with viewing television violence: the learning of aggressive attitudes and behaviors, fear, desensitization or loss of sympathy toward victims of violence.

• Recognize that different kinds of violent programs pose different risks.

The *National Television Violence Study Executive Summary 1994–95* is published by Mediascope, Inc., and is available for $10 prepaid. For further information, contact Mediascope at 12711 Ventura Boulevard, Studio City, CA 91604; 818-508-2080; fax 818-508-2088; e-mail: mediascope@mediascope.org

It's Hard to Do Day Care Right—and Survive

Sue Shellenbarger

Staff Reporter of The Wall Street Journal

Donna Krause is in a cutthroat business. When she raises prices just 3%, she loses customers to cheaper competitors. While she tries to provide high-quality service, she can't pay enough to keep trained workers. To cut costs, she has professional employees scrub toilets and mop floors, and she spends her evenings shopping for cheap supplies. Still, twice in the past month she has had to dip into her personal savings just to meet the payroll.

Ms. Krause's business: She cares for children. "There just aren't enough resources to go around," says the owner and director of Creative Learning and Child Care Center in Dundalk, Md. "We drive ourselves crazy and we drive our parents crazy" trying to make ends meet.

U.S. child care is increasingly under attack by researchers as mediocre or even harmful to children. A new generation of studies concludes that only a small minority of the estimated nine million children in child care outside their homes get the nurturing attention they need. "Compared with what we used to see in the 1970s, I would have to say that the quality of child care is declining," says Carollee Howes, a professor at the University of California, Los Angeles, and a leading child-care researcher.

A close look at the economics of child care suggests that quantum leaps in quality won't come soon. A vast underground market for cheap, unregulated care acts as a ball-and-chain on centers' prices. Most experts believe that low teacher turnover, staff training, ample materials and a planned curriculum help to achieve quality day care. But despite their good intentions, directors of child-care centers must make excruciating tradeoffs to attain even one or two of these goals.

Ms. Krause, who has a master's degree in education, pours all the resources she can into teacher pay and training. She spent $2,000 last year to expand an in-house teacher resource center and runs training courses. She ekes out 25- to 50-cent-an-hour annual raises for her teachers, who start at a minimum of $4.50 an hour, partly by spending her evenings shopping for cheap cleaning fluids and sink strainers. Last year, when the center finished the year with a small profit, she split it among the teachers.

But giving raises is getting harder each year. When Ms. Krause raised tuition just 50 cents a day a few years ago to $70 a week, she lost six families from her 90-child center. So she badgers her parents to help fix gate latches and donate toys, and she runs constant fund-raisers, blanketing the neighborhood with kids selling candy bars. To make ends meet, she had to fire the cleaning service and ask teachers to wash cots and scrub toys. "That's a dirty job for someone who has a degree," she says. Asked where the next budget cut will come from, she says, "There is no other" that can be made.

Increasingly, her teachers are quitting for higher-paying jobs. When one teacher left abruptly earlier this year to take a temporary job at General Motors for $13 an hour, painful ripples spread through the center. "Her partner cried all day" out of a sense of betrayal and frustration that she would have to train a new co-worker in the thousands of details of running a classroom, Ms. Krause says. Worse yet, "boom, she's out of the lives of the kids."

Mary Wortman's three-year-old, one of the children in the room, "just doesn't understand where [his teacher] went. He wants to see her," his mother says. Ms. Wortman, a first-grade teacher and former child-care worker herself, worries that if too many important people depart from a preschooler's life, "it becomes very hard for a child to trust anybody."

Some centers, particularly nonprofit centers that receive donated space, manage to hold teacher turnover down by using as much as 80% of their budgets for salaries. Still, they often have to sacrifice basic equipment. Bob French, director of three nonprofit centers in New Bedford, Mass., holds turnover to 10% a year partly by starting staff at $8.32 an hour. He has put together a "tattered patchwork" of subsidies and grants by working seven days a week. But he can't afford to put in a playground at one center even though he has the space; children have to walk to a neighborhood park instead.

Sue Britson, director of the nonprofit Step One School in Berkeley, Calif., pays well enough to attract experienced teachers with college degrees. But she spent a week recently trying to shave $1,000 off the center's insurance costs. She also had to make painful cuts in materials, using recycled toys and cheap art supplies. "Kids get less interested in painting" with poor paints, she says. "They have to work so much harder to get a lousy watercolor to perform for them."

Among the 35% of child-care centers that operate for profit, many don't make any money. Others eke out slim margins by paying teachers less, while a few target the small proportion of more affluent parents who will pay higher tuition.

Despite the improving economy, center directors say parental resistance to higher prices is intensifying. For many years, Ms. Britson, whose school is in an affluent area, raised tuition 4.5% annually to finance 6% teacher-pay raises. But this year, the formula no longer works. Parents "squeezed their time down to fewer hours so they didn't need full-time care" anymore, she says.

The Economics Of Child Care

Where the Revenue Comes From ...

Tuition	93%
In-kind donations*	5
Fund-raisers	1
Parent fees for extra services	1

*Services, supplies and equipment donated by parents and director

... And Where It Goes

Staff pay and benefits	70%
Rent	15
Supplies	5
Staff training and materials	3
Loans and bank fees	3
Utilities	2
Insurance	1
Miscellaneous	1

Source: Creative Learning and Child Care Center, Dundalk, Md.

Nancy Doniger

Inflation-adjusted pay for the lowest-paid assistant teachers has actually fallen 1.5% since 1988 to an average of $5.08 an hour, or $8,890 a year, a 1992 study by the Child Care Employee Project shows, leaving many child-care workers below the poverty line. Renee Sutton, a Raleigh, N.C., child-care worker, had to support herself and her two daughters on food stamps while working full-time at $5.40 an hour for a child-care chain.

And annual teacher turnover, already about 25% to 40% industrywide, threatens to get worse as service industries generate more jobs paying $5 to $8 an hour. Ms. Krause has lost two of her 10 teachers in the past month. When she advertises, she fights a losing battle for applicants with a new Home Depot store nearby.

Consuelo Marie Sullivan, one of the teachers leaving Ms. Krausë's center, loves the work and moonlighted 16 hours a week selling shoes to pay for night classes in child development. "When parents say, 'Christopher talked about this today,' I can say to myself, 'I taught

him that,' " she says. But she is getting married next year and wants to save money, so she has taken a higher-paying job in retailing. "I gotta do what I gotta do," she says.

The best teachers often leave first. Kevin Becketti, a bearded six-footer who works at Step One School, has a talent for working with aggressive kids. He plays basketball with them and tells stories that help them develop self-control. At parties, he delights them by donning a pirate suit. "He is a fabulous teacher," says his boss, Ms. Britson.

But come fall, Mr. Becketti will leave Step One. The only car he can afford, an aged Volkswagen van, can't even make it to the top of the hill where the school is located. "I can't maintain this [salary] and do any of the things I might want to do later on, like have a better car and maybe a house one day," he says.

Though advocacy groups have campaigned to get parents to pay more for child care, parents resist. They are already paying 6% to 30% of their income for day care and either can't or won't pay more. Child care is seen as a low-paying

service, "and changing it is not just a matter of changing people's moral sensibility," says James Greenman, a vice president of Resources for Child Care Management, Morristown, N.J.

And unlike France, Belgium, Sweden and Finland, where child care is part of public education, the U.S. leaves child care mostly to the private sector. Day-care costs for some poor families are subsidized, but few people expect government to start financing universal child care.

Improved management alone isn't the answer either. A three-year study at 20 Minneapolis-area child-care programs found that improving management increased resources about 10%. "You're going to need a lot more than a 10% increase in the budget to get those teachers up to $9 or $10 an hour," says Nancy Johnson, director of center-management services for the nonprofit Greater Minneapolis Day Care Association.

"The problem is much bigger," Ms. Johnson says. "This is a failure in the marketplace."

NAEYC Position Statement: Technology and Young Children— Ages Three through Eight

Adopted April 1996

In this position statement, we use the word technology *to refer primarily to computer technology, but this can be extended to include related technologies, such as telecommunications and multimedia, which are becoming integrated with computer technology.*

Technology plays a significant role in all aspects of American life today, and this role will only increase in the future. The potential benefits of technology for young children's learning and development are well documented (Wright & Shade 1994). As technology becomes easier to use and early childhood software proliferates, young children's use of technology becomes more widespread. Therefore, early childhood educators have a responsibility to critically examine the impact of technology on children and be prepared to use technology to benefit children.

Market researchers tracking software trends have identified that the largest software growth recently has been in new titles and companies serving the early childhood educational market. Of the people who own home computers and have young children, 70% have purchased educational software for their children to use (*SPA Consumer Market Report* 1996). While many new titles are good contributions to the field, an even larger number are not (Haugland & Shade 1994).

Early childhood educators must take responsibility to influence events that are transforming the daily lives of children and families. This statement addresses several issues related to technology's use with young children: (1) the essential role of the teacher in evaluating appropriate uses of technology; (2) the potential benefits of appropriate use of technology in early childhood programs; (3) the integration of technology into the typical learning environment; (4) equitable access to technology, including children with special needs; (5) stereotyping and violence in software; (6) the role of teachers and parents as advocates; and (7) the implications of technology for professional development.

NAEYC's position

Although now there is considerable research that points to the positive effects of technology on children's learning and development (Clements 1994), the research indicates that, in practice, computers supplement and do not replace highly valued early childhood activities and materials, such as art, blocks, sand, water, books, exploration with writing materials, and dramatic play. Research indicates that computers can be used in developmentally appropriate ways beneficial to children and also can be misused, just as any tool can (Shade & Watson 1990). Developmentally appropriate software offers opportunities for collaborative play, learning, and creation. Educators must use professional judgment in evaluating and using this learning tool appropriately, applying the same criteria they would to any other learning tool or experience. They must also weigh the costs of technology with the costs of other learning materials and program resources to arrive at an appropriate balance for their classrooms.

1. In evaluating the appropriate use of technology, NAEYC applies principles of developmentally appropriate practice (Bredekamp 1987) and appropriate curriculum and assessment (NAEYC & NAECS/SDE 1992.) In short, NAEYC believes that in any given situation, a professional judgment by the teacher is required to determine if a specific use of technology is age appropriate, individually appropriate, and culturally appropriate.

The teacher's role is critical in making certain that good decisions are made about which technology to use and in supporting children in their use of technology to ensure that potential benefits are achieved.

Teachers must take time to evaluate and choose software in light of principles of development and learning and must carefully observe children using the software to identify both opportunities and problems and make appropriate adaptations. Choosing appropriate software is similar to choosing appropriate books for the classroom—teachers constantly make judgments about what is age appropriate, individually appropriate, and culturally appropriate. Teachers should look for ways to use computers to support the development and learning that occur in other parts of the classroom and the development and learning that happen with computers in complement with activities off the computer. Good teaching practices must always be the guiding goal when selecting and using new technologies.

2. Used appropriately, technology can enhance children's cognitive and social abilities.

Computers are intrinsically compelling for young children. The sounds and graphics gain children's attention. Increasingly, young children observe adults and older children working on computers, and they want to do it, too. Children get interested because they can make things happen with computers. Developmentally appropriate software engages children in creative play, mastery learning, problem solving, and conversation. The children control the pacing and the action. They can repeat a process or activity as often as they like and experiment with variations. They can collaborate in making decisions and share their discoveries and creations (Haugland & Shade 1990).

Well-designed early childhood software grows in dimension with the child, enabling her to find new challenges as she becomes more proficient. Appropriate visual and verbal prompts designed in the software expand play themes and opportunities while leaving the child in control. Vast collections of images, sounds, and information of all kinds are placed at the child's disposal. Software can be made age appropriate even for children as young as three or four.

When used appropriately, technology can support and extend traditional materials in valuable ways. Research points to the positive effects of technology in children's learning and development, both cognitive and social (Clements 1994; Haugland & Shade 1994). In addition to actually developing children's abilities, technology provides an opportunity for assessment. Observing the child at the computer offers teachers a "window" onto a child's thinking. Just as parents continue to read to children who can read themselves, parents and teachers should both participate with children in computer activities and encourage children to use computers on their own and with peers.

Research demonstrates that when working with a computer children prefer working with one or two partners over working alone (Lipinski et al. 1986; Rhee & Chavnagri 1991; Clements, Nastasi, & Swaminathan 1993). They seek help from one another and seem to prefer help from peers over help from the teacher (King & Alloway 1992; Nastasi & Clements 1993). Children engage in high levels of spoken communication and cooperation at the computer. They initiate interactions more frequently and in different ways than when engaged with traditional activities, such as puzzles or blocks. They engage in more turn taking at the computer and simultaneously show high levels of language and cooperative-play activity.

Technology extends benefits of collaboration beyond the immediate classroom environment for children in the primary grades who can already read and write. With the potential of access to the Internet or other on-line "user friendly" networks, young children can collaborate with children in other classrooms, cities, counties, states, and even countries. Through electronic field trips in real time or via diskette, children are able to share different cultural and environmental experiences. Electronic mail and telecommunications opportunities through the Internet facilitate direct communication and promote social interactions previously limited by the physical location of participating learners.

3. Appropriate technology is integrated into the regular learning environment and used as one of many options to support children's learning.

Every classroom has its own guiding philosophies, values, schedules, themes, and activities. As part of the teacher's overall classroom plan, computers should be used in ways that support these existing classroom educational directions rather than distort or replace them. Computers should be integrated into early childhood practice physically, functionally, and philosophically. Teachers can accommodate integration in at least five ways:

• Locate computers in the classroom, rather than in a separate computer lab (Davis & Shade 1994).

• Integrate technology into the daily routine of classroom activity. For example, a teacher might introduce musical rhythm with actions, recordings, and a computer used as an electronic rhythm-matching game. The children then would work in small groups with the computer program serving as one of several learning centers.

• Choose software to enrich curriculum content, other classroom activities, or concepts. For example, the program in the computer learning center might allow children to invent their own rhythms that they could simultaneously hear played back and see displayed graphically. They could edit these rhythms on the computer, hearing and seeing the changes.

• Use technology to integrate curriculum across subject-matter areas. For example, one group of children used the computer to make signs for a restaurant in their dramatic-play area (Apple Computer Inc. 1993). The rhythm program helps children connect mathematical patterns to musical patterns.

• Extend the curriculum, with technology offering new avenues and perspectives. For example, exploring shapes on the computer provides opportunities to stretch, shrink, bend, and combine shapes into new forms. Such activities enrich and extend children's activities with physical manipulatives.

4. **Early childhood educators should promote equitable access to technology for all children and their families. Children with special needs should have increased access when this is helpful.**

Educators using technology need to be especially sensitive to issues of equity.

A decade of research on the educational use of computers in schools reveals that computers maintain and exaggerate inequalities (Sutton 1991). Sutton found gender, race, and social-class inequalities in the educational uses of computers, which Thouvenelle, Borunda, and McDowell summarize below.

• Girls used computers in and out of school less often than did boys.

• African American students had less access to computers than did White students.

• Presence of computers in a school did not ensure access.

• Teachers, while concerned about equity, held attitudes that hindered access—they believed that better behaved students deserved more computer time and that the primary benefit of computers for low-achieving students was mastery of basic skills (i.e., drill-and-practice software).

• Richer schools bought more equipment and more expensive equipment. (1994, 153–54)

These findings identify trends that, unchecked, will almost certainly lead to increased inequity in the future. Early childhood educators must find ways to incorporate technology into their classrooms that preserve equity of access and minimize or even reverse the current trends. For example, anecdotal reports indicate that preschool-age boys and girls show equal interest in computers, but as they grow older girls begin to spend less time with

computers than do boys. There are a number of ways educators can proactively work to maintain girls' interest in computers and technology: (1) consider girls' interests and interaction styles when selecting and evaluating software for classroom use; (2) model the use of the computer as a learning and productivity tool and invite children, especially girls, to observe and assist them in the work; and (3) promote equity by offering special times for "girls only" use of computers, which permits girls to explore the computer without having to directly compete with boys (Thouvenelle, Borunda, & McDowell 1994).

Considerations of equity in curriculum content require qualitative judgments. For example, research evidence indicates that children who are economically disadvantaged have less access to computers at home and at-home access is related to attitudes and competence (Martinez & Mead 1988). If schools wish to provide equity to children of low-income families, with respect to their confidence and competence concerning computer learning, these children need to be provided more in-school computer access (Sutton 1991). And that access must be meaningful, moving beyond rote drill-and-practice usage.

Preschool-age children spend time in a variety of diverse settings (e.g., homes, child care centers, family child care), which further complicates the issues of equity and access. Some of these settings have considerable access to technology while others lack the very basics. The more early childhood educators believe in the benefits of appropriate use of technology at the preschool age, the more responsibility we bear in ensuring equity and access to this important learning tool.

Efforts should be made to ensure access to appropriate technology for children with special needs, for whom assistive technologies may be essential for successful inclusion.

For children with special needs, technology has many potential benefits. Technology can be a powerful compensatory tool—it can augment sensory input or reduce distractions; it can provide support for cognitive processing or enhance memory and recall; it can serve as a personal "on-demand" tutor and as an enabling device that supports independent functioning.

The variety of assistive-technology products ranges from low-tech toys with simple switches to expansive high-tech systems capable of managing complex environments. These technologies empower young children, increasing their independence and supporting their inclusion in classes with their peers. With adapted materials, young children with disabilities no longer have to be excluded from activities. Using appropriately designed and supported computer applications, the ability to learn, move, communicate, and recreate are within the reach of all learners.

Yet, with all these enhanced capabilities, this technology requires thoughtful integration into the early childhood curriculum, or it may fall far short of its promise. Educators must match the technology to each child's unique special needs, learning styles, and individual preferences.

5. **The power of technology to influence children's learning and development requires that attention be paid to eliminating stereotyping of any group and eliminating exposure to violence, especially as a problem-solving strategy.**

Technology can be used to affirm children's diversity.

Early childhood educators must devote extra effort to ensure that the software in classrooms reflects and affirms children's diverse cultures, languages, and ethnic heritages. Like all educational materials, software should reflect the world children live in: It should come in multiple languages, reflect gender equity, contain people of color and of differing ages and abilities, and portray diverse families and experiences (Derman-Sparks & A.B.C. Task Force 1989; Haugland & Shade 1994).

Teachers should actively select software that promotes positive social values.

Just like movies and television today, children's software is often violent and much of it explicit and brutally graphic, as in most of the best-selling titles for the popular game machines. But, often, violence is presented in ways that are less obvious. In all of its forms, violence in software threatens young children's development and challenges early childhood educators, who must take active steps to keep it out of their classrooms (see the *NAEYC Position Statement on Violence in the Lives of Children* 1994).

Some software programs offer children the opportunity to get rid of mistakes by "blowing up" their creations—complete with sound effects—instead of simply erasing or starting over. As a metaphor for solving problems or getting rid of mistakes, "blowing up" is problematic. In the context of a computer software experience, it is more troubling than in the context of television or video. Children control the computer software, and, instead of being passive viewers of what appears on the screen, with the computer they become active decisionmakers about what takes place on the screen. Software programs that empower children to freely blow up or destroy without thought of the actual consequences of their actions can further the disconnection between personal responsibility and violent outcomes.

Identifying and eliminating software containing violence is only one of the challenges facing early childhood educators. A related, opposite challenge is discovering software programs that promote positive social actions. For example, software has the potential to offer children opportunities to develop sensitivities to children from other cultures or to children with disabilities. Much could be done to help children develop positive responses to cultural and racial diversity by offering software programs that enable children to explore the richness within their own and different cultures.

6. **Teachers, in collaboration with parents, should advocate for more appropriate technology applications for all children.**

The appropriate and beneficial use of technology with young children is ultimately the responsibility of the early childhood educator, working in collaboration with parents. Parents and teachers together need to make better choices as consumers. As they become educated on the appropriate uses of technology, parents and teachers are more likely to make informed decisions and to make it known to developers of technology when they are unhappy with products. Working together, parents and teachers are a large consumer group wielding greater influence on the development of technology for young children. Following are specific recommendations for early childhood professionals as they advocate for more appropriate technology applications for all children.

• Provide information to parents on the benefits and use of appropriate software.

• Advocate for computer hardware that can be upgraded easily as new technology becomes available.

• Encourage software publishers to make previewing of software easier for parents and educators.

• Advocate for a system of software review by educators.

• Promote the development of software and technology applications that routinely incorporate features that cater to the needs of learners with different abilities.

• Advocate for software that promotes positive representation of gender, cultural and linguistic diversity, and abilities. Software publishers should create a balance of programs that appeal to both boys and girls.

• Encourage software publishers to create programs that support collaboration among learners rather than competition. Fostering cooperative learning enhances the acceptance of the abilities of all learners.

• Encourage software publishers to develop programs that reflect appropriate, nonviolent ways to solve problems and correct mistakes.

• Develop formal and informal information sharing and support for teachers, parents, and appropriate organizations and community-based programs. Encourage free community access to technology through libraries, schools, and so forth.

• Support policies on federal, state, and local levels that encourage funding that supports equity in access to technology for young children and their families.

7. **The appropriate use of technology has many implications for early childhood professional development.**

> *As early childhood educators become active participants in a technological world, they need in-depth training and ongoing support to be adequately prepared to make decisions about technology and to support its effective use in learning environments for children.*

To achieve the potential benefits of technology, both preservice and inservice training must provide early childhood educators with opportunities for basic information and awareness. These efforts must address the rapid proliferation and fast-paced change within the technology arena. Opportunities that emphasize evaluating the software in relation to children's development are essential.

Institutions of higher education and other organizations and groups that provide preservice and inservice education have a responsibility to

• incorporate experiences that permit educators to reflect on the principles of early childhood education and how technology can support and extend these principles;

• give teachers concentrated time to focus on how best to use educational technology and to develop a plan for the use of educational technology in a school or early childhood program;

• provide hands-on training with appropriate software programs to assist teachers in becoming familiar and comfortable with the operation and features of hardware and software; and

• provide on-site and school-based training on effectively integrating technology into the curriculum and assessment process.

At the classroom level, teachers need staff-development experiences (Kearsley & Lynch 1992) that permit them to

• use teaching techniques that fully use the technology;

• encourage parental involvement with technology;

• match technology applications to the learning needs of individual children;

• look for cross-curriculum/cross-cultural applications;

• facilitate cooperative interactions among children; and

• use technology to improve personal efficiency.

The potentials of technology are far-reaching and ever changing. The risk is for adults to become complacent, assuming that their current knowledge or experience is adequate. "Technology is an area of the curriculum, as well as a tool for learning, in which teachers must demonstrate their own capacity for learning" (Bredekamp & Rosegrant 1994, 61). As teachers try out their new knowledge in the classroom, there should be opportunities to share experiences and insights, problems and challenges with other educators. When teachers become comfortable and confident with the new technology, they can be offered additional challenges and stimulated to reach new levels of competence in using technology.

> *Early childhood educators should use technology as a tool for communication and collaboration among professionals as well as a tool for teaching children.*

Technology can be a powerful tool for professional development. Software can provide accessible information and tools for classroom management, planning, and creation of materials. Telecommunications and the Internet can enable teachers to obtain information and new ideas from around the world and to interact with distant experts and peers. Early childhood educators can incorporate principles of cooperative learning as they assist distant peers in acquiring new skills; share curriculum ideas, resources, and promising practices; exchange advice; and collaborate on classroom and professional development projects. Providing training and support for access to services available via on-line networks and the Internet has the potential of opening the doors to worlds of additional classroom resources. With a responsive on-line system, mentors can assist novices in becoming more technology literate and more involved in actively using technology for professional benefits. As educators become competent users of technology for personal and professional growth, they can model appropriate use for young children.

References

Apple Computer Inc. 1993. *The adventure begins: Preschool and technology.* Videocassette. (Available from NAEYC.)

Bredekamp, S., ed. 1987. *Developmentally appropriate practice in early childhood programs serving children from birth through age 8.* Exp. ed. Washington, DC: NAEYC.

Bredekamp, S., & T. Rosegrant. 1994. Learning and teaching with technology. In *Young children: Active learners in a technological age,* eds. J.L. Wright & D.D. Shade, 53–61. Washington, DC: NAEYC.

Clements, D.H. 1994. The uniqueness of the computer as a learning tool: Insights from research and practice. In *Young children: Active learners in a technological age,* eds. J.L. Wright & D.D. Shade, 31–50. Washington, DC: NAEYC.

Clements, D.H., B.K. Nastasi, & S. Swaminathan. 1993. Young children and computers: Crossroads and directions from research. *Young Children* 48 (2): 56–64.

Davis, B.C., & D.D. Shade. 1994. Integrate, don't isolate!—Computers in the early childhood curriculum. *ERIC Digest* (December). No. EDO-PS-94-17.

Derman-Sparks, L., & the A.B.C. Task Force. 1989. *Anti-bias curriculum: Tools for empowering young children.* Washington, DC: NAEYC.

Haugland, S.W., & D.D. Shade. 1990. *Developmental evaluations of software for young children: 1990 edition.* New York: Delmar.

Haugland, S.W., & D.D. Shade. 1994. Software evaluation for young children. In *Young children: Active learners in a technological age,* eds. J.L. Wright & D.D. Shade, 63–76. Washington, DC: NAEYC.

Kearsley, G., & W. Lynch. 1992. Educational leadership in the age of technology: The new skills. *Journal of Research on Computing in Education* 25 (1): 50–60.

King, J.A., & N. Alloway. 1992. Preschooler's use of microcomputers and input devices. *Journal of Educational Computing Research* 8: 451–68.

Lipinski, J.A., R.E. Nida, D.D. Shade, & J.A. Watson. 1986. The effect of microcomputers on young children: An examination of free-play choices, sex differences, and social interactions. *Journal of Educational Computing Research* 2 (2): 147–68.

Martinez, M.E., & N.A. Mead. 1988. *Computer competence: The first national assessment.* Tech report no. 17-CC-01. Princeton, NJ: National Educational Progress and Educational Testing Service.

NAEYC position statement on violence in the lives of children. 1994. Washington, DC: NAEYC.

NAEYC, & NAECS/SDE (National Association of Early Childhood Specialists in State Departments of Education). 1992. Guidelines for appropriate curriculum content and assessment in programs serving children ages 3 through 8. In *Reaching potentials: Appropriate curriculum and assessment for young children, volume 1,* eds. S. Bredekamp & T. Rosegrant, 9–27. Washington, DC: NAEYC.

Nastasi, B.K., & D.H. Clements. 1993. Motivational and social outcomes of cooperative education environments. *Journal of Computing in Childhood Education* 4 (1): 15–43.

Rhee, M.C., & N. Chavnagri. 1991. *4 year old children's peer interactions when playing with a computer.* ERIC, ED 342466.

Shade, D.D., & J.A. Watson. 1990. Computers in early education: Issues put to rest, theoretical links to sound practice, and the potential contribution of microworlds. *Journal of Educational Computing Research* 6 (4): 375–92.

SPA consumer market report. 1996. Washington, DC: Software Publishers Association (SPA).

Sutton, R.E. 1991. Equity and computers in the schools: A decade of research. *Review of Educational Research* 61 (4): 475–503.

Thouvenelle, S., M. Borunda, & C. McDowell. 1994. Replicating inequities: Are we doing it again? In *Young children: Active learners in a technological age,* eds. J.L. Wright & D.D. Shade, 151–66. Washington, DC: NAEYC.

Wright, J.L., & D.D. Shade, eds. 1994. *Young children: Active learners in a technological age.* Washington, DC: NAEYC.

Child Development and Families

Startling information about brain development has been released that has brought on a flurry of speculation about the best ways to prepare children for a lifetime of learning. The information pediatric neurobiologists now have indicates that the types of experiences children have prior to the age of 10 can affect their future capacity to learn. Early experiences, once thought to be useless, now have been found to help support the developing neurons in a child's brain. These neurons, which make successful complete connections when a child is young, will be used in the future to work complicated mathematical problems, learn a second language, or play a musical instrument.

Knowledge of the way a child's brain develops led the writers of the Carnegie Corporation Starting Points Report to conclude, "How children function from the preschool years all the way through adolescence, and even adulthood, hinges in large part on their experiences before the age of three." This information is exciting to early childhood professionals. It has been the focus for over a year of planning on a public engagement campaign that started in the spring of 1997. This campaign will educate parents and the general public on the importance of a young child's early years to future learning. The care and education received prior to the age of three can deter-

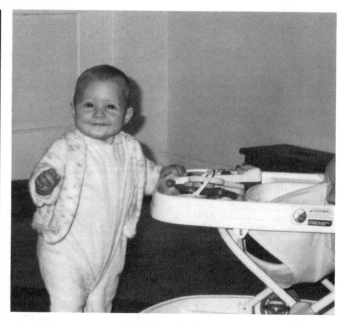

mine the success a child will have in developing new skills. There is a danger that parents and others will try to push learning on a young child. What the findings on brain development do indicate is that experiences that allow a child to investigate and explore a variety of sounds, objects, and materials can foster the development of neurons. It is also important to note that parents who did not provide for a stimulating early environment for their children should not be seen as failures. Learning experiences that will affect future learning can be offered throughout life.

We cannot separate the child from his or her family or home environment. Therefore, for professionals in early childhood education, much of what is done involves the child's family. Families come in many different arrangements, and the more familiar teachers and caregivers are with the people the child sees on a regular basis, the easier communication with those individuals will be. Professionals who are aware of the enormously varied life circumstances that children and parents experience today are mindful not to offer a magic formula, quick remedies, or simplistic solutions to complicated, long-standing problems. Instead, parents appreciate a sense that they are respected and given up-to-date, objective information about their child.

"Creativity and the Child's Social Development" by Martha Nabors and Linda Edwards answers questions that teachers have about the best strategies for supporting the young child's creative and social development. These strategies can be shared with families. The terms *building* and *bridging* are used in the titles of two of the articles in this unit. Collaborative efforts to build bridges between home and school allow for maximized learning for all children.

Looking Ahead: Challenge Questions

Why is it important for teachers and caregivers to know about major changes affecting young children and their families?

What steps should educators take when labeling a young child for special education services?

How does the absence of a father affect a child's development academically, socially, and emotionally?

How can the cultural values emphasized in each family help children to develop a sense of who they are and to assist them in learning?

What strategies have been found to be successful when working with children of different intelligences?

Educational Implications of Developmental Transitions
Revisiting the 5- to 7-Year Shift

Understanding the nature of the 5- to 7-year shift is a major prerequisite if educators are to help children make a successful transition into elementary school, the authors maintain.

By Arnold Sameroff and Susan C. McDonough

ARNOLD SAMEROFF is a professor of psychology and a research scientist in the Center for Human Growth and Development at the University of Michigan, Ann Arbor, where SUSAN C. McDONOUGH is an assistant professor in the School of Social Work.

Illustration by Kay Salem

WHEN OUR child was 7 years old and experiencing the enlightenment provided by the local school system, she came home tearfully one day to question us about something we had protected her from since birth. Her classmates had informed her that there was no Santa Claus. When we admitted that what she had heard was true, she stared at us dolefully as she came to an even more disheartening conclusion. "This probably means that there is no Easter Bunny or Tooth Fairy either!" she charged.

Many of us have witnessed a child's sad discovery that a favorite belief is not true. But what is especially interesting in the above vignette is that a normative, but often unnoticed, intellectual extension — one that should frame educational theory — has taken place. The child revealed a belief in the existence of a conceptual category that included unseen figures who bring gifts. When it was discovered that one of these figures did not really exist, she made the logical extension that other members of this cognitive category did not exist.

These kinds of observations provide evidence of what developmental psychologists have called the 5- to 7-year shift. Children's thinking after age 7 seems to be quite different from their thinking before age 5.

What we will present here is a discussion of a different shift: a shift in the way the 5- to 7-year transition is understood by developmentalists. Current developmentally appropriate practices are based on Piagetian theory, in which the education of the child depends on a match between the curriculum and the child's emerging mental abilities.[1]

Piaget resolved the classic nature/nurture debate by arguing that every educational achievement was a developmental achievement. In Piaget's view, learning was the result neither of some intellectual trait native to the child, as believed in the United States and in some European countries, nor of the excellence of the education system, as believed in most Asian countries.[2] Instead, learning was a co-construction of the child and the teacher. New knowledge was the result of a creative activity in which the child built on prior mental constructions and the teacher provided the appropriate building material. Successful learning required a match between the curricular material and the state of the child's understanding. Revisions of Piagetian theories are changing the way we understand this match and are leading to new versions of nativism and environmentalism. Neo-Piagetian reformulations are changing our understanding of what capacities the child brings to the school on the nature side and of what makes a successful educator on the nurture side. These theoretical developments may have major implications for future educational theory, practice, and training.

Understanding developmental changes in the child during the 5- to 7-year period is especially important for educators because these are the years during which institutionalized schooling generally begins. Although the 5- to 7-year shift was not officially christened until 1965, when Sheldon White gave it that label, this developmental change, which is the basis for most formal educational systems, has long been recognized.[3] In his historical analysis of childhood, Philippe Ariés quotes a 14th-century poem that sets the limits of childhood, after which the child was immediately absorbed into the world of adults.

The first six years of life on earth
We to January would compare
For in that month strength is as rare
As in a child six years from birth.[4]

From ancient times there was a widespread cultural awareness that differences in children's behavior around 6 years of age permitted them to take on adultlike roles. These included care of other children, hunting and gathering, and, in industrial societies, child labor. Anthropological studies have found that most cultures begin formal training around age 6. Barbara Rogoff and her colleagues examined ethnographies from 50 communities around the world to determine at what age the expectations for children's roles and responsibilities underwent major changes.[5] They found a modal pattern of such changes when children were between 5 and 7 years of age, after which children were given increased responsibility for taking care of younger children, tending animals, and doing household chores. Most important, from an educational perspective, children were also expected to be teachable. In general, children after the age of 7 were thought to have common sense or rationality.

The 5- to 7-Year Shift

White provided a wealth of evidence to support the positing of this transition. He analyzed 21 kinds of developmental studies in a variety of cognitive, linguistic, and perceptual domains, showing that children younger than 5 behaved in one way while those older than 7 behaved in another. Among the architects of those studies, White noted Piaget, who in 1965 was just beginning to make an impression on mainstream American psychological studies and educational practice.[6] It was Piaget, of course, who placed at the center of his theory of cognitive development the 5- to 7-year shift — a period during which children move from dependence on appearance to an understanding of reality, from centering on single aspects of a situation to the ability to coordinate multiple perspectives, and from an egocentric focus on their own points of view to an appreciation that other minds have alternative outlooks on the world.

The water-glass problem is perhaps the best known of Piaget's examples of how children's logic changes during this age period. The younger child believes that, if water is poured from a short, fat glass into a tall, thin one, there is more water because the level is higher. The older child recognizes a relationship between multiple dimensions, in which the increase in height is compensated for by a decrease in width, and will frequently state a logical principle: "Because nothing was added or taken away, there must be the same amount of water." In classification tasks the older child is able to consider more than one level at a time in a conceptual hierarchy and knows the difference between *all* and *some*. When younger children are shown a bouquet of roses and daffodils and asked whether there are more roses or more flowers, they frequently reply that there are more roses. A 7-year-old will say that all of them are flowers but that only some of them are roses, so there cannot be more roses than flowers.

Piaget did not believe that the advanced intellectual performance of the older child was the result of learning. He viewed it as the result of developmental processes. Children younger than 5 used a different system of logic than children older than 7, and they needed to develop in order to move ahead. Learning taught a child the names of flowers, and more learning meant more names. But it was *development* that led a child to know that there were more flowers than roses. Moreover, according to Piaget, these changes in the logic of thinking were not restricted to school topics. Developmental advances in the understanding of the physical world were matched by advances in the logic children applied to social situations, especially in the area of rules and moral judgments. Whereas younger children believed that what was right and wrong depended on the consequences — whether or not they were punished — older children recognized the existence of a system of morality based on social agreement.

The implications of Piaget's work were not lost on educators, who soon began to create Piagetian curricula and assessments in which the details of children's knowledge were regarded as secondary to the logical processes by which children arrived at these details. Through the Sixties and Seventies and up to his death in 1980, Piaget's theories dominated the environment of those interested in the cognitive development of children.

However, at about the same time as his physical demise, Piaget's work was undergoing a major theoretical demise in scientific circles. The post-Piagetian critique came from two directions: a nativist position arguing that Piaget was wrong in believing that younger children could not engage in logical thinking and an environmental position arguing that Piaget had ignored major environmental influences that produced developmental changes in thought.

Nature: Performance Versus Competence

The heart of the Piagetian position is that children's intelligence develops over time, moving through successive stages, each one building on the achievements of the previous one. Furthermore, Piaget believed that, when children moved from one stage of development to another — for example, from preoperational to operational intelligence — behavior in every cognitive domain changed as they consolidated their new intellectual capacities. The first group of neo-Piagetians argued that there was no general change in children's logic from one stage to the next. There may be stage-like transitions in individual domains of behavior — such as classification problems or the understanding of number concepts or even moral judgment — but these changes were seen to be content-specific and not evidence for a universal shift based on a single central process of cognitive reorganization.[7] Children did not change their thinking across all areas at once; they might be quite advanced in some areas but somewhat delayed in others.

Then an even more serious set of criticisms argued that what Piaget believed to be changes in the cognitive competence of the child, even within individual domains, were only changes in performance. What Piaget had seen as new intellectual breakthroughs by the 5- to 7-year-old child were already within the capacity of much younger children and were perhaps even innate.[8] Complex understanding of number concepts, spatial transformations, and causality could be found in preschoolers and even in infants. These critics argued that Piaget confused performance with competence — that children had more cognitive abilities than Piaget could detect in his research because his experiments restricted their ability to show their competence. Experiments designed especially to reveal the logical capacities of young children revealed a surprising precocity, even in moral judgment.

Does this mean that there is no 5- to 7-year shift? Not exactly. If the question is whether younger children demonstrate these precocious capacities in their general behavior, then the answer is no. Early indicators of intellectual competence appeared only when the situation was right, when the environmental stimuli and required responses were highly simplified, and when the child's emotional and attentional conditions were optimized. When the task was to educate groups of children in a school setting with socially relevant and useful lessons, starting after age 6 still seemed to work best.

A good example of this situation is the child's ability to consider multiple dimensions at the same time in a conceptual task, such as whether a balance scale will go up or down. To answer correctly, the child must consider both the dimension of weight and the distance from the fulcrum. Robert Siegler found that 5-year-olds showed this talent when conditions were simplified. However, they did not when a task was unfamiliar, required a quantitative comparison between alternatives, and included a dominant dimension that led them to the wrong answer. In other words, when asked to solve the problem in a typical classroom situation, 5-year-olds could not do so. For children to demonstrate this talent regularly, they had to be older than 7.[9]

Nurture: Narration and Activities

The second revision of Piagetian theory stems from the environmentalist view that Piaget did not pay enough attention to the effects of children's experiences on the course of their cognitive development. These experiences might arise in the family, in the community, or in the classroom. For example, the shift in thinking between 5 and 7 may be a consequence of schooling rather than a prerequisite for schooling. This hypothesis is very difficult to test in a society in which all children begin school at about the same age.

However, some ingenious researchers found a way to overcome this problem. In a unique set of studies Fred Morrison and Elizabeth Griffith compared two groups of children of nearly the same age: one group whose birthdays were just before the cutoff for entry into kindergarten and another group whose birthdays were just after the cutoff.[10] As most educators would predict, after two years the re-searchers found that schooling accounted for a number of differences in behavior between the two groups. Those who had been in classrooms for two years, kindergarten and first grade, had a number of memory, language, and quantitative skills that exceeded those of children who had been kept out of school for the first year and had completed only kindergarten. But another set of memory, language, and number skills were no worse in the group of children who were held out of school for another year. The latter findings provide evidence for a developmental effect independent of classroom experience. What such research is revealing is that there is no simple formula for distinguishing in advance the intellectual skills that the child brings to school from those that are produced by the school.

However, the experience of schooling is only one element in the learning environment of the child. Early experiences in the home may be another determinant of the child's developmental progress. Recent research on the development of memory is a good example of an unexpected environmental effect. Changes in the ability to remember may be related to the extent to which memories are shared with others.

A general finding in research on memory is that there is an infantile amnesia; people cannot remember anything about their lives before about age 3. The original explanation was that young children did not have good memories, but more recent research has found that infants can remember events for up to two years. That is, they will show recognition when placed in similar situations. What they lack is the ability to recall such early events when they have grown older, a capacity that appears to be intimately connected to their experience with narration.[11]

Parents play an active role in framing and guiding their children's descriptions of what happened. Through conversations with their parents, children learn simultaneously how to talk about memories and how to formulate their own memories as narratives for themselves. Parents who are more elaborative — who ask their children what happened when, where, and with whom — have children who have more extensive memories. Preschool children do not remember specific events for long periods of time unless they have the opportunity to talk about them with their teacher or parent. The beginning of autobiographical memory in early childhood, which has been viewed as the result of brain maturation processes, can also be viewed as the result of specific experiences in a social context. The educational implication is that memory skills in children can be enhanced by fostering narrative exchanges between children and others.

The changes in memory during the 5- to 7-year shift are a further elaboration of the use of language as a tool for thinking. Prior to this time of life, children use language primarily for communication and secondarily for cognitive organization. During this period, however, language becomes a tool for reflecting on thought and action, enabling the child to call to mind and reexperience events from the past. Membership in a linguistic community provides a tool for further advances in cognition and memory. However, because such advances are a consequence of the experience of narrating memories to others, the age range when these new capacities emerge is wide and depends on the opportunities provided for such experiences. For example, the average age for the beginning of autobiographical memory is around 3, but the range is from 2 to 8, and there is also wide variation in the number of early memories. To the extent that parents and educators encourage narration, children's memory capacities may be precocious. To the extent that children are placed in passive roles in educational settings, memory and cognitive development may be delayed.

Cultural factors add another level of environmental influence on children's cognitive abilities. From a contextualist perspective, the abilities of children cannot be understood apart from their participation in the ongoing activities of their family and cultural group. The age at which a shift will occur depends on the social activities of the child.

Barbara Rogoff, a strong proponent of this position, argues that changes in children's abilities can be understood only in terms of their sociocultural activities.[12] In her cross-cultural comparisons she had found that some societies began formal education with 2-year-olds and some with 15-year-olds. To understand this wide range in age of onset of schooling requires attention to the beliefs, practices, needs, and resources of each culture. She argues for a shift in focus from what children *can* think to what they *do* think. Changes in what children do think between 5 and 7 vary widely across different cultures that engage children in different kinds of social activities.

Rogoff argues that the age when a child moves from one stage to another depends on the meaning and support given that transition in the life of that culture. One example is the age at which children begin to take care of other children. The major cognitive requirement for such a role is that the caregiver be able to assume the perspective of the younger child in order to understand the child's signals and ensure its well-being. In industrial societies, such perspective taking is not found until after the 5- to 7-year shift, and children usually do not become babysitters until they are at least 10 years old. Among the Mayan villagers of Guatemala, 3- to 5-year-olds are able to be babysitters because of the social organization of family roles and the cultural expectations of that community. Rogoff suggests that this difference is to be found in the Mayan training of children to become interdependent members of the community, while children in the U.S. are encouraged to assert individuality and be competitive.

The consequences of these differing social values were observed during home visits. Preschool Mayan caregivers were seen to give over whatever their younger siblings wanted, whereas middle-class U.S. preschoolers negotiated or tussled with babies over toys until parents intervened. Similarly, children as young as age 3 in other cultures are found to have the cognitive abilities to engage in skilled gardening and household work and the social abilities to engage in complex social interactions both within and outside of the family. What is significant in the sociocultural perspective is that developmental transitions are seen to be neither solely within the child nor solely within the education system. Rather, developmental transitions result from shifts in the roles and responsibilities associated with participation in a social group.

Shifts in Social and Emotional Behavior

White's proposal of a 5- to 7-year shift in behavior was originally restricted to cognitive functioning, but it has been extended by a new generation of developmental scientists into social and emotional domains, especially with regard to self-concept. Similarly, educators are aware that the social and emotional condition of the child is a major determinant of whether schooling will be effective. Therefore, awareness of changes in these capacities in the child is an important at-

tribute of the successful teacher of young children. Although there is still considerable debate about the relative contributions of social and school experience to cognitive development, there is far more agreement that, in the social/emotional domain, a child's experiences of relationships are major determinants of a child's behavior.

If child development is a function of a child's engagement in cultural activities, then schooling must be reframed as a social activity whose significance goes beyond the training of children in reading, writing, and arithmetic. The characteristics of school activities will have an impact not only on what children learn, but also on how children evaluate themselves as learners — that is, on their self-concepts.

The most detailed descriptions of shifts in self-understanding between ages 5 and 7 have been provided in the studies of Susan Harter.[13] Shifts occur in the nature of self-attributes, in the structure and organization of the self, in the understanding of combined and conflicting emotions, in the balance between positive and negative attributes, in the emergence of self-affects, and in the ability to be self-critical. The self-attributes used by preschoolers refer to their behavior: "I can jump high. I like pizza. I have a dog." School-age children use more higher-order generalizations that are more trait-like to describe themselves: "I am smart. I am popular." Preschoolers do not believe that you can have two emotions at the same time, whereas school-age children know that they can both like and dislike the same person and can describe themselves as both smart and dumb, depending on the subject. In addition, whereas preschoolers are generally positive in their self-descriptions, school-age children are more balanced, offering both positive and negative descriptions. Finally, it is not until about age 8 that children can verbalize their sense of self-esteem — whether or not they like themselves and how much.

In this shift in self-understanding, what is especially salient for educators is the emergence of the self-affects, pride and shame. Although these are experienced as young as infancy, it is not until after the 5- to 7-year shift that children express these emotions verbally. Moreover, the degree to which a child feels and expresses pride or shame is strongly determined by the action of others — parents, teachers, and friends. Changes in the behavior of important adults are among the environmental experiences of children entering school. In the elementary school classroom increasing attention is paid to social comparisons rather than to individual accomplishments. No matter how high the quality of a child's school activities, they are judged relative to the activities of other children in the class. How these comparisons are handled by the teacher has consequences for the child's sense of self-worth.

Although the quality and importance of social relationships does not change during the 5- to 7-year shift, the child's social network goes through a major expansion, including new settings, new classmates, and new teachers. Given responsive and friendly interactions, the child's self-concept can follow a positive course, whereas teasing and criticism will produce the opposite. The major developmental difference is that, as children grow older, it becomes more and more difficult to change their self-concepts. For the younger child, where the self-system and the social setting are less structured, it is easier to feel bad in one situation but good in another. For the older child, where the self-system is gaining in coherence and consistency, negative experiences and negative reputations can become far more pervasive and even overwhelming in their effects on self-esteem.

Shifts in School Experience

The 5- to 7-year shift for most children in this country involves a transition from the experiences of the preschool to those of the elementary school. Children do not enter kindergarten with a clean slate. Based on their previous time spent in school-like settings, they have many expectations about the experiences they will encounter. Just as teachers need to be aware of the quality and range of intellectual capacities children bring to the classroom, they also need to be aware of the quality and range of children's social experiences. The child's prior experience with social interactions, social comparisons, and self-esteem experiences in the home, in day care, and in the preschool are especially important. There are general differences in these settings that produce problems for children who expect the elementary school experience to be a continuation of the preschool experience.

Social interactions in the home and in the preschool tend to have been collaborative, whereas in the elementary school pressure for individual behavior and self-control increases. When children talk with one another and share activities with other children, it may be less a sign of disrespect for the elementary teacher than the consequence of previous classroom experience. In the elementary school new enrollees may be confused about the new conditions they face. In preschool, the focus is not on comparisons with other children in the class. Children new to elementary school may perceive that their teacher believes that doing things faster and getting higher scores than other children are more important than doing a good job. All these changes have an impact on the self-esteem of children. Parents of children new to elementary school are often asked, "Why wasn't I a bad girl in preschool?" The only meaningful answer educators can provide is through teaching without producing such self-concepts in children.

Reframing the 5- to 7-Year Shift

Current thinking about behavioral shifts between the ages of 5 and 7 has moved away from a belief in a cognitive reorganization that permits the child to be educated. When the logical structure of any particular skill is analyzed, precursors and analogs can be found in much younger children if task conditions are simplified and motivation is maximized. Preschoolers can be taught to speak in complex sentences, to read, and even to solve mathematical puzzles. But these achievements require individual attention, sensitivity, and devotion on the part of the educator. What appears to be unique about the period between 5 and 7 is that for most children task conditions do not need to be simplified, and motivation does not have to be maximized.

Preschoolers can be taught the skills needed to engage in useful work in the home and in the field. But these achievements require a culture that integrates the child into meaningful social activities. After the 5- to 7-year shift, most children can learn things that have no obvious social connection. In the typical classroom situation, academic skills are learned apart from a meaningful cultural context. The primary achievement of this age period may be the attainment of this capacity for abstraction, the capacity to learn for learning's sake.

Understanding the nature of the 5- to 7-year shift is a major prerequisite if educators are to help children make a successful transition into the elementary school. The timing and quality of this shift is influenced by characteristics of the child, the home environment, the cultural context, and previous experiences with group learning. When the resulting heterogeneity of children's characteristics and capacities is met by a uniformity of teacher expectations and behavior, many children become cognitive and social casualties. If we wish to change these outcomes, then the elementary school must become much more attuned to the individuality that each child brings to the classroom. The existence of the 5- to 7-year shift is evidence for what *is* rather than what *could be*.

1. David Elkind, "Developmentally Appropriate Practice: Philosophical and Practical Implications," *Phi Delta Kappan*, October 1989, pp. 113-17.

2. Harold W. Stevenson, Chuansheng Chen, and Shin-Ying Lee, "Mathematics Achievement of Chinese, Japanese, and American Children: Ten Years Later," *Science*, vol. 259, 1993, pp. 53-58.

3. Sheldon H. White, "Evidence for a Hierarchical Arrangement of Learning Processes," in Lewis P. Lipsitt and Charles C. Spiker, eds., *Advances in Child Development and Behavior* (New York: Academic Press, 1965), pp. 187-220.

4. Philippe Ariés, *Centuries of Childhood: A Social History of the Family* (New York: Vintage, 1962).

5. Barbara Rogoff et al., "Age of Assignment of Roles and Responsibilities to Children," *Human Development*, vol. 18, 1975, pp. 353-69.

6. Jean Piaget, *The Psychology of Intelligence* (London: Routledge and Kegan Paul, 1950).

7. Charles Brainerd, "The Stage Question in Cognitive Developmental Theory," *Behavioral and Brain Sciences*, vol. 1, 1978, pp. 173-82.

8. Rochel Gelman and Renée Baillargeon, "A Review of Some Piagetian Concepts," in Paul H. Mussen, ed., *Handbook of Child Psychology*, vol. 3 (New York: Wiley, 1983), pp. 167-230.

9. Robert Siegler, "Five Generalizations About Cognitive Development," *American Psychologist*, vol. 38, 1983, pp. 263-77.

10. Fred Morrison and Elizabeth M. Griffith, "Nature-Nurture in the Classroom: Entrance Age, School Readiness, and Learning in Children," *Developmental Psychology*, in press.

11. Katherine Nelson, "Towards a Theory of the Development of Autobiographical Memory," in Andrew Collins et al., eds., *Theoretical Advances in the Psychology of Memory* (Hillsdale, N.J.: Erlbaum, 1993), pp. 116-65.

12. Barbara Rogoff, *Apprenticeship in Thinking: Cognitive Development in Social Context* (New York: Oxford University Press, 1993).

13. Susan Harter, "Causes, Correlates, and the Functional Role of Global Self-Worth: A Life-Span Perspective," in John Kolligan and Robert Sternberg, eds., *Perceptions of Competence and Incompetence Across the Life Span* (New Haven, Conn.: Yale University Press, 1990).

A baby's brain is a work in progress, trillions of neurons waiting to be wired into a mind. The experiences of childhood, pioneering research shows, help form the brain's circuits—for music and math, language and emotion.

Your Child's Brain

Sharon Begley

YOU HOLD YOUR NEWBORN SO his sky-blue eyes are just inches from the brightly patterned wallpaper. *ZZZt:* a neuron from his retina makes an electrical connection with one in his brain's visual cortex. You gently touch his palm with a clothespin; he grasps it, drops it, and you return it to him with soft words and a smile. *Crackle:* neurons from his hand strengthen their connection to those in his sensory-motor cortex. He cries in the night; you feed him, holding his gaze because nature has seen to it that the distance from a parent's crooked elbow to his eyes exactly matches the distance at which a baby focuses. *Zap:* neurons in the brain's amygdala send pulses of electricity through the circuits that control emotion. You hold him on your lap and talk . . . and neurons from his ears start hard-wiring connections to the auditory cortex.

And you thought you were just playing with your kid.

When a baby comes into the world her brain is a jumble of neurons, all waiting to be woven into the intricate tapestry of the mind. Some of the neurons have already been hard-wired, by the genes in the fertilized egg, into circuits that command breathing or control heartbeat, regulate body temperature or produce reflexes. But trillions upon trillions

more are like the Pentium chips in a computer before the factory preloads the software. They are pure and of almost infinite potential, unprogrammed circuits that might one day compose rap songs and do calculus, erupt in fury and melt in ecstasy. If the neurons are used, they become integrated into the circuitry of the brain by connecting to other neurons; if they are not used, they may die. It is the experiences of childhood, determining which neurons are used, that wire the circuits of the brain as surely as a programmer at a keyboard reconfigures the circuits in a computer. Which keys are typed—which experiences a child has—determines whether the child grows up to be intelligent or dull, fearful or self-assured, articulate or tongue-tied. Early experiences are so powerful, says pediatric neurobiologist Harry Chungani of Wayne State University, that "they can completely change the way a person turns out."

By adulthood the brain is crisscrossed with more than 100 billion neurons, each reaching out to thousands of others so that, all told, the brain has more than 100 trillion connections. It is those connections—more than the number of galaxies in the known universe—that give the brain its unrivaled powers. The traditional view was that the wiring diagram is predetermined, like one for a new house,

by the genes in the fertilized egg. Unfortunately, even though half the genes—50,000—are involved in the central nervous system in some way, there are not enough of them to specify the brain's incomparably complex wiring. That leaves another possibility: genes might determine only the brain's main circuits, with something else shaping the trillions of finer connections. That something else is the environment, the myriad messages that the brain receives from the outside world. According to the emerging paradigm, "there are two broad stages of brain wiring," says developmental neurobiologist Carla Shatz of the University of California, Berkeley: "an early period, when experience is not required, and a later one, when it is."

Yet, once wired, there are limits to the brain's ability to create itself. Time limits. Called "critical periods," they are windows of opportunity that nature flings open, starting before birth, and them slams shut, one by one, with every additional candle on the child's birthday cake. In the experiments that gave birth to this paradigm in the 1970s, Torsten Wiesel and David Hubel found that sewing shut one eye of a newborn kitten rewired its brain: so few neurons connected from the shut eye to the visual cortex that the animal was blind even after its eye was reopened.

The Logical Brain

SKILL: Math and logic

LEARNING WINDOW: Birth to 4 years

WHAT WE KNOW: Circuits for math reside in the brain's cortex, near those for music. Toddlers taught simple concepts, like one and many, do better in math. Music lessons may help develop spatial skills.

WHAT WE CAN DO ABOUT IT: Play counting games with a toddler. Have him set the table to learn one-to-one relationships—one plate, one fork per person. And, to hedge your bets, turn on a Mozart CD.

Such rewiring did not occur in adult cats whose eyes were shut. Conclusion: there is a short, early period when circuits connect the retina to the visual cortex. When brain regions mature dictates how long they stay malleable. Sensory areas mature in early childhood; the emotional limbic system is wired by puberty; the frontal lobes—seat of understanding—develop at least through the age of 16.

The implications of this new understanding are at once promising and disturbing. They suggest that, with the right input at the right time, almost anything is possible. But they imply, too, that if you miss the window you're playing with a handicap. They offer an explanation of why the gains a toddler makes in Head Start are so often evanescent: this intensive instruction begins too late to fundamentally rewire the brain. And they make clear the mistake of postponing instruction in a second language (see box, "Why Do Schools Flunk Biology?"). As Chugani asks, "What idiot decreed that foreign-language instruction not begin until high school?"

Neurobiologists are still at the dawn of understanding exactly which kinds of experiences, or sensory input, wire the brain in which ways. They know a great deal about the circuit for vision. It has a neuron-growth spurt at the age of 2 to 4 months, which corresponds to when babies start to really notice the world, and peaks at 8 months, when each neuron is connected to an astonishing 15,000 other neurons. A baby whose eyes are clouded by cataracts from birth will, despite cataract-removal surgery at the age of 2, be forever blind. For other systems, researchers know what happens, but not—at the level of neurons and molecules—how. They nevertheless remain confident that cognitive abilities work much like sensory ones, for the brain is parsimonious in how it conducts its affairs: a mechanism that works fine for wiring vision is not likely to be abandoned when it comes to circuits for music. "Connections are not forming willy-nilly," says Dale Purves of Duke University, "but are promoted by activity."

Language: Before there are words, in the world of a newborn, there are sounds. In English they are phonemes such as sharp ba's and da's, drawn-out ee's and ll's and sibilant sss's. In Japanese they are different—barked *hi's*, merged rr/ll's. When a child hears a phoneme over and over, neurons from his ear stimulate the formation of dedicated connections in his brain's auditory cortex. This "perceptual map," explains Patricia Kuhl of the University of Washington, reflects the apparent distance—and thus the similarity—between sounds. So in English-speakers, neurons in the auditory cortex that respond to "ra" lie far from those that respond to "la." But for Japanese, where the sounds are nearly identical, neurons that respond to "ra" are practically intertwined, like L.A. freeway spaghetti, with those for "la." As a result, a Japanese-speaker will have trouble distinguishing the two sounds.

Researchers find evidence of these tendencies across many languages. By 6 months of age, Kuhl reports, infants in English-speaking homes already have different auditory maps (as shown by electrical measurements that identify which neurons respond to different sounds) from those in Swedish-speaking homes. Children are functionally deaf to sounds absent from their native tongue. The map is completed by the first birthday. "By 12 months," says Kuhl, "infants have lost the ability to discriminate sounds that are not significant in their language. And their babbling has acquired the sound of their language."

Kuhl's findings help explain why learning a second language after, rather than with, the first is so difficult. "The perceptual map of the first language constrains the learning of a second," she says. In other words, the circuits are already wired for Spanish, and the remaining undedicated neurons have lost their ability to form basic new connections for, say, Greek. A child taught a second language after the age of 10 or so is unlikely ever to speak it like a native. Kuhl's work also suggests why related languages such as Spanish and French are easier to learn than unrelated ones: more of the existing circuits can do double duty.

With this basic circuitry established, a baby is primed to turn sounds into words. The more words a child hears, the faster she learns language, according to psychiatrist Janellen Huttenlocher of the University of Chicago. Infants whose mothers spoke to them a lot knew 131 more words at 20 months than did babies of more taciturn, or less involved, mothers; at 24 months, the gap had widened to 295 words. (Presumably the findings would also apply to a father if he were the primary caregiver.) It didn't matter which words the mother used—monosyllables seemed to work. The sound of words, it seems, builds up neural circuitry that can then absorb more words, much as creating a computer file allows the user to fill it with prose. "There is a huge vocabulary to be acquired," says Huttenlocher, "and it can only be acquired through repeated exposure to words."

Music: Last October researchers at the University of Konstanz in Germany reported that exposure to music rewires neural

The Language Brain

SKILL: Language

LEARNING WINDOW: Birth to 10 years

WHAT WE KNOW: Circuits in the auditory cortex, representing the sounds that form words, are wired by the age of 1. The more words a child hears by 2, the larger her vocabulary will grow. Hearing problems can impair the ability to match sounds to letters.

WHAT WE CAN DO ABOUT IT: Talk to your child—a lot. If you want her to master a second language, introduce it by the age of 10. Protect hearing by treating ear infections promptly.

---

circuits. In the brains of nine string players examined with magnetic resonance imaging, the amount of somatosensory cortex dedicated to the thumb and fifth finger of the left hand—the fingering digits—was significantly larger than in nonplayers. How long the players practiced each day did not affect the cortical map. But the age at which they had been introduced to their muse did: the younger the child when she took up an instrument, the more cortex she devoted to playing it.

Like other circuits formed early in life, the ones for music endure. Wayne State's Chugani played the guitar as a child, then gave it up. A few years ago he started taking piano lessons with his young daughter. She learned easily, but he couldn't get his fingers to follow his wishes. Yet when Chugani recently picked up a guitar, he found to his delight that "the songs are still there," much like the muscle memory for riding a bicycle.

Math and logic: At UC Irvine, Gordon Shaw suspected that all higher-order thinking is characterized by similar patterns of neuron firing. "If you're working with little kids," says Shaw, "you're not going to teach them higher mathematics or chess. But they are interested in and can process music." So Shaw and Frances Rauscher gave 19 preschoolers piano or singing lessons. After eight months, the researchers found, the children "dramatically improved in spatial reasoning," compared with children given no music lessons, as shown in their ability to work mazes, draw geometric figures and copy patterns of two-color blocks. The mechanism behind the "Mozart effect" remains murky, but Shaw suspects that when children exercise cortical neurons by listening to classical music, they are also strengthening circuits used for mathematics. Music, says the UC team, "excites the inherent brain patterns and enhances their use in complex reasoning tasks."

The Musical Brain

SKILL: Music

LEARNING WINDOW: 3 to 10 years

WHAT WE KNOW: String players have a larger area of their sensory cortex dedicated to the fingering digits on their left hand. Few concert-level performers begin playing later than the age of 10. It is much harder to learn an instrument as an adult.

WHAT WE CAN DO ABOUT IT: Sing songs with children. Play structured, melodic music. If a child shows any musical aptitude or interest, get an instrument into her hand early.

Emotions: The trunk lines for the circuits controlling emotion are laid down before birth. Then parents take over. Perhaps the strongest influence is what psychiatrist Daniel Stern calls attunement—whether caregivers "play back a child's inner feelings." If a baby's squeal of delight at a puppy is met with a smile and hug, if her excitement at seeing a plane overhead is mirrored, circuits for these emotions are reinforced. Apparently, the brain uses the same pathways to generate an emotion as to respond to one. So if an emotion is reciprocated, the electrical and chemical signals that produced it are reinforced. But if emotions are repeatedly met with indifference or a clashing response—Baby is proud of building a skyscraper out of Mom's best pots, and Mom is terminally annoyed—those circuits become confused and fail to strengthen. The key here is "repeatedly": one dismissive harrumph will not scar a child for life. It's the pattern that counts, and it can be very powerful: in one of Stern's studies, a baby whose mother never matched her level of excitement became extremely passive, unable to feel excitement or joy.

Experience can also wire the brain's "calm down" circuit, as Daniel Goleman describes in his best-selling "Emotional Intelligence." One father gently soothes his crying infant, another drops him into his crib; one mother hugs the toddler who just skinned her knee, another screams "It's your own stupid fault!" The first responses are attuned to the child's distress; the others are wildly out of emotional sync. Between 10 and 18 months, a cluster of cells in the rational prefrontal cortex is busy hooking up to the emotion regions. The circuit seems to grow into a control switch, able to calm agitation by infusing reason into emotion. Perhaps parental soothing trains this circuit, strengthening the neural connections that form it, so that the child learns how to calm herself down. This all happens so early that the effects of nurture can be misperceived as innate nature.

Stress and constant threats also rewire emotion circuits. These circuits are centered on the amygdala, a little almond-shaped structure deep in the brain whose job is to scan incoming sights and sounds for emotional content. According to a wiring diagram worked out by Joseph LeDoux of New York University, impulses from eye and ear reach the amygdala before they get to the rational, thoughtful neocortex. If a sight, sound or experience has proved painful before—Dad's drunken arrival home was followed by a beating—then the amygdala floods the circuits with neurochemicals before the higher brain knows what's happening. The more often this pathway is used, the easier it is to trigger: the mere memory of Dad may induce fear. Since the circuits can stay excited for days, the brain remains on high alert. In this state, says neuroscientist Bruce Perry of Baylor College of Medicine, more circuits attend to nonverbal cues—facial expressions, angry noises—that warn of impending danger. As a result, the cortex falls behind in development and has trouble assimilating complex information such as language.

Movement: Fetal movements begin at 7 weeks and peak between the 15th and 17th weeks. That is when regions of the brain controlling movement start to wire up. The critical period lasts a while: it takes up to two years for cells in the cerebellum, which controls posture and movement, to form functional circuits. "A lot of organization takes place using information gleaned from when the child moves about in the world," says William Greenough of the University of Illinois. "If you restrict activity you inhibit the formation of synaptic connections in the cerebellum." The child's initially spastic movements send a signal to the brain's motor cortex; the more the arm, for instance, moves, the stronger the circuit, and the better the brain will become at moving the arm intentionally and fluidly. The window lasts only a few years: a child immobilized in a body cast until the age of 4 will learn to walk eventually, but never smoothly.

THERE ARE MANY MORE CIRCUITS to discover, and many more environmental influences to pin down. Still, neuro labs are filled with an unmistakable air of optimism these days. It stems from a growing understanding of how, at the level of nerve cells and molecules, the brain's circuits form. In the beginning, the brain-to-be consists of only a few advance scouts breaking trail: within a week of conception they march out of the embryo's "neural tube," a cylinder of cells extending from head to tail. Multiplying as they go (the brain adds an astonishing 250,000 neurons per minute during gestation), the neurons clump into the brain stem which commands heartbeat and breathing, build the little cerebellum at the back of the head which controls posture and movement, and form the grooved and rumpled cortex wherein thought and perception originate. The neural cells are so small, and the distance so great, that a neuron striking out for what will be the prefrontal cortex migrates a distance equivalent to a human's walking from New York to California, says developmental neurobiologist Mary Beth Hatten of Rockefeller University.

Only when they reach their destinations do these cells become true neurons. They grow a fiber called an axon that carries electrical signals. The axon might reach only to a neuron next door, or it might wend its way clear across to the other side of the brain. It is the axonal connections that form the brain's circuits. Genes determine the main highways along which axons travel to make their connection. But to reach particular target cells, axons follow chemical cues strewn along their path. Some of these chemicals attract: this way to the motor cortex! Some repel: no, *that* way to the olfactory cortex. By the fifth month of gestation most axons have reached their general destination. But like the prettiest girl in the bar, target cells attract way more suitors—axons—than they can accommodate.

How does the wiring get sorted out? The baby neurons fire electrical pulses once a minute, in a fit of what Berkeley's Shatz calls auto-dialing. If cells fire together, the target cells "ring" together. The target cells then release a flood of chemicals, called trophic factors, that strengthen the incipient connections. Active neurons respond better to trophic factors than inactive ones, Barbara Barres of Stanford University reported in October. So neurons that are quiet when others throb lose their grip on the target cell. "Cells that fire together wire together," says Shatz.

The same basic process continues after birth. Now, it is not an auto-dialer that sends signals, but stimuli from the senses. In experiments with rats, Illinois's Greenough found that animals raised with playmates and toys and other stimuli grow 25 percent more synapses than rats deprived of such stimuli.

Rats are not children, but all evidence suggests that the same rules of brain development hold. For decades Head Start has fallen short of the high hopes invested in it: the children's IQ gains fade after about three years. Craig Ramey of the University of Alabama suspected the culprit was timing: Head Start enrolls 2-, 3- and 4- year-olds. So in 1972 he launched the Abecedarian Project. Children from 20 poor families were assigned to one of four groups: intensive early education in a day-care center from about 4 months to age 8, from 4 months to 5 years, from 5 to 8

Why Do Schools Flunk Biology?

LYNNELL HANCOCK

BIOLOGY IS A STAPLE AT MOST American high schools. Yet when it comes to the biology of the students themselves—how their brains develop and retain knowledge—school officials would rather not pay attention to the lessons. Can first graders handle French? What time should school start? Should music be cut? Biologists have some important evidence to offer. But not only are they ignored, their findings are often turned upside down.

Force of habit rules the hallways and classrooms. Neither brain science nor education research has been able to free the majority of America's schools from their 19th-century roots. If more administrators were tuned into brain research, scientists argue, not only would schedules change, but subjects such as foreign language and geometry would be offered to much younger children. Music and gym would be daily requirements. Lectures, work sheets and rote memorization would be replaced by hands-on materials, drama and project work. And teachers would pay greater attention to children's emotional connections to subjects. "We do more education research than anyone else in the world," says Frank Vellutino, a professor of educational psychology at State University of New York at Albany, "and we ignore more as well."

Plato once said that music "is a more potent instrument than any other for education." Now scientists know why. Music, they believe, trains the brain for higher forms of thinking. Researchers at the University of California, Irvine, studied the power of music by observing two groups of preschoolers. One group took piano lessons and sang daily in chorus. The other did not. After eight months the musical 3-year-olds were expert puzzlemasters, scoring 80 percent higher than their playmates did in spatial intelligence—the ability to visualize the world accurately.

This skill later translates into complex math and engineering skills. "Early music training can enhance a child's ability to reason," says Irvine physicist Gordon Shaw. Yet music education is often the first "frill" to be cut when school budgets shrink. Schools on average have only one music teacher for every 500 children, according to the National Commission on Music Education.

Then there's gym—another expendable hour by most school standards. Only 36 percent of schoolchildren today are required to partic-

The Windows of Opportunity

PRENATAL	BIRTH	1 YEAR OLD	2 YEARS	3 YEAR
	Motor development			
	Emotional control			
	Vision			
	Social attachment			
	Vocabulary			
	Second language			
		Math/logic		
				Music

ipate in daily physical education. Yet researchers now know that exercise is good not only for the heart. It also juices up the brain, feeding it nutrients in the form of glucose and increasing nerve connections—all of which make it easier for kids of all ages to learn. Neuroscientist William Greenough confirmed this by watching rats at his University of Illinois at Urbana-Champaign lab. One group did nothing. A second exercised on an automatic treadmill. A third was set loose in a Barnum & Bailey obstacle course requiring the rats to perform acrobatic feats. These "supersmart" rats grew "an enormous amount of gray matter" compared with their sedentary partners, says Greenough.

Of course, children don't ordinarily run such gauntlets; still, Greenough believes, the results are significant. Numerous studies, he says, show that children who exercise regularly do better in school.

The implication for schools goes beyond simple exercise. Children also need to be more physically active in the classroom, not sitting quietly in their seats memorizing subtraction tables. Knowledge is retained longer if children connect not only aurally but emotionally and physically to the material, says University of Oregon education professor Robert Sylwester in "A Celebration of Neurons."

Good teachers know that lecturing on the American Revolution is far less effective than acting out a battle. Angles and dimensions are better understood if children chuck their work sheets and build a complex model to scale. The smell of the glue enters memory through one sensory system, the touch of the wood blocks another, the sight of the finished model still another. The brain then creates a multidimensional mental model of the experience—one easier to retrieve. "Explaining a smell," says Sylwester, "is not as good as actually smelling it."

Scientists argue that children are capable of far more at younger ages than schools generally realize. People obviously continue learning their whole lives, but the optimum "windows of opportunity for learning" last until about the age of 10 or 12, says Harry Chugani of Wayne State University's Children's Hospital of Michigan. Chugani determined this by measuring the brain's consumption of its chief energy source, glucose. (The more glucose it uses, the more active the brain.) Children's brains, he observes, gobble up glucose at twice the adult rate from the age of 4 to puberty. So young brains are as primed as they'll ever be to process new information. Complex subjects such as trigonometry or foreign language shouldn't wait for puberty to be introduced. In fact, Chugani says, it's far easier for an elementary-school child to hear and process a second language—and even speak it without an accent. Yet most U.S. districts wait until junior high to introduce Spanish or French—after the "windows" are closed.

Reform could begin at the beginning. Many sleep researchers now believe that most teens' biological clocks are set later than those of their fellow humans. But high school starts at 7:30 a.m., usually to accommodate bus schedules. The result can be wasted class time for whole groups of kids. Making matters worse, many kids have trouble readjusting their natural sleep rhythm. Dr. Richard Allen of Johns Hopkins University found that teens went to sleep at the same time whether they had to be at school by 7:30 a.m. or 9:30 a.m. The later-to-rise teens not only get more sleep, he says; they also get better grades. The obvious solution would be to start school later when kids hit puberty. But at school, there's what's obvious, and then there's tradition.

Why is this body of research rarely used in most American classrooms? Not many administrators or school-board members know it exists, says Linda Darling-Hammond, professor of education at Columbia University's Teachers College. In most states, neither teachers nor administrators are required to know much about how children learn in order to be certified. What's worse, she says, decisions to cut music or gym are often made by noneducators, whose concerns are more often monetary than educational. "Our school system was invented in the late 1800s, and little has changed," she says. "Can you imagine if the medical profession ran this way?"

With PAT WINGERT *and* MARY HAGER *in Washington*

Circuits in different regions of the brain mature at different times. As a result, different circuits are most sensitive to life's experiences at different ages. Give your children the stimulation they need when they need it, and anything's possible. Stumble, and all bets are off.

4 YEARS	5 YEARS	6 YEARS	7 YEARS	8 YEARS	9 YEARS

years, or none at all. What does it mean to "educate" a 4-month-old? Nothing fancy: blocks, beads, talking to him, playing games such as peek-a-boo. As outlined in the book "Learningames,"* each of the 200-odd activities was designed to enhance cognitive, language, social or motor development. In a recent paper, Ramey and Frances Campbell of the University of North Carolina report that children enrolled in Abecedarian as preschoolers still scored higher in math and reading at the age of 15 than untreated children. The children still retained an average IQ edge of 4.6 points. The earlier the children were enrolled, the more enduring the gain. And intervention after age 5 conferred no IQ or academic benefit.

All of which raises a troubling question. If the windows of the mind close, for the most part, before we're out of elementary school, is all hope lost for children whose parents did not have them count beads to stimulate their math circuits, or babble to them to build their language loops? At one level, no: the brain retains the ability to learn throughout life, as witness anyone who was befuddled by Greek in college only to master it during retirement. But on a deeper level the news is sobering. Children whose neural circuits are not stimulated before kindergarten are never going to be what they could have been. "You want to say that it is never too late," says Joseph Sparling, who designed the Abecedarian curriculum. "But there seems to be something very special about the early years."

And yet . . . there is new evidence that certain kinds of intervention can reach even the older brain and, like a microscopic screwdriver, rewire broken circuits. In January, scientists led by Paula Tallal of Rutgers University and Michael Merzenich of UC San Francisco described a study of children who have "language-based learning disabilities"—reading problems. LLD affects 7 million children in the United States. Tallal has long argued that LLD arises from a child's inability to distinguish short, staccato sounds—such as "d" and "b." Normally, it takes neurons in the auditory cortex something like .015 second to respond to a signal from the ear, calm down and get ready to respond to the next sound; in LLD children, it takes five to 10 times as long. (Merzenich speculates that the defect might be the result of chronic middle-ear infections in infancy: the brain never "hears" sounds clearly and so fails to draw a sharp auditory map.) Short sounds such as "b" and "d" go by too fast—.04 second—to process. Unable to associate sounds with letters, the children develop reading problems.

The scientists drilled the 5- to 10-year-olds three hours a day with computer-produced sound that draws out short consonants, like an LP played too slow. The result: LLD children who were one to three years behind in language ability improved by a full two years after only four weeks. The improvement has lasted. The training, Merzenich suspect, redrew the wiring diagram in the children's auditory cortex to process fast sounds. Their reading problems vanished like the sounds of the letters that, before, they never heard.

Such neural rehab may be the ultimate payoff of the discovery that the experiences of life are etched in the bumps and squiggles of the brain. For now, it is enough to know that we are born with a world of potential—potential that will be realized only if it is tapped. And that is challenge enough.

With MARY HAGER

*Joseph Sparling and Isabelle Lewis (226 pages. Walker. $8.95).

Labeled for life?

Over two million kids are termed **"learning disabled."** But this and other tags are often **inaccurate** and always **damaging.**

BY NAOMI BARKO

Naomi Barko writes frequently on education.

Vicki LaFarge was devastated when a preschool psychologist suggested that her 4-year-old daughter, Adrienne, had Asperger's disorder, a mild form of autism. She had taken the child for independent testing after a nursery-school teacher said she wasn't interacting normally with other kids. "If the autism label wasn't scary enough," says Vicki, "the tests said she was acting at a low-normal level of intelligence!"

Terrified, Vicki took her daughter to the Developmental Consultation Services at the Harvard Community Health Plan, in Somerville, Massachusetts, for a second opinion. "They took one look at her and said, 'She does not have autism or low-normal intelligence. It may be a subtle learning disorder. Or it may

be that she is just developing socially at a different rate. We won't know until she's in regular school and is faced with more learning challenges.'" Happily, Vicki reports, "We are working on Adrienne's social skills and she's doing much better."

At age 5, Kenny Ridenour, of Bellflower, California, was diagnosed with attention deficit/hyperactivity disorder (ADHD), and his pediatrician prescribed Dexedrine. Always a good student, Kenny had never had learning problems. But when he was around 8 his school began to complain that he refused to complete writing assignments, and began labeling him "noncompliant."

"Kenny would cry and say that he hated school, even though he had always loved it before," says his mother, Phyllis. Then she transferred him to the Child Development Center of the University of California, Irvine.

He was taken off Dexedrine and taught how to work and interact by employing behavior-modification techniques. Now 9, Kenny is flourishing and doing work above his grade level.

Are we treating kids for disorders they don't have?

Welcome to the era of psychological evaluations, where schools, psychologists, and physicians freely attach such labels to small children, with potentially grave consequences. Yet parents need to be aware that in many cases, the methods used to make these evaluations are not definitive, which leaves them in a quandary. While it's damaging to have a problem misdiagnosed, it's equally tragic not to seek specialized help for a child who is truly struggling, since early treatment can make all the difference in school success.

No one is suggesting that these problems don't exist, but experts are admitting that detecting them is an inexact science, and warning parents to be vigilant before letting anyone label their child.

"The evaluations children are getting throughout the United States are often problematic," says Mel Levine, M.D., professor of pediatrics at the University of North Carolina at Chapel Hill and president of All Kinds of Minds, a nonprofit institute for the understanding of differences in learning. "Some of the most misleading testing is done for preschoolers. I can say this because I've developed some of those tests myself. They're not fine-grained enough. There are some kids who look as if they're in trouble at age 4 and they're great at 8 or 9. It's difficult to evaluate learning disabilities in preschoolers because they are not faced with complex language and conceptual challenges until later in school."

"Our testing instruments are simply not refined enough to differentiate slow learners and low achievers from the truly learning disabled," says James Ysseldyke, Ph.D., professor of educational psychology at the University of Minnesota.

If preschoolers are so difficult to diagnose accurately, why all the interest in having them evaluated? "Labels are convenient for schools, or for getting reimbursements from managed-care or insurance companies," explains Levine. "But in no way do they fit all kids." By school age, he says, "kids are reduced to a test score or a simplistic label, without focusing on their strengths and weaknesses."

Learning and behavior problems can be misread

The sheer number of "problem kids" is staggering. Some 2.5 million children—about 5 percent of the school population—are labeled as having learning disabilities, a loose term for a group of disorders that cause significant difficulty in listening, speaking, reading, writing, reasoning, or mathematical abilities.

LDs often overlap with attentional dysfunctions, though they are two separate problems. ADD (attention deficit disorder) is a neurological disorder characterized by an inability to focus attention and a tendency to be easily distracted; ADHD is the same as ADD, but with hyperactivity nd impulsivity.

The number of ADD and ADHD diagnoses has grown so dramatically that since 1990, production of Ritalin—a brain stimulant used to treat ADHD—has increased sixfold. It is now estimated that some 1.3 million American children be-

tween ages 5 and 14 are taking it.

Experts fear that many kids are being medicated for a disorder they may not have. ADHD is especially difficult to diagnose because doctors haven't successfully defined hyperactivity. So a common error that professionals make is "turning normal variations of temperament into abnormalities," says William Carey, M.D., clinical professor of pediatrics at the Children's Hospital of Philadelphia. "In fact, half of normal children are more or less active than average, but that doesn't mean they have something wrong with their brain."

"Forty percent of the so-called ADHD cases I see are kids who are suffering from anxiety caused by family tensions," adds Boston child psychiatrist Arnold Kerzner, M.D. He recalls an 8-year-old whose pediatrician put him on Ritalin after his teacher said he had sudden outbursts of anger.

"I found he was suffering from severe anxiety caused by his parents' marital problems," says Kerzner. "I took him off Ritalin and counseled the family. After six months the symptoms disappeared."

The biggest problem is the evaluation process itself. "Most ADHD diagnoses are not made by psychologists or other mental-health professionals," reports Russell Barkley, Ph.D., professor of psychiatry and neurology at the University of Massachusetts Medical Center, in Worcester. "They are made mainly on the basis of a brief interview with parents by a pediatrician. And rarely is there any contact between the doctor and the teacher."

Our health-care system may be contributing to these quick diagnoses, which may become even more common as doctors join HMOs, warns Barkley: "Managed care can demand that a pediatrician spend less than 20 minutes with a patient."

"Spending time with a family, counseling them and educating them, is expensive," adds Levine. Unfortunately, the most efficient and "most reimbursable thing you can do is put a child on drugs."

Is it really dyslexia or just poor teaching?

There is more controversy over a common LD, dyslexia, a disorder characterized by inaccuracy and slowness in reading. "Sixty to 80 percent of children identified as learning disabled in school have reading as their primary difficulty," says Reid Lyon, Ph.D., director of research programs on learning disabilities at the National Institute of Child Health and Human Development, in Washington, D.C.

But not all reading difficulties mean dyslexia. "It seems that any kid who has a reading problem is labeled as dyslexic," says Frank Vellu-

tino, Ph.D., director of the Child Research and Study Center at the State University of New York, Albany. "If what you mean by 'dyslexic' is a basic neurological or genetic inadequacy, then only 3 to 5 percent of children are truly dyslexic."

In a six-year study involving 1,400 children, Vellutino selected a group of 76 of his worst first-grade readers, some of whom had already been labeled dyslexic. With intensive one-on-one teaching for half an hour a day, about 70 percent of the children were brought up to an average reading range in just one semester. "These children are not dyslexic," he claims. "You might say they just got off to a poor start."

Are some kids more likely to be labeled? There are indicators, says Ysseldyke. "A kid who bothers the teacher will get referred for testing, yet another kid who may

How reliable are IQ tests?

Tests for giftedness can be as misleading as tests for learning disabilities. According to current estimates, 5 percent of children (preschoolers through high school)—roughly 2.5 million—are gifted and talented. But experts believe many of them are never identified.

Though IQ tests were once viewed as an absolute measure of intelligence, many educators have questioned their validity and fairness. Still, most schools use tests (such as the Stanford-Binet or Wechsler scale) as part of the screening process for gifted-and-talented programs, says Ellen Winner, Ph.D., author of *Gifted Children: Myths and Realities*

(Basic Books) and a professor of psychology at Boston College.

"IQ measures verbal, numerical, and some spatial ability," says Winner. "But it's narrow because it doesn't take into account visual, musical, athletic, leadership, or social ability."

"The IQ test is not in itself an indication of giftedness; it is only one of a series in the identification process," adds Peter D. Rosenstein, executive director of the National Association for Gifted Children (NAGC), in Washington.

Other gifted kids may fall through

the cracks because they don't fit the "bookworm" stereotype.

"A precocious child who is not being challenged may act up in class and show behavior problems associated with ADHD," says Rosenstein. (Many bright kids can also have LDs, and their giftedness can often be overlooked.)

If you think your child may be gifted, experts recommend getting an individual evaluation by a trained professional who will administer a series of tests beyond the IQ measurement. For more information, call the NAGC at 202-785-4268.

have real problems won't get referred because she's quieter." These "troublesome" kids usually turn out to be boys, who until recently were reported to have four times the reading problems of girls. However, says Lyon, "NIH has found that girls have almost as many reading problems as boys."

Still, schools alone can't be blamed for rampant misdiagnosis, say critics. Ironically, the problem may be the federal law that was designed to help children. The Individuals With Disabilities Education Act (IDEA), enacted in 1975 to assure a free, appropriate public education for kids with physical and learning disabilities, distributes about $2 billion nationally each year for special education.

"Public schools aren't getting money for smaller classes, better-trained teachers, or aides to help kids who fall behind," says Ysseldyke. "But they can get money for special education, and the only way they can get it under federal law is to test a child

and label him—and 'learning disabled' is the most convenient."

IDEA has fueled the learning-disabilities issue. "The law defines an LD as a 'significant discrepancy' between a child's IQ and achievement as measured on a test or shown by his performance in school," says Susan Vess, Ph.D., president of the National Association of School Psychologists. This discrepancy or gap between how capable a child seems and how he is performing is what school psychologists are looking for when they test. "But that difference can vary from state to state," adds Vess. "So a child who is borderline could be learning disabled in one state, but not in another."

Why your pediatrician's opinion isn't enough

If you think you see early signs of learning problems, start by discussing

them with your child's pediatrician and preschool teachers, advises Betty Osman, Ph.D., a psychologist affiliated with the White Plains Medical Center, in White Plains, New York. "Parents are often the first to notice these things, and in most cases they and their child's teachers can intervene to resolve many social or learning problems." However, in severe cases–if there is a significant language delay by age 3 or difficulties with motor skills–she advises consulting a speech or physical therapist.

School-age kids (and some preschoolers, depending on the problem) should be evaluated by a multidisciplinary team—a school psychologist, a speech therapist, a teacher, and sometimes a developmental pediatrician.

"What's crucial is to get a picture of the whole child," says Claire Wurtzel, chair of special education at the Bank Street College of Education, in New York, and a member of the advisory

board of the National Center for Learning Disabilities. "A child should be seen over a period of time to study his development. The parents should always be involved. And you need a teacher's assessment: If you change the method of teaching, does the problem persist, change, or even disappear?"

Christine Lord, of Washington, D.C., knows the value of getting other opinions. When her daughter, Elicia, was entering fourth grade, she was diagnosed with ADD and put on Ritalin. But Christine decided to see a new doctor, who found the real problem: a mild form of epilepsy. "Elicia was having trouble paying attention because she was having seizures," says Christine. "Now she's getting the proper medication, and she's doing great."

Christine's advice? "Don't be afraid to be a pushy parent. If you don't believe the experts, get more opinions. You know your child better than anyone else."

Creativity and the child's social development

MARTHA L. NABORS
LINDA C. EDWARDS

Martha L. Nabors, Ph.D., and *Linda C. Edwards*, Ed.D., are associate professors of early childhood education at the College of Charleston in South Carolina.

Two-year-old Alex is playing alone at the block center, exploring the various shapes and sizes of colorful blocks. He picks up a shiny red block and turns it over and over in his hands. After a minute or two he looks over in the housekeeping center where he sees his friend Joe. Suddenly, Alex stands up and toddles over to the housekeeping center, carrying the red block. He approaches the miniature ironing board and uses the block to carefully iron his laundry. Noticing that Alex has removed a block from the block center, Mrs. Whisdale immediately reprimands him for taking a block from its proper center and tells him, in front of the other children: "Blocks belong in the block center! I want you to put it back on the shelf now."

Psychosocial development

Let us consider how Mrs. Whisdale's behavior may affect Alex's social development, in light of Erikson's *psychosocial theory*, which categorizes social development into eight conflicts or crises (Erikson, 1963, 1968, 1975). (See figure 1.) Alex was playing alone and exploring the world of blocks. Asserting his will, he

made the choice to take a block into the dramatic play, or "housekeeping," center. Once there, his imagination transformed the block into an iron and he explored the new function of the block. According to Erikson (1963), Alex was developing some degree of independence and autonomy. Mrs. Whisdale gave Alex the clear message that he could not make choices. When caregivers consistently restrict children's environment by exerting external control over their play, they can plant the seeds of shame and doubt. The negative outcome of this crisis is loss of self-esteem. Mrs. Whisdale discouraged independence that could have led to Alex having feelings of pride and good will. Alex learned to doubt his own judgment.

Lakesha is a bright, energetic five-year-old who loves to wear polka dots. She also loves her kindergarten teacher. The children have been learning about herbs and spices and how to grow herb gardens. The class was given a large section of the outdoor play area for use as a garden. Mr. Thomas, Lakesha's teacher, announced that each child would have her own section in the class garden. He asked children to think about how they would plant their sections and the herbs they would like to grow. Lakesha decided to plant her seeds in circles.

Planting day arrived. Mr. Thomas reviewed all they had learned about planting herb gardens. Each child was given a packet of seeds, a trowel for digging, and a cup of water. Using her finger, Lakesha

began to make little circles in the dirt in preparation for planting her seeds. She made three little circles: one for basil, one for rosemary, and one for mint. Then she planted her seeds, each variety in its own special circle. As Lakesha was covering the last of her seeds, Mr. Thomas approached and said: "Lakesha, where are your straight rows?" Lakesha began to explain how her seeds were planted in circles like the polka-dots on her blouse. Mr. Thomas told her that herb gardens are always planted in straight rows and that she must replant her seeds. Lakesha's chin dropped to her chest and she started to cry.

Lakesha had taken initiative while using her motor and intellectual abilities to create a unique herb plot. She was exploring her environment and assuming responsibility for carrying out her own plans. She was pleased with the pattern of her garden. By not accepting Lakesha's initiative, Mr. Thomas instilled feelings of failure and guilt in a once excited little girl. Erikson's psychosocial theory (1963) asserts that if a task is not mastered, and the conflict of initiative versus guilt is not satisfactorily resolved, the ego is damaged in the process.

Jane is a seven-year-old second-grader with a wonderful sense of humor. One Wednesday afternoon, during a lesson in a unit about animals, the teacher gave each child a lump of clay and told them to make animals. For what seemed like a long time, Jane just looked at the clay. Finally, she

From *Dimensions of Early Childhood*, Fall 1994, pp. 14-16, 48. © 1994 by the Southern Early Childhood Association. Reprinted by permission.

began to pull and poke at it and eventually she started to model it into a form. Her teacher, Mrs. Barto, was pleased to see that Jane was finally working with her clay. Jane laughed out loud as an idea for her animal came to mind. She would make a "bird-dog," a creature with a beak, wings, and a long tail. When all the children had finished making their animals, Mrs. Barto asked them to tell the class about their animals. Timmy made a huge elephant with a long trunk. Peter made a cat. The twins, Marty and Linda, made monkeys. When Jane's turn came to share, she giggled as she proudly held up her "bird-dog." It had a long beak like a hummingbird, wings like an eagle, a big, massive body and a long, skinny tail.

This fun-loving girl glanced over at Mrs. Barto for approval and her eyes were met with a cold stare. Mrs. Barto admonished the children for giggling with Jane and told Jane to go back to her desk and make a real animal.

It was clear that Jane had not met the demands or expectations of her teacher. Any feelings of self-worth Jane may have felt because of her creation were wiped out by the teacher's comment, which could have made Jane feel inferior to her classmates. Erikson (1963) stresses that repeated frustration and failure may lead to feelings of inadequacy and inferiority, thereby negatively affecting one's view of self.

The classroom experiences of Alex, Lakesha, and Jane illustrate that Eriksons' crises (1963) can occur during everyday interactions with others. The outcomes of these crises can be positive or negative in their effects on self-esteem. Such typical psychosocial conflicts also can affect young children's creative development.

Creative development

Research literature essentially agrees that there are four basic phases in the creative process (Wallas, 1926; Patrick, 1937; Kneller, 1965; Boles, 1990; Sapp, 1992) and four basic characteristics of creativity (Barron, 1969, 1978; MacKinnon, 1976, 1978; Torrance, 1962, 1979, 1981a, 1981b, 1984). (See Figures 2 and 3.) In the experiences of Alex, Lakesha, and Jane, creative development is contingent upon the positive solution of each child's psychosocial conflict. The negative reso-

Psychosocial Conflict (Crisis)	Age
Trust versus mistrust	Birth to 18 months
Autonomy versus shame or doubt	18 months to three years
Initiative versus guilt	Three to six years
Industry versus inferiority	Six to 12 years
Identity versus role confusion	Adolescence
Intimacy versus isolation	Young adulthood
Generativity versus stagnation	Mature adulthood
Integrity versus despair	Old age

Figure 1: The eight stages of development in Erikson's Theory of Psychosocial Development. Adapted from Erikson, 1963.

lution of their psychosocial conflicts resulted in the stifling of the creative development of each child. Alex's play with the block demonstrated several characteristics of creativity (Figure 3). Alex was *fluent* in his approach to the possibilities the block held for him. He was *flexible* as he experimented with different ways of using the block. While his idea may not have been completely *original*, he did transform the block into an iron. For Alex, this was a novel idea! When Mrs. Whisdale interrupted his ironing, she also denied him the opportunity to build on his idea. No *elaboration* occurred.

The first three phases in the creative process (Figure 2), also pertain to Alex's situation. He *prepared* by exploring with blocks of different shapes, sizes, and colors. Alex's ideas for using the block could have been *incubating* as he turned the block over and over in his hand before wandering into the housekeeping center. His "'a-ha' moment" (*illumination*) occurred as he changed an ordinary wooden block into an iron. But excitement (*verification*) was short-lived. Mrs. Whisdale made sure her blocks remained in the block center where she thought they belonged. Alex was denied verification of his creative idea.

Lakesha also experienced fluency as she thought about the possibility of a circular garden. She was flexible as she explored different ways of making her circles. Her idea was so original, it conflicted with Mr. Thomas' understanding of garden design. He interrupted her attempt at elaboration.

Like Alex, Lakesha was successful in her preparation phase. She thought about making a circular garden to match the polka-dots on her dress. The polka-dots gave her the information she needed to get started. For Lakesha, incubation occurred as she made circles in the dirt with her fingers in preparation for planting the herbs. Lakesha might have thought: "How perfect. Three circles for three herbs." Illumination had happened; her garden came together. Unfortunately, verification never occurred for Lakesha. Mr. Thomas' insistence upon straight rows prevented Lakesha from any verification of her exciting idea.

Jane was successful in three of the four basic characteristics of creativity. Fluency and flexibility were evident as she poked and pulled at her clay. She was thinking of ways to create her animal. "A bird-dog. What a clever idea!" Jane clearly expressed originality; she put a new stamp on an existing animal. One cold stare from an inflexible Mrs. Barto blocked all chances of Jane being allowed to elaborate on her creation. During the preparation phase of the creative process, Jane drew on her sense of humor and her knowledge of hunting dogs. Staring at the clay and poking it with her fingers provided an incubation period. Jane's ideas jelled. Her "Eureka!" came when she invented her own pun: a "bird-dog." As with elaboration, Mrs. Barto's stare and comment prevented verification form occurring.

The connection between psychosocial development and creative development

A careful examination of Erikson's theory of psychosocial development (1963), the characteristics of creativity (Torrance, 1984), and the phases in the creative process (Sapp, 1992), strongly suggest that the positive resolution of the psychosocial conflict is central to successful creative development. Likewise, experiences in creative development can lead to the positive resolution of the central psychosocial conflicts. In Alex's, Lakesha's, and Jane's stories, a positive psychosocial-creative connection almost occurred. The inability of each child to progress through elaboration and verification had a negative impact on the resolution of their psychosocial conflict. At the same time, the negative resolution of the psychosocial conflict interrupted completion of their creative development. Mrs. Whisdale could have facilitated the connection between Alex's psychosocial and creative development simply by allowing Alex to use the block as an iron in the housekeeping center. Had she let him use the block for his own idea, Mrs. Whisdale would have encouraged autonomy. She could have encouraged his creativity by letting him elaborate on his idea and by giving him time for verification—as eas-

---

Preparation
Gathering materials and ideas to begin

Incubation
Letting ideas "cook" and develop

Illumination
The "a-ha" moment when ideas and materials jell; the "light bulb" phenomenon

Verification
When the exhilaration of the moment has passed and only time will confirm the efforts

---

Figure 2: Phases in the creative process. Adapted from Wallas, 1926; Patrick, 1937; Kneller, 1965; Boles, 1990; Sapp, 1992.

ily as she stopped Alex from using the block as an iron.

Mr. Thomas should have recognized and respected Lakesha's layout of her herb plot. He was in a perfect position to praise her initiative. He could have said: "I like your circular garden. What a great idea!" Simple words like these could have

---

Fluency
To allow ideas and thoughts to flow freely

Flexibility
To explore various ways of using ideas and materials

Originality
To have a new or novel idea or to put a new stamp on something that already exists

Elaboration
Adding finishing touches or decoration

Figure 3: Characteristics of creativity. Adapted from Barron, 1969, 1978; MacKinnon, 1976, 1978; Torrance, 1962, 1979, 1981a, 1981b, 1984.

also been instrumental in Lakesha's development of elaboration and verification.

Jane was also unable to complete the process through elaboration and verification. Mrs. Barto should have recognized that Jane's sense of humor guided her in making such a creative animal. Clearly, when Mrs. Barto told Jane to go back to her table and make a "real" animal, Jane must have felt inferior to her peers. Instead of a cold stare, Mrs. Barto could have joined in the fun with a wink and a smile. This same response could have led Jane to feelings of industry. It also would have opened a door for Jane to elaborate and, finally, to verify her "bird-dog" animal.

Each child could have made a positive connection between psychosocial development and creative development. Teachers and caregivers can encourage children and foster learning environments so that these connections can occur. These suggestions can guide adults in supporting the marriage of psychosocial and creative development:

- Be flexible.
- Consider children's feelings.
- Encourage time for preparation and incubation.
- Foster independence.
- Give children adquate time to complete their projects.
- Recognize children's novel ideas.
- Embrace the "'a-ha' moments."
- Value autonomy.
- Praise industry.
- Acknowledge competence.

References

Barron, F. (1969). *Creative person and creative process.* New York: Holt, Rinehart and Winston.

Barron, F. (1978). An eye more fantastical. In G.A. Davis and J.A. Scott (Eds.), *Training creative thinking.* Melbourne, FL: Krieger.

Boles, S. (1990). A model of routine and creative problem-solving. *Journal of Creative Behavior, 24*(3), 171-189.

Erikson, Erik H. (1963). *Childhood and society.* (2nd ed.). New York: Norton.

Erikson, Erik H. (1968). *Identify, youth, and crisis.* New York: Norton.

Erikson, Erik H. (1975). *Life history and the historical moment.* New York: Norton.

Kneller, G.F. (1965). *The art of science and creativity.* New York: Holt, Rinehart and Winston.

MacKinnon, D.W. (1976). Architects, personality types, and creativity. In A. Rothenberg and C.R. Hausman (Eds.), *The creativity question.* NC: Duke University Press.

MacKinnon, D.W. (1978). Educating for creativity: a modern myth? In G.A. Davis and J.A. Scott (Eds.), *Training creativity thinking.* Melbourne, FL: Krieger.

Patrick, C. (1937). Creative thought in artists. *Journal of Psychology, 4,* 35-67.

Sapp, David D. (1992). The point of creative frustration and the creative process: a new look at an old model. *The Journal of Creative Behavior, 26*(1), 21-28.

Torrance, E.P. (1962). *Guiding creative talent.* New Jersey: Prentice Hall.

Torrance, E.P. (1979). *The search for satori and creativity.* New York: Creative Education Foundation.

Torrance, E.P. (1981a). Non-test ways of identifying the creatively gifted. In J.C. Gowan, J. Khatena, and E.P. Torrance (Eds.), *Creativity: Its educational implications.* Iowa: Kendall/Hunt.

Torrance, E.P. (1981b). *Thinking creativity in action and movement.* Illinois: Scholastic Testing Service.

Torrance, E.P. (1984). Teaching gifted and creative learners. In M. Wittrock (Ed.), *Handbook of research on teaching.* Chicago: Rand-McNally.

Wallas, G. (1926). *The art of thought.* New York: Harcourt, Brace.

Families and Schools
Building Multicultural Values Together

Kevin J. Swick, Gloria Boutte and Irma Van Scoy

Kevin Swick is Professor, Gloria Boutte is Assistant Professor and Irma Van Scoy is Assistant Professor, Early Childhood Education Program, College of Education, University of South Carolina, Columbia.

A society's culture encompasses its citizens' efforts to develop meaning about individual and collective values, beliefs and actions (Slonim, 1991). It serves as a continuing reference point through which people construct their perceptions about and reactions to the environment. Families and schools in a democratic, multicultural society must promote a positive climate in which children learn to appreciate not only their own culture, but also cultures of other people (Fu, Stremmel & Treppte, 1992).

Indeed, the current social context throughout the world suggests an urgent need for multicultural learning. The rise in hate groups, distorted perceptions of people of different cultures, ethnic-related crime and many other antisocial patterns must be countered by families and schools working together to build a social fabric that values cultural diversity (Swick, Van Scoy & Boutte, 1994). Before a proactive multicultural learning environment can be developed, parents and teachers must recognize both its importance, and the barriers that prevent its achievement.

The Rationale for Multicultural Citizens

Csikszentmihalyi (1993) challenges the myopic view that multicultural learning is only important for minority populations. He notes that progressive societies succeed because their people can "transcend themselves" and relate to the environment in more sensitive and humane ways. This challenge is relevant to the growth and development of everyone in the global community. Pursuing unity through diversity calls for total involvement. Gary Howard (1993) stresses, "The future calls each of us to become partners in the dance of diversity, a dance in which everyone shares the lead" (p. 17). Multicultural learning must begin at birth and be continually nurtured through intentional family-school efforts.

Most important cultural understandings are shaped during the early childhood years. Thus, adult modeling of proactive multicultural values is critical for children. Hohensee and Derman-Sparks (1992) note that:

Numerous research studies about the process of identity and attitude development conclude that children learn by observing the differences and similarities among people and by absorbing the spoken and unspoken messages about these differences. The biases and negative stereotypes about various aspects of human diversity prevalent in our society under-cut all children's healthy development and ill-equip them to interact effectively with many people in the world. (p. 1)

Barriers to a Proactive Multicultural Learning Framework

Many individual and cultural variables interact to impede the development of culturally sensitive individuals, including: cultural stereotypes, social isolation, tradition and excessive conformity. All of these factors have a powerful influence on children's understanding of racial, ethnic and cultural perspectives and behaviors (Banks, 1993).

Cultural stereotypes arise from incomplete and often distorted conceptions of people and events. They tend to emerge when people are insecure, have low self-esteem and are isolated from people of other cultures (Hilliard, 1992). Such contexts often create intergenerational racism and/or culturally destructive attitudes. Isolation and tradition often serve to reinforce ignorance and, thus, further exacerbate prejudices (Derman-Sparks, 1991). Social isolation reduces children's opportunities to learn about culturally different people. Tradition may actually even encourage the continuation of erroneous beliefs. Without understanding the need to become multicultural, many people conform to long-lasting beliefs that are racist, sexist or highly prejudicial.

Barriers of cultural conformity, tradition and related exclusionary practices daily convey a distorted and inequitable picture of people from different backgrounds and contexts. Men, for example, still hold most leadership positions while many women are subtly isolated from mainstream political life. Minorities still compose a disproportionate segment of low-paying positions. Television often presents incomplete and distorted views of minority cultures, offering prime-time programs filled with sexist humor, distorted ethnic characterizations and superficial presentations of illnesses like AIDS (Diaz, 1992).

These barriers are maintained and reinforced by individual, family, school and community patterns (Ramsey & Derman-Sparks, 1992). The family learning system, for example, may distort a child's images of people from other cultures (Slonim, 1991). Insecure adults pass on their distorted views to their children through the family socialization process. Insecure and fearful children are likely to form rigid conceptions of people different from themselves.

Schools also need to recognize the effect they have on children's multicultural development (Boutte, La Point & Davis, 1993). Some teachers have limited understanding of their students' cultural backgrounds. The resulting erroneous beliefs must be transcended through staff development, personal reading and enrichment, and through personal growth

What kind of citizens do we need to foster a truly proactive multicultural society?

experiences. Institutional practices of tracking, ability grouping and rigidly defined graded systems need to be replaced with more inclusionary strategies such as multiage grouping, cross-cultural peer learning and more personalized instruction. Unquestioned rituals and policies imprison culturally different children within an inequitable and insensitive environment (Swick, Van Scoy & Boutte, 1994). For example, the failure to use bilingual teaching strategies and resources can impede academic and social growth (Diaz, 1992). Inappropriate and inaccurate labeling has led many children to years of academic failure.

A Developmental Framework for Multicultural Learning

Learning new concepts, attitudes, skills and behaviors requires awareness, exploration and experimentation, systematic development, and integration of newly acquired knowledge (Hohensee & Derman-Sparks, 1992). Family-school collaboration is essential to actualizing these processes in ways that create meaningful multicultural learning.

Awareness. The initial step in this learning process is awareness of desired outcomes and potential barriers (Hohensee & Derman-Sparks, 1992). Critical questions to ask are: What kind of citizens do we need to foster a truly proactive multicultural society? And, what conditions support the development of this kind of person? We must be aware of the need for a multicultural learning vision and the strategies for achieving it (Gay, 1992).

Permeating this awareness process is our understanding of the cultural values and behaviors that we model for children and parents (Hilliard, 1992). Other important aspects of the awareness process include:

- *Examining how self-esteem is developed:*
  How do people feel about themselves?
  What do they know about their own culture?
- *Probing people's perceptions of different cultures, lifestyles and contexts:*
  What do people know about other cultures?
  What are their attitudes toward people from diverse cultures?
  What stereotypes and biases do people have about other cultures?
- *Examining the ingrained cultural habits of a society, particularly with regard to inequities in jobs, roles, salaries, status symbols and related rituals:*
  Are people from different cultures equitably represented in public roles?
  Do the housing and living patterns in our community reflect patterns of discrimination?
  Do employers, schools and business practice systematic discrimination?

- *Analyzing the ways families socialize children about culture:*
  Are parents educating children about their cultural heritage in appropriate ways?
  Are parents modeling culturally sensitive and enriching behaviors and attitudes for children?
- *Probing the substance of school and classroom practices relative to multicultural learning:*
  Are staff exemplary models of multicultural learning?
  Do school artifacts, policies and learning activities reflect equity and proactive multicultural learning?
- *Studying the biases, inequities and related issues of cultural distortion that may pervade our daily lives:*
  Are families providing equitable and respectful roles and relationships?
  Are schools providing quality learning arrangements for all children?
  Are communities actively seeking policies that support equity and justice for all citizens?

Awareness depends upon a climate of openness that can be created to strengthen attitudes, knowledge and skills that foster more sensitive and enriching interrelationships (Banks, 1993). Family and school frameworks need to encourage open discussion and analysis of cultural understanding, behavior patterns and relationship patterns.

Dialogue about how we live with and relate to each other should also include an assessment of specific family, school and community habits (Hilliard, 1992). For example, parent education could help adults assess the ways they teach their children to view themselves and others, especially people from different cultural contexts. Teach-

ers can enrich this process by using proactive multicultural teaching methods.

Exploration and experimentation. Exploration and experimentation with new ways of building multicultural learning environments is the second step in a multicultural learning process (Hohensee & Derman-Sparks, 1992). Attempts to gain everyone's involvement in culturally sensitive activities are typical of this effort. Parents and teachers can involve children in volunteer activities, for example, that broaden their cultural understanding and increase their self-efficacy. These activities might include service at a homeless shelter, participation in programs that serve special populations and social awareness field trips.

Teachers might develop regular activities that enrich children's perspectives, such as highlighting a "culture of the week," visiting community cultural events, involving parents and children in multicultural social and educational activities, hosting parent study groups that focus on multicultural issues, and offering teacher development programs on curriculum issues and community awareness activities that bring people of different cultures together in meaningful ways (Boutte & McCormick, 1992).

This exploratory phase of multicultural learning stimulates interest in learning about others in a positive and enjoyable way. The main focus in this effort is to help people realize the importance and enrichment possibilities of living in a multicultural environment (Banks, 1993).

Systematic development. Systematic multicultural development is the phase in which communities of people intentionally recognize and act on a transformational vision. The community focuses on building multicultural

learning communities in which beliefs, perceptions and actions create a flow of cultural habits that help people understand, value, support and learn from each other (Csikszentmihalyi, 1993). Formalized family and school collaboration incorporates planning, design and implementation of multicultural learning systems into daily life.

The initial step in this development phase is to review, refine and integrate proactive multicultural attitudes, knowledge and skills into all facets of the family-school-community learning system (Banks, 1993). Clearly, the major impediment to a fully functioning multicultural world is the lack of accurate representation and involvement of diverse peoples. Hilliard (1992) notes the pervasiveness of this impediment in global actions:

Those who have studied worldwide liberation struggles know that the manipulation of information, including propaganda and misinformation, are primary tactics employed in the domination process. Oppressive populations defame, stigmatize, stereotype and distort the reality of dominated populations. Ultimately, if the curriculum is centered in truth, it will be pluralistic, for the simple fact is that human culture is the product of the struggles of all humanity, not the possession of a single racial or ethnic group. (pp. 157-158)

In this context, it is critical that families and schools assess all aspects of their cultural functioning. For example, families need to examine how they relate to each other in terms of multicultural learning (Swick, Van Scoy & Boutte, 1994). At school, classroom content, teacher-child interactions and significant processes and rituals (such as grouping patterns, treatment of all children, involvement of families and the overall school culture) should be continuously reviewed for accuracy, cultural inclusion and degree of collaboration and individuality (Derman-Sparks, 1991).

Some specific actions that can promote this systematic effort include:

- Joint parent-teacher planning of activities and strategies that integrate multicultural learning into children's daily experiences
- Teacher assessment and refinement of instructional and curricular content, process and actions relative to providing accurate and comprehensive multicultural experiences
- School ecology team actions to develop policies that promote equity, cultural enrichment and individual sensitivity to cultural differences and commonalities.

Formalized planning brings systematic attention to all aspects of multicultural learning in order to promote accurate representations of culturally diverse people and promote a proactive multicultural orientation within family, school and community (Hilliard, 1992). Planners must develop goals, an action plan, strategies and tools for continually monitoring and refining the entire system. Nothing less than a comprehensive and collaborative approach to addressing multicultural learning needs can achieve the goal of a more sensitive and nurturing citizenry.

Swick, Van Scoy and Boutte (1994) suggest five "opportunities for multicultural learning" that can be initiated with children from birth through age 7: 1) educating parents about their role in building children's self-esteem, 2) helping children explore their own culture through family and school activities, 3) training parents and teachers to assess their multicultural

competence, 4) supporting families' and schools' development of skills and strategies for promoting multicultural learning and 5) initiating intense teacher education about multicultural learning. The

positive multicultural learning relies upon a foundation of being valued within the family, meaningfully guided in school and engaged in helpful community rituals.

following sampling of strategies highlights the importance of a comprehensive approach:

- Teachers can share multicultural information with parents by lending them relevant books, articles and videos; posting information and suggestions on parent bulletin boards; offering monthly parenting programs; and publishing newsletters that report on multicultural activities within the school and community.
- Classroom displays should represent diverse ethnic, racial and cultural backgrounds. Also, these displays should include children's personal work. Parents can participate by helping to acquire materials and by volunteering in the classroom.
- Teachers can ask families to share pictures, family recipes, dramatic play props, family experiences,

books and other print materials, stories and other artifacts that reflect their cultures.

Integration of multicultural learning. This step is necessary to build a cooperative and proactive society (Byrnes & Kiger, 1992). This phase of multicultural development filters every aspect of social functioning through the lenses of equity, sensitivity, understanding and cultural enrichment. Families and schools will eventually internalize multicultural values so that these filtering actions become natural and sustaining behaviors. Four behavior patterns are essential: 1) nurturing authentic and positive self-esteem; 2) promoting a sharing, nurturing and positive self-other relationship syndrome; 3) nurturing the cultural strengths of all people and 4) promoting collaborative relationships among different cultures (Swick & Graves, 1993).

Low self-esteem is the most prevalent obstacle to building proactive multicultural communities (Slonim, 1991). Children and adults need contexts that build self-esteem. Positive multicultural learning relies upon a foundation of being valued within the family, meaningfully guided in school and engaged in helpful community rituals. The secure and valued "self" is the basis for cultural competence (Neugebauer, 1992).

Learning about others through nurturing, sharing and positive relationships can foster critical prosocial skills (Hilliard, 1992). Regular opportunities for people to meet, and learn from, culturally diverse people in positive ways must be available. Cooperative learning, cross-age grouping and networking activities are strategies that support this process.

Culturally different people are too often viewed from the perspective of the dominant culture, which is often deficit-focused (Neugebauer, 1992). An attitude of strength through diversity, by contrast, celebrates the multiple talents of all people. Likewise, collaborative relationships are critical to sustaining proactive multicultural learning (Oliver & Howley, 1992).

Systematic effort can facilitate integration of multicultural learning into family, school and community habits. This process must be revisited frequently to combat the often subtle forms of prejudice, racism, sexism and classism (Boutte, La Point & Davis, 1993).

Collaboration and Advocacy Is Essential

Every effort to promote a culturally sensitive and enriching world is empowering. Family-school collaboration, however, enables people to transform themselves in ways that can extend multicultural constructs toward full societal implementation. This collaboration process can occur in many ways: within the family, in collaboration between family and school and in societal planning and advocacy activities (Hilliard, 1992).

Collaborative schemes work best in small social units (e.g., teams of teachers, neighborhood action teams and community innovation groups). The power of small groups is evident in school events that focus on cultural celebrations, antibias committees and multicultural learning teams (Banks, 1993). Face-to-face interactions bring about the most powerful transformations and understandings. It is only through working together that we really come to understand one another. The important elements of these small social action units are: commitment to a common goal, continuous membership, specific roles for members, a detailed plan on how to achieve identified goals and a system for continued nurturance of the group's original mission (Csikszentmihalyi, 1993). Creating networks with like-minded groups can increase each group's influence, if system flexibility within the smaller units is maintained.

Advocacy is critical to the long-term promotion of multicultural values. Families, schools and communities need to monitor their systems to ensure cultural accuracy and to maintain supports that foster integrative multicultural learning habits. For example, education programs can highlight multicultural learning experiences that families can carry out on a regular basis. Schools and community groups can serve as anti-bias watchdogs. The best hope for cultural harmony that respects positive individuality is collaborative advocacy. We must be continually reminded of the urgency and need for attention to our cultural knowledge, attitudes and skills.

◆

References

Banks, J. (1993). Multicultural education for young children: Racial and ethnic attitudes and their modification. In B. Spodek (Ed.), *Handbook of research on the education of young children* (pp. 236-251). New York: Macmillan.

Boutte, G. S., La Point, S., & Davis, B. (1993). Racial issues in education: Real or imagined? *Young Children, 49*(1), 19-22.

Boutte, G., & McCormick, C. (1992). Authentic multicultural activities: Avoiding pseudomulticulturalism. *Childhood Education, 68,* 140-144.

Byrnes, D., & Kiger, G. (Eds.). (1992). *Common bonds: Anti-bias teaching in a diverse society.* Wheaton, MD: Association for Childhood Education International.

Csikszentmihalyi, M. (1993). *The evolving self.* New York: HarperCollins.

Derman-Sparks, L. (Ed.). (1991). *Antibias curriculum: Tools for empowering young children.* Washington, DC: National Association for the Education of Young Children.

Diaz, C. (Ed.). (1992). *Multicultural education for the 21st century.* Washington, DC: National Education Association.

Fu, V., Stremmel, A., & Treppte, C. (Eds.). (1992). *Multiculturalism in early childhood programs.* Urbana, IL: ERIC Clearinghouse on Elementary and Early Childhood Education.

Gay, G. (1992). Effective teaching practices for multicultural classrooms. In C. Diaz (Ed.), *Multicultural education for the 21st century* (pp. 38-56). Washington, DC: National Education Association.

Hilliard, A. (1992). Why we must pluralize the curriculum. *Educational Leadership, 49*(4), 157-160.

Hohensee, J., & Derman-Sparks, L. (1992). *Implementing an anti-bias curriculum in early childhood classrooms.* Champaign, IL: ERIC Clearinghouse on Early Childhood Education. ED 351146.

Howard, G. (1993). Whites in multicultural education: Rethinking our role. *Phi Delta Kappan, 75*(1), 36-41.

Neugebauer, B. (Ed.). (1992). *Alike and different: Exploring our humanity with young children.* Washington, DC: National Association for the Education of Young Children.

Oliver, J.-P., & Howley, C. (1992). *Charting new maps: Multicultural education in rural schools.* Charleston, WV: ERIC Clearinghouse on Rural and Small Schools. ED 348196.

Ramsey, P., & Derman-Sparks, L. (1992). Multicultural education reaffirmed. *Young Children, 47*(2), 10-11.

Slonim, M. (1991). *Children, culture, and ethnicity.* New York: Garland.

Swick, K., Van Scoy, I., & Boutte, G. (1994). Multicultural learning through family involvement. *Dimensions of Early Childhood, 22*(4), 17-21.

Swick, K., & Graves, S. (1993). *Empowering at-risk families during the early childhood years.* Washington, DC: National Education Association.

LIFE WITHOUT FATHER

In exclusive excerpts from 'Fatherless America,' to be published Tuesday, the author argues that fathers are an endangered species — and offers a plan to save them

DAVID BLANKENHORN

The author of these excerpts is chairman of the National Fatherhood Initiative, one of several groups attempting to call attention to the importance of fathers in solving today's most pressing social problems. Board members range from former U.S. Education Secretary William Bennett to actor James Earl Jones. Blankenhorn lives in New York with his wife, Raina, and their 4-year-old son, Raymond.

The United States is becoming an increasingly fatherless society. A generation ago, a child could reasonably expect to grow up with his or her father. Today, a child can reasonably expect not to. Fatherlessness is approaching a rough parity with fatherhood as a defining feature of childhood.

This astonishing fact is reflected in many statistics, but here are the two most important: Tonight, about 40 percent of U.S. children will go to sleep in homes in which their fathers do not live *(see chart, opposite page)*. More than half of our children are likely to spend a significant portion of childhood living apart from their fathers. Never before in this country have so many children been voluntarily abandoned by their fathers. Never before have so many children grown up without knowing what it means to have a father.

Fatherlessness is the most harmful demographic trend of this generation. It is the leading cause of the decline in the well-being of children. It is also the engine driving our most urgent social problems, from crime to adolescent pregnancy to domestic violence. Yet, despite its scale and social consequences, fatherlessness is frequently ignored or denied. Especially within our elite discourse, it remains a problem with no name.

Surely a crisis of this scale merits a name — and a response. At a minimum, it requires a serious debate: Why is fatherhood declining? What can be done about it? Can our society find ways to invigorate effective fatherhood as a norm of male behavior? Yet, to date, our public discussion has been remarkably weak and defeatist. There is a prevailing belief that not much can or even should be done to reverse the trend.

As a society, we are changing our minds about men's role in family life. Our inherited understanding of fatherhood is under siege. Men are increasingly viewed as superfluous to family life: either expendable or part of the problem. Masculinity itself often is treated with suspicion, and even hostility, in our cultural discourse. Consequently, our society is unable to sustain fatherhood as a distinctive domain of male activity.

'Fatherlessness is the engine driving our most urgent social problems, from crime to adolescent pregnancy to domestic violence'

The core question is simple: Does every child need a father? Increasingly, our society's answer is "no." Few idea shifts in this century are as consequential as this one. At stake is nothing less than what it means to be a man, who our children will be and what kind of society we will become.

My book is a criticism not simply of fatherlessness but of a *culture* of fatherlessness. For, in addition to fathers, we are losing something larger: our idea of fatherhood. Unlike earlier periods of father absence in our history, such as wartime, we now face more than a physical loss affecting some homes. The 1940s child could say: My father had to leave for a while to do something important. The '90s child must say: My father left me permanently because he wanted to.

This is a cultural criticism because fatherhood, much more than motherhood, is a cultural invention. Its meaning is shaped less by biology than by a cultural script, a societal code that guides — and at times pressures — a man into certain ways of acting and understanding himself.

Like motherhood, fatherhood is made up of both a biological and a social dimension. Yet, across the world, mothers are far more successful than fathers at fusing these dimensions into a coherent identity. Is the nursing mother playing a biological or a social role? Feeding or bonding? We can hardly separate the two, so seamlessly are they woven together. But fatherhood is a different matter. A father makes his sole biological contribution at the moment of conception, nine months before the infant enters the world. Because social paternity is linked only indirectly to biological paternity, a connection cannot be assumed. The phrase "to father a child" usually refers only to the act of insemination, not the responsibility for raising the child. What fathers contribute after conception is largely a matter of cultural devising.

Moreover, despite their other virtues, men are not ideally suited to responsible fatherhood. Men are inclined to sexual promiscuity and paternal waywardness. Anthropologically, fatherhood constitutes what might be termed a necessary problem. It is necessary because child well-being and societal success hinge largely on a high level of paternal investment: men's willingness to devote energy and resources to the care of their offspring. It is a problem because men frequently are unwilling or unable to make that vital investment.

Because fatherhood is universally problematic, cultures must mobilize to enforce the father role, guiding men with legal and extralegal pressures that require them to maintain a close alliance with

DISAPPEARING DADS

U.S. KIDS LIVING WITH ...	1960	1980	1990
Father and mother	80.6%	62.3%	57.7%
Mother only	7.7	18	21.6
Father only	1	1.7	3.1
Father and stepmother	0.8	1.1	0.9
Mother and stepfather	5.9	8.4	10.4
Neither parent	3.9	5.8	4.3

Sources: *America's Children* by Donald Hernandez; U.S. Census Bureau. Because the statistics are from separate sources, they don't total 100%.

their children's mother and invest in their children. Because men don't volunteer for fatherhood as much as they are conscripted into it by the surrounding culture, only an authoritative cultural commitment to fatherhood can fuse biological and social paternity into a coherent male identity. For exactly this reason, anthropologist Margaret Mead and others have observed that the supreme test of any civilization is whether it can socialize men by teaching them to nurture their offspring.

The stakes could hardly be higher. Our society's conspicuous failure to sustain norms of fatherhood reveals a failure of collective memory and a collapse of moral imagination. It undermines families, neglects children, causes or aggravates our worst social problems and makes individual adult happiness, both female and male, harder to achieve.

Ultimately, this failure reflects nothing less than a culture gone awry, unable to establish the boundaries and erect the signposts that can harmonize individual happiness with collective well-being. In short, it reflects a culture that fails to "enculture" individual men and women, mothers and fathers.

In personal terms, the main result of this failure is the spread of a me-first egotism hostile to all except the most puerile understandings of personal happiness. In social terms, the results are a decline in children's well-being and a rise in male violence, especially against women. The most significant result is our society's steady fragmentation into atomized individuals, isolated from one

12 WAYS TO PUT FATHERS BACK IN THE PICTURE

25 PERCENT OF U.S. BABIES born in 1993 were to unmarried mothers who ran their households alone, Blankenhorn estimates. To create a stronger national focus on the value of fatherhood, he recommends:

■ A coalition of civic groups should ask every man to pledge that "every child deserves a father, marriage is the pathway to effective fatherhood, part of being a good man is being a good father, and America needs more good men."

■ The president, acting through the White House Domestic Policy Council, should issue a brief annual report to the nation on the state of fatherhood.

■ A few good men should create Fathers' Clubs in their communities.

■ Congress should assist community organizers, clergy members and other local leaders who are serious about creating higher standards of male responsibility.

■ Community organizers and veterans of the poor people's and civil rights movements should help build the infrastructure for a new grass-roots movement to empower families and strengthen community life.

■ Policies should be changed to encourage a higher percentage of married couples in public housing.

■ An interfaith council of religius leaders should speak up and act up on behalf of marriage.

■ Congress should pass, and the president should support, a resolution stating that policymakers' first question about domestic legislation should be whether it will strengthen the institution of marriage.

■ Local officials across the nation should follow the example of the Hennepin County (Minn.) Board of Commissioners by issuing a "vision statement" that urges citizens to move toward a community in which a "healthy family structure is nurtured."

■ States should regulate sperm banks, prohibiting the sale of sperm to unmarried women and limiting artificial insemination to infertile married couples.

■ Well-known pro athletes should organize a public service campaign on the importance of fatherhood.

■ Prominent family scholars should write better high school textbooks about marriage and parenthood.

another and estranged from the aspirations and realities of common membership in a family, a community, a nation, bound by mutual commitment and shared memory.

Many voices today, including many expert voices, urge us to accept the decline of fatherhood with equanimity. Be realistic, they tell us. Divorce and out-of-wedlock childbearing are here to stay. Growing numbers of children will not have fathers. Nothing can be done to reverse the trend itself. The only solution is to remedy some of its consequences: More help for poor children. More sympathy for single mothers. Better divorce. More child-support payments. More prisons. More programs aimed at substituting for fathers.

Yet what Abraham Lincoln called the better angels of our nature always have guided us in the opposite direction. Passivity in the face of crisis is inconsistent with the American tradition. Managing decline never has been the hallmark of American expertise. In the inevitable and valuable tension between conditions and aspirations — between the social "is" and the moral "ought" — our birthright as Americans always has been our confidence that we can change for the better.

Does every child need a father? Our current answer hovers between "not necessarily" and "no." But we need not make permanent the lowering of our standards. We can change our minds. We can change our minds without passing new laws, spending more tax dollars or empaneling more expert commissions. Once we change our philosophy, we might well decide to pass laws, create programs or commission research. But the first and most important thing to change is not policies, but ideas.

Our essential goal must be the rediscovery of the fatherhood idea: For every child, a legally and morally responsible man.

If my goal could be distilled into one sentence, it would be this: A good society celebrates the ideal of the man who puts his family first. Because our society is lurching in the opposite direction, I see the Good Family Man as the principal casualty of today's weakening focus on fatherhood. Yet I cannot imagine a good society without him.

Bridging Home and School Through Multiple Intelligences

Judith C. Reiff

Judith C. Reiff is Associate Professor, Department of Elementary Education, University of Georgia, Athens.

Children's learning styles are as different as the colors of the rainbow. All people have different, distinct personalities, preferences and tastes. When we understand the various ways in which children learn, we are better able to 1) prevent discipline problems, 2) communicate with parents, 3) reduce teacher burn-out and parent frustration, 4) organize the classroom and 5) help children reach their potential (Reiff, 1992).

Howard Gardner's theory of multiple intelligences (1987, 1993) enables us to discuss positive strengths in all children and to plan appropriate learning strategies for a more effective classroom environment. Gardner maintains that intelligence is something more complex than can ever be reflected by a test score, and that the Western education system overemphasizes the linguistic and logical/mathematical intelligences. At least five other intelligences are present in everyone to some degree; therefore, our classrooms should include activities, materials and assessment that respond to all intelligences (Faggella & Horowitz, 1990; Lazear, 1992).

By sharing this information with parents and involving them in the learning process, parents are recognized and valued as collaborators in their children's education. Teachers can explain these intelligences or domains to parents in a brochure or pamphlet (Reiff, 1995), at an Open House or during a parent/teacher conference. The specific terms are not as important as the idea that all of us need to be appreciated for our strengths, which might be in different areas. Parents should be encouraged to provide different activities to discover and nurture their child's own intelligences. This article provides the classroom teacher with instructional strategies for each domain and additional activities for parents.

Linguistic Learners

These children have a sensitivity to the meaning, sounds and rhythms of words. They enjoy storytelling, wordplay and creative writing. They love reading, poetry, tongue twisters, puns and humor, and find pleasure in working puzzles and solving riddles. Teachers should be sensitive to the language and questioning patterns used in the home.

Suggestions for teachers. Activities for linguistic learners could include reading/writing workshops, book sharing, dialogue writing, book-tape stories, word processing and newspaper activities.

Suggestions for parents. Read with your children. Listen intently to their questions, concerns and experiences. Provide ample books and paper for reading and writing activities. Encourage your children to tell you about the stories they read or to share something they have written. A tape recorder is a helpful aid. Provide opportunities to visit the public library and local bookstores. Games such as Scrabble™, Hangman, Boggle™ and Yahtzee™ are ideal for linguistic learners.

Logical-Mathematical Learners

These children enjoy number games, problem solving, pattern games and experimenting. They have strong reasoning skills and ask questions in a logical manner. Activities that are more ordered and sequential appeal to these children.

Suggestions for teachers. Challenge these children with problem solving and patterning activities. They will enjoy experiments, computer instruction and syllogism. Use graphic organizers, number sequences and pattern games, and show relationships to help them learn.

Suggestions for parents. Let your children experiment! Invite them to help you bake a cake or make new colors by mixing paints. Show them how to use a calculator. Allow your children to help with the family budget and to budget their own allowances. Setting the table, sorting clothes or organizing the desk drawer are ideal activities. Games such as UNO™, checkers and chess will tap a logical-mathematical intelligence.

Spatial Learners

Spatial learners respond to visual cues and are image-oriented. They often are daydreamers and have a talent for art. These children like to invent and design. They enjoy creating visual patterns and need visual stimulation. Visual word cues assist these individuals. Maps, charts, diagrams, puzzles and mazes are excellent resources. Provide opportunities to create with various arts and crafts.

Suggestions for teachers. Use color in your activities. Verbs could be blue, nouns red, antonyms orange and synonyms purple, for example. Mathematical symbols could be color-coded as well. Provide manipulatives and use guided imagery and mind-mapping.

Suggestions for parents. Provide opportunities for solving puzzles or inventing. Let children with spatial intelligence choose the colors for their bedrooms and design the furniture arrangement. A spatial learner will enjoy mapping the bedroom to show where everything belongs or arranging items on a table or shelf. Visiting art museums and taking photographs are appropriate activities. Provide a variety of art mediums such as paints, crayons and magic markers. Play games such as Pictionary™ or cards.

Musical Learners

These children thoroughly enjoy playing instruments, singing songs, drumming, etc. They like the sounds of the human voice, environmental sounds and instrumental sounds. They can learn easier if things are set to music or to a beat.

Suggestions for teachers. "Note" the volume and pitch of your voice. Use descriptive and rhythmic words to enhance communication. Use a variety of music in the classroom as background and to teach skills. Play musical chairs, have listening centers and tape-record storybooks. Be attentive to environmental sounds and how they might interfere with children's learning.

Suggestions for parents. Allow musical children to select a recording at the local music store. Encourage your children to sing along or clap to the rhythm. If possible, involve your children in some type of music lessons. Provide opportunities to attend concerts and musicals. Have sing-alongs.

Bodily-Kinesthetic Learners

These children are athletic and active. They enjoy creative dramatics, role-playing, dancing and expressing themselves with movement and bodily action. These children derive much of what they learn through physical movement and from touching and feeling. They use movement, gesture and physical expression to learn and solve problems. They may touch while talking.

Suggestions for teachers. Provide physical exercise and hands-on activities. Walk through difficult problems and ideas, such as subtraction and addition. Use materials such as fabric, clay, blocks and other manipulatives.

Suggestions for parents. Involve your children in dancing, acting or sports activities. Provide a variety of manipulatives for experimentation. Walk, jog, hike, play tennis, bowl or bike as a family. These children will enjoy swings, riding toys and slides. Play games such as charades, Simon says and hide-and-seek. Provide chores such as sweeping, setting the table and emptying the trash cans.

Interpersonal Learners

These children are very social and intuitive about others' feelings. They are "people persons" because they can "read" others' feelings and behaviors. They are excellent leaders, have empathy for others, enjoy being part of a group and are street smart. They can help peers and work cooperatively with others.

Suggestions for teachers. Arrange for these children to be peer tutors or buddies to younger children. These children would enjoy skits, plays, group work, discussions, debates or cooperative learning.

Suggestions for parents. Play a family game. Encourage your children to participate in group activities. Encourage discussions and problem solving.

Intrapersonal Learners

Intrapersonal children like to work independently. They "march to a different drummer" and are very self-motivated, preferring solitary activities. They have the ability to understand their own feelings, motivations and moods. They may be daydreamers.

Suggestions for teachers. Provide a quiet area for independent work, encourage writing in a personal journal, discuss thinking strategies, facilitate metacognition techniques and suggest independent projects.

Suggestions for parents. Give your children quality time to work or play alone because individual time is very important to these children. Ask them to make something for the whole family to enjoy. Provide a time for reflection. Encourage your children to keep a diary or journal.

Conclusion

Teachers must recognize and admit that schools traditionally value certain intelligences over others. Some children identified as "at risk" might be considered gifted in a different situation or context. It is important, therefore, to carefully observe each child to identify where their key intelligences lie. A profile representing the child's spectrum of intelligences can be a valuable resource at a parent/teacher conference (Krechevsky, 1991). Parents can help teachers by providing insight into the domains in which the child excels at home. The goal of education should be to provide an equitable environment for all children; one way of accomplishing this is to value the multiple intelligences in all of us.

Children should not be "tracked" according to a specific intelligence, nor should they be excluded from enjoying activities in other intelligences. Instead, all children must be provided an equal opportunity for succeeding within the context of the classroom.

References

Faggella, K., & Horowitz, J. (1990). Different child different style. *Instructor, 100*(2), 49-54.

Gardner, H. (1987). *Multiple intelligences: The theory in practice.* New York: Basic Books.

Gardner, H. (1993). *Frames of mind* (rev. ed.). New York: Basic Books.

Krechevsky, M. (1991). Project spectrum: An innovative assessment alternative. *Educational Leadership, 48*(5), 135-138.

Lazear, D. (1992). *Teaching for multiple intelligences.* Bloomington, IN: Phi Delta Kappa.

Reiff, J. (1992). *What research says to teachers: Learning styles.* Washington, DC: National Education Association.

Reiff, J. (1995). *Multiple intelligences: Different ways of learning.* Pamphlet for parents. Wheaton, MD: Association for Childhood Education International.

Educational Practices

Educational practices with young children seem to be always changing, yet always the same. The notion of what is good practice in early childhood education seems to vary between two extremes. One approach is traditional, with an emphasis on skill and drill methods, segmented curriculum, and accuracy in work. The other approach, which includes curricular integration and an emphasis on play, is more constructive. These two approaches coexist in early childhood but are based in very different philosophies of how teaching and learning occur. So the dilemma is to determine which educational practice is most appropriate for children.

How does a person recognize good practice? Basically, look for action in the learning environment. *Appropriate practice is children in action.* Children are busy constructing with blocks, working puzzles, and creating with multimedia. They invent, cook, and compose throughout the day. When children are interested and begin to experiment in the learning environment, they develop understanding. This process of active learning is described by Christine Chaillé and Steven B. Silvern in their essay "Understanding through Play."

Appropriate practice is teachers in action. Teachers are busy holding conversations, guiding activities, and questioning children. They observe, draw conclusions, plan, and monitor the activities throughout the day. Learning how to teach well means that teachers must go through a change process. Gaye Gronlund provides a clear model for change in her article, "Bringing the DAP Message to Kindergarten and Primary Teachers." She emphasizes that teachers, like children, learn appropriate practice through doing.

Appropriate practice means teaching children, not curriculum. Sandra J. Stone's "Strategies for Teaching Children in Multiage Classrooms," tackles ways to individualize teaching for groups of children who stay with the same teacher for several years. A vital element of making multiage classrooms work is to use a process approach to learning, with plenty of opportunities for open-ended projects based on integrated curriculum. To accomplish this approach, the teacher takes on the role of learning facilitator. Such a flexible role allows children to engage in planning and carrying out their learning activities.

Appropriate practice means authentic assessment of children's progress. Several articles in this unit address best assessment practices. In a series of to-the-point strategies, Lilian Katz, Sylvia Chard, and Celia Genishi outline the

essence of authentic assessment. Learning how to observe children, record anecdotes, and display children's learning provide useful tools for teaching well. One technique currently being used by teachers is the assessment portfolio, which is a good way to archive the work done by children. Keeping periodic records of children's development along with their work aligns well with appropriate practice. This variety of assessment methods provides a much broader picture of children's performance than is available in programs that are test-driven. This unit concludes with Ellen Booth Church's insightful "Your Learning Environment: A Look Back at Your Year." She recommends taking time to ask specific in-depth questions at the end of the year. This is a valuable way to get an accurate evaluation of the entire learning environment. From the answers to questions about the centers and activities of the program, planning begins for the next year. Good practice, appropriate for children's development and based on active play, has no shortcuts and cannot be trivialized. It takes careful thought and planning, using the latest knowledge of early childhood education, to make curriculum and practice choices. By working out specifics of routines and procedures, curriculum, and assessment suitable for young children, the early childhood professional strengthens skills in decision making. These are crucial tasks for a teacher interested in developmentally appropriate practice.

Looking Ahead: Challenge Questions

How do young children arrive at understanding something?

What does integration or inclusion mean?

Analyze the ramifications of this statement: It's not what I *cover* that is important, it's what students *discover*.

Comment on the idea that there are multiple ways of being intelligent.

What items might be included in a portfolio?

Understanding Through Play

Christine Chaillé and
Steven B. Silvern

*Christine Chaillé is Professor, Curriculum and Instruction,
Portland State University, Portland, Oregon. Steven B. Silvern is Professor,
Early Childhood Education, Auburn University, Auburn, Alabama.*

A visitor walks into a kindergarten classroom and observes the children scattered about the room, playing in various areas. In one area a child is playing with a magnetic toy. The toy consists of four magnets embedded in a plastic base and hundreds of tiny metal parallelograms that can be formed into larger forms above the magnets in the base. The child has constructed an arch between two of the magnets. He then takes one tiny parallelogram and tries to stick it onto another one that he holds in his hand. When he tries to stick the combination onto the arch with one hand, one parallelogram falls to the floor. He picks it up and then presses the two objects together harder, as though trying to make them stick together by the force of his hand pressure.

This child is displaying *understanding*. When we speak of "understanding" we are referring to the active construction of meaning. Children arrive at understanding by creating hypotheses about items and events that they find interesting. They test hypotheses as they actively interact with the materials and events in their environment (Chaillé & Britain, 1991). The child in the above scenario was testing his hypothesis that each individual metal piece would stick to any other one.

The idea that these understandings *belong* to each child, individually, is important when discussing children's understanding. While the actions described above are familiar to teachers, not every child will act with the same understandings. As the child acts, familiar tools are applied to unfamiliar ideas. In the above example, when the two pieces did not stick together, the child attempted to make them stick in the same way that he would try to make a piece of paper stick with glue.

Sometimes these familiar tools do not *work* in the way that an adult would consider to be correct. Once the two pieces did not stick together, for example, an adult would not consider trying to use more force to try and make them stick. Nevertheless, some tools may work for the child. That is, although the hypothesis may not be totally correct, it has enough correctness to be satisfying to the child. Therefore, the child has an understanding; in this case, an understanding about things sticking together. It is not completely correct, but it is correct enough that the child is satisfied with the result. Only if the child sees a discrepancy in his reasoning will he be motivated to modify his reasoning, and ultimately his answer. Thus, when the piece fell a second time, the child abandoned his strategy and placed the individual pieces one at a time on the arch.

Piaget refers to the intentional social process of constructing understanding (partially described above) as active education (DeVries & Kohlberg, 1987). Active education involves four elements: interest, play, genuine experimentation and cooperation. In this article, the authors contend that interest, experimentation and cooperation are joined within the context of play. They first examine the kinds of play and the relation of these kinds of play to active education. Then, they place these kinds of play into particular learning contexts, intending to show that through play, children achieve all the elements of active education through play.

It is important to remember, however, that play may take two different forms, one of which is not active learning. When children are interested and applying attention to their play, they are engaging in active education. If, however, their play involves a simple manipulation of materials, without applying mental activity, it is unlikely that knowledge construction will take place. This is why constructivists caution against simply giving children materials to manipulate. Little understanding can occur without interest, experimentation and cooperation.

Play and Active Education

Piaget (1962) identified four kinds of play: practice play, symbolic play, games with rules and constructions. (Piaget, in fact, separates constructions as a unique form of play that leads to adapted behaviors.) Opportunities for active education exist within each of these kinds of play.

■ *Practice play.* Practice play is the "... exercise [of] structures for no other purpose than the pleasure of functioning" (Piaget, 1962, p. 110). This definition stresses the importance of pleasure over the learning of a new behavior. According to this definition, learning does not necessarily take place in practice play. We can imagine, however, many instances of adult play in which the same ability is exercised and we do construct a "new" behavior. While we ski to get pleasure from the activity, for example, each time we do so we attempt to gain more control or, perhaps, more speed. So, too, as we watch our children and their friends jump rope or use a pogo stick, we can see them attempting to gain more control as they exercise their ability. They seem to ask the implicit questions: Can I jump longer? Can I jump farther? Can I jump two ropes going in different directions? Some intent to learn appears present even in practice play.

Other elements of active education, certainly interest, are present in practice play. Children will not continue to jump without an interest evidenced either internally or through peer relations. Active experimentation occurs as children attempt to go beyond what they can already do, even if that is only an attempt to maintain "social position" (by jumping longer, for example). Interestingly, children often

adapt rules during practice play. When jumping rope, for example, they may decree that children cannot monopolize the jump rope longer than the jump rope chant permits. The social negotiation that occurs around the act of jumping then involves the cooperation necessary for further understanding. In this case, it may not be further understanding of jumping, but instead an understanding of interactions that allows everyone to jump without becoming bored with turning the rope or waiting one's turn.

■ *Symbolic play.* As the children in one kindergarten class prepared to act out "Little Red Riding Hood," Shuwan said, "I'll be the chopper and this is my ax, OK? Pretend my hand is the ax." This is an example of symbolic play. Such play "... impl[ies] representation of

> **A**ctive experimentation occurs as children attempt to go beyond what they can already do, even if that is only an attempt to maintain "social position."

an absent object . . . [and] make-believe representation . . . " (Piaget, 1962, p. 111). It is impossible to represent or make believe without applying active thought. Therefore, symbolic play would seem to be the epitome of active interest. Children cannot simply manipulate something that is not present, nor can an object be substituted for another without some mental effort. Interest, then, is implied when children engage in symbolic play.

Ample opportunity for genuine experimentation exists during symbolic play, although it does not always occur. Experimentation is possible whenever children construct props for their symbolic play. Granny's house in "Little Red Riding

Hood," for example, had to be built tall enough for the wolf to hide behind, yet be stable enough that it would not topple easily. Another kind of experimentation involves modes of communication. Whenever children seek alternate means for communicating their intent, as with Shuwan and his hand/ax, they are experimenting to find out if their actions/representations communicate.

Cooperation among children lies at the core of the negotiations that must occur whenever symbolic play occurs in groups of children. Rubin (1980) and Williamson and Silvern (1992) identify the discussions that occur within symbolic play as the impetus for thinking. During symbolic play children disagree, discuss the problem and come to agreement so that the play can continue. Children come to see other points of view during this exchange and learn to understand the others' reasoning.

■ *Games with rules.* Games with rules are defined as " ... prescribed acts, subject to rules, generally penalties for the infringement of rules and the action proceeds in a formal evolution until it culminates in a given climax . . ." (*Encyclopedia Americana*, 1957, p. 266, cited in DeVries, 1980, p. 1). In games with rules, children willingly submit themselves to the rules so that the game can continue. Interest and cooperation are evident within this context for, without either, the game cannot continue. The concept of genuine experimentation is not as commonplace. Children do experiment in games with rules when they try alternate means of achieving an end. In marbles, for example, the child may ask himself, "Can I make my marble skip over another? Can I hit one marble hard enough so that it will hit into other marbles?"

■ *Constructions.* While not identified by Piaget as a kind of play itself, constructions are seen as a midway point between play and work. Children might use materials to represent reality, for example, by carving wood to represent a boat, instead of simply taking a block of wood and pretending it is a boat (Piaget, 1962). It is perhaps easiest for teachers to see active education in constructions. Clearly, when a child is engaged in making something for the pleasure of making it, he or she is active and engaged in genuine experimentation. When the constructions take on a group form (e.g., block constructions), cooperation is also present.

Play and Content

Although play is one of the richest contexts for observing children's construction of understanding, it is important for teachers to be able to recognize the different types of knowledge that are being constructed through play. Teachers will then be able to identify the "content" that children are understanding through play, and relate it to the curricular goals of the classroom.

■ *Play and physical knowledge.* Numerous interesting problems arise in the context of play that lead to experimentation, creative problem solving and cooperation; all these behaviors contribute to the construction of understanding. When two preschool children are devising a drawbridge at the entry to their pretend castle, for example, they must figure out how to connect the drawbridge on each end, and be able to move one end up and down over the "moat." They may draw on a range of possible solutions, use a variety of materials and engage in substantial trial-and-error as they

seek a solution. Highly motivated children will work on the problem for longer periods of time and with less frustration than if the task were part of a decontextualized problem.

Similarly, 2nd-graders constructing marble roll-ways using cardboard tubes will encounter numerous situationally determined tasks, or problem-solving situations, that will lead to active experimentation and, ultimately, the construction of understanding. The idea that the steeper the ramp, the faster the marble will roll, becomes concrete as children try to get the marble to roll up a hill at the other end.

■ *Play and logico-mathematical knowledge.* Play also helps children construct understanding of relationships, which is the heart of logico-mathematical knowledge. Think of children constructing a tower from unit blocks. If they run out of big blocks, they must eventually figure out that two of the smaller blocks together will match one of the larger ones. Or think of older children trying to figure out how many weights to put on top of a pendulum to make it swing far enough to knock down a target. After each weight is placed on the pendulum bob, they swing it to see how it moves. They then add one weight at a time until the target is reached. Here, children are demonstrating their interest and cooperation in play.

The motivated construction of relationships that occurs in the context of play is also evident when children are sharing materials: dividing up the play dough and comparing amounts, sorting through the crayons or serving up the "dinner" at the pretend restaurant. And it is in the context of games that children, particularly older children, are challenged to incorporate scoring systems that provide a meaningful context for the use of arithmetic (Kamii & DeVries, 1980).

■ *Play and language.* Some of the most interesting developments

in relation to both oral and written language happen in the context of play. In the arena of oral language, children have an opportunity to explore language without the fear of correction or constraint. One of the characteristics of play is the "suspension of belief" (Garvey, 1977), which makes it possible for a 5-year-old girl to "become" an old man in speech and mannerisms. We see much experimentation with language patterns and sounds through dramatic play, both in solitary and in social dramatic play.

It is in the context of social dramatic play, however, that we observe the role of communicative competence and the instrumental use of language to accomplish shared goals. Collaboration in an imaginary context requires a good deal of language use to establish the scene, verify the pretend context and guide each other's actions. "You be the doctor, okay? And this is the blood pressure thing, right?" Language takes on the important role of marking pretense, as well as labeling objects and actions.

Similarly, in other types of play oral language use, though not as necessary as in the pretend mode, becomes important as children function together (e.g., in the building of a model). Older children in particular use language for planning play actions. The 2nd-graders working on the marble roll-way may "talk out" their predictions about whether and how a particular structure will work; preschoolers might talk less and do more.

Construction of understanding through written language also occurs in the play context. Print can be incorporated into younger children's play in many ways. "Stop" and "Go" signs used with toy cars, for example, can signify for young children the basic idea that print has meaning. Older children may use written language to codify the rules of a game and introduce modifications. In addition, many games themselves directly involve language, including numerous board games such as Scrabble™. Many in the field of language arts (Wilde, 1991) view invented spelling as the best way of learning to become a good speller. This practice can be viewed as a playful approach to the act of writing itself.

■ *Play and curricular integration.* Segmenting the curriculum according to what children are learning, and monitoring that learning in the classroom, leads us to analyze play and understanding in terms of separable content areas: language, mathematics and science. One of the most salient characteristics of the play environment, however, is that it facilitates the cross-fertilization of ideas and connections across content areas. Literacy and spatial relations come together in play when a child builds a set of gears and labels each part to keep track of where they belong. Mathematics and oral communication occur simultaneously as children play an exciting card game and debate the ways to keep score.

The separations of curricular domains fade when children are actively engaged, self-directed and highly motivated—as they are when they play. As we move toward projects and integrated themes in preschool and elementary curriculum development, we need to keep in mind that in play, projects and curriculum integration happen as a matter of course. We can facilitate the construction of understanding by encouraging children to engage in all forms of play.

■ *Play and the sociomoral environment.* The elements of interest, experimentation and cooperation must be present in order for active learning, or understanding, to occur through play. An appropriate sociomoral environment is essential if these elements are to come together. The classroom's culture needs to be one in which children feel ownership and responsibility

for their own actions. They must feel a sense of community and safety in having their own ideas and trying them out, and they must feel good and caring about each other and share ideas in collaborative activity. Without such a classroom culture, the children will not manifest experimentation, engagement and interest.

Why is the classroom climate or the sociomoral environment so necessary for these elements to come together in constructing understanding? Children need to feel the safety and confidence that permits them to take risks, as they do in their play. Children's understandings (everyone's new understandings, for that matter) are tentative and fragile. Conflict must be experienced in order for learning and growth to take place. Children need to feel safe enough to go out on a limb and confident that falling will not matter. The role of sociocognitive conflict, so necessary for cognitive growth and learning, can seamlessly occur without affective disturbance, in large part because of the framework of play.

Think of the child rolling play dough out with a roller, making a smooth flat surface. He announces that he wants to make a line across it, "to make a road." A girl offers him a roller with spokes in it that, if rolled across a surface, would leave dots and indentations, not a line. He rolls it across, and the two children declare that they have made a "bumpy road." They have changed their "task" based on the outcome of their incorrect prediction. The play context allows the conflict between the prediction, the spoke will make a road when you roll it across the play dough, and the reality, the spoke makes bumps across the play dough, to be assimilated into a new goal. Because the goal is of their choosing to begin with, and because the play context allows for self-directed flexibility, it truly does not matter. Nonetheless, the chil-

dren have acquired a deeper understanding of the relationship between the marks on the roller and the action of rolling it on play dough—a relationship they can build on in their future hypotheses.

Play, then, offers the child the opportunity to make sense out of the world by using available tools. Understanding is created by doing, by doing with others and by being completely involved in that doing. Through play, the child comes to understand the world and the adult comes to understand the child.

◆

References

Chaillé, C., & Britain, L. (1991). *The young child as scientist.* New York: HarperCollins.

DeVries, R. (1980). Good group games: What are they? In C. Kamii & R. DeVries (Eds.), *Group games in early education: Implications of Piaget's theory* (pp. 1-9). Washington, DC: National Association for the Education of Young Children.

DeVries, R., & Kohlberg L. (1987). *Programs of early education: The constructivist view.* White Plains, NY: Longman.

Garvey, C. (1977). *Play.* Cambridge, MA: Harvard University Press.

Kamii, C. K. (1985). *Young children reinvent arithmetic: Implications of Piaget's theory.* New York: Teachers College Press.

Kamii, C., & DeVries, R. (Eds.). (1980). *Group games in early education: Implications of Piaget's theory.* Washington, DC: National Association for the Education of Young Children.

Piaget, J. (1962). *Play, dreams and imitation in childhood.* New York: Norton.

Rubin, K. H. (1980). Fantasy play: Its role in the development of social skills and social cognition. In K. H. Rubin (Ed.), *Children's play* (pp. 69-84). San Francisco: Jossey-Bass.

Wilde, S. (1991). *You kan red this! Spelling and punctuation for whole language classrooms K-6.* Portsmouth, NH: Heinemann.

Williamson, P. A., & Silvern, S. B. (1992). "You can't be grandma; you're a boy": Events within the thematic fantasy play context that contribute to story comprehension. *Early Childhood Research Quarterly, 7,* 75-93.

Bringing the DAP Message to Kindergarten and Primary Teachers

Gaye Gronlund

Gaye Gronlund, M.A., is an early child-hood education consultant in India-napolis and works with school and district agencies around the country. She is a national faculty member for the Work Sampling System developed by the Assessment Project at the University of Michigan.

M y work as an early child-hood education consult-ant gives me the oppor-tunity to interact with kinder-garten and primary teachers around the country. In those in-teractions I am often introducing NAEYC's *Developmentally Appro-priate Practice* (DAP) (Bredekamp 1987) and explaining how those practices are effective with 5-through 8-year-olds.

I have learned that teachers really appreciate pictures of practice in action, whether those pictures be video, slides, or dem-onstrations that they can ob-serve and then participate in themselves. But, along with those pictures must be some philosophical foundation, some structure that provides the rea-sons and justifications for the recommended choices to make with children. Highlighting three key elements in DAP has helped me build this foundation for kin-dergarten and primary teachers. These key elements have been the lightbulbs of understanding for many—the "Ahas" as they in-tegrate their own extensive knowledge of children's learning with the newer ideas in *Develop-mentally Appropriate Practice.*

> **Children learn by doing, through active engagement. Many adults can identify with this because they see that they also learn in this way.**

The first key element

The first key element has been the notion that *children learn by doing, through active engagement.* Many adults can identify with this element because they see that they also learn this way. I use the example of someone trying to show you how to use the copy machine. You stand off to the side and listen, but finally, in frustra-tion say, "Let *me* do it!" And, then, you exclaim, "Oh . . . now I get it!" This story is greeted with warm laughter as teachers recognize themselves in familiar situations.

When we make the connection to children and think of *all* or at least most of their learning occur-ring through active participation, folks really stop and pause. How much time in their classrooms is spent on sitting and listening or on paper-and-pencil skill and drill, as opposed to exploring and dis-covering, organizing and discuss-ing, building and creating, ques-tioning and thinking, reading and writing, measuring and comput-ing, and so on? I often introduce teachers to several classroom schedules that illustrate using blocks of time for active learning (David Birchfield's from the video by NCREL [1992], Selma Wasser-mann [1990], the Indiana Depart-ment of Education [1989]) for them to consider and compare to their own daily routines.

Engagement is also a critical part of an active learning environ-ment. Asking teachers if they know when their children are engaged brings forth interesting responses. Many describe the children's eyes—when they're engaged, their eyes "sparkle," "there's a fire for learning." When not engaged, those same eyes "glaze over" or "stare into space." Measuring again the time they estimate children are excited about learning in their classrooms often does cause folks to think seriously about the teach-ing approaches they are using.

Some "Yes . . . buts" often are raised at this point in discussions:

"But I have so much curriculum to
   cover."

"But I'm accountable to the state-
   mandated standardized tests given
   for one week in March."

"But it's not my job to entertain kids."

"Kids have to learn this is the *real*
   world where work is hard, not fun."

These are some very serious concerns on the part of teachers. As a facilitator, I have found no perfect response to any of them. However, when I see a group be-gin to ask these difficult ques-tions, I get excited. Their anxiety indicates to me that they are se-riously considering these new ideas. I see the rightness of DAP as its match to children. And, I believe that most kindergarten and primary teachers are folks who care deeply about children.

However, in my opinion, teach-ers have concluded that they are only accountable to parents, the school district administration, and the community. They receive messages constantly that reinforce that idea. But the most important people in the whole process have been left out of the accountability picture—*the children!*

When we discuss active learning and engagement, both such easily measurable and observable factors in a classroom, we bring the children back into the picture. Teachers who care deeply about young children want to do right by them as well as be accountable to the other elements of public education. My job as a consultant is to help them combine new ideas with their anxiety-provoking concerns, blending the very-real demands that are placed upon them day in and day out with the understanding of how children learn best.

I propose that kindergarten and primary teachers' vision is to help children learn, grow, and develop to their full potential. In all of the groups with whom I have worked, this vision has been agreed upon. But asking teachers to help children in active learning environments in which children are engaged in exploration and discovery is frightening.

"Where do I start?"

"What do my lesson plans look like?"

"How do I know they're learning anything?"

"Won't it be chaos?"

"What will others (colleagues, parents, administrators) think?"

These questions evidence a cry for the skills needed to set up and manage a DAP classroom.

My excitement, then, as a facilitator, when I see this anxiety, is that I have a clear directive from the group: "Give me the skills I need to use these teaching practices, so I can be accountable to the children I care about as well." I know we've got a good beginning and a clear direction from here.

The second key element

The second key element that I have found successful with kindergarten and primary teachers is introducing the idea of *play with intent and purpose*. Those of us who have been in the field of early childhood education for awhile have heard the criticisms, "Oh, all they do in *that* classroom is play; they don't learn anything" or "That's a play-based curriculum, not an academic one." We have had to become excellent communicators to explain the value of learning through play to others who did not evaluate children's active involvement with the same understandings we did. Elizabeth Jones and Gretchen Reynolds give the following explanation of the value of play:

Young children . . . play in order to find their way around in what is for them the foreign country of adults, to master its daily scripts . . . . Pretending enables children to represent problems and practice solving them, to ask questions and learn about the world in terms they can understand. Play is self-motivated practice in meaning-making; its themes are repeated over and over until the child is satisfied that she's got *this* figured out. In the process, she is acquiring learning strategies, knowledge, and skills. Issues of right and wrong arise as children negotiate with each other and as adults mediate. Shapes, colors, and numbers are embedded in the properties of dishes and blocks, puzzles and paints . . . . (1992, 10)

Teachers who are considering DAP in their classrooms are anxious about those criticisms. They say, "At least when I'm teaching the whole group from the teacher's manual, I know I've *covered* the material I'm supposed to for *all* the children" [emphasis theirs]. I often ask if I may change the emphasis on that statement and note *who* did the covering—"I know *I've* covered the material"—and also point out the meaning of *cover* as opposed to *uncover* or *discover*. The final question I pose is, "How do you know *all* of the children understand or grasp the material?"

Folks often admit they don't know for sure. Observing a group of passive learners as one gives new information does not yield total assurance that all grasped the concepts. When teachers think in these terms, the "letting go" involved in running an active learning environment does not seem quite so frightening. In ad-

© The Growth Program

dition, when children are engaged in learning by doing, they can demonstrate their new understanding in so many different ways: sorting, organizing, grouping, naming, identifying, questioning, measuring, computing, reading, recording, creating, applying, and so on.

Selma Wassermann's book *Serious Players in the Primary Classroom* has been an invaluable tool to me in moving teachers beyond the notion of DAP as "just play." She states, "It is one thing to believe in the importance of play but another to consider how play may help stimulate intellectual development in the classroom" (1990, xi). She describes play as purposeful engagement in inquiries that children have invented. The defining aspect of such play is that it's open-ended. There are many potential ways to use the materials that teacher and/or child have chosen. Wassermann

designs "Inquiry Studies" to focus children's investigative play in certain ways. But the teacher-designed focus still allows for a variety of uses of the materials, as well as conclusions. The play activity, says Wassermann, "should not set narrow parameters that

Introduce teachers to the idea of play with intent and purpose.

limit the play, nor should it lead pupils to 'correct answers'. . . . A good indicator of the effectiveness of the play activity is the extent to which it stimulates children's investigations" (1990, 100). Through careful planning and questioning techniques before, during, and after the child's involvement, she defines the intent and purpose for the child, allows him to add to that intent and purpose with his own

interests and creative ideas, and assesses the child's learning through observing his interaction with the materials and answers to debriefing questions.

A very simple example of a language arts inquiry study suggested by Wassermann (1990) contrasts beautifully with a common approach to teaching children to recognize rhyming words. Many of us, myself included, have spent hours creating "word-family wheels" with cute animals or figures as the base for the wheel ("Dog" for the "og" family; "Cat" for the "at" family, and so on). Children sit with the wheel, turning it, changing the initial consonant to form a new word in the family, and reading the words as they go.

Wassermann's Inquiry Study allows children to move to higher levels of learning. She suggests that the teacher write individual words of many rhyming families on index cards and give them to the children with the question, "How can you organize these word cards?" Children then demonstrate their understanding of a

© The Growth Program

© The Growth Program

variety of concepts. One child may group by initial consonants, another by rhyming words. Further questioning by the teacher, such as "Are there other ways?" or even directive questioning, "Can you group them by rhyming word families?" can help define the intent and purpose and assist the teacher in the assessment of children's understanding.

But the beauty of the Inquiry Study, as opposed to the rhyming-word wheels, is the active involvement of the child in setting up the actual learning for herself. The child with the wheel is playing a far more passive role

© BmPorter/Don Franklin

Figure 1. Framework-Based Problems for Nurturing and Assessing Place Value Understanding

	Pre-place value Level 1-1	Initial place value Level 1-2	Extended place value 1 Level 2-1	Extended place value 2 Level 2-2
Counting	We found 9 meatballs on the grass and 2 on the sidewalk. How many meatballs did we find?	After a big storm, meatballs were packed in bags of 10. There were 6 bags, 2 extra. How many? Add 1 more bag. How many now?	On Monday it rained 33 meatballs in Henry's yard. On Tuesday it rained 30 more. How many then?	By the end of the week we had 172 meatballs. Over the weekend we found 210 more. How many then?
Partitioning	There are 10 biscuits hidden in these 2 bags. How many could be in each bag?	You can buy loose biscuits or bags of 10. We need 68 for a party. How could they be bought?	I need 87 biscuits for a party. I have 64. How many more are needed?	The 4-H group made 134 biscuits. They need 260. How many still need to be made?
Grouping	Here are 5 brussels sprouts (cubes in the open hand). Take a handful of your own. About how many? Count them. How could you place them to make it quick and easy for me to count?	Enter the festival contest. Pick up 2 handfuls of brussels sprouts (cubes). About how many? Count them. How could you place them to make it quick and easy for me to count?	Grandma wants to buy some of the brussels sprouts that rained last night. This bag is 25¢; the bigger one is 38¢. Grandma only has 70¢. Does she have enough for both? How do you know?	The General Store of Chewandswallow has 2 baskets for brussels sprouts. One holds 175, the other 150. Henry wants to buy 330 for a party. Will the 2 baskets be enough? How do you know?
Number relationships	Spin the wheel for the number of pancakes you'll take from the roof. Tell how many more or less than 5(10) that number is.	At the pancake breakfast, Henry wrote the numbers between 60 and 69. Help him reverse the digits and tell which of the numbers becomes bigger, gets smaller.	At the Maple Syrup Festival, Grandpa picked 2 numbers from a 100s Chart and added them. Help him reverse the digits of the 2 numbers and add again. Which sum is greater?	The pancake cook posed a riddle. Write a number so that when you • reverse the digits and • add to the first number, • the sum is between 25 and 50.

Note: All problems are based on the story Cloudy with a Chance of Meatballs *(Barrett 1978), which is read prior to the problem solving.*

3. EDUCATIONAL PRACTICES

than the one involved in the Inquiry Study. Defining as many open-ended, higher-learning-level activities in a variety of curricular areas is really helpful to kindergarten and primary teachers in allaying their concerns about setting up an active learning environment and planning accordingly.

The third key element

The third key element that has really helped many teachers embrace DAP more enthusiastically has been the idea of *moving from the simple to the complex* in planning for learning in active and engaging ways. The idea of play with intent and purpose instead of "just play" leads itself to the idea that children's learning through play will move along a continuum from simpler understanding to ever-increasing complexity. Therefore, teachers must plan activities that will help children move along this continuum, realizing that each child will do so at his own pace. In *Dimensions of Teaching–Learning Environments*, Jones and Prescott define different ways of complicating learning through the environment and teacher behaviors: "A simple environment contributes to children's focus on completion of closed tasks . . . . A complex environment contributes to innovation and the development of imagination" (1984, 33). Wassermann says the same thing in a different way: "The richer the play, the more potential it has for concept development, creative and investigative opportunities, and the examination of issues of substance" (1990, 27).

Instead of textbook writers and publishers determining scope and sequence, developmentally appropriate kindergarten and primary teachers do so themselves to truly meet the individual as well as the age-appropriate needs of the children from year to year. Jones and Pres-

cott's continuum idea helps folks see that within a classroom one can plan for children's learning to occur at different points on a continuum from simple to complex. A teacher must constantly think of varying learning behaviors that build toward understanding a concept. He must find ways to develop behaviors that demonstrate understanding and ways a child can apply that knowledge with ever-increasing complexity and sophistication.

An example of this movement from simple to complex in planning for primary students can be found in the teaching of place value in first, second, and third grades. Constance Kamii (1985) and others have cited numerous research studies that indicate that primary children are *not* grasping the concept of place value; only 42% of third graders studied demonstrated understanding of numeral placement (Jones & Thornton 1993). Kamii advocates not teaching place value at all but posing situations in which children will discover it for themselves. She emphasizes the simpler concept of number sense as being essential before moving on to understanding place value. Jones and Thornton (1993) even break down the development of number sense into

four levels that build toward understanding of place value (Figure 1). Both Kamii and Jones and Thornton suggest active learning opportunities, such as games with playing cards and manipulatives and integrated units related to children's literature and classroom problem solving (e.g., planning for a party).

One second-grade teacher told me that she realized she had been moving much too fast on place value in her class. She had been concentrating her efforts on numerical representation of addition and subtraction problems that required trading to and

Figure 2. Managing Complex Change

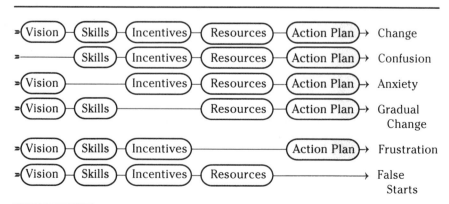

Reprinted with permission of the Houston-based American Productivity & Quality Center Consulting Group.

from the 10s column. She reported that many children were confused by the concepts involved and did not seem to understand place value at this abstract, complex level. After learning a variety of simple to increasingly complex games and activities, she decided to offer several of these activities in her classroom to meet the needs of all of the children at all levels in her class. She included grouping actual objects (buttons, paper clips) by 4s, 5s, and 6s (for those who were not ready to group by 10s), as well as grouping objects by 10s. She added games with place-value mats and cups for placing groups of 10 objects, addition and subtraction with real objects, followed by numerical recording. In this case, the continuum from simple to complex moved from manipulating real objects to manipulating abstract numerals. This teacher wisely identified her children's needs and backed up on that continuum to offer more hands-on activities to build the number sense needed to grasp place value at more abstract levels.

All curricular areas can be viewed on this simple to complex continuum. Textbook scope-and-sequence charts can be used as resources, as well as child development information (see *The Primary Program: Growing and Learning in the Heartland* [Nebraska Department of Education et al. 1993] for the Appendix "Widely Held Expectations, Ages Birth through 13"), and other information about each specific group of children. These resources can assist teachers in planning the following:

1. Activities that build skills and understandings necessary to grasp concepts.
2. Ways to practice those new understandings.
3. Ways to challenge the children to apply their new knowledge in

similar and different situations.

Kindergarten and primary teachers have a professional responsibility to look at their particular group of children and determine the range of activities that will best meet their needs. But, also, they have a responsibilty to be always complicating the learning, moving the children along in their development toward competency in a variety of areas.

This idea of challenging children has been a surprise to many of the teachers with whom I work. When they first consider play and exploration in active learning environments, they assume these approaches are the opposite of traditional academic teaching methods. With the ideas of play with intent and purpose that continually move toward the complex and challenging, teachers see the academic side of DAP. Content of the curriculum is not necessarily changed by changing teaching approaches nor are expectations for children's learn-

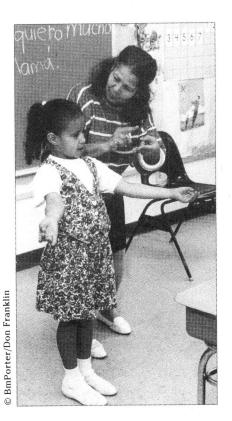

© BmPorter/Don Franklin

ing and performance. Instead, the environment, daily schedules, use of materials, teacher planning, and children's and teachers' behaviors in classrooms are changed. For many folks, this realization has been a major piece of the puzzle for them to fit into their notion of developmentally appropriate practice, and it is not a comfortable piece. When people are asked to change themselves, disequilibrium, if not total rejection, occurs. But identifying the three key elements cited above provides a beginning for teachers to consider for themselves.

The change process

A model for managing complex change in organizations from the American Productivity and Quality Center is very helpful (see Figure 2). In this model, effective change will occur when each piece of the process is in place. The necessary pieces for change are the following: Vision, Skills, Incentives, Resources, and Action Plan. When a piece is missing, other problems will arise and effective change will not result. The problems include these: Confusion, Anxiety, Gradual Change, Frustration, and False Starts. According to this model, when anxiety appears, people are evidencing the need for skills. Their vision or goals are intact, but the second piece of the change process is missing. If confusion arises, the vision is not clear. If there is only gradual change, perhaps incentives are not great enough. If there is frustration, the problem lies with resources being available. And finally, if there are false starts, a clear action plan is needed.

I have used this model in analyzing teacher reactions to the message I have been bringing about developmentally appropriate practices. The most common reaction from teachers is anxiety, so I conclude that I need to focus on the development of skills. Thus, some of my inservice workshops now focus on very specific topics, such as "Managing an Active Learning K–3 Classroom by Giving Children Choices," with all sorts of real teacher stories to document ways of sharing power with children, paying attention to individual learning styles, and not having total chaos in a classroom. In this way I can answer teachers' cries for help by focusing on their growing classroom management skills. I have also found this model very useful in analyzing the change process with administrators. Perhaps there has not been a clear statement of vision on the part of a district or program, and therefore people are confused. Or perhaps incentives have not been high enough, and the pace of change is very slow. Principals and curriculum directors have responded very favorably to this way of analyzing their situations and helping the change process along.

Time is an imperative part of the process of change so that new ideas can be incorporated with teachers' extensive experience base with children, and new approaches can be tried out in ways that are not confusing or anxiety provoking. Just as children learn by doing, so do adults. Giving teachers opportunities to explore and play with DAP in their own classrooms is essential to building the skills they need to use these approaches successfully.

I have been fortunate to work with school districts that have been committed to supporting teachers in their change efforts *over time*. As teachers are introduced to these new ideas, they are given time to experiment in their own classrooms, whether that experimentation involves just thinking about changes as they become more aware of their own practices or involves moving toward more active learning through play and exploration, inquiry studies, and so on. Teachers, then, return for further inservice and discussion, comparing notes on their new thoughts and practices, sharing frustrations and solutions. In this way each person can grow individually with her own unique style of DAP for her particular group of children.

One group of teachers reached some interesting conclusions after considering these approaches over a semester. I asked them to list what they saw as the advantages and disadvantages of DAP (Figure 3). I served as scribe for their ideas. When they finished giving their suggestions, I stepped back and asked them to look for any commonalities or themes in their ideas. All of us were amazed at how the list of advantages showed the overwhelming benefits *for children* and the list of disadvantages focused on problems *for the adults involved*. This group of teachers found this list humorous and profound. They believed deeply that the focus of their work was the children. To see that their list of disadvantages did not include a single one that primarily affected children but, rather, included items that mainly affected teachers really seemed a powerful conclusion to all of their learning about developmentally appropriate practice. One teacher said it for us all, "I think we should call it Developmentally Cool!"

Many teachers struggle with these ideas, however. Change is a difficult process for human beings and often takes place slowly. Teachers who have embraced DAP at the kindergarten and primary levels have reported that their adaptation of their own teaching approaches has taken two to three years, and their development of a comfort level with DAP has taken five years. Empathizing with folks as they consider

---

Figure 3. Developmentally Appropriate Practice

What are the advantages?
• children learning to manage themselves
• children taking risks, feeling more competent
• children gaining self-confidence, self-esteem going up.
• children happier, feeling more valued and in control
• no failure resulting
• being individualized

What are the disadvantages?
• evaluating
• managing behavior
• dealing with change
• needing extra time for planning and making materials

---

educating children in active, playful, and challenging ways and assuring them that time is a necessary part of their own growth and development can be helpful.

Encouraging teachers to take small steps rather than to change dramatically has been successful. One third-grade teacher announced that he would try to offer choices to the children in his classroom for one hour a

---

Instead of textbook writers and publishers determining scope and sequence, developmentally appropriate kindergarten and primary teachers do so themselves to truly meet the individual as well as the age-appropriate needs of the children from year to year.

week. A kindergarten teacher started a Journal Writing Time for one-half hour a day. Children could choose their own topics and explore writing through inventive spelling, scribble writing, and pictorial representation. In a second-grade classroom, children chose a variety of thematically related learning centers for one or two weeks each month. The other two weeks, the teacher used more whole-group, skill-based instruction. For some teachers, moving desks together to form learning groups might be a major step. Placing materials on shelves and allowing children to get what they need can be the first move in the process of "letting go" and employing developmentally appropriate practices.

In *The Primary Program* (Nebraska Department of Education et al. 1993), the authors have developed a "Continuum of Change" (Figure 4). I have used this continuum to help people see how the change process occurs and identify the many steps involved. Some teachers react negatively to the idea of "appropriate practices" versus "inappropriate practices." They see themselves using many teaching strategies that are labeled "inappropriate," and they reject the

© The Growth Program

whole idea of DAP out of self-defense. As an alternative approach, I have asked teachers to identify their thinking on the

---

Figure 4. A Continuum of Change for Kindergarten and Primary Classrooms

From less-appropriate practices:	To more-appropriate practices:
Child adapts	Schools adapt
Child as passive and dependent	Child as active partner in learning
Whole-group instruction	Whole-group, small-group, and individual instruction
Individual tasks	Balanced small groups, cooperative and individual tasks
Preset material covered	Children's capacity to learn extended
3Rs instructional focus	Focus on concepts, skills, processes, and attitudes
Separate subjects	Integrated subjects
Workbooks	Concrete materials, quality literature, and a variety of resource materials
Verbal information emphasis	Constructivist, problem-solving, thinking emphasis
Single correct answers	Alternative solutions generated
Work and play divided	Play as one condition of learning
Holiday rituals marked	Multicultural content based on the study of social experience
Teacher as the sole arbitrator of what is correct	Children as theory builders and negotiators
Grouping by ability or age	Group developed by interest, motivation, and learning needs
Assessment of what a child already knows	Assessment focusing on how a child learns and what a child "can do"
Assessment for classification and reporting	Assessment ongoing for purposes of instructional decisionmaking
Child as the recipient of the teacher's teaching	Child as collaborator in own learning
Answers valued	Questions valued
Paper-and-pencil representations	Multiple ways of representing knowledge

Adapted by permission of the Nebraska Department of Education from *The Primary Program: Growing and Learning in the Heartland.* First published in D.P. Fromberg, "Kindergarten: Current Circumstances Affecting Curriculum," *Teachers College Record* 90 (1989): 392–403.

"Continuum of Change" chart by marking where they see themselves in the shift from left side to the right (from inappropriate to more developmentally appropriate teaching practices). They analyze each left-to-right item as having a range of possibilities for its particular aspect of DAP, and they rank themselves by making a mark on the dotted line to represent where they see their own practice. For example, one group of kindergarten teachers saw children as active partners in learning; therefore, they marked themselves far to the right on the dotted line. However, they still saw work and play as divided, and they grouped children by ability. On these two items, they marked themselves to the far left. This exercise gave them the option to say, "Well, I haven't changed very much on this item. However, I am moving toward this one. Oh, and I am way over here on this one! I guess I am in the process of change." Not feeling quite so defensive then about their present approaches, teachers are more open to consider new ideas.

But, most importantly, reminding them of the vision or purpose of their work can provide a strong foundation upon which they can stand. Referring back to our model for Managing Complex Change (Figure 2), without vision people become confused. In my work I am continually impressed with the clarity of purpose and dedication demonstrated by kindergarten and primary teachers. They care deeply about reaching children and helping them reach their potential as learners. With such a strong foundation, developmentally appropriate practice is recognized as a tool to help make that vision a reality.

Finding the commonality of purpose, providing pictures of practice in action to help teachers see DAP more clearly, giving them key philosophical elements to guide the choices they make with and for children, and building skills for them to implement these practices in their own classrooms over time can be helpful strategies in reaching out to teachers who have not heard the DAP message before.

Learning is finding out what you already know.

Doing is demonstrating that you know it.

Teaching is reminding others that they know just as well as you.

You are all learners, doers, teachers. (Bach 1977)

References

Bach, R. 1977. *Illusions.* New York.

Barrett, J. 1978. *Cloudy with a chance of meatballs.* New York: Macmillan Children's Group.

Bredekamp, S., ed. 1987. *Developmentally appropriate practice in early childhood programs serving children from birth through age 8.* Exp. ed. Washington, DC: NAEYC.

Indiana Department of Education. 1989. *Kindergarten guide.* Indianapolis: Center for School Improvement & Performance, PRIME TIME Unit.

Jones, E., & E. Prescott. 1984. *Dimensions of teaching–learning environments: A handbook for teachers in elementary schools and day care centers.* Pasadena, CA: Pacific Oaks College.

Jones, E., & G. Reynolds. 1992. *The play's the thing: Teachers' roles in children's play.* New York: Teachers College Press.

Jones, G.A., & C.A. Thornton. 1993. Research in review. Children's understanding of place value: A framework for curriculum development and assessment. *Young Children* 48 (5): 12–18.

Kamii, C. 1985. *Young children re-invent arithmetic: Implications of Piaget's theory.* New York: Teachers College Press.

Nebraska Department of Education, Iowa Department of Education, Iowa Area Education Agencies, & Head Start–State Collaboration Project. 1993. *The primary program: Growing and learning in the heartland.* Lincoln: Nebraska Department of Education.

NCREL (North Central Regional Educational Laboratory). 1992. *Meeting children's needs: Conference # 5.* Video. Chicago: Author.

Wassermann, S. 1990. *Serious players in the primary classroom: Empowering children through active learning experiences.* New York: Teachers College Press.

For further reading

Bredekamp, S., & T. Rosegrant, eds. 1992. *Reaching potentials: Appropriate curriculum for assessment for young children.* Vol. 1. Washington, DC: NAEYC.

Fourth-Grade Slump: The Cause and Cure

A new study reveals the impact of children's early childhood experience on their later achievement.

REBECCA A. MARCON

Rebecca A. Marcon is a developmental psychologist and associate professor of psychology at the University of North Florida in Jacksonville.

Parents, teachers, and administrators are often perplexed by what is often referred to as "fourth-grade slump." Why do so many bright, achieving children in the primary grades have difficulty making the transition to the upper elementary grades?

Although a number of ideas have been put forward, recent research suggests that the root of the difficulty lies in children's early childhood experiences, which influence how young children approach learning tasks. The impact is especially noticeable during the transition to fourth grade, which for many children is cognitively difficult because of increased expectations for independent thought, applications of previously learned concepts to new problems, and mastery of more complex skills and ideas. The transition can also be socially difficult because of increased expectations of maturity.

The latest results of an ongoing study in the District of Columbia Public Schools address this crucial transition period by comparing the outcomes of different models of early childhood education.

In the initial study, prompted by an unacceptably high first-grade retention rate, we set out in 1986–87 to examine the impact of different preschool models on the school success of inner-city, public school children. We studied the progress of four-year-olds enrolled in the District's prekindergarten or Head Start programs. The children were predominantly minority students (97 percent African American) and poor (76 percent qualified for subsidized lunch). More than two-thirds lived in single-parent families.

Three Early Childhood Models

A preliminary survey, based on classroom observations and teacher responses, identified three different preschool models operating in the D.C. school system:

- The *child-initiated* classrooms, called Model CI, had child-development-oriented teachers who allowed children to select the focus of their learning.
- The *academically directed* classrooms, or Model AD, had academically oriented teachers who preferred more teacher-directed instruction.
- The *middle-of-the-road* classrooms, called Model M, represented teaching beliefs and practices which fell between.

> "Pushing children too soon into 'formalized academics' can actually backfire when children move into the later childhood grades where they are required to think more independently."

Our initial findings showed that children enrolled in the more child-development-oriented Model CI actually mastered more basic skills than those in Model AD or Model M classrooms. Furthermore, the Model M compromise approach did not work for any of the four-year-olds. By the end of the preschool year, Model M children were significantly behind the others in language, social, and motor development, as well as overall adaptive functioning and mastery of basic skills.

In the second and third years of the study, Model M children remained behind their peers as they moved into kindergarten and first grade, where Model CI children continued to excel while Model AD children's social development declined, along with their mastery of first-grade reading and math objectives.

As a result of the initial three-year study, we now knew that previous, inappropriate early learning experiences in many of the District's early childhood programs clearly hindered children's progress in the preprimary and pri-

From *Principal*, May 1995, pp. 17, 19-20. © 1995 by the National Association of Elementary School Principals. All rights reserved. Reprinted by permission.

mary years, and we had a clearer notion of the type of early childhood program that was needed.

Examining Fourth-Grade Transition

We continued to study the impact of early childhood experiences even as the District of Columbia system responded to the initial findings by instituting reforms in its early childhood programs. Having discovered ways to increase children's chances of making a successful transition from preschool to first grade, we now focused on the progress of the original study groups as they advanced through the primary grades.

The negative impact of overly academic early childhood programs on achievement and social development was clearly apparent by the fourth grade. Children who had attended Model AD prekindergarten programs were scoring noticeably lower in the fourth grade despite their adequate performance on third-grade standardized achievement tests. The Model AD children were also developmentally behind their peers and displayed notably higher levels of maladaptive behavior (*i.e.*, defiant behavior, anxiety, and distractibility).

As shown in *Figure 1*, children whose preschool experience was academically focused showed the greatest decline in school grades between third and fourth grades. At the same time, the long-term positive effects of a more active, child-initiated preschool experience showed up most clearly during this transition. Patterns of developmental change were more difficult to identify, although children with overly academic preschool experiences had not advanced as rapidly in social development by the fourth grade.

In comparing children's academic progress since first grade, the study found that while all children's grades were typically lower by fourth grade, the three-year drop in performance was especially disconcerting for Model AD children. Their overall grade-point average dropped 22 percent from first to fourth grades, compared to only 5 and 6 percent for Model C and M children. More specifically, Model AD grades decreased by 36 percent in math, 32 percent in reading and language, 30 percent in spelling and social studies, 23 percent in science, and 16 percent in health and physical education.

Ending Fourth-Grade Slump

Our findings show that fourth-grade slump can be traced back to inappropriate early childhood learning experiences for many children. The findings indicate that preschool programs are most successful when they correspond to children's level of development and natural approach to learning, and that children's academic and developmental progress through the elementary grades is enhanced by active, child-initiated early learning experiences.

The study also shows that later progress is slowed for most children when formal learning experiences are introduced too early. Pushing children too soon into "formalized academics" can actually backfire when children move into the later childhood grades where they are required to think more independently. This is because teacher-directed early childhood approaches that tell young children what to do, when to do it, and how to do it curtail development of autonomy.

According to developmental authority Constance Kamii, such teacher-directed approaches produce passive students who wait to be told what to think and do next. Therefore, it is not surprising that children who lack the early foundations of autonomy—the root of critical thinking and effective choice making—find the transition to fourth grade difficult.

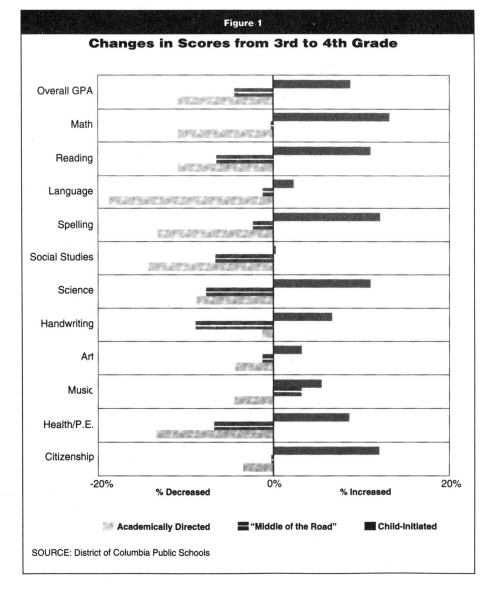

Figure 1

Changes in Scores from 3rd to 4th Grade

SOURCE: District of Columbia Public Schools

While the benefits of developmentally appropriate early childhood experiences may take a while to unfold, they become especially prominent by fourth grade, if not sooner. As we work to assure that all our children start school *ready to learn* by 2000, it is equally important that our schools be *ready to receive* these eager young learners. If we wish children to be independent and self-reliant, to choose wisely between options, and to think critically, our teaching styles and curricular focus must better reflect those desired outcomes. The early childhood years can either foster children's sense of autonomy or curtail it. As educators, the choice is ours.

REFERENCES

Elkind, D. "In Defense of Early Childhood Education." *Principal* 65:5 (May 1986): 6–9.

Kamii, C. "One Intelligence Indivisible." *Phi Delta Kappan* 65 (January 1984): 410–415.

Marcon, R. "Differential Effects of Three Preschool Models on Inner-city 4-year-olds." *Early Childhood Research Quarterly* 7:4 (1992): 517–530.

Marcon, R. "Socio-emotional Versus Academic Emphasis: Impact on Kindergartners' Development and Achievement." *Early Child Development and Care* 96 (December 1993): 81–91.

Marcon, R. "Doing the Right Thing for Children: Linking Research and Policy Reform in the District of Columbia Public Schools." *Young Children* 50:1 (November 1994): 8–20.

Schweinhart, L. J.; Barnes, H. V.; Weikart, D. P. *Significant Benefits: The High/Scope Perry Preschool Study through Age 27.* Ypsilanti, Mich.: High/Scope Educational Research Foundation, 1993.

Schweinhart, L. J.; Weikart, D. P.; Larner, M. B. "Consequences of Three Preschool Curriculum Models through Age 15." *Early Childhood Research Quarterly* 1:1 (1986): 15–45.

Sykes, M. R. "Creating a Climate for Change in a Major Urban School System." *Young Children* 50:1 (November 1994): 4–7.

Woods, C. "Responsive Teaching: Creating Partnerships for Systemic Change." *Young Children* 50:1 (November 1994): 21–28.

Zigler, E. "Should Four-year-olds Be in School?" *Principal* 65:5 (May 1986): 10–14.

A Blueprint for Change

During the school year 1986–87, the District of Columbia Public Schools responded to a high first-grade retention rate by initiating a three-year study to evaluate and determine the impact of early learning programs on children's long-term school success. The resulting 1990 report concluded that children enrolled in child-centered classrooms, where developmentally appropriate practices were implemented, had a higher passing rate in first grade than their peers in academically-oriented programs.

The district also authorized a three-year follow-up study that compared the previously studied children as they progressed from the primary to the upper elementary grades. This study indicated that by the age of 9 students from academically-oriented programs were clearly behind.

Because the evidence showed that child-initiated early childhood programs were effective, our next step was to develop a pilot project based on continuous progress and performance assessment. We began by allowing seven schools to replace skill-oriented academic programs with child-initiated, integrated, thematic learning programs from prekindergarten to third grade. The program has been expanded to include about half of our elementary schools and will eventually include all pre-K through third grades.

The program is success-oriented, capitalizing on the interests and capabilities of students while considering individual learning rates and styles. Our decision to emphasize social, emotional, and cognitive development in the early learning years is based on a growing body of evidence supporting such practices for young children, as well as increasing awareness that early retention is detrimental to a child's academic success.

Early on, we realized the need for authentic assessment instruments that would accurately reflect actual learning experiences while providing information about a child's overall development—social, emotional, physical, aesthetic, and cognitive. Research led us to the Work Sampling System developed by Samuel Meisels and others at the University of Michigan. The system's three-pronged performance assessment approach, which we've adapted, uses developmental checklists, portfolios, and summary reports. Because it provides a comprehensive overview of children's developmental progress, the system is not only highly effective, but popular with many teachers, students, and parents.

Overall, we have been pleased with our new approach to early childhood education. Based on the findings of our studies, we feel our youngest students will now be better prepared for the academic challenges ahead.

Franklin L. Smith
Superintendent
District of Columbia Public Schools

FOR FURTHER INFORMATION

The full report on which this article is based, *Early Learning and Early Identification Follow-Up Study: Transition from the Early to the Later Childhood Grades 1990-93*, by Rebecca A. Marcon, is available for $14 from the District of Columbia Public Schools, Center for Systemic Educational Change, 415 12th Street, N.W., Washington, D.C. 20004; (202) 724-4099.

Strategies for Teaching Children in Multiage Classrooms

Sandra J. Stone

Sandra J. Stone is Assistant Professor, Early Childhood/Literacy Education, Center for Excellence in Education, Northern Arizona University, Flagstaff.

The multiage classroom is becoming an increasingly popular way to restructure schools. Kentucky, for example, has mandated multiage classrooms in all primary grades (K-3). Mississippi and Oregon have similar mandates. Alaska, California, Florida, Georgia, New York, Pennsylvania, Tennessee and Texas are also considering implementation of multiage classrooms (Gaustad, 1992; Kentucky Department of Education, 1992; Lodish, 1992).

In a multiage classroom a group of mixed-age children stay with the same teacher for several years. Typical primary grade age groups are 5-6-7, 6-7-8 or 7-8-9. The children spend three years with the same teacher (Connell, 1987). While the current multiage movement generally focuses on the primary years, multiage classrooms are also being implemented in upper elementary classes with age groups of 8-9-10 and 9-10-11.

Multiage teachers are frequently asked, "How does one teach students with such a wide range of abilities?" The question implies that teaching several grades of children is impractical and too difficult. On the surface, teaching mixed ages does appear to be overwhelming.

Successful multiage classrooms require teachers to shift attention from teaching *curriculum* to teaching *children*. A multiage class requires teachers to consider children as individuals, each with his or her own continuum of learning. Teachers who try to teach grade-specific curriculum to multiple-grade classrooms may become frustrated and often return to same-age classrooms. Teachers who have instituted appropriate instructional strategies, however, find multiage classes to be exhilarating and professionally rewarding. What are some teaching strategies that will help make multiage classroom teaching successful?

Process Approach to Learning

A key factor in multiage classrooms' success is the use of a process approach to education. This approach emphasizes teaching children, rather than curriculum. Each child is treated as a whole person with a distinct continuum of learning and developmental rate and style. The teacher focuses on developing children's social skills and on teaching broad academic subjects such as reading, writing and problem-solving. Each goal reflects a developmental process, not the learning of discrete skills in a prescribed curriculum.

To facilitate the writing process, for example, the teacher provides daily opportunities to write. First, she models writing and includes broad-based writing conventions. The children's writing is based on their individual developmental continuum. The younger child may write one sentence, using only beginning sounds, while the older child may write paragraphs.

Rather than acting simply as the "giver of knowledge," she must facilitate each child's growth . . .

The teacher also provides daily opportunities for children to read. Children read independently and in large and small groups. In large groups, the teacher presents a shared reading experience and focuses on broad-based skills, such as recognizing initial consonants, predicting outcomes and finding compound words. In small groups, the teacher chooses teaching points to fit the children's individual needs, nurturing effective reading strategies and increased comprehension.

Opportunities for children to use math are also available. Children studying dinosaurs, for example, may choose to set up a dinosaur store. Younger children learn to distinguish between nickels and dimes or to compute how many dimes are needed to buy a 30-cent dinosaur. Older children may try more complex calculations, such as adding a series of numbers.

A teacher using the process approach provides opportunities, open-ended activities, experiences or projects in which all the children can participate on their own devel-

From *Childhood Education*, Winter 1994/95, pp. 102-105. © 1994 by the Association for Childhood Education International, 11501 Georgia Avenue, Suite 315, Wheaton, MD. Reprinted by permission.

opmental levels. The strategy is to provide the context where the learning process occurs. Children learn to read by reading, and to write by writing, in meaningful and relevant contexts. The process approach helps children to see themselves as progressive, successful learners.

Facilitator of Learning

The teacher must become a facilitator of learning in order to successfully implement a multiage classroom. A teacher must guide, nurture and support the learning process. Rather than acting simply as the "giver of knowledge," she must facilitate each child's growth in all areas according to individual developmental needs and interests. Therefore, teachers must *know the children*. A teacher can guide a younger child to use beginning sounds in writing only if she *knows* where the child is in the writing process. By facilitating learning, the teacher focuses on teaching children, not curriculum.

An Integrated Curriculum

Teachers choose an integrated curriculum in multiage classrooms that not only applies a holistic approach to learning, but also provides an excellent context for the process of learning. Teachers and/or children select a yearly, quarterly, monthly or even weekly theme. Children's reading, writing, problem-solving, graphing, measuring, painting and playing are based upon that thematic choice. As Connell (1987) notes, "integrating a curriculum around a theme allows children of different ages and stages to work together in a group as well as to practice skills at different levels" (p. 24).

Appropriate Learning Environment

The learning environment should permit all children to engage in the processes of learning. Such an environment includes active, hands-on learning experiences that are based on children's interests and choices. The center and/or the project approach is very effective in multiage

classrooms. Centers may include library, writing, listening, art, play, science, social science, social studies, math, drama and computers.

Using bears as a theme, children at the writing center might create stories based on a group reading of "Goldilocks and the Three Bears." At the listening center, children may choose from a selection of fictional and nonfictional stories about bears or related themes. Younger children at the science center could clas-

*T*he center and/or project approach allows children to be involved in active, hands-on learning within the social context of mixed ages.

sify bears by type, while older children write descriptive paragraphs for each bear. At the play center, children of mixed ages can dramatize "Goldilocks and the Three Bears." Mixed-age groups could also design and build bear habitats or create a poster campaign to inform the public about endangered bear species.

Children choose their own open-ended activities and monitor their own time. The teacher is free to work with the children in small groups or individually as they become autonomous learners in charge of their own learning. The center and/or project approach allows children to be involved in active, hands-on learning within the social context of mixed ages.

Cross-age Learning

An effective multiage classroom encourages opportunities for cross-age learning. Social interaction in mixed-age groupings positively affects all areas of a child's development. Vygotsky (1978) suggests that children's learning can be enhanced by adults or more capable peers. In a multiage classroom where cooperation replaces competition, older

children become mentors to younger children. A multiage classroom is not effective if the children are predominantly isolated in same-age groups or even same-ability groups. Cooperative learning groups and peer tutoring are effective strategies. Collaboration through social interaction positively affects the children's learning.

Flexible Groupings

The predominant instructional strategy in multiage classrooms relies on small, flexible groupings. Children spend most of their class time in small groups, pairs or on their own.

While children participate in independent, cooperative groupings at centers or projects, the teacher works with small groups characterized by student needs or interests. For example, a teacher may conduct a literature study with a mixed-ability grouping, gather beginning readers together for support on using reading strategies and engage another group that showed interest in solving a particular problem. She may work individually with a child needing help in letter recognition. The breakdown of small groupings and independent study is not based on a predetermined, prescribed curriculum, but rather on the needs and interests of the children.

There is very little large-group instruction in the multiage classroom. Large group instruction times do provide a forum for broad-based skills. These instructional times allow for a wider curriculum presentation. Multiage teachers are amazed at how opening up the curriculum engages children to whom they ordinarily would not have presented certain concepts or skills.

Portfolio Assessment

Because the multiage classroom approach frees teachers to see children as individuals and relies on process learning, a new type of assessment is necessary. Portfolio assessment is an ideal strategy for documenting the progress of each child. Children are assessed according to their own achievement and potential and not in comparison with other children (Goodlad & Anderson, 1987). The teacher holds different expectations for different children, does not grade portfolios and relies on using report cards that are narrative, rather than traditional.

Portfolios also help the teacher support and guide instruction. The authentic assessments in the portfolio enable teachers to know their students' strengths as well as areas that need further development. Portfolio assessment is an excellent tool for communicating with children and parents. It allows children to see themselves as successful learners and parents to better understand the learning process.

Conclusion

Strategies such as the process approach to learning, teacher as facilitator, appropriate learning environments, cross-age learning, flexible groupings and portfolio assessment all help teachers focus on teaching *children*. These strategies support the implementation of a successful and effective multiage program.

References and Other Resources

American Association of School Administrators. (1992). *The nongraded primary: Making schools fit children.* Arlington, VA: Author.

Anderson, R. H., & Pavan, B. N. (1993). *Nongradedness: Helping it to happen.* Lancaster, PA: Technomic Press.

Barbour, N. H., & Seefeldt, C. (1993). *Developmental continuity across preschool and primary grades: Implications for teachers.* Wheaton, MD: Association for Childhood Education International.

Bredecamp, S. (Ed.). (1987). *Developmentally appropriate practice in early childhood programs serving children from birth through age 8* (expanded edition). Washington, DC: National Association for the Education of Young Children.

Connell, D. R. (1987). The first 30 years were the fairest: Notes from the kindergarten and ungraded primary (K-1-2). *Young Children, 42*(5), 30–39.

Cushman, K. (1990). The whys and hows of the multi-age classroom. *American Educator, 14,* 28–32, 39.

Elkind, D. (1989). Developmentally appropriate practice: Philosophical and practical implications. *Phi Delta Kappan, 17*(2), 113–117.

Gaustad, J. (1992). Nongraded primary education: Mixed-age, integrated and developmentally appropriate education for primary children. *Oregon School Study Council Bulletin, 35*(7).

Goodlad, J. I., & Anderson, R. H. (1987). *The non-graded elementary school* (rev. ed.). New York: Teachers College Press.

Kasten, W. C., & Clarke, B. K. (1993). *The multiage classroom.* Katonah, NY: Richard C. Owen.

Katz, L. G., & Chard, S. C. (1989). *Engaging children's minds: The project approach.* Norwood, NJ: Ablex.

Katz, L. G., Evangelou, D., & Hartman, J. A. (1990). *The case for mixed-age grouping in early education.* Washington, DC: National Association for the Education of Young Children.

Kentucky Department of Education. (1992). *Kentucky's primary school: The wonder years.* Frankfort, KY: Author.

Lodish, R. (1992). The pros and cons of mixed-age grouping. *Principal, 71*(6), 20–22.

Oberlander, T. M. (1989). A nongraded, multiage program that works. *Principal, 68*(5), 29–30.

Vygotsky, L. S. (1978). *Mind in society: The development of psychological processes.* Cambridge, MA: Harvard University Press.

Preschool Integration
Strategies for Teachers

Sarah H. Stafford and
Virginia P. Green

Sarah H. Stafford is a Prekindergarten Teacher, Caroline Brevard Elementary School, Tallahassee, Florida. Virginia P. Green is Professor, Early Childhood Education, Florida State University, Tallahassee.

Two small boys

on the stage that night

Each child aware

of the eyes and lights

The program begins

the story is told

Children burst forth

as their song unfolds

One small boy

stands as if beguiled

Another tiny hand

joins with this child

To bring comfort

through a shared rapport

A friendship dawns

with care and support.

◆

This scenario, captured in verse, makes apparent the benefits of integration in Early Childhood Education (ECE) and Early Childhood Special Education (ECSE) programs. At a prekindergarten program for parents, two small boys who might never have met shared the spotlight and companionship. Because two teachers saw the inherent possibilities of an integrated program, one "regular ed" child and one "special ed" child had the opportunity to become partners in a school setting.

ECE and ECSE educators have long recognized the importance of early intervention with developmentally delayed children. The long-term benefits associated with early quality preschool programs include: 1) increased IQ scores, 2) decreased time spent in special education classes, 3) reduced education costs, 4) reduced crime and delinquency, 5) fewer teen pregnancies and 6) improved socialization (Schweinhart, Berrueta-Clement, Barnett, Epstein & Weikart, 1985). Research indicates that preschool integration positively influences children with disabilities as well as children with regular needs, helping both groups develop positive attitudes and social interaction, and increase their language and skill acquisition (Hanline & Murray, 1984).

When the Head Start Program received funding in 1964, the importance of early schooling began receiving national recognition. Educators envisioned early programs as powerful tools against poverty and illiteracy. Early intervention for developmentally delayed young children became a feature of Public Law 99-457, The Education of the Handicapped Act Amendments of 1986 (Cook, Tessier & Klein, 1992). Further federal legislation helped serve a greater diversity of children, including those designated as at-risk for developmental delays or disabilities (P.L. 100-297, P.L. 101-476 and P.L. 102-119). When the National Education Goals Panel set guidelines in 1989, it stated, as its first goal, that "all children will start school ready to learn" by the year 2000. Terms such as "least restrictive environment" (LRE) and "Individualized Family Service Plans" (IFSPs) are now commonly used.

While teachers and administrators clearly would like to integrate prekindergarten programs, strategies for doing so are only fledgling. Part of the problem is the lack of pertinent information for implementing integrated programs on a specific day-to-day basis.

From *Childhood Education*, Summer 1996, pp. 214-218. © 1996 by the Association for Childhood Education International, 11501 Georgia Avenue, Suite 315, Wheaton, MD. Reprinted by permission.

Successful programs should "adapt curricula to meet the needs of children with a wide range of differences in skills, learning styles, background and potential" (Cook, Tessier & Klein, 1992, p. 34). Planning and implementation of such programs will require a deliberate integration process coordinated by early childhood education teachers, special education teachers, school administrators and parents. A number of professional organizations, including the Association for Childhood Education International, have published position papers in support of the rights of children and their families to receive educational services (Association for Childhood Education International/Sexton, Snyder, Sharpton & Stricklin, 1993).

What Does Integration/Inclusion/ Mainstreaming/LRE Mean?

One widely accepted definition of "integration" specifies primary placement in a self-contained special education classroom during at least one half of the school day, with opportunities for interactions with nondisabled peers. Such an approach is frequently referred to as a least restrictive environment (LRE). "Inclusion" refers "to the education of all students in neighborhood classrooms and schools" (Stainback & Stainback, 1992). "Mainstreaming" is "the temporal, instructional and social integration of eligible exceptional children with normal peers . . . " (Kaufman, Gottlieb, Agard & Kukic, 1975). Mainstreaming requires placing an individual child in a regular classroom, with more than 50 percent of the child's school day spent in that classroom.

Effective Strategies for Integration

Two teachers, one in a Chapter 1 ECE program and the other in an ECSE program, collaborated on developing strategies for classroom integration. The Chapter 1 ECE class (with one teacher and two instructional aides) consisted of 19 children who scored below average on the DIAL-R Preschool Screening Instrument and/or lived in a low socioeconomic neighborhood. The ECSE class (with one teacher, a behavioral specialist and one aide) contained nine children identified as extremely language delayed or exhibiting challenging behaviors. These teachers found the following ten strategies to be beneficial in implementing a successful integration effort.

1. Instructional methods. Integrated classrooms should have instructional methods based on combining the developmental approach of ECE and the more structured approach of ECSE. Teachers who work together in joint programs incorporate developmental activities and structured, direct instruction into a complementary learning network for students with

and without disabilities (Kugelmass, 1989; Poresky & Hooper, 1984; Rule, Stowitschek, Innocenti, Striefel, Killoran & Swezey, 1987; Stevenson & Dondey, 1987).

The Activity-Based Intervention Approach recommended by Bricker and Cripe supports the use of direct instruction for teaching receptive and expressive vocabulary acquisition. Acquisition of generalizations increased significantly under such an activity-based approach (Bricker & Cripe, 1992). This study emphasizes the need for clarifying program goals prior to embarking on the plan.

2. Children's participation in planning. The highest priority when implementing an integration program is to include children from each classroom in the planning stage. In one prekindergarten integration model, teachers of ECE and ECSE classes introduced their students to the idea of integrating with one another. The teachers initiated a discussion with each class on the definition of "needs." Each class identified children's needs, and then individually stated their own unique special needs. Eventually, the classes discussed integration with another class and the "special needs" each class might have. A follow-up discussion of "friends helping friends" emphasized positive goals.

3. Structured integration situations. While proximity is not generally recognized as an important factor for increasing interaction, it was effective with this group of children. The teachers set up a shared breakfast time in which they seated children from both classes next to each other to encourage social skills

*T*he highest priority when implementing an integration program is to include children from each classroom in the planning stage.

development. Later, the children were allowed to choose their own seats. Aides were assigned to each table of eight and the two teachers moved about the room. Other opportunities for providing structured integration included shared lunch or snack times, in which paired children set the tables and served food. Children made comments in this setting such as, "Nakin give Thomas his napkin to wipe milk off his shirt" and "I opened the windows and door on Kaylin's milk."

4. Teachers modeling appropriate behavior. Teachers participated with the children during morning playground time in ball games, sand activities and interplay on the climbing equipment. The teachers took advantage of these opportune times to unobtrusively bring children together through play and emphasizing shared interests with remarks such as "Kyle, would you like to play London Bridge with Johnny and me?" or "Kyle, come and see what Michael's building in the sand."

5. Shared classroom and play yard space. As activities rotated between the ECE and ECSE classrooms, play areas provided a sense of sharing and ownership for all the children. Sharing began prior to the program's total integration, as students shuttled between the classrooms for

more appropriately in groups of two or four—sharing ("Tonya, here diaper for you' baby"), discussing ("What you putting on you' pizza, cheese?"), creating ("Look, look, me and Lemetrix made a slide from blocks!") and exploring ("Come see, come see, Latavia and me got water in our hole!"). When children were grouped by three, two of the children would often "gang up" against the other one unless an adult was actively involved, as these recorded conversations indicate: "We gonna be the mommas and you gotta do what we say!" and "Suzie and me don' want you playin' in home livin'!"

8. Appropriate behaviors praised. When first integrated, the children often engaged in parallel play. Teachers were quick to praise interactive behavior: "Manuel and Jose, you are being good friends putting your blocks together to make a zoo." Such encouragement helped develop interactive play. Using an instant camera, teachers photographed instances of appropriate interactive play. These pictures gave the children immediate positive reinforcement and were placed in the classroom photograph album for subsequent viewing and discussion. Appropriate play interactions were also recorded on video, generating a great deal of positive response and discussion from the children.

9. Opportunities provided for imitative behavior. The teachers made available sets of toys or activities (such as Mr. Potato Head, pattern blocks, stringing beads, clay centers and finger paint trays) for children to work with beside each other. Teachers recognized not only accomplishments, but also attempts to play together: "Keyona and Shawn are working on matching

necklaces with the stringing beads!" Providing ample materials for play often led to children imitating others' work and assisting one another. Fluids and tactile mixtures, including sand, rice and bean mixtures, water, shaving cream, corn starch, paint, etc., encouraged shared experiences with a minimum of teacher intervention.

10. Cooperative learning activities. Cooperative activities appeared to establish a rapport between children and a sense of support for each other. During parachute play, for example, children spontaneously shared handle grips on the parachute with "new" friends. "Come hold my 'chute, Latrice!" or "Here's one for you!" A particularly special moment developed during a balloon activity. Two new friends who had been playing catch joined hands on their balloon and together placed it in the box when the color of their balloon was called. They then turned to each other, smiled and found a seat in the circle beside each other, happy in their new friendship and content with their accomplishment.

Group participation in parachute, bean bag toss, balloon, ball and musical activities appeared to foster trust within the group. A class listening center was set up so children had to share when listening to a book or using a computer. The children did in fact take turns turning the pages on the book in the listening center and offered advice when a friend needed help on the computer.

Barriers to Integration

Attitude is critical to planning and implementing a successful preschool integration effort. A national survey of parents, policy officials, and program directors of child care and Head Start centers indicated that approximately 60 percent of those surveyed cited negative attitudes toward integration as a barrier (Rose & Smith, 1993). Possible

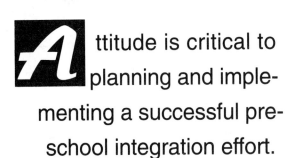

*A*ttitude is critical to planning and implementing a successful preschool integration effort.

stories, socio-dramatic events and group-to-group introductions.

6. Play groups arranged. Each child from the Chapter 1 prekindergarten class chose a companion from the self-contained prekindergarten special education class. The children would take turns introducing their companion to activities in their respective classrooms. This shared activity gave each child an opportunity to become a leader and spokesperson for his/her own classroom.

7. Centers and play areas arranged for small groups. Play areas or centers limited to several children were more successful than those designed for larger numbers of children. Children interacted

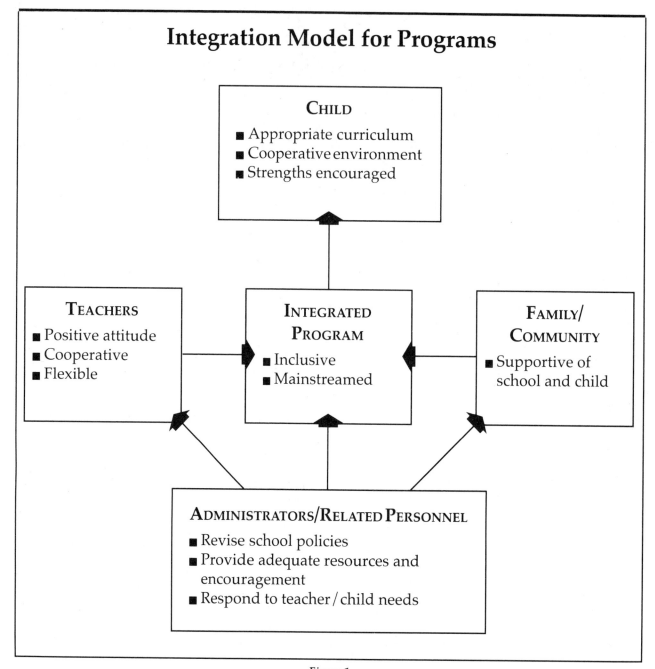

Figure 1

reasons for teachers' negative attitudes may be founded in a lack of knowledge about disabilities, uncertainty about dealing with children who have disabilities and frustration about the extra effort they imagine would be involved.

Teachers express concerns about "turf, teacher preparedness, awareness, someone will lose, and communication/respect" (Rose & Smith, 1993, p. 59). Positive teacher attitude, however, is essential to successful integration. Teachers with positive attitudes toward integration are more likely to have open communication with parents, administrators and support personnel. Asking for teacher input about possibile integration is the first step toward encouraging such positive attitudes.

Three possible concerns for ECE and ECSE teachers are: philosophical differences regarding instructional strategies, instructional planning and classroom management. ECE programs embrace a child-centered approach in which children explore, discover and absorb the learning environment at their own developmental levels. ECSE programs identify children's specific needs and design a curriculum to provide structured learning experiences. While ECE educators incorporate individualization into the thematic and play curriculum, ECSE teachers typically prepare IFSPs and Individual Educational Plans (IEPs). Classroom management strategies also differ. ECSE teachers often rely on rules, rewards and punishment, while ECE teachers are more likely to use behavioral programs centered on relationship-listening skills.

How can these barriers be overcome? Odom and McEvoy (1990) recommend encouraging positive teacher attitudes with: 1) supportive policy statements on preschool mainstreaming from national early childhood organizations, 2) supportive policy statements on preschool mainstreaming from local early childhood administrators (see Figure 1), 3) staff members who are committed to the mainstream program, 4) official recognition of mainstream staff, 5) establishment of an ongoing inservice program, 6) establishment of a realistic teacher-child ratio and 7) instructional support and teacher training for special education teachers. Teachers who are trained in effective early intervention methods and supported by peers, administrators and parents develop positive attitudes that enable them to meet classroom challenges and recognize the unique potential of each child regardless of ability or disability.

Conclusion

The successful integration of Early Childhood and Early Childhood Special Education programs requires careful planning, flexibility and initiative from cooperative teachers. Successful programs can be easily designed to nurture a learning environment that is founded in exploration and discovery, yet provides structural boundaries as well.

As interactive play between students in regular and special education classes does not occur naturally, it must be initiated through subtle teacher interaction (Hanline, 1985).

All children benefit from positive peer role models, leadership opportunities, acceptance of unique needs and friendships. Certain strategies and activities that only require a minimum of teacher intervention can help develop positive sustaining behaviors. Carefully chosen games for developing cooperative behaviors can encourage problem-solving skills rather than a sense of competition (Stainback & Stainback, 1990). A program's strength relies on a teacher-student ratio that ensures each child is nurtured, supported and encouraged in such a way to achieve maximum development. Finally, high quality early childhood programs recognize the inherent differences among children and provide a natural environment for early integration.

References

Association for Childhood Education International/Sexton, D., Snyder, P., Sharpton, W., & Stricklin, S. (1993). Infants and toddlers with special needs and their families. *Childhood Education*, 69, 278-276.

Bricker, D., & Cripe, J. J. W. (1992). *An activity-based approach to early intervention.* Baltimore, MD: Paul H. Brookes.

Cook, R. E., Tessier, A., & Klein, M. D. (Eds.). (1992). *Adapting early childhood curricula for children with special needs.* New York: Merrill.

Hanline, M. F. (1985). Integrating disabled children. *Young Children,* 40(2), 45-48.

Hanline, M. F., & Murray, C. (1984). Integrating severely handicapped children into regular public schools. *Phi Delta Kappan,* 66, 273-276.

Kaufman, M. J., Gottlieb, J., Agard, J.

A., & Kukic, M. B. (1975). Mainstreaming: Toward an explication of the construct. *Focus on Exceptional Children*, 7, 1-12.

Kugelmass, J. W. (1989). The "shared classroom": A case study of interactions between early childhood and special education staff and children. *Journal of Early Intervention*, 13(1), 36-44.

Odom, S. L., & McEvoy, M. A. (1990). Mainstreaming at the preschool level: Potential barriers and tasks for the field. *Topics in Early Childhood Special Education*, 10(2), 48-61.

Poresky, R. H., & Hooper, D. J. (1984). Enhancing prosocial play between handicapped and nonhandicapped preschool children. *Psychological Reports*, 54, 391-402.

Rose, D., & Smith, B. (1993). Preschool mainstreaming: Attitude barriers and strategies for addressing them. *Young Children*, 48(4), 57-62.

Rule, S., Stowitschek, J., Innocenti, M., Striefel, S., Killoran, J., & Swezey, K. (1987). The social integration program: An analysis of the effects of mainstreaming handicapped children into daycare centers. *Education and Treatment of Children*, 10(2), 175-192.

Schweinhart, L. J., Berrueta-Clement, J. R., Barnett, W. S., Epstein, A. S., & Weikart, D. P. (1985). The promise of early childhood education. *Phi Delta Kappan*, 66, 545-547.

Stainback, W., & Stainback, S. (Eds.). (1990). *Support networks for inclusive schooling.* Baltimore, MD: Paul H. Brookes.

Stainback, W., & Stainback, S. (1992). *Controversial issues confronting special education: Divergent perspectives.* Needham Heights, MA: Allyn & Bacon.

Stevenson, S. E., & Dondey, C. (1987). *Forming cooperative programs for mainstreaming preschool children with severe behavior disorders: Policy, programmatic and procedural issues.* Paper presented at the annual conference of the Association for the Severely Handicapped, San Francisco, CA.

NURTURING KIDS'
Seven Ways
of Being
Smart

How to develop your students' multiple intelligences

Kristen Nelson

KRISTEN NELSON *is a sixth-grade teacher at Ambuel Elementary in the Capistrano unified school district in Orange County, California. She is also a mentor teacher and consultant on multiple intelligences in the classroom.*

Throughout my teaching career I've been perplexed and fascinated by students who perform poorly in math and language activities, and appear unmotivated—yet thrive outside of the classroom. I'd see these "underachievers" in the streets after school, their faces lit with laughter and enthusiasm for whatever they were doing. They were engaged, expert, joyful—why couldn't I bring this out of them in class? Dr. Howard Gardner's Multiple Intelligences Theory nudged me toward the answer: I could reach many of these turned-off kids if I discovered their special ways of being smart.

You're probably familiar with Gardner's theory, but here's a refresher of his basic premise: Individuals don't have one fixed intelligence, but at least seven distinct ones that can be developed over time—linguistic, logical-mathematical, spatial, musical-rhythmic, bodily-kinesthetic, interpersonal, and intrapersonal. See the box ("The Seven Intelligences") and the clip-and-save chart [in this article] for more details about these seven kinds of smarts.

HOW MY TEACHING CHANGED

Gardner's theory is a dream come true for teachers—because it means intelligences can be nurtured. And with that in mind, I reinvented my curriculum and the way I taught it so that it met the needs of a wider range of learning styles—which, as educator Thomas Armstrong says, are "the intelligences put to work."

The strategies you can use to put the Multiple Intelligences Theory into play in your own classroom are limitless. To add to your thinking, here are two approaches that have had a big impact on my students' achievement: one is a focused unit that introduces kids to the concept of diverse strengths; the other is an open-ended exploration of the seven intelligences through classroom flow areas, which are similar to learning centers.

7 Smarts: An 8-Day Unit

Think a kindergartner will have trouble grasping the theory of Harvard psychologist Gardner? Think again. As a mentor teacher on multiple intelligences, I work with children throughout grades K–6, and even the youngest students naturally take to the idea that there are multiple ways of being intelligent.

I begin the unit by asking students what being smart

From *Instructor,* July/August 1995, pp. 26-30, 34. © 1995 by Scholastic, Inc. Reprinted by permission.

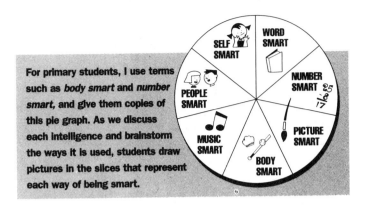

For primary students, I use terms such as *body smart* and *number smart*, and give them copies of this pie graph. As we discuss each intelligence and brainstorm the ways it is used, students draw pictures in the slices that represent each way of being smart.

means to them, and then list their replies on the board. Since their answers usually revolve around reading, writing, and math, we discuss the importance of these subjects in school success.

Next, I ask them to brainstorm other ways a person can be smart, conveying the idea that humans have proven time and again that although having strong math and language skills is important, it is not the only predictor of success in life. With grades 3 to 6, I discuss famous people who performed poorly in school but were smart in other ways. Albert Einstein and Pablo Picasso—who both disliked

school rules and dropped out to study under experts—are two good examples to use. With younger students, we talk about the fact that not everyone likes school all of the time.

As we continue our discussion, I give kids lots of examples of skills, activities, and professions that make use of each intelligence area.

EXAMINING STRENGTHS

After the introductory lesson, I focus on a different intelligence area for each of the next seven days. For example, on a spatial intelligence day with fourth graders, I might have students draw

floor plans of the Spanish mission we are studying and have them practice picturing numbers in their minds as we do oral calculations in math. On body-kinesthetic day, we role-play a scene from a novel we're reading, and learn a new sport. Each day, I also devote 45 minutes to exploring the famous people, book characters, and historical figures who are good role models in that intelligence.

By now, students are not only familiar with the different ways they're smart, but they are now ready and usually very willing to use their intelligences in daily work.

NURTURING KIDS ALL YEAR

After the opening unit, I integrate Multiple Intelligences Theory into my lesson plans for the rest of the year, adapting activities to meet various learning styles. For example, a child who is strong in spatial intelligence and is a visual learner can strengthen her reading and writing skills by drawing a picture before writing about a book she's reading. See the chart Draw Out Your Students' Strengths for

The Seven Intelligences

As you explore these seven intelligences with your students, keep in mind that Gardner's theory should not be used as another way to pigeonhole students as "spatial," "musical," and so forth. Students need to perceive themselves as having a combination of these intelligences, capable of growth in all areas.

Bodily-Kinesthetic: involves using the body to solve problems, create products, and convey ideas and emotions.

Interpersonal-Social: refers to the ability to work effectively with others; to understand them; and to notice their goals, motivations, and intentions.

Intrapersonal-Introspective: involves the ability to be deeply aware of inner feelings, intentions, and goals.

Logical-Mathematical: involves the ability to reason deductively or inductively and to recognize and manipulate abstract patterns and relationships.

Musical-Rhythmic: includes sensitivity to pitch, timbre, and rhythm of sounds, and responsiveness to music.

Verbal-Linguistic: involves ease with reading and writing skills, and sensitivity to the nuances, order, and rhythm of words.

Visual-Spatial: involves the ability to create visual-spatial representations of the world and to transfer those representations mentally or concretely—to think in pictures.

Adapted from "Seven Ways of Knowing" by David Lazear; *If Minds Matter: A Forward to the Future*, Vol. II (IRI/Skylight Publishing)

more ideas on how to build on your kids' multiple intelligences.

Flow Areas Foster Intelligence

Using multiple intelligences in your teaching has to go beyond detecting strengths in students and flexing just those intellectual muscles. You need to give students the opportunity to explore all seven domains. Setting up flow areas—which are centers organized around the seven intelligences—will help you accomplish this.

The concept of *flow* was developed by Mihaly Csikszentmihalyi, Ph.D., professor of human development at the University of Chicago, who describes flow as a state of complete absorption in something, to the point where one loses track of time. Csikszentmihalyi first observed flow when studying artists; he then looked for and found it in dancers, athletes, scientists, musicians, and talented people in many other fields.

In the classroom, flow areas provide students with the space, materials, time, and challenging activities that spark deep involvement while strengthening children's intelligences.

GO WITH THE FLOW

The very nature of flow areas is flexible, and they can be designed in numerous ways. Sometimes you'll want to set up flow areas for four to six weeks, and at other times just for a week or two. How you guide students to use them will vary, too. You'll want children to work in them solo, with partners, and in small groups; you can have children use them only when they're finished with their class work, or you can rotate students through the areas on a regular schedule. Try to block out a period of at least 30 minutes for kids, so they have a chance to get lost in their endeavor.

You can set up flow areas as centers independent of what students

are studying, or you can link them to your curriculum.

21 FLOW-AREA IDEAS
Verbal-Linguistic

1. Set up a language lab with a cassette player, cassettes, earphones, and talking books. Invite students to tape themselves reading a story or poem they've written, to share with others.
2. Establish a writing center with a computer, writing supplies, and examples of different types of writing. A fourth grader I taught used this area to write letters to local land developers to discuss her environmental concerns.
3. Organize a tutoring station where older children volunteer to help younger students with reading and writing. One sixth grader who lacked confidence in his reading gained more self-assurance when he helped a first grader learn to read.

CLIP AND SAVE

Draw Out Your Students' Strengths

Intelligence Area:	Is Strong In:	Likes to:	Learns Best Through:	Famous Examples:	Common Misbehaviors:
Verbal/ Linguistic	Reading, writing, telling stories, memorizing dates, thinking in words	Read, write, tell stories, talk, memorize, do word puzzles	Reading, hearing, and seeing words; speaking; writing; discussions	T. S. Eliot, Maya Angelou, Abraham Lincoln	Passing notes, reading during lessons
Logical/ Mathematical	Math, reasoning, logic, problem-solving, patterns	Solve problems, question, reason, work with numbers, experiment, use computers	Working with patterns and relationships, classifying, abstract thinking	Albert Einstein, John Dewey, Susanne Langer	Working on math or building things during lessons
Visual/ Spatial	Reading, maps, charts, drawing, puzzles, imagining things, visualization	Design, draw, build, create, daydream, look at pictures	Working with pictures and colors, visualizing, drawing	Pablo Picasso, Frank Lloyd Wright, Georgia O'Keeffe, Bobby Fischer	Doodling, drawing, daydreaming
Bodily/ Kinesthetic	Athletics, dancing, acting, crafts, using tools	Play sports, dance, move around, touch and talk, use body language	Touching, moving, processing knowledge through bodily sensations	Charlie Chaplin, Michael Jordan, Martha Graham	Fidgeting, wandering around the room
Musical/ Rhythmic	Singing, picking up sounds, remembering melodies, rhythms	Sing, hum, play an instrument, listen to music	Rhythm, melody, singing, listening to music and melodies	Leonard Bernstein, Mozart, Ella Fitzgerald	Tapping pencil or feet
Interpersonal/ Social	Understanding people, leading, organizing, communicating, resolving conflicts	Have friends, talk to people, join groups	Sharing, comparing, relating, interviewing, cooperating	Mohandas Gandhi, Ronald Reagan, Mother Teresa	Talking, passing notes
Intrapersonal/ Introspective	Understanding self, recognizing strengths and weaknesses, setting goals	Work alone, reflect, pursue interests	Working alone, self-paced projects, reflecting	Eleanor Roosevelt, Sigmund Freud, Thomas Merton	Conflicting with others

How to Enhance Your Teaching Smarts

☑ **Invite guest speakers.** Show students the relevance of each intelligence by inviting parents and community members as guest speakers—their professions can highlight specific intelligences. For example, a local architect described to my students how he designed a building they pass every day on their way to school—the kids were fascinated.

☑ **Create a video.** Have your students plan and execute a video to inform parents or other classes about the many ways of being smart.

☑ **Encourage individual projects.** Have students choose an intelligence area in which they would like to complete a one- to two-week project.

☑ **Honor overlooked intelligences.** Remember to recognize students that excel in bodily-kinesthetic, interpersonal, and intrapersonal intelligences.

☑ **Assess your own intelligences.** Think about how your strengths and weaknesses in the seven intelligences influence your teaching. Look at your lesson plans. Beside each activity, write the initials of the intelligences exercised—you will be able to see your dominant intelligence areas as well as the areas you need to enhance. Share your strengths and weaknesses with students.

☑ **Stretch yourself.** Instead of accepting the belief that you don't excel in certain areas, attend workshops and read books that can help strengthen these skills.

☑ **Team teach.** Use fellow teachers who have different intelligence strengths to plan lessons and activities. Rotating students can allow you to teach to your strengths and loves, while providing students with different styles of teaching and learning.

☑ **Update your professional portfolio.** Set your sights on having a portfolio that contains examples of lessons that use each intelligence area.

Math-Logic

4. Make a math lab with manipulatives, calculators, objects to measure and graph, and so on. My younger students love to use the area to classify pattern blocks, buttons, and coins. One older student calculated the expenses of an upcoming family trip and planned an itinerary.

5. Put together a science lab with simple hands-on experiments and science books. A flower-dissection lab—which I set up when we're learning about plant reproduction—is a favorite of my students.

6. Create a logic-challenge center. For example, I invited my fifth graders to develop a mystery-based board game. When I challenged my sixth graders to design a way to teach a blind person geometric shapes, they collected yardsticks and made giant squares, triangles, and parallelograms on the playground.

Spatial

7. Enrich an art area with paints, pencils, different types of paper, clay, and various objects students can use as models for still-life drawings. Display examples of famous artists' work for students to study. My students loved it when I brought in a large shell and invited them to do a painting of it in the style of Georgia O'Keeffe.

8. Stock a visual media center with a video camera, VCR, and videotapes. Invite groups of students to make a short classroom documentary. My students chose topics of concern to them, like getting along with parents.

9. Fill an architecture center with pencils, rulers, and large sheets of paper. Invite students to draw the floor plan of anything. A fourth grader planned, designed, and built a futuristic mission for space exploration.

Bodily-Kinesthetic

10. Put together a hands-on center with materials such as clay, blocks, and craft materials. While studying Michelangelo's sculpting style, my students decided to make chess sets out of clay.

11. Enrich a drama center with play books and ideas for student performances or puppet theater. One student wrote his own version of a Greek tragedy, selected his cast, and performed it for other classes.

12. Create an open space for creative movement (mini-trampoline, juggling equipment, drama area, and so on). Or set up an outside flow area that can be monitored by a parent volunteer. I've seen students use this area to learn how to juggle (which increases eye-hand coordination) and teach jazz and country dances to their peers.

Musical

13. Set up a music lab with cassettes, earphones, and various tapes to compare and contrast. For example, students can compare Mozart's "Symphony No. 39" with Garth Brooks's "The Thunder Rolls" and the Beatles' "Paperback Writer."

14. Display lyrics for students to analyze. Fill a listening lab with sound-related items such as a stethoscope, walkie-talkies, and a conch shell.

15. Invite students to compose their own songs and write the lyrics. A fourth grader composed a song for the violin that represented the tone and feeling of the book *Where the Red Fern Grows* by Wilson Rawls.

Interpersonal

16. Create a flow area with a round table—to encourage group discussions. You can write curriculum-based discussion ideas on cards and place them in the center, or let students choose their own topics.

17. Establish a debate center where students form teams and choose a subject to debate. Give kids ten minutes to prepare for the debate. Rain-forest preservation versus local economic needs, and whether or not kids should be allowed to ride in-line skates to school are two topics that sparked heated discussions among students.

18. Give students an index card stating a common school-related problem. Challenge them to work together to come up with solutions. A group of second graders discussed how to resolve arguments that developed in their handball games. They wrote rules to share with other students.

Intrapersonal

19. Create a selection of self-esteem activities. For example, ask students to list ten of their strengths or have them write out specific ways they are a good friend to others. Encourage journal writing.

20. Invite kids to draw a picture that describes a mood or feeling. I've found this really helps older students to become aware of their fluctuating moods and to reflect on how their moods affect their daily lives.

21. Design study nooks for individual work. Use beanbag chairs to make them cozy spaces. A third grader who had difficulty controlling his anger used this nook often as a cooling-off location.

Personalized Learning

The biggest impact that the Multiple Intelligences Theory has had in my classroom is that it has helped me create an individualized learning environment. I no longer expect students to think exactly alike in order to be *right*. I am more comfortable with my students' individualistic thinking—and my own. In personalizing each student's education experience, I find that an increasing percentage of students discover their own strengths, put more effort into improving their weaker areas, and feel better about themselves.

a Profile of every child

As you get to know each child in your program, you are building a foundation for authentic assessment that can last throughout the year. Observing, documenting, collecting children's work, and communicating are the building blocks. LILIAN KATZ, SYLVIA CHARD, and CELIA GENISHI share insights and strategies you can use to make these tools a dynamic part of your classroom.

Observation: *Watching children in action*

LILIAN G. KATZ

Lilian G. Katz, Ph.D., is a Professor of Early Childhood Education at the University of Illinois, Urbana, and Director of the ERIC Clearinghouse.

Observation must be intentional. As a teacher, you know you can't possibly observe everything. Intentional observation, as part of your daily routine, is perhaps the most authentic form of assessment. Intentional observation is seeing children in a *real* context, rather than a contrived situation. Observing what children actually do every day is the best place to start when creating a real-life profile of each child and planning for each child's success.

Why Observe?
There are several reasons for you to practice this vital technique:
You will increase your knowledge of each child. You will understand how each child interacts with materials, with one another, with your classroom, and with adults.

You can let the child's actions lead your assessment, and so be less con-

cerned with how the child compares to a formal standard or measure of achievement.

You can learn more by observing the process of an activity than by seeing only the end product.

You can make more informed decisions. These might include:
■ choosing curriculum activities that work successfully for each child.
■ identifying children who work best together and children who belong together in group activities.
■ identifying those children who need more guidance and those who need more independence.

What to Observe
What, exactly, are you looking for when you observe?

Dispositions. A disposition is a trend in behavior or activity that reflects a particular motivation to learn, explore, or investigate a particular thing. Dispositions are different from the skills

or abilities that are so often assessed. Having a certain disposition doesn't mean that a child *can* do something but that he or she actually *does* it on a regular basis.

Coping strategies. Watch for evidence of problem solving. How does a child cope when things aren't working right?

Withdrawal or isolation. Observing a child over a number of days can help you determine his or her place or even reputation within the group. You can then look for opportunities to make sure no child gets left out or locked into a certain status that may be limiting.

Key attributes. You can't observe everything about a child, so try to identify and list the attributes you are most interested in. You might focus on these questions, which can be best answered through observation:
■ Does each child show satisfaction in what he or she is doing or learning?

■ Does each child persist at a task or give up easily?

3. EDUCATIONAL PRACTICES

■ Does each child enjoy interacting with other children?

How to Observe
Observe regularly and intentionally. Don't leave this to chance.

Observe your children at different times of the day, not just at activity time. If you aren't free to observe a child, then ask another adult to help you.

Observe the children in different settings — on the playground, in the hallways, on the bus, at the front door — throughout the school or center.

Observe what the child is usually like. Don't get bogged down in unusual behavior or bad days.

Observe for new possibilities. If a child is having trouble in a certain area, imagine how that child might behave if things were different. If the environment or circumstances changed, how might he move or talk or act differently?

How to Record Your Observations
Your observations increase in value when you record and share them. Consider these strategies:

■ Jot down anecdotes or quick notes about *what* you see, *when* you see it.
■ Record your observations on a checklist you have created or adapted. Make sure you do this regularly, not just once.
■ If you don't have the time to record your observations during the day, record the day's highlights at the end of each day.
■ Let the children in on your observations and talk with them about what you observe. It is vitally important to involve children in self-reflection and self-assessment.
■ Take frequent photographs of situations. Sometimes it is easier to snap a picture than to jot down notes.

Creating and Using Anecdotes

Teachers often use anecdotes (short written descriptions of behavior or events) to make note of their observations.

■ While observing, write just enough to jog your memory later when you have time to elaborate.

■ Try to keep objective descriptions of behavior separate from subjective interpretations or inferences.

■ Keep handy your materials for writing down anecdotes. Hang a small notebook on a string around your neck, or place index cards in key areas around the room.

Documentation: *Displaying children's learning*

SYLVIA C. CHARD

Syvia C. Chard, Ph.D., is an Associate Professor in the Department of Education at the University of Alberta, Canada.

Many early childhood programs have traditionally encouraged and practiced observation of children and extensive record keeping. However, the preprimary schools in the northern Italian city of Reggio Emilia have centered their curriculum on the documentation of children's experiences, memories, thoughts, and ideas. This city's unique contribution to early childhood education is the use of documentation of children's experiences as a standard part of classroom practice.

The documentation of Reggio Emilia typically includes samples of a child's work at different stages of completion, photographs showing the work in progress, comments written by the teacher or other adults, transcripts of children's discussions about their activity, and comments made by the parents. Examples of the children's work are displayed in classrooms or hallways. These documents reveal how the children planned, carried out, and completed the displayed work.

Documentation of children's work and ideas can contribute to the quality of your early childhood program in many ways:

Enhancing children's learning.
Preparing and displaying examples of children's experience and effort provides a means of debriefing or revisiting experience, enabling new understandings to be clarified and strengthened.

2 **Taking children's ideas and work seriously.** Careful and attractive displays can convey to children that their efforts, intentions, and ideas are taken seriously.

3 **Involving children in planning and evaluation.** Over a period of several days or weeks, you can examine the work and discuss with children their evolving ideas and the possibilities of new prospects or activities for the following days.

4 **Fostering parent participation.** Documentation clearly and graphically shows parents what their children are doing. It may inspire them to participate or to contribute ideas for field experiences, especially when they can offer help in gaining access to a site or expert.

5 **Awareness of the learning process.** The final product of a child's work rarely illustrates the child's false starts and persistent efforts. By documenting the steps taken by children during their investigations and representational work, teachers and parents can appreciate the uniqueness of each child's learning.

Note: These six benefits of documentation were adapted from the April 1996 ERIC digest, The Contribution of Documentation to the Quality of Early Childhood Education, *by Lilian G. Katz and Sylvia C. Chard. To receive a free copy, call the ERIC/EECE Clearinghouse at (800) 583-4135.*

6 **Making children's learning visible.** Documenting children's work in a wide variety of media provides compelling public evidence of the intellectual powers of young children.

Why Document?
Documentation gives you a focus for reflecting on your own work. As you become increasingly sensitized to children's interests and how these facilitate their learning, you can better plan all aspects of your program.

Documentation helps build bridges of communication between teachers and families. It helps you to show parents what their children are learning and how it relates to their experience outside the school setting.

Documentation helps children make sense of their experience. It provides a concrete way for them to reflect on their own learning.

What to Document
It is important to document changes that can be observed each day or each week. And it is not only what the children do that is interesting. It is what you do, as well! Parents want to know how you value the experiences offered to children and how you guide the children with materials and equipment.

You can display many different kinds of evidence of learning. Much of what

children learn is represented in products — drawings, paintings, collage, and models — that can be collected, labeled, and displayed on bulletin boards or shelves. And some learning experiences can be recorded through a sequence of photographs.

Useful documentation is possible only when children are engaged in interesting projects and activities worthy of display. If much of children's time is devoted to making the same pictures about the same topics, you have little to document and little to provide rich content for discussions with children and parents.

How to Document
The staff member recording the work can be responsible for creating a display on the walls, in journals, or in portfolios that can be available to children, parents, and other teachers. The staff member should write captions to explain the significance of the material displayed.

Remember that your documents or displays should tell a story. They might describe a sequence of events or be illustrated with pictures, diagrams, and lists that fill in background detail.

In all these different ways you can help your coworkers, the children, and their parents to have a thorough understanding of what is going on in the classroom. Good documentation gives a positive and constructive commentary on children's lives and learning that helps them to progress with confidence day by day into their own future.

Portfolios: *Collecting children's work*

CELIA GENISHI

Celia Genishi, Ph.D., is Professor of Education and Chairperson of Curriculum and Teaching at Columbia University Teachers College.

Like an artist's portfolio, a young child's assessment portfolio should contain a wide range of work. It is individualized and can take various forms. In a preschool classroom or child-care center, each child's cubby might function as a portfolio because it holds products that

have accumulated over time. Or you may use a folder or actual portfolio.

Many teachers and caregivers use portfolios for two major functions:

To illustrate the kinds of things the child is able to do, which would include his or her "best" or most complete and satisfying products, as well as developing or less-developed examples.

To use as the basis for sharing with others, including parents, administrators,

other teachers, and the child himself, how he has developed and what he has learned over time.

A portfolio is infinitely adaptable to your goals, as well as to each child's strengths and abilities. It can reflect many facets of the children and of your classroom's curriculum. And so each portfolio will be unique. The portfolios you assemble will contain contrasting items and items unique to each child.

You can reflect various segments of the daily schedule in these portfolios. Your own goals and preferences, and the goals of your school or center, will determine whether the portfolio will represent all aspects of the curriculum for every child or will instead focus on each child's main interests.

For example, in schools in which administrators look for consistency throughout kindergarten classrooms, there may be a requirement to include specific products that illustrate each child's artwork, dictated stories, and oral development. Another program might take a different approach and expect teachers to focus on each child's most notable strengths and weaknesses.

Portfolio assessment is a comprehensive process that reflects your own, your administrators', or even your parents' preferences. Together, you must decide what kind of portfolio is the most informative, useful, and authentic for your program. The portfolio, after all, is a culmination of authentic assessment. It is highly individualized and useful for improving all aspects of a child's learning. Like other methods of authentic assessment, it is extremely valuable in givingh a unique profile of each child — whether the child is "average," "difficult," or "advanced" or has special needs.

How to Create Portfolios

Remember, portfolio assessment:
- happens as a process over time.
- is coordinated by teachers but involves children.

- is about each individual child's progress.

Make use of the following questions and strategies to help you begin your own system of portfolio assessment:

1 Decide what you want to assess: Spoken language? Art? Early literacy? Symbolic play? Motor skills? Math concepts?

2 Decide which documents best demonstrate development: drawings, paintings, other artwork, photos, dictated stories, book choices, teacher's notes, audiotape or videotape recordings, graphs, checklists.

3 Regularly collect samples with children's input — adding the dates when children did them and comments children may have about them.

4 Decide how to store the samples: a homemade folder (made of construction paper or oaktag), a plastic box or container to be kept in each child's cubby, one or more file folders, an artist's portfolio, or accordion file.

5 See if there are gaps in the "developmental story." Do you have work that shows the full range of what each child can do? Are there samples of work or notes from the beginning, middle, and end of the period of time you've selected? Do the samples tell

you where the child has been, where she or he is now, and where she or he should go next?

6 See if what you have collected will tell a clear story to the audience. This includes parents, other teachers, the child, the administrator, and you!

What a Portfolio Might Contain

Here are some samples of what you might include in a portfolio. Remember, the contents of each portfolio will reflect the individuality of the child — no two will be alike!

- **dictated story**
- **audiotape**
- **paintings or drawings**
- **ceramic piece**
- **photographs of projects or activities**
- **writing samples, such as the child's name**
- **self-portrait**

Questions About Portfolio Assessment

1. What are your main reasons for creating a portfolio for each child? What are you trying to learn?

2. Who will decide what goes into each portfolio?

3. What will the criteria be for selection? You might consider:

• what is typical of the child's play or work.

• what is unique (something that seems especially informative, whether it represents a bare beginning or a fully developed sample).
• how a product documents specific curricular objectives or goals.

4. What is the child's role? Have you allowed for authentic self-evaluation? Is the child able to select products based on her or his own reasons or preferences?

5. How will the child's self-evaluation come about?

• through a scheduled "conference" with one or more children?
• by selecting and discussing the products in the portfolio?

6. With whom will you share the portfolio? Parents, administrators, future teachers, other children?

Communication: *Involving children and families*

CELIA GENISHI

Cecilia Genishi, Ph.D., is Professor of Education and Chairperson of Curriculum and Teaching at Columbia University Teachers College.

You are not alone in assessing the children in your classroom or center! Both the parents and the children themselves are your partners in this vital task.

The Parents

Parents can be your most helpful ally in accurately and sensitively assessing your students. Here's how to effectively communicate with parents about your assessment of their child:

1 Be upbeat. Authentic child-centered assessment must accentuate the positive.

2 Communicate often. Make it clear to parents that you believe communication is the foundation of authentic assessment:
■ Build "assessment comments" about how a child is doing into the day-to day conversations you have with parents.

■ Explain your approach to assessment at a parent meeting or workshop; be clear about the differences between standardized tests and authentic assessment.
■ Write about assessment in a newsletter or a special letter home.

3 Be respectful. Show that you value parents' knowledge about their children:
■ Treat them as respected consultants on their child's behavior or progress.
■ Support what you say with documentation, perhaps a portfolio, of what the child has accomplished over time.

The Children

Everyone has a view of a child's abilities, preferences, and performance, including the child. Here's how to effectively involve the children in their own assessment:

1 Observe and document things the children say and do. Seemingly random statements like "I was this big on my last birthday; now I'm THIS big" are evidence that children are capable of assessing what they can do and how they are changing. Children may demonstrate their awareness of their own capabilities by how quickly they jump into new activities.

2 Ask children about themselves. Often, children will tell you what they like to do or what they don't like to do. Some children may talk about what they do as they are doing or completing it; others may be pleased by a conference or interview situation in which they receive your undivided attention. Use your own judgment as to when and where to ask children about themselves.

3 Ask children to evaluate their work. When you are deciding what to include in children's portfolios, ask them to help you choose. You can also ask children why they choose what they do or how one piece of work is different from another. Some children may give elaborate responses, whereas others may shrug. Respect their responses as a reflection of their own views.

4 Let children take pictures of their most prized work from time to time. They can then make a bulletin board display of their specially chosen "picture portfolio."

Material by Celia Genishi on pages 103–105 was adapted from Teacher Workshop: Observation and Assessment *by Celia Genishi, part of the Scholastic Early Childhood Workshop (Professional Resource Library, Scholastic Inc.: 1995).*

Your Learning Environment

A look back at your year

by Ellen Booth Church

When you assess your children's growth and learning, set aside some time to also evaluate your learning environment. You'll find that an end-of-year review is a great tool — one you can use to plan an even better classroom and curriculum for next year.

GETTING STARTED
On the following pages you'll find questions to get you started in evaluating five key classroom learning centers. You probably have other learning centers to look at, and you may wish to generate additional questions that refer to specific learning goals for your children. So use the questions that follow as a framework, which you can customize for your classroom.

Make use of all the tools you have available to help you in your evaluation. These include your own thoughts and memories and also the documentation you have collected, such as your anecdotal notes, portfolios, and other records of children's work. You might even want to make use of a video camera to get an accurate look at what's really happening in your centers.

Also, seek out feedback from people who know your classroom well, including, if appropriate, your director or principal, parents, and colleagues. Finally, don't forget your children! Their perspectives offer valuable information and can serve as a barometer of how well your learning centers worked this year. Ask them questions such as these: *What was your favorite center and why? What didn't you like about school this year? What suggestions do you have for next year's children? What new things do you think we need in the classroom?*

Now, let's take an indepth tour through your learning environment.

From *Early Childhood Today*, May/June 1996, pp. 28-35. © 1996 by Scholastic, Inc. Reprinted by permission.

Literacy: Bringing Language to Life

Your language and literacy activities may be integrated in one place or consist of a separate library corner, writing center, listening center, and/or group-meeting area. But however the literacy center is designed, it should help children understand the forms and functions of spoken and written language; give them meaningful experiences with reading, writing, speaking, and listening; help them master early-literacy skills; and foster a love of books.

■ How many opportunities did children have every day to read? To write? Was there enough time and enough materials every day to accommodate all children who were interested?

■ How many opportunities did children have to make use of environmental print? Was the print meaningful to them? What percentage of the words that surrounded children were written or dictated by them?

■ How did your center resources demonstrate the connections between reading and writing and all the other areas of your curriculum? Did you use, for example, song charts, science vocabulary, or books about current themes?

■ What was the balance of large-group, small-group, and individual reading activities?

■ Were activities readily available in the classroom to reinforce specific age-appropriate literacy skills, such as sequencing picture stories for younger children and matching sounds with letters for kindergartners?

■ How would you describe your book collection in terms of quality, quantity, and variety? Are the books age-appropriate? Do they reflect the cultures of your children?

■ How did your environment communicate to parents and visitors information about children's literacy experiences? Were samples of individual children's writing displayed? What about class books and experience charts?

■ Did you offer materials to reinforce literacy at home? How did families respond?

■ Did children have frequent opportunities to see their ideas written down through dictation and invented spelling?

■ Was there a place for children to record and read back new vocabulary words of interest to them?

■ Were children free to play with language, its sounds and meaning?

PLANNING TIPS

● Make sure there is enough room for children to access all needed materials.

● Avoid clutter by using hanging storage pockets (such as clear shoe or clothing bags) for writing, listening, and language-game materials.

A LOOK AT SYSTEMS

Your management systems allow your learning centers to operate smoothly. In a child-centered environment, they also enable children to manage themselves as much as possible.

Did children feel empowered by your systems and routines? Could they independently check in to learning centers, choose their own activities, and take out and put away materials by themselves?

Were systems easy to follow? If you had to explain procedures repeatedly, your systems need work. Review procedures that were difficult, and think about ways to simplify them or to alter the environment to help.

Did your environment provide visual or tactile cues? If children were confused, mark shelves and materials with matching symbols. Post pictorial daily schedules and signs in each center so that children know what to expect.

● Augment your literacy space (and reinforce the connections between literacy and other learning) by adding paper and writing materials to other areas.

● Use bins to store books in other learning centers — books about building in the block area, for example.

● Check that all children in your room can see themselves respectfully represented in books, songs, and discussions.

Manipulatives: Making Math Work

Your math and manipulative center is where children use materials to explore and discover concepts that help them organize their world. Because math is integral to many other activities — art, music, science — your math center also functions as a storehouse for portable materials that can be used around the room.

■ What range of materials did you have that could be used for sorting and classifying? For seriating? For measuring weight and dimensions? For making patterns? For exploring number and spatial concepts? Did you have materials that could be used in a variety of ways?

■ What was the balance of teacher-directed and child-directed math activities?

■ How did your activities in this center encourage children to use math to reason, communicate ideas, make connections, and solve problems?

■ How did the environment facilitate bringing math materials to other areas of the room for activities like measuring and making patterns?

■ How did your environment help children learn the language of math, such as the terms *more* and *less* for younger children, and *add* and *plus* for kindergartners?

■ What opportunities did children have to record and review the results of their problem solving?

PLANNING TIPS

● Limit materials and games to those related to math concepts, such as links, cubes, and objects for sorting. Keep non-math-related games elsewhere.

● Supply multiples of manipulatives that are particularly popular or are necessary for developing particular skills, especially for kindergartners.

● Keep tabletops orderly by offering children trays or mats to work on.

● Rotate manipulatives and materials often enough to spark children's interest.

● Offer basic information and structure so that children understand some ways they can use the materials. Then encourage and accept children's own innovations.

Art: An Invitation to Creativity

Art is one of many languages children use to express their feelings and ideas. Your art area can support children's developing creativity by offering the materials, time, and space for them to explore freely. Activities should be open-ended and emphasize process rather than just product.

■ How many open-ended materials (paper, crayons and markers, wood, recycled objects) were available to children on a daily basis? Was there a wide variety of each?

■ How often did you introduce new or innovative materials to the art area? How much time did children have to fully explore these items?

■ How did you help children learn specific art skills, such as printing or using scissors?

■ Did behavior problems arise in your art area due to children's boredom with the materials, frustration over scarcity of materials, or insufficient space?

■ Which of your children visited the art area frequently? Occasionally? Not at all?

■ Was there freedom to create on a variety of surfaces, like easels and the floor?

■ Was there space to store works-in-progress? To continue projects over time?

■ How did you provide space

to display two- and three-dimensional creations?

PLANNING TIPS

● Check your art area regularly to make sure it is well-stocked and orderly.

● Try integrating curriculum themes and activities based on raw art materials —

paper, paint, or string — into all your learning centers.

● Stock materials such as fabrics, buttons, beads from many cultures, and crayons and paints in different skin tones, to help all children feel at home in the art area. Encourage donations from families.

● Engage the interest of children who rarely choose art by offering activities such as driving toy cars through paint to make tire prints.

● Have smocks and extra play clothes available so children who are not dressed for messy play can feel free to participate.

A LOOK AT FLOW

Traffic problems can undermine an engaging curriculum and well-planned routines.

Was there too much running in your classroom? There may be too large an open space or a runway through your room. Expand your learning centers to incorporate some of the extra space.

Were children in quiet work areas disturbed by children in other areas? Group quieter centers, such as literacy and math away from noisier activities like blocks, dramatic play, and music. Define the centers' borders clearly with rugs, shelving, or tape.

Dramatic Play: Acting Out of the World

In your dramatic-play area, children have an opportunity to explore their imaginations and practice language and social skills by playacting meaningful events and characters in their lives.

■ Were play themes and props age-appropriate, focusing on home, families, and friends for preschoolers, and expanding to include community, adventure, and fantasy themes for older fours, fives, and kindergartners?

■ What was the balance of child-initiated and teacher-initiated play themes? How successfully did each one work?

■ Did you change themes or props often enough to sustain children's interest? Too often to allow for in-depth exploration by children?

■ Were social conflicts caused by too little space? By arguments over sharing props?

■ How did children apply literacy and math concepts in their dramatic play? What props in the area encouraged these behaviors?

■ What did you do to make sure your dramatic-play area reflected the home environments of all your children? What more might you do next year?

PLANNING TIPS

● Provide enough space and materials for children to free-

ly interact and recreate meaningful experiences.

● Expand your supply of props by enlisting the help of families and visiting tag sales and flea markets.

● Assemble dramatic-play "prop boxes" for different themes children have enjoyed.

● Store large blocks near the dramatic-play area so that children can create their own play structures.

● Look for meaningful ways to foster age-appropriate skills. Include literacy props such as books, telephones, message pads, and markers. Offer props that promote math skills, including a clock, a cash register with play money, and a balance scale.

Science: Making New Discoveries

In a child-centered program, science is individualized to accommodate all learning styles and enable children to explore their interests in their own way. Yet, the goal for all children is to practice using basic science skills and processes — observation, prediction, experimentation, and evaluation — to help understand the world around them.

■ What specific materials and activities in your science area encouraged children to observe, predict, experiment, and evaluate?

■ Did children have many opportunities to record their science findings through drawing, writing, or creating charts and graphs? Did opportunities match your children's varying literacy and math abilities?

■ Did you adequately introduce new concepts and techniques in mini-lessons to help children who needed more structure? Did you then allow everyone plenty of opportunity for free exploration?

■ How often could you accommodate children's desires to test out their ideas? Were you able to provide them with the necessary materials and time?

■ How did you use your observations of children's experiments in this center and around the room to offer activities that built on their natural curiosity?

■ Did you provide activities in this center that responded to a specific experience of children's — for example, seeing "cracks" (erosion) produced by rain on the playground?

■ Did your science tools and materials support a range of scientific experiences, from physics to plant and animal studies to chemical reactions?

■ Did your science center seem more like just a museum than a laboratory for active learning? How could you change this?

PLANNING TIPS

● Provide bins of materials for children to use in creating self-directed explorations and experiments.

● Make sure that your science center includes things to *do*, not just to look at. Stock it with science tools such as magnifying glasses and magnets. Prepare discovery trays of materials and tools like metal and nonmetal objects and a magnet. Add pictorial cards that present problem-solving experiments children can conduct.

● Set up your science area so that it invites several children to actually sit, spend time, and work there together.

● Watch for children using materials inappropriately — as pretend weapons, for example. To redirect children, spark their interest by interacting with them in the activities you've set out.

● Consider other science-related areas and activities when planning your science-center curriculum. These can include the outdoors, your sand and water tables, cooking, and art.

A LOOK AT TONE

Children's emotions, behavior, and interactions are strongly influenced by your program and space, and can indicate aspects of your learning environment that need improvement. Your answers to the questions below can serve as a barometer of your classroom's tone.

• Was the general tone of the classroom happy, balanced, energetic, or chaotic?

• Were most children excited about activities and school in general?

• Were many children anxious to go home throughout the day?

• Were children generally focused or were they easily distracted?

• What was the quality of children's interactions? Was there a great deal of fighting or shouting?

• What was the quality and quantity of adult-child interactions?

• Were children relatively independent or always needing assistance?

As you assess your learning environment, make note of the things that worked really well, even as you look at the things that you could (or should) do better. Then set realistic goals that will keep you moving forward, and look for fun things that you can do over the summer to enrich your program next year. And remember, a classroom environment with your own personal touches will make for a more successful, exciting year to come for you and your children!

Ellen Booth Church is an early childhood consultant for the New York State Department of Education and for early childhood programs across the country.

Your Environment for
CHILDREN WITH SPECIAL NEEDS

Children with special needs may be included in your classroom along with those who do not require special accommodation. Take some time to look at how your room has specifically enabled children with disabilities to meet the following special challenges:

Visual Challenges: Well-planned learning centers with clearly defined borders can do wonders to make the classroom more navigable. In each learning center, ask yourself how you can add texture to items to make them identifiable through more than one sense.

Hearing Challenges: Do your planned activities and materials enable hearing-impaired children to manage independently? Place simple drawings and symbols in centers, bathrooms, and hallways to remind them and all children about procedures and routines.

Physical Challenges: Are your learning areas arranged for comfort and support? Heavy, stable furniture placed on a carpet that won't slide is a must.

Cognitive/Intellectual Challenges: Did you design activities that complement children's various developmental stages? Look for more ways to develop your learning centers and your curriculum to provide repetition. Present new information and materials in manageable pieces so that children can experience frequent success.

Social/Emotional Challenges: Did some children get overstimulated or confused? Consider making aspects of your environment less stimulating, limiting some choices, and varying the length of time for activities. Make sure your environment accommodates your spending one-on-one time with children who need extra support.

Talented and Gifted: Restlessness and misbehavior can be signs of boredom. Increase individual responsibility and adjust the complexity of projects and materials to motivate children who have special gifts.

Guiding and Supporting Young Children

No subject in early childhood education seems to attract the attention of teachers and parents more than how to guide behavior. New teachers are concerned that they will not be able to keep the children "under control." Mature teachers wrestle with the finer points of how to guide behavior positively and effectively. Parents have strong feelings on the subject of behavior, often based on their own childhood experiences. Teachers spend many hours thinking and talking about the best ways to guide young children's behavior: *What should I do about the child who is out of bounds? What do I say to parents who want their child punished? Is punishment the same as discipline? How do I guide a child who has experienced violence and now acts out violently?*

From their wealth of experience with young children, Alice S. Honig and Donna S. Wittmer offer suggestions for schools and families to foster positive social development. They urge schools to work closely with families to plan a prosocial curriculum and establish community rituals that acknowledge children. In these times when violence and unethical actions are so prevalent, it is vital for the entire community to promote positive behavior. Cele M. McCloskey shows how this is possible. In "Taking Positive Steps toward Classroom Management in Preschool: Loosening Up without Letting It All Fall Apart," she provides eight basic steps to foster a positive preschool environment. Mutual respect and consistency are two of her keys to successful classroom management.

The outcome of domestic violence or abuse on young children is often inappropriate behavior or lack of control. Violent experiences can alter children's behavior and lower their self-esteem. In an early childhood setting, it is difficult for these children to cope with others and to express their emotions. Some children who have been affected by violence may be extremely angry and display unacceptable behaviors. Others may be pessimistic and act out in self-destructive ways.

Teachers find that guiding the behavior of children who have suffered abuse is a complicated task. Lorraine B. Wallach's article, "Breaking the Cycle of Violence," addresses ways in which teachers can successfully guide children who endure different types of violence. She advises us that the basis for working with these children is through relationships. Teachers must be models for affection and respect, communicating belief in children's abilities. Above all, consistency and care are necessary for children to learn. Wallach emphasizes the value of playing out bad experiences in order to learn to manage anger, fear, and anxiety. Dictating stories and art activities are also good outlets for feelings. Beyond the classroom, Wallach calls for closer attention by community organizations to curbing violence. This comes about only when politicians and policymakers know that educators and families support efforts to fight crime and violence.

Dan Gartrell in "Misbehavior or Mistaken Behavior?" clearly pictures two extremes of discipline—one based on punishment and the other on guidance. He cautions us to recognize the difference between the two and to choose the positive form. Because such terms as "misbehavior" make us think of punishment, a better term is "mistaken" behavior. Gartrell sorts out three levels of mistaken behavior—strong needs, socially influenced, and experimentation—that identify the types of problems children are likely to experience. Giving alternatives is an effective way to guide children as worthwhile individuals who make mistakes.

Schools that include families in significant ways find that problems decrease and academic performance increases. This is the premise of David M. Rosenthal and Julanne Young Sawyers' report, "Building Successful

Home/School Partnerships." Teachers and families both benefit from an open exchange of information. To assist in improving collaboration, they provide excellent strategies for conducting parent-teacher conferences.

As with all areas of early childhood education, a high-quality, effective plan for guiding behavior does not arrive prepackaged for the teacher's immediate use. Guiding and disciplining are hard work, requiring careful attention to individual children and differing situations. The work is not complete until teachers examine their own sense of control and feelings about children's behavior. Anger and disrespect have no place in a positive environment. When feelings are brought out into the open and discussed calmly, teachers create an atmosphere where everyone is able to speak and act responsibly. This is the basis for a caring, helping environment for young children.

Looking Ahead: Challenge Questions

What classroom rituals or routines have you observed that create a climate of caring and affirmation?

In what ways is young children's emotional development jeopardized when they live with violence?

What is the difference between misbehavior and mistaken behavior? How is the difference reflected in a teacher's approach to classroom guidance?

Brainstorm five or six rules appropriate for a group of kindergarten children. What rewards and consequences would be powerful motivators for young children?

How can schools be more family-friendly?

Helping Children Become More Prosocial:
Ideas for Classrooms, Families, Schools, and Communities

Alice S. Honig and Donna S. Wittmer

Alice Sterling Honig, Ph.D., professor of child development at Syracuse University in Syracuse, New York, was program director for the Family Development Research Program and has authored numerous books, including Parent Involvement in Early Childhood Education *and* Playtime Learning Games for Young Children. *She directs the annual Syracuse Quality Infant/Toddler Caregiving Workshop.*

Donna Sasse Wittmer, *Ph.D., is assistant professor in early childhood education at the University of Colorado in Denver. She has had extensive experience directing, training in, and conducting research in early childhood care and education programs.*

P art 1 of this review of strategies and techniques to enhance prosocial development focused on techniques that teachers and parents can use with individual children or small groups of children (see Wittmer & Honig, Encouraging Positive Social Development in Young Children, *Young Children* 49 [5]: 4–12). Part 2 offers suggestions for involving whole classrooms, entire school systems, parents, and communities in creating classroom and home climates for kindness, cooperation, generosity, and helpfulness.

Child-sensitive, high-quality care in classrooms promotes prosocial behaviors

If you thought so, you were right. Here is more information to back you up. Peaceful play and cooperation are more likely to occur when teachers set up developmentally appropriate classrooms (Bredekamp & Rosegrant 1992). Staff competence and years of teacher experience are significant factors in ensuring such quality care. In one research study the more highly trained and stable the preschool staff were, the *lower* were teacher-rated and observed preschool aggression scores, despite children's varying histories of full-time or part-time nonparental care during infancy and toddlerhood (Park & Honig 1991). In another study 4-year-olds in a constructivist classroom, given many opportunities for choices and autonomous construction of attitudes, principles, and social problem-solving strategies, showed higher social-cognitive skills than their peers from another preschool program with whom they played board games (DeVries & Goncu 1990).

Children in strongly adult-directed preschool classrooms engage in less prosocial behavior than do children in classrooms that encourage more child-initiated learning and interactions (Huston-Stein, Friedrich-Cofer, & Susman 1977). In a longitudinal study of 19-year-olds who had attended either a highly adult-directed preschool or a program

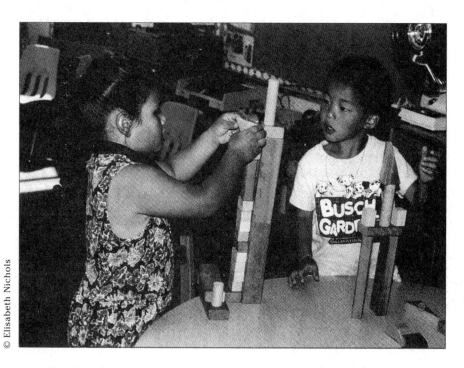

© Elisabeth Nichols

that emphasized child initiations much more, the teenagers who had been in the latter program were more socially competent and had fewer juvenile delinquency convictions (Schweinhart, Weikart, & Larner 1986).

Howes and Stewart (1987) discovered that children who experience high-quality child care and supportive parents acquire the *ability to decode and regulate emotional signals in peer play.* Social sensitivity to others' cues and needs is a good predictor of positive peer relations. Unfortunately, the researchers also found that families who are the most stressed choose the lowest quality child care arrangements, are the most likely to change arrangements, and have children with the lowest levels of competence during social play with peers. A community resource-and-referral agency may be the best source of materials and information to help families recognize and choose high-quality child care and to inform parents about NAEYC accreditation.

Emphasize cooperation rather than competition

Every experienced preschool teacher surely wants young children to be prepared to succeed in their school learning careers. Competitive classrooms result in some children becoming tense, fearing failure, and becoming less motivated to persist at challenging tasks. In a cooperative-interaction classroom, the emphasis is on children working together to accomplish mutual goals (Aronson, Bridgeman, & Geffner 1978). Even toddlers can work together in cooperative play. For example, if each grasps the opposite end of a towel and both coordinate efforts, they can keep a beach ball bouncing on the towel.

Every child has an essential and unique contribution to make

to class learning. One teaching tool has been called the "jigsaw technique" because the teacher provides each child with one piece of information about a lesson; then the children must work cooperatively with each other to learn all the material and information necessary for a complete presentation by the group (Aronson et al. 1978).

We have referred here only to a few studies emphasizing the positive outcomes of cooperative learning environments, but surely our readers have read about this in numerous books and articles in recent years!

Teach cooperative and conflict-resolution games and sports

Caregiver creativity in initiating group games and in devising conflict-resolution games promotes peace in the classroom (Kreidler 1984). New games and variations of traditional children's games and sports that encourage cooperation rather than competition facilitate prosocial interactions (Orlick 1982, 1985; Prutzman et al. 1988). When Musical Chairs is played so that each time a chair is taken away, the "leftover" child must find a lap to sit on rather than be forced out of the game, no child feels left out or a failure. Bos (1990) provides examples of such games. In Spider Swing one child sits on the lap of another, with legs hanging out the back of the swing. Bos calls games in which children play cooperatively together to create pleasure and fun "coaction." Why not try these and invent some of your own?

Of course, even more important than an occasional game is helping children live cooperatively in the classroom every day and resolve personal conflicts peaceably.

Set up classroom spaces and play materials to facilitate cooperative play

Arrangements of space and varieties of toys and learning materials affect whether children act more aggressively or cooperate more peacefully. A small, cluttered play area can lead to more tension and fights. A group seesaw, a tire-bouncer, or a nylon parachute encourage group cooperation because the children *need* each other to maximize their enjoyment.

In the research we reviewed, more prosocial responses were given by young children attending child care or nursery school programs when (1) a variety of age-appropriate materials were available and (2) space was arranged to accommodate groups of varying sizes (Holloway & Reichhart-Erickson 1988). Children who played with large hollow blocks and unit blocks in a large block area of their preschool learned and practiced positive social problem-solving skills rather than aggression (Rogers 1987). Yet, where preschoolers are crowded together in a narrow area with large blocks, there is greater pressure to use the blocks as missiles or pretend guns.

Classroom layout affects children's emotional security and sense of free choice in play. Combine your environmental design skills with your expertise in early childhood education to arrange class traffic patterns that maximize peaceful interactions. Think through the placement of clearly defined and well-supplied interest centers; provide unobstructed access to materials; give aesthetic attention to color and wall decorations; and decrease clutter. Arrange inviting spaces with soft cushions for children to nestle on when they need to calm down or rest when distressed.

Your executive space-planning skills can promote more comfortable feelings conducive to a more harmonious, cooperative classroom climate.

Use bibliotherapy: Incorporate children's literature to enhance empathy and caring in daily reading activities

A growing number of preschool and primary teachers do use bibliotherapy. If you do not, you may find this a good time to begin!

Choose children's literature for prosocial themes and characters that provide altruistic models. *Two Good Friends* (by Judy Delton) is the charming story of how two friends—Bear, who is messy but a fine cook, and Duck, who is tidy but a poor cook—care for each other lovingly and generously. Dr. Seuss's Horton the Elephant is that kind of prosocial character in the books *Horton Hears a Who* and *Horton Hatches an Egg*. So is the king's young page boy in Seuss's *The King's Stilts*. And so is *The Little Engine That Could*, as she chugs courageously up and over a very tall mountain to bring toys to boys and girls. Sucking his thumb vigorously, one little boy listened enraptured as his caregiver read the story of the brave little engine who did not want to disappoint the children. The child kept nodding his head and whispering to himself, "That was very nice of her! That was very nice of her!"

McMath (1989) suggests asking open-ended questions that help children think about and understand the motives and actions of storybook characters. When skilled adults read stories that feature altruistic characters, they promote children's ability to grasp socioemotional motivations and motivate children to imitate empathic and helpful responses (Dreikurs, Grunwald, & Pepper 1982). Many publishers, such as the Albert Whitman Company, provide children's books that adults can read to young chil-

dren to help them cope with and find adaptive solutions to disturbing personal concerns, such as living with family alcoholism, parental divorce, or domestic violence.

Actively lead group discussions on prosocial interactions

Some teachers focus on developing supportive classroom communities. Discussion of social interactions within the group is usually a central part of the curriculum in this kind of classroom.

Sharing increases among preschool children whose teachers give them explanations as to *why* sharing is important and *how* to share (Barton & Osborne 1978). Some second-grade teachers daily set aside brief classroom time to encourage children to discuss specific incidents in which they and their classmates were helpful and kind with one another. After one month, prosocial interactions increased about twofold among these children, compared with a randomly assigned group of control children (Honig & Pollack 1990).

As a teacher, you have learned a great deal about the individual interests and talents of your children. During show-and-tell circle times you can extend group discussion to increase children's awareness of *distributive justice*—how goods and benefits are distributed justly among people with varying needs, temperaments, talents, and troubles. Lively discussions can center around what is "fair" or not so fair. Children between 4 and 8 years old are busy learning rules for games and rules for social relations, and they are often concerned about fairness and who gets advantages. Yet, preschoolers are capable of realizing, for example, that at meal and snack times, rigid equality in distributing food would not be the best plan if one child habitu-

ally comes to school without breakfast and is very hungry.

Young children often protest if there is not strict equality in distributing goodies. Many a teacher or parent has heard the protest, "That's not fair. He got more than me!" Through discussions, children can move from a position of belief in strict equality in treat or toy distribution toward awareness of the concepts of *equity and benevolence*—that is, the idea that the special needs of others must be taken into account (Damon 1977).

Talk about taking turns and about *different* ways each child gets some special time or privilege, although not exactly the same as another receives. These talks can be especially helpful for preschoolers who are distressed because Mama is now nursing a new baby and seemingly gives lots more time and attention to the tiny new stranger. Caregiver kindness lies not only in providing extra nurturing for that preschooler during this difficult time but also in assisting all the children to think through issues of neediness and fairness. As you help children to learn about "turn taking" through group discussions, you increase their understanding of fairness. Although in some families it may be a new baby's turn to get special attention, such as nursing, preschoolers now get other kinds of special attention from parents, such as a story reading at bedtime or a chance to help with cooking, a household repair job, or some other special activity in which a baby cannot participate.

Encourage social interaction between normally developing children and children with special needs

Teachers must initiate specific friendship-building strategies when atypical children in an inclusive classroom exhibit low-level prosocial skills. Activities to promote classroom friendship are available (Fox 1980; Smith 1982; Edwards 1986; Wolf 1986). Children with disabilities need your inventive interventions to learn how to make a friend, use positive and assertive techniques to enter a play group, and *sustain* friendly play bouts with peers (Honig & Thompson 1994). Promotion of specific friendship skills to enhance the social integration of typical and atypical children requires well-planned teacher strategies and initiatives. Prosocial interactions of children with disabilities may need a boost. Some typical preschoolers also may need a boost in their sensitivity to others' difficulties *and* competencies (Gresham 1981; Honig & McCarron 1990).

More than other children, a child with a disability may need help from classmates and the teacher or extra time to finish a project. If you are making preparations to create an inclusive classroom that integrates atypical and typical children, then class discussions about fairness become particularly urgent. Children will need to talk about and struggle with a new idea: strict equal apportionment according to work done may not be the kindest or most prosocial decision in special cases. If a child with cerebral palsy and marked difficulties in hand coordination finishes far fewer placemats than the other children in a class project, she or he has tried just as hard as the others and should receive the same share of any "profits" from the class craft sale.

Develop class and school projects that foster altruism

With the help of a caring teacher, children can think about and decide on a class project to help others (Solomon et al. 1988). Some classes prominently label and display a jar in which they put pennies to donate to hungry children or to families in need at holiday time. When the jar is full, children count the money and compose a joint class letter to the organization to which they are contributing. Other class projects can arise from children's suggestions during group discussion times about troubles that faraway or nearby children are having. Prosocial projects include cleaning up the schoolyard, writing as pen pals to children in troubled lands, collecting toys or food for individuals in need, and making friends with older people during visits to a home for the aged.

Your perceptive knowledge about individuals in the class is especially useful when you encourage each child to generate personal ideas for sharing kindness and caring in her or his own family. As a group, the children may decide to draw their own "helping coupons." Each child creates a gift book with large, hand-drawn coupons. Every coupon promises a helpful act to a parent or family member. Some of the coupons could be "reading my baby sister a story," "setting the table," "sorting socks from the laundry basket into pairs," "sharing my toy cars with my brother," and "brushing my teeth all by myself while Papa puts the baby to bed." Young children dictate their helpful offers for you to write down and then illustrate the coupons with signs and pictures that remind them of what sharing or caring action their coupon represents. Children generously give the coupons to family members as personal gifts—promises of help.

Encourage cooperative in-classroom activities that require several children's joint productive efforts. Ideas include drawing a group mural, building a large boat or space station with blocks and Tinkertoys, planning and producing a puppet show, and sewing a yarn picture that has been outlined on both sides of burlap.

Move very young children with peers to the next age group

Toddlers adjust more positively to movement from one group to a slightly older group in center care when they move with peers. Howes (1987) found that children who stayed in the same child care center with the same peer group increased their proportion of complementary and reciprocal peer play more than did children who changed peer groups within their center. Continuity of quality child care and continuity of peer group relationships are important in the development of a child's feelings of security and social competence. Consider security needs and friendship patterns rather than rigid age criteria in moving young children to a new classroom.

Arrange regular viewing of prosocial media and videogames

Viewing prosocial videos and television programs increases children's social contacts as well as fosters smiling, praising, hugging (Coates, Pusser, & Goodman 1976), sharing, cooperating, turn taking, positive verbal/physical contact (Forge & Phemister 1987), and willingness to help puppies in need (Poulds, Rubinstein, & Leibert 1975). Regular viewing of prosocial television, particularly *Mister Rogers' Neighborhood*, has resulted in higher levels of task persistence, rule obedience, and tolerance of delayed gratification. Children from low-socioeconomic families who watched this program daily showed increased cooperative play, nurturance, and verbalization of feelings (Friedrich & Stein 1973). In contrast, children who were exposed to aggressive videogames donated less to needy children than did children who played prosocial videogames (Chambers 1987).

Invite moral mentors to visit the class

Damon (1988) urges teachers actively to recruit and involve *moral mentors* in the classroom. Invite individuals who have contributed altruistically to better the lives of others in the community to come in and talk about their lives and experiences. Children may be eager to nominate someone in their own family to tell about how they help others. Perhaps Aunt Esther visits a nursing home and livens up senior citizens' days. Perhaps Uncle Irving outfitted the family station wagon with a ramp so he can take people in wheelchairs to weekend ball games. Children learn to reframe their ideas about community helpfulness and personal generosity toward others in trouble if a special guest—a high school swimming star who volunteers as a coach for children with physical impairments, for example—comes to visit and talks about her or his experiences helping others.

Work closely with families for prosocial programming

Families need to know that prosocial interactions are an integral curriculum component of your child care program. As a practicing professional, you use your prosocial skills to support and affirm family members of each child in your classroom. And, of course, you know how your close contact with parents provides you with insight and more sensitive understanding of each child. Parents also need you to share your concern for and emphasis on prosocial classroom activities and goals. During informal greetings at the beginning of the day or at end-of-day pickup times, you may want to affirm how special each parent's role is

in promoting care and concern for others at home (Barnett et al. 1980). Yarrow and colleagues (in Pines 1979) revealed that parents who exhibit tender concern when their very young children experience fright or upset and who firmly discourage aggressive actions to solve squabbles have children who show very early signs of concern and empathy for others' troubles. These personal examples of "baby altruism" persist into elementary school (Pines 1979).

In interviews 10 years after graduation from a program that emphasized caring and prosocial development in outreach with families as well as in high-quality group care, teenagers and their families reported that they felt more family support, closeness, and appreciation than did control youth. Compared with members of the control group, the adolescents also had far lower rates of juvenile delinquency (Lally, Mangione, & Honig 1988).

Establish a parent resource lending library

Interested parents will appreciate being able to browse through prosocial articles in your child care facility. For example, make available a copy of Kobak's (1979) brief article on how she embeds caring and awareness of positive social interactions in all classroom activities, dialogues, and projects. Her concept of a *caring quotient* (CQ) classroom emphasizes the importance of children learning positive social interaction skills as well as intellectual (IQ) skills. Social problem solving by a class must take into consideration that the child whose problem is being brainstormed has to feel that the class members *care* about him or her as they explore ways to resolve a problem, such as chronic truancy or a book borrowed from a teacher and never returned.

Convince parents of the importance of a specific focus on prosocial as well as cognitive curriculum through displays of brief, easy-to-read reports of research articles. The Abecedarian program provides powerful research findings (Finkelstein 1982). Children who had attended this infant and preschool program that emphasized cognitive development were 15 times more aggressive with kindergarten peers than a control group of children who had not been in child care or who had attended community child care. A prosocial curriculum was then instituted for future waves of children in the program; the difference in aggression between program children and their peers in kindergarten subsequently disappeared, according to later evaluations.

Promote a bias-free curriculum

A bias-free curriculum promotes more prosocial interactions among children despite multicultural differences in ethnicity, language, or family background (Derman-Sparks & the A.B.C. Task Force 1989). Emphasize how all children and adults feel better and get a fairer chance when others treat them courteously and kindly. Children who feel that others are *more,* rather than less, similar to themselves behave more prosocially toward them (Feshbach 1978). During class meeting times, children discover how much alike they are—in having special family members they feel close to, in enjoying a picnic or an outing with family, in playing with friends, and in wanting to feel safe, well-loved, and cared about.

Require responsibility: Encourage children to care for younger children and classmates who need extra help

Anthropologists, studying six different cultures, noted that when children help care for younger siblings and interact with a cross-age variety of children in social groups in nonschool settings, then children feel more responsible for the welfare of the group and gain more skills in nurturing (Whiting & Whiting 1975).

Children should be given responsibility, commensurate with their abilities, to care for and help teach younger children or children who may need extra personal help in the classroom. In a long-term study of at-risk infants born on the island of Kauai, children who carried out such caring actions of *required helpfulness* were more likely 32 years later to be positively socially functioning as family members and as community citizens (Werner 1986).

Become familiar with structured curriculum packages that promote prosocial development

Complete program packages are available with materials and specific ideas as well as activities for enhancing prosocial behaviors in the classroom. Shure's (1992) daily lesson plans give step-by-step techniques for teaching how the feelings or wishes of one child may be the same or different from those of another child and how to challenge children to think of the consequences of their behaviors and to think up alternatives to inappropriate or hurtful behaviors in solving their social problems. *Communicating to Make Friends* (Fox 1980) provides 18 weeks of planned activities to promote peer acceptance. Dinkmeyer and Dinkmeyer's *Developing Understanding of Self and Others* (1982) provides puppets, activity cards, charts, and audiocassettes to promote children's awareness of others' feelings and social skills. The Abecedarian

program instituted *My Friends and Me* (Davis 1977) to promote more prosocial development.

Arrange Bessell and Palomares's (1973) Magic Circle lessons so that children, each day during a safe, nonjudgmental circle time, feel *secure enough to share* their stories, feelings, and memories about times they have had troubles with others, times when they have been helped by others, and times when they have been thoughtful and caring on behalf of others.

Commercial sources also provide some materials that directly support teacher attempts to introduce peace programs and conflict-resolution programs in their classrooms (e.g., Young People's Press, San Diego). Sunrise Books (Provo, Utah) is a commercial source of book and video materials for teachers and parents to promote positive discipline and conflict resolution. One book by Nelson (n.d.) features the use of class meetings, a technique that builds cooperation, communication, and problem solving so that classmates' mutual respect and accountability increase.

Watkins and Durant (1992) provide pre-K to second-grade teachers with specific classroom techniques for prevention of antisocial behaviors. They suggest the right times to *ignore* inappropriate behavior and specify other situations when the teacher must use *control*. Teachers are taught to look for signs that they may actually be rewarding socially inappropriate behavior by their responses. The use of subtle, nonverbal cues of dress, voice control, and body language are recommended in order to promote children's more positive behaviors.

Implement a comprehensive school-based prosocial program that emphasizes ethical teaching

John Gatto, a recipient of the

New York City Teacher of the Year award in 1990, admitted, "The children I teach are cruel to each other, they lack compassion for misfortune, they laugh at weakness, they have contempt for people whose need for help shows too plainly" (Wood 1991, 7).

Wood urges teachers to conceptualize a more ethical style of teaching that he calls " maternal teaching." He suggests that teachers develop a routine of morning meetings that involve greetings and cooperation, as in singing together. Children feel personally valued when they are greeted by name as they enter a school. Classes can create rules of courtesy for and with each other, and the rules should be prominently posted. Wood urges teachers to "figure out a way to teach recess and lunch . . . . When children come in from recess, the teacher often can spend another half hour of instructional time sorting out the hurt feelings and hurt bodies and hurt stories she wasn't even there to see or hear" (1991, 8). Children can be taught the power of "please" and "thank you." Role playing helps them become aware of how hurtful name-calling and verbal put-downs are. You, of course, are a powerful positive model of social courtesies as you listen to each child's ideas and give each a turn to talk at mealtime and grouptime. Help children feel all-school ownership. Flowers and tablecloths in school lunchrooms can be incentives for making lunchtime a friendly and positive experience.

Brown and Solomon (1983) have translated prosocial research for application throughout school systems. In the California Bay Area, they implemented a comprehensive program in several elementary schools to increase prosocial attitudes and behavior among the children and their families. In the program the following occur:

Suggested Books for Classroom Parents' Library

Bos, B. 1990. *Together we're better: Establishing a coactive learning environment.* Roseville, CA: Turn the Page Press.

Briggs, D. 1975. *Your child's self-esteem.* New York: Dolphin.

Crary, E. 1990. *Kids can cooperate: A practical guide to teaching problem solving.* Seattle, WA: Parenting Press.

Damon, W. 1988. *The moral child: Nurturing children's natural moral growth.* New York: Free Press.

Feshbach, N., & S. Feshbach. 1983. *Learning to care: Classroom activities for social and affective development.* Glenview, IL: Scott Foresman.

Finkelstein, N. 1982. Aggression: Is it stimulated by day care? *Young Children* 37 (6): 3–13.

Gordon, T. 1975. *Parent effectiveness training.* New York: Plume.

Honig, A. 1996. *Developmentally appropriate behavior guidance for infants and toddlers from birth to 3 years.* Little Rock, AR: Southern Early Childhood Association.

Kobak, D. 1970. Teaching young children to care. *Children Today* 8 (6–7): 34–35.

Orlick, T. 1985. *The second cooperative sports and games book.* New York: Pantheon.

Shure, M. 1994. *Raising a thinking child: Help your young child to resolve everyday conflicts and get along with others.* New York: Henry Holt.

Smith, C. 1993. *The peaceful classroom: 162 easy activities to teach preschoolers compassion and cooperation.* Mount Rainier, MD: Gryphon House.

Wolf, P., ed. 1986. *Connecting: Friendship in the lives of young children and their teachers.* Redmond, WA: Exchange Press.

1. Children from about age 6 onward, with adult supervision, take responsibility for caring for younger children.

2. Cooperative learning requires that children work with each other in learning teams within classes.

3. Children are involved in structured programs of helpful and useful activities, such as visiting the elderly or shut-ins, making toys for others, cleaning up or gardening in nearby parks and playgrounds.

4. Children of mixed ages engage in activities.

5. Children help with home chores on a regular basis with parental approval and cooperation.

6. Children regularly role-play situations in which they can experience feelings of being a victim *and* a helper.

7. The entire elementary school recognizes and rewards caring, helping, taking responsibility, and other prosocial behaviors, whether they occur at home or at school.

8. Children learn about prosocial adult models in films, television, and their own community. The children watch for such models in the news media and clip newspaper articles about prosocially acting persons. They also invite such models to tell their stories in class.

9. Empathy training includes children's exposure to examples of animals or children in distress, in real life or staged episodes. They hear adults comment on how to help someone in trouble, and they watch examples of helpfulness.

10. Continuity and total saturation in a school program create a climate that *communicates prosocial expectations and supports children's learning and enacting prosocial behaviors* both at home and in school.

Train older children as peer mediators

In some New York City schools and elsewhere in the United States, the Resolving Conflict Creatively Program (RCCP) trains fifth-graders as peer mediators to move to situations of social conflict, such as a playground fight, and help the participants resolve their problems. RCCP rules mandate that each child in a conflict be given a chance by the peer mediators to describe and explain the problem from her or his viewpoint and to try to agree on how to settle the problem. Peer mediators are trained in nonviolent and creative ways of dealing with social conflicts (RCCP, 163 Third Avenue # 239, New York, NY 10003).

Teachers of kindergarten and primary children may want to look into this. Think how much influence the "big kids" would have on *your* children!

Cherish the children: Create an atmosphere of affirmation through family/classroom/ community rituals

Loving rituals—such as a group greeting song that names and welcomes each child individually every morning, or leisurely and soothing backrubs given at naptime in a darkened room—establish a climate of caring in the child care classroom.

College students who scored high on an empathy scale remembered their parents as having been empathic and affectionate when the students were younger (Barnett et al. 1980). Egeland and Sroufe (1981), in a series of longitudinal research studies, reported devastating effects from the lack of early family cherishing of infants and young children. (Of course, therapists' offices and prisons are full of people who were not loved in their early years.)

A warm smile or an arm around the shoulder lets a child know he or she is valued and cared for. Encourage children to tell something special about their relationship to a particular child on that child's birthday. Write down these birthday stories in a personal book for each child. An attitude of affirmation creates an environment in which children feel safe, secure, accepted, and loved (Salkowski 1991). Special holiday celebration times, such as Thanksgiving, Abraham Lincoln's birthday, Father's Day, and Mother's Day, offer opportunities to create ritual class activities and to illustrate ceremonies and appropriate behaviors for expressing caring and thankfulness.

Teachers are bombarded with books and articles about the importance of developing positive self-esteem in each child and how to attempt to instill it. Many of these sources contain important and helpful ideas (see Honig & Wittmer 1992).

Sometimes children come into care from such stressful situations that it is hard for them to control their own sadness and anger. One teacher uses a "Magic Feather Duster" to brush off troubles and upsets from children. A preschooler arriving in child care aggravated and upset announces, "Teacher, I think you better get the Magic Feather Duster to brush off all the 'bad vibes'!" After the teacher carefully and tenderly uses her magic duster, the child sighs, relaxes, and feels ready to enter into the atmosphere of a caring and peaceful classroom. Each teacher creates her or his own magic touches to help children feel secure, calm, and cooperative.

The more cherished a child is, the less likely he or she is to bully others *or* to be rejected by other children. The more nurturing parents and caregivers are—the more positive affection and responsive, empathic care they provide—the more positively children will relate in social interactions with teachers, caring adults, and peers and in coooperating with classroom learning goals, as well.

References

Aronson, E., D. Bridgeman, & R. Geffner. 1978. Interdependent interactions and prosocial behavior. *Journal of Research and Development in Education* 12 (1): 16–27.

Aronson, E., C. Stephan, J. Sikes, N. Blaney, & M. Snapp. 1978. *The jigsaw classroom.* Beverly Hills, CA: Sage.

Barnett, M., J. Howard, L. King, & G. Dino. 1980. Empathy in young children: Relation to parents' empathy, affection, and emphasis on the feelings of others. *Developmental Psychology* 16: 243–44.

Barton, E.J., & J.G. Osborne. 1978. The development of classroom sharing by a teacher using positive practice. *Behavior Modification* 2: 231–51.

Bessell, H., & U. Palomares. 1973. *Methods in human development: Theory manual.* El Cajun, CA: Human Development Training Institute.

Bos, B. 1990. *Together we're better: Establishing a coactive learning environment.* Roseville, CA: Turn the Page Press.

Bredekamp, S., & T. Rosegrant, eds. 1992. *Reaching potentials: Appropriate curriculum and assessment for young children.* Vol. 1. Washington, DC: NAEYC.

Brown, D., & D. Solomon. 1983. A model for prosocial learning: An in-progress field study. In *The nature of prosocial development: Interdisciplinary theories and strategies,* ed. D.L. Bridgeman. New York: Academic.

Chambers, J. 1987. The effects of prosocial and aggressive videogames on children's donating and helping. *Journal of Genetic Psychology* 148: 499–505.

Coates, B., H. Pusser, & I. Goodman. 1976. The influence of "Sesame Street" and "Mr. Rogers' Neighborhood" on children's social behavior in the preschool. *Child Development* 47: 138–44.

Damon, W. 1977. *The social world of the child.* San Francisco, CA: Jossey-Bass.

Damon, W. 1988. *The moral child: Nurturing children's natural moral growth.* New York: Free Press.

Davis, D.E. 1977. *My friends and me.* Circle Pines, MN: American Guidance Service.

Derman-Sparks, L., & the A.B.C. Task Force 1989. *Anti-bias curriculum: Tools for empowering young children.* Washington, DC: NAEYC.

DeVries, R., & A. Goncu. 1990. Interpersonal relations in four-year-old dyads from constructivist and Montessori programs. In *Optimizing early child care and education,* ed. A.S. Honig, 11–28. London: Gordon & Breach.

Dinkmeyer, D., & D. Dinkmeyer, Jr. 1982. *Developing understanding of self and others (Rev. DUSO-R).* Circle Pines, MN: American Guidance Service.

Dreikurs, R., B.B. Grunwald, & F.C. Pepper. 1982. *Maintaining sanity in the classroom: Classroom management techniques.* New York: Harper & Row.

Edwards, C.P. 1986. *Social and moral development in young children: Creative approaches for the classroom.* New York: Teachers College Press.

Egeland, B., & A. Sroufe. 1981. Developmental sequelae of maltreatment in infancy. *Directions for Child Development* 11: 77–92.

Feshbach, N. 1978. Studies of empathetic behavior in children. In *Progress in experimental personality research,* Vol. 8, ed. B. Maher, 1-47. New York: Academic Press.

Finkelstein, N. 1982. Aggression: Is it stimulated by day care? *Young Children* 37 (6): 3–13.

Forge, K.L., & S. Phemister. 1987. The effect of prosocial cartoons on preschool children. *Child Study Journal* 17: 83–88.

Fox, L. 1980. *Communicating to make friends.* Rolling Hills Estates, CA: B.L. Winch.

Friedrich, L.K., & A.H. Stein. 1973. *Aggressive and prosocial television programs and the natural behavior of preschool children.* Monographs of the Society for Research in Child Development, vol. 38, issue 4, no. 151. Chicago: University of Chicago Press.

Gresham, F. 1981. Social skills training with handicapped children: A review. *Review of Educational Research* 51: 139–76.

Holloway, S.D., & M. Reichhart-Erickson. 1988. The relationship of day care quality to children's free-play behavior and social problem-solving skills. *Early Childhood Research Quarterly* 3: 39–53.

Honig, A., & P. McCarron. 1990. Prosocial behaviors of handicapped and typical peers in an integrated preschool. In *Optimizing early child care and education,* ed. A.S. Honig. London: Gordon & Breach.

Honig, A., & B. Pollack. 1990. Effects of a brief intervention program to promote prosocial behaviors in young children. *Early Education and Development* 1: 438–44.

Honig, A.S., & A. Thompson. 1994. Helping toddlers with peer entry skills. *Zero to Three* 14 (5): 15–19.

Honig, A.S., & D.S. Wittmer. 1992. *Prosocial development in children: Caring, sharing, and cooperating: A bibliographic resource guide.* New York: Garland Press.

Howes, C. 1987. Social competence with peers in young children: Developmental sequences. *Developmental Review* 7: 252–72.

Howes, C., & P. Stewart. 1987. Child's play

with adults, toys, and peers: An examination of family and child care influences. *Developmental Psychology* 23 (8): 423–30.

Huston-Stein, A., L. Friedrich-Cofer, & E. Susman. 1977. The relation of classroom structure to social behavior, imaginative play, and self-regulation of economically disadvantaged children. *Child Development* 48: 908–16.

Kobak, D. 1979. Teaching children to care. *Children Today* 8 (6/7): 34–35.

Kreidler, W. 1984. *Creative conflict resolution.* Evanston, IL: Scott Foresman.

Lally, J.R., P. Mangione, & A.S. Honig. 1988. The Syracuse University Family Development Research Program: Long range impact of an early intervention with low-income children and their families. In *Parent education as early childhood intervention: Emerging directions in theory, research, and practice,* ed. D. Powell, 79–104. Norwood, NJ: Ablex.

McMath, J. 1989. Promoting prosocial behaviors through literature. *Day Care and Early Education* 17 (1): 25–27.

Nelson, J. n.d. *Positive discipline in the classroom featuring class meetings.* Provo, UT: Sunrise.

Orlick, T. 1982. *Winning through cooperation: Competitive insanity—cooperative alternatives.* Washington, DC: Acropolis.

Orlick, T. 1985. *The second cooperative sports and games book.* New York: Pantheon Press.

Park, K., & A. Honig. 1991. Infant child care patterns and later teacher ratings of preschool behaviors. *Early Child Development and Care* 68: 80–87.

Pines, M. 1979. Good samaritans at age two? *Psychology Today* 13: 66–77.

Poulds, R., E. Rubinstein, & R. Leibert. 1975. Positive social learning. *Journal of Communication* 25 (4): 90–97.

Prutzman, P., L. Sgern, M.L. Burger, & G. Bodenhamer. 1988. *The friendly classroom for a small planet: Children's creative response to conflict program.* Philadelphia: New Society.

Rogers, D. 1987. Fostering social development through block play. *Day Care and Early Education* 14 (3): 26–29.

Salkowski, C.J. 1991. Keeping the peace: Helping children resolve conflict through a problem-solving approach. *Montessori Life* (Spring): 31–37.

Schweinhart, L.J., D.P. Weikart, & M.B. Larner. 1986. Consequences of three curriculum models through age 15. *Early Childhood Research Quarterly* 1: 15–45.

Shure, M. 1992. *I can problem solve: An interpersonal cognitive problem-solving program.* Champaign, IL: Research Press.

Smith, C.A. 1982. *Promoting the social development of young children: Strategies and activities.* Palo Alto, CA: Mayfield.

Solomon, D., M.S. Watson, K.L. Delucci, E. Schaps, & V. Battistich. 1988. Enhancing children's prosocial behavior in the classroom. *American Educational Research Journal* 25 (4): 527–54.

Watkins, K.P., & L. Durant. 1992. *Complete early childhood behavior management guide.* West Nyack, NY: Center for Applied Research in Education.

Werner, E. 1986. Resilient children. In *Annual editions: Human development,* eds. H.E. Fitzgerald & M.G. Walraven. Sluice-Dock, CT: Dushkin.

Whiting, B., & J. Whiting. 1975. *Children of six cultures: A psychocultural analysis.* Cambridge, MA: Harvard University Press.

Wittmer, D., & A. Honig. 1994. Encouraging positive social development in young children, Part 1. *Young Children* 49 (5): 4–12.

Wolf, P., ed. 1986. *Connecting: Friendship in the lives of young children and their teachers.* Redmond, WA: Exchange Press.

Wood, C. 1991. Maternal teaching: Revolution of kindness. *Holistic Education Review* (Summer): 3–10.

Encouraging Positive Social Development in Young Children

Donna Sasse Wittmer and Alice Sterling Honig

Donna Sasse Wittmer, *Ph.D., is assistant professor in early childhood education at the University of Colorado in Denver. She has had extensive experience directing, training in, and conducting research in early childhood care and education programs.*

Alice Sterling Honig, *Ph.D., professor of child development at Syracuse University in Syracuse, New York, was program director for the Family Development Research Program and has authored numerous books, including* Parent Involvement in Early Childhood Education *and* Playtime Learning Games for Young Children. *She directs the annual Syracuse Quality Infant/ Toddler Caregiving Workshop.*

Editor's note: *This two-part review presents techniques for teachers and parents, schools and communities, to promote young children's social development. Supportive research findings are often cited to back up the techniques suggested. In Part 1, suggestions refer to interpersonal interactions of caregivers with individual children or small groups of children. Techniques in Part 2 (. . . published in a subsequent issue of* Young Children) *target entire classrooms as well as broader systems, such as centers, schools, families, and communities.*

An earlier version of this article was presented at NAEYC's Annual Conference in Denver, Colorado, in November 1991. Portions of this article have been adapted from Prosocial Development in Children: Caring, Sharing, & Cooperating: A Bibliographic Resource Guide *by Alice Sterling Honig and Donna Sasse Wittmer (1992).*

A toddler, reaching for a toy, got his finger pinched in the hinge on the door of a toy shelf in his child care classroom. He cried loudly; his pacifier fell from his mouth. Another toddler, obviously distressed by the sounds of pain coming from his playmate, picked up the pacifier and held it in the crying toddler's mouth in an apparent attempt to help and comfort the injured toddler.

This example, shared by a child care provider, is one of many exciting prosocial events that have been observed in young toddlers, preschoolers, and primary-age children as they interact together in group settings. Caregivers of young children notice events such as the one above as they live and work with very young children. If adults implement curriculum that promotes interpersonal consideration and cooperation in children, we see even more of these behaviors.

Social development was seen as the core of the curriculum in nursery schools and kindergartens until a cognitive emphasis was brought into the field in the late 1960s; social development has recently been getting renewed attention by early childhood education leaders. Skilled teachers of young children implement prosocial goals for young children as they attempt to facilitate children's positive social interactions. Prosocial goals that teachers emphasize include

- showing sympathy and kindness,
- helping,
- giving,
- accepting food or toys,
- sharing,
- showing positive verbal and physical contact,
- comforting another person in distress,
- donating to others who are less fortunate,
- showing concern
- responding to bereaved peers,
- taking the perspective of another person,
- showing affection, and
- cooperating with others in play or to complete a task.

The adults in children's lives play an important role in helping children develop these prosocial attitudes and behaviors.

Not surprisingly, if caregivers and teachers take time to encourage, facilitate, and teach prosocial behaviors, children's prosocial interactions increase and aggression decreases (Honig 1982). In an interesting study, children who attended, from 3 months to kindergarten, an experimental child care program that focused on intellectual growth were rated by their kindergarten teachers as more aggressive than a control group of children who attended community child care programs during their preschool years for less amount of time (Haskins 1985). But when a prosocial curriculum entitled "My Friends and Me" was implemented, the next groups of child care graduates did not differ in aggression rates from control-group children. Emphasizing and encouraging prosocial behaviors made a difference in how children learned to interact and play with each other. A number of other intriguing research studies concerning teacher educators and curriculum intended to enhance positive social development in young children are described in our book *Prosocial Development in Children: Caring, Sharing, & Cooperating.*

© The Growth Program

Social development was seen as the core of the curriculum in nursery schools and kindergartens until a cognitive emphasis was brought into the field in the late 1960s; social development has recently been getting renewed attention by early childhood education leaders.

Focus on prosocial behaviors: Value, model, and acknowledge

Need it be said? What the adults who are important in children's lives value, model, and encourage in children influences them. What values do we value and encourage?

Value and emphasize consideration for others' needs. Children become aware at an early age of what aspects of life their special adults admire and value. Research on toddlers (Yarrow & Waxler 1976) and boys with learning disabilities (Elardo & Freund 1981) shows that when parents encourage their children to have concern for others, the children behave more prosocially.

As every experienced teacher knows, emphasizing the importance of children helping others whenever possible results in children undertaking more helping activities (Grusec, Saas-Kortsaak, & Simultis 1978). Children whose parents esteem altruism highly are more frequently considered

by peers as highly prosocial (Rutherford & Mussen 1968).

Model prosocial behaviors. "Practice what you preach," "Do as I say, not as I do," and "Monkey see, monkey do" are tried-and-true sayings that remind us that children model many behaviors that we do—and do not!—want them to imitate. Adults who model prosocial behaviors influence children's willingness to behave prosocially (Bandura 1986). A teacher who patiently tied his toddlers' shoelaces day after day observed that toddlers who saw a peer tripping over laces would bend down and try to twist their

friend's sneaker laces in an attempt to help. Bryan (1977) stresses that children imitate helping activities whether the models are living people or fictional characters. Over the years, modeling has proven more powerful than preaching. Traditionally we have called it *setting a good example.* How caregivers and parents act—kind, considerate, and compassionate, or cruel, thoughtless, and uncaring—influences young children to imitate them.

Children who frequently observe and are influenced by family members and teachers who behave prosocially will imitate those special adults. "Mama," ob-

---

If adults implement curriculum that promotes interpersonal consideration and cooperation in children, we see even more of these behaviors.

---

served 3-year-old Dana, "that was a very good job you did buckling my seat belt." How often Mama had used just such encouraging words with her preschooler!

Label and identify prosocial and antisocial behaviors. We all love it when our positive deeds are acknowledged. Notice the positive interactions, however small, that occur between children and encourage them through your comments. When adults label behaviors, such as "considerate toward peers" and "cooperative with classmates," children's dialogues and role-taking abilities increase (Vorrath 1985). Rather than just saying "That's good" or "That's nice" to a child, be specific in identifying prosocial behaviors and actions for children. Saying

"You are being helpful" or "You gave him a tissue, he really needed it to wipe his nose" will be most helpful to children.

Attribute positive social behaviors to each child. Attributing positive intentions, such as "You shared because you like to help others" or "You're the kind of person who likes to help others whenever you can," results in children donating more generously to people in need (Grusec, Kuczynski, Rushton, & Simultis 1978; Grusec & Redler 1980).

After 8-year-olds had shared their winnings from a game with "poor" children, the children who were given positive attributions (e.g., "You're the kind of person who likes to help others whenever you can"), as op-

posed to social reinforcers (just being told that it was good to share with others), were more likely to share at a later time (Grusec & Redler 1980).

Skilled teachers personalize attributions so that each child feels special. Say such things as "You are a very helpful person," "You are the kind of person who likes to stick up for a child who is being bothered," and "You really try to be a buddy to a new child in our class who is shy at first in finding a friend."

Children from punitive homes may need help understanding how to make attributions that are true rather than assuming that others have evil intentions. For example, you might ask, "Did your classmate step on your homework paper in the school-yard to be mean or to keep it from blowing away?" Focus children's thinking on attributes and intentions of others' actions as a way to prevent children from unthinkingly lashing out at others in angry response.

Notice and positively encourage prosocial behaviors, but do not overuse external rewards. In research by Rushton and Teachman (1978), social reinforcement for sharing increased sharing among young children even when the experimenter was no longer present. Goffin (1987) recommends that teachers notice when children share mutual goals, ideas, and materials, as well as when they negotiate and bargain in decision making and accomplishing goals. When caregivers and parents use external reinforcement too much, however, children's prosocial behaviors may decrease. Fabes, Fultz, Eisenberg, May-Plumlee, and Christopher (1989) reported that mothers who like using rewards may undermine their children's internalized *desire* to behave prosocially by increasing the salience of external rather than internal rewards.

Teachers have reported that offering stickers for prosocial be-

As every experienced teacher knows, emphasizing the importance of children helping others whenever possible results in children undertaking more helping activities. Children whose parents esteem altruism highly are more frequently considered by peers as highly prosocial.

haviors to one child in a classroom often backfires when other children become upset that they didn't also get stickers. A kindergarten child went home from school one day and told his grandmother, "I've got it figured out now. First you have to be bad, and then good, and then you get a sticker." Commenting on positive behaviors and attributing positive characteristics to children rather than using external rewards help young children internalize prosocial responses.

Encourage understanding of children's own and others' feelings and perspectives

Skilled teachers understand how to do these things:

Acknowledge and encourage understanding and expression of children's feelings. The ability to empathize with a peer who is experiencing sadness, anger, or distress may depend on a child having had a prior similar experience with those feelings (Barnett 1984). Children from ages 3 to 8 are becoming aware of *happy feelings* (3½ years), *fear* (3½ to 4 years), and *anger and sadness* (3 to 8 years) (Borke 1971).

Caregivers need to help children put feelings into words and to understand their feelings. Teachers can acknowledge and reflect children's feelings by making comments such as "It seems as if you are feeling so sad" or "You look like you are feeling angry. You want my attention *now*. As soon as I change

Luanne's diaper, I can read to you." This calm observation by a child care provider wiped the thunder off a toddler's face. He looked amazed that his teacher had understood his feelings. He relaxed when she reassured him with a promise to come back in a few minutes and read with him.

Facilitate perspective- and role-taking skills and understanding others' feelings. Helping young children notice and respond to the feelings of others can be quite effective in teaching them to be considerate of others. A preschool teacher kneeled to be at eye level with a child who had just socked another child during a struggle for a bike. The teacher pointed out the feelings of the other child: "He's very sad and hurt. What can you do to make him feel better?" The aggressor paused, observed the other child's face, and offered the bike to the crying child.

A child's ability to identify accurately the emotional state of another, as well as the empathic ability to experience the feelings of another, contribute to prosocial behavior. Children who are altruistic and more willing to help others display more empathy and perspective-taking skills (a cognitive measure) (Chalmers & Townsend 1990).

Feshbach (1975) reported that two training techniques that promoted understanding in children of other children's feelings were *role playing* and *maximizing the perceived similarity* between the observer and the stimulus person. The latter is what antibias education is about.

Encourage children to act out stories dramatically. Children who act out different stories become aware of how the characters feel. Switching roles gives children a different perspective on the feelings and motives of each character. Acting out roles, as in "The Three Billy Goats Gruff" or "Goldilocks and the Three Bears" gives children a chance to understand each story character's point of view (Krogh & Lamme 1983). A first- or second-grade class may want to write a letter of apology from Goldilocks to the Bear family!

Trovato (1987) created the puppets "Hattie Helper," "Carl Defender," "Robert Rescuer," "Debra Defender," "Kevin Comforter," and "Sharon Sharer" for adults to use to help young children learn prosocial behaviors with other children. Crary (1984) also promotes the use of puppets for teachers and children to use in role playing different social situations that may arise in the classroom.

Perspective taking is not enough to ensure children's development of prosocial behaviors. Children who are low in empathy but high in perspective taking may demonstrate Machiavellianism (a tendency to take advantage in a negative way of knowledge concerning another person's feelings and thoughts) (Barnett & Thompson 1985). Although Howes and Farber's (1987) research with toddlers ages 16 to 33 months of in child care showed that 93% of toddlers responded prosocially to peers who showed distress, George and Main (1979) reported that abused toddlers looked on impassively or reacted with anger when a playmate was hurt or distressed. Vulnerable children urgently need help understanding and acknowledging their range of often very strong feelings and empathizing with other people's feelings.

Helping young children notice and respond to the feelings of others can be quite effective in teaching them to be considerate of others.

***Use victim-centered discipline
and reparation: Emphasize consequences.*** Other-oriented techniques focus a child on the effects of hurtful and antisocial behaviors, such as hitting or pinching. Results of a study of how children learned altruism at home revealed that parents of the most prosocial toddlers had emphasized the negative consequences of their toddlers' aggressive acts on other children (Pines 1979). Point out the consequences of the child's behavior. Emphasize to the aggressor the results of hurtful actions upon another person. Choose statements such as "Look—that hurt him!" "He is crying" and "I cannot let you hurt another child, and I do not want anyone to make you hurt; we need to help each other feel happy and safe in this class."

Help children become assertive concerning prosocial matters. If a child has high-perspective-taking skills and is assertive, then the child is likely to be prosocial. In contrast, if a child has high-perspective-taking skills and is timid, then the child is less likely to be prosocial (Barrett & Yarrow 1977). In the book *Listen to the Children* (Zavitkovsky, Baker, Berlfein, & Almy 1986, 42), the authors shared a true story about two young girls, Dolores and Monica, who were washing their hands before lunch. Eric was waiting for his turn to wash his hands. Out of the blue, he shouted crossly into Monica's face, "You're not pretty." The author and observer reported that out of the stillness came Dolores's firm voice, "Yes, she is. She looks just right for her." Dolores was demonstrating both perspective-taking skills—knowing that Monica's feelings were hurt—and prosocial defending skills. As teachers notice and acknowledge prosocial behaviors, children's self-confidence concerning prosocial interactions will increase.

© The Growth Program

Acknowledge and encourage understanding and expression of children's feelings. Facilitate perspective- and role-taking skills and understanding others' feelings.

Encourage problem solving and planfulness for prosocial behaviors

You have heard this before, but it takes time, effort, and planfulness to *do* it.

Encourage means–ends and alternative-solution thinking in conflict situations. Help children think through, step-by-step, their reasoning about how to respond when they are having a social problem with a peer. What are the steps by which they figure out how to get from the conflict situation they are in to peaceful, friendly cooperation or a courteous live-and-let-live situation?

Shure (1992) provides daily lessons for teachers to help children discover when their feelings and wishes are the *same* or *different* from other children's, or whether *some* or *all* of the children want to play the game that *one* prefers. Teachers who use these daily lesson plans with emphasis on encouraging children to think of alternative solutions to their social conflicts and to imagine the consequences of each behavior or strategy they think of can help aggressive and shy children become more positively social within three months. Increased positive social functioning is associated with children's ability to think of more strategies rather than with the quality of the social solutions they devise (Shure & Spivak 1978).

Use Socratic questions to elicit prosocial planfulness and recognition of responsibility. When a child is misbehaving in such a way as to disturb his own or class progress, quietly ask, "How does that help you?" This technique, recommended by Fugitt (1983), can be expanded to encourage group awareness by asking the child, "How is that helping the group?" or "How is that helping your neighbor?" This strategy is designed to help children recognize and take responsibility for their own behaviors.

Show pictured scenes of altruism, and ask children to create verbal scenarios. Show children pictured scenes of children being helpful, cooperative, generous, charitable, patient, courteous, sharing, and kind. Working with a small group of children, call on each child to make up a scenario or story about the child or children in the picture. Ask, "What do you think is happening here?" Be sure to help children become aware of how the child being helped feels and how the child who has been helpful or generous will feel about herself or himself.

Provide specific behavioral training in social skills. Cartledge and Milburn (1980) recommend defining skills to be taught in behavioral terms assessing children's level of competence. Then teach the skills that are lacking, evaluate the results of teaching, and provide opportunities for children to practice and generalize the transfer of these new social skills to other situations.

McGinnis and Goldstein use structured "skillstreaming" strategies to teach prosocial skills to preschool (1990) and elementary

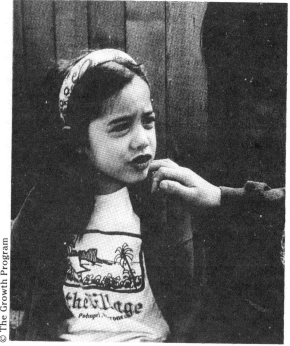

© The Growth Program

Encourage means–ends and alternative-solution thinking in conflict situations. Help children think through, step-by-step, their reasoning about how to respond when they are having a social problem with a peer. What are the steps by which they figure out how to get from the conflict situation they are in to peaceful, friendly cooperation or a courteous live-and-let-live situation?

school (1984) children. Skills such as listening, using nice talk, using brave talk, saying thank you, asking for help, greeting others, reading others, waiting one's turn, sharing, offering help, asking someone to play, and playing a game are a few of the "beginning social skills" and "friendship making skills." Other skills help children deal with feelings and provide them with alternatives to aggression. Preschool children who received training and were encouraged to (1) use politeness words, (2) listen to who is talking, (3) participate with a peer in an activity, (4) share, (5) take turns, and (6) help another person have fun were more sociable in the training classroom and at follow-up (Factor & Schilmoeller 1983).

Teaching concern for others is a familiar idea to teachers of children from infancy through 8 years!

Place a child who is experiencing social problems with a friendly, socially skilled playmate, preferably a younger one, to increase the social isolate's positive peer interactions.

Use positive discipline for promoting prosocial behaviors and less aggression

We have to educate children about socially desirable behaviors, as about many other things.

Use positive discipline strategies, such as induction and authoritative methods. When teachers use positive discipline techniques—such as reasoning, use of positive reinforcement, and empathic listening—and *authoritative* strategies (Baumrind 1977)—loving, positive commitment to the child plus use of firm, clear rules and explanations—children are more likely to behave prosocially. The more nonauthoritarian and nonpunitive the parent, the higher the child's level of reasoning (Eisenberg, Lennon, & Roth 1983). Discipline that is *emotionally intense but nonpunitive* is effective with toddlers (Yarrow & Waxler 1976).

Positive discipline: A protection against media violence. As one might guess, a relationship has been found between parents' positive discipline techniques and the effects of prosocial and antisocial television programs on children. Using Hoffman's terms to describe parenting styles, Abelman (1986) reported that parents who are most *inductive* (who use reasoning) and who rarely use love withdrawal or power assertion have children who are *most* affected by prosocial and *least* affected by antisocial television. The reverse is also true. Positive discipline, then, is a powerful buffer against the negative effects of antisocial media materials.

Respond to and provide alternatives to aggressive behaviors. This has been a basic principle of nursery and kindergarten education since their beginning. Writing much more recently, Caldwell (1977) advises caregivers not to ignore aggression or permit aggression to be expressed and assume that this venting will "discharge the tension." For example, bullying that is ignored does not disappear. Caldwell writes, "In order to control aggression, we must strengthen altruism" (1977, 9). Teach children what they can do to help others feel good.

Redirect antisocial actions to more acceptable actions. A child who is throwing a ball at someone may be redirected to throw a beanbag back and forth with another child.

Teach angry, acting-out children to *use words* to express feelings. When children are feeling aggrieved, tell them, "Use your words" instead of hurtful actions. Help children learn "I" statements to express their feelings or wishes and to express how they perceive a situation of distress or conflict (Gordon 1970). Give children words and phrases to use, such as "I feel upset when our game is interrupted," "I cannot finish my building if you take away these blocks," or "I was using that Magic Marker first. I still need it to finish my picture."

Ask children to restate classroom rules about not hitting or hurting others (Honig 1985). Preschool children, however, may interpret the rules from an egocentric viewpoint and not always understand the reasons for rules. Deanna, a preschooler, went home from school and told her mother, "Matthew pinched me." After talking about the classroom rule, "Don't pinch or hit back," Deanna's mother tried to get Deanna to problem-solve other solutions to the problem, such as telling Matthew that it hurt when he pinched. The next day, when her mom picked her up from school, Deanna reported angrily, "Matthew pinched me back." When asked why she pinched him, Deanna restated the classroom rule, "That doesn't matter; he's not supposed to pinch me back."

Offer children choices. This is another "basic" of professional work with young children. Toddlers and preschoolers struggling to assert newly emergent autonomy cooperate more easily with caregiver requests if they feel empowered to make choices. Adults can decide on the choices to be offered. For the toddler having trouble settling at naptime, the offer "Would you like to sleep with your head at this end of your cot or the other end?" may empower him enough to decide cheerfully just how he wants to lie down for naptime. Gilligan observed that "The essence of the moral decision is the exercise of choice and the willingness to accept responsibility for that choice" (1982, 58). Often adults forget that if they carefully craft choices, children may more readily cooperate in the home and in the classroom. During snacktime adults can offer a choice of "darker or lighter toast," "apple or orange juice" to the finicky eater who generally resists food simply set down without her being allowed some choice. When children want to practice throwing a small basketball into a preschooler-size net, discuss the need for a turn-taking rule and offer a choice: "Do you want to take two or three throws for your turn?" Later, comment on how the children followed the rule. Ask them how they think the rule helped their game go more peaceably.

Provide opportunities for social interactions through play—pair "social isolates" with sociable children

Place a child who is experiencing social problems with a friendly, socially skilled playmate, preferably a younger one, to increase the social isolate's positive peer interactions (Furman, Rahe, & Hartup 1978). Pair an assertive, gregarious, but gentle child (who is the recipient of many prosocial overtures and is likely to offer help and friendliness) with a very shy child.

Create good adult–child relationships

Children learn to enjoy being with other people when they experience adults who are positive, caring, loving, and responsive. When adults respond to a child in affectionate, kind, empathetic ways, the child learns how to be a communicative partner who knows how to take turns, listen, negotiate, and help others; common sense tells us that this is logical. Park and Waters (1989)

found that two children who had experienced affirmative first relationships with their mothers engaged in more harmonious, less controlling, more responsive, and happier play together than did children who had not experienced positive first relationships.

Provide body relaxation activities

Create a relaxed classroom climate to further harmonious interactions. Relaxation exercises can restore harmony when children are fussy or tense. Back rubs help. Sand play and water play promote relaxation in some children who have a difficult time acting peaceably.

Offer children choices. This is another "basic" of professional work with young children. Toddlers and preschoolers struggling to assert newly emergent autonomy cooperate more easily with caregiver requests if they feel empowered to make choices. Adults can decide on the choices to be offered.

© The Growth Program

Children may lie down on mats and wiggle each limb separately, in turn, to relax and ease body tension. Many classical music pieces, such as the Brahms *Lullaby* or Debussy's *Reverie*, can be useful in helping children imagine peaceful scenes. Focused imagery activities can reduce tensions. Have children close their eyes and imagine being in a quiet forest glade, listening to a stream flow nearby and feeling the warm sunshine on their faces.

Group movement to music adds another dimension of relaxation. Dancing partners need to tune in to each other's motions and rhythmic swaying as they hold hands or take turns imitating each other's gestures.

Use technology to promote prosocial behaviors

Unlike most of the familiar principles for promoting social development reviewed in this article, *this* idea will be new to many teachers. Videotape children who are behaving prosocially to facilitate sharing. A video camera in the classroom can help promote altruism. Third-grade children viewed videotapes of themselves and models in situations involving sharing. This technique was effective in increasing sharing immediately following training and one week later (Devoe & Sherman 1978). Maybe some teachers who like trying new things will try this idea with *younger* children.

Conclusion

As teachers focus on and facilitate prosocial behaviors, the whole ambience of a classroom may change. As teachers model kindness and respect, express appreciation for prosocial actions, promote cooperation, teach children how their behaviors affect others, point out each child's prosocial behaviors with admiration to the other children, and encourage children to help each other, prosocial deeds and attitudes will increase. Adults' interactions with young children make a powerful difference in the atmosphere and climate of the classroom.

References

Abelman, R. 1986. Children's awareness of television's prosocial fare: Parental discipline as an antecedent. *Journal of Family Issues* 7: 51–66.

Bandura, A. 1986. *The social foundation of thought and action: A social cognitive theory.* Englewood Cliffs, NJ: Prentice Hall.

Barnett, M. 1984. Similarity of experience and empathy in preschoolers. *The Journal of Genetic Psychology* 145: 241–50.

Barnett, M., & S. Thompson. 1985. The role of perspective-taking and empathy in children's Machiavellianism, prosocial behavior, and motive for helping. *The Journal of Genetic Psychology* 146: 295–305.

Barrett, D.E., & M.R. Yarrow. 1977. Prosocial behavior, social inferential ability, and assertiveness in young children. *Child Development* 48: 475–81.

Baumrind, D. 1977. Some thoughts about childrearing. In S. Cohen & T.J. Comiskey (Eds.), *Child development: Contemporary perspectives.* Itasca, IL: F.E. Peacock.

Borke, H. 1971. Interpersonal perception of young children: Egocentrism or empathy? *Developmental Psychology* 5: 263–9.

Bryan, J.H. 1977. Prosocial behavior. In H.L. Hom, Jr., & P.A. Robinson, eds. *Psychological processes in early education.* New York: Academic.

Caldwell, B. 1977. Aggression and hostility in young children. *Young Children* 32 (2): 4–14.

Cartledge, G., & J.F. Milburn, eds. 1980. *Teaching social skills to children.* New York: Pergamon.

Chalmers, J., & M. Townsend. 1990. The effects of training in social perspective taking on socially maladjusted girls. *Child Development* 61: 178–90.

Crary, E. 1984. *Kids can cooperate: A practical guide to teaching problem solving.* Seattle, WA: Parenting Press.

Devoe, M., & T. Sherman. 1978. A microtechnology for teaching prosocial behavior to children. *Child Study Journal* 8 (2): 83–92.

Eisenberg, N., R. Lennon, & K. Roth. 1983. Prosocial development: A longitudinal study. *Developmental Psychology* 19: 846–55.

Elardo, R., & J.J. Freund. 1981. Maternal childrearing styles and the social skills of learning disabled boys: A preliminary investigation. *Contemporary Educational Psychology* 6: 86–94.

Fabes, R.A., J. Fultz, N. Eisenberg, T. May-Plumlee, & F.S. Christopher. 1989. Effect of rewards on children's prosocial motivation: A socialization study. *Developmental Psychology* 25: 509–15.

Factor, D., & G.L. Schilmoeller. 1983. Social skill training of preschool children. *Child Study Journal* 13 (1): 41–56.

Feshbach, N. 1975. Empathy in children: Some theoretical and empirical considerations. *The Counseling Psychologist* 5: 25–30.

Fugitt, E. 1983. *"He hit me back first!" Creative visualization activities for parenting and teaching.* Rolling Hills Estates, CA: Jalmar.

Furman, W., D.F. Rahe, & W.W. Hartup. 1978. Rehabilitation of low-interactive preschool children through mixed-age and same-age socialization. In H. McGurk, ed., *Issues in childhood social development.* Cambridge: Methuen.

George, C., & M. Main. 1979. Social interactions of young abused children: Approach, avoidance, and aggression. *Child Development* 50: 306–18.

Gilligan, C. 1982. *In a different voice.* Cambridge, MA: Harvard University Press.

Goffin, S.G. 1987. Cooperative behaviors: They need our support. *Young Children* 42 (2): 75–81.

Gordon, T. 1970. *Parent effectiveness training.* New York: Wyden.

Grusec, J.E., & E. Redler. 1980. Attribution, reinforcement, and altruism. *Developmental Psychology* 16: 525–34.

Grusec, J., P. Saas-Kortsaak, & Z. Simultis. 1978. The role of example and moral exhortation in the training of altruism. *Child Development* 49: 920–3.

Grusec, J., J. Kuczynski, P. Rushton, & Z. Simultis. 1978. Modeling, direct instruction, and attributions: Effects on altruism. *Developmental Psychology* 14: 51–7.

Haskins, R. 1985. Public school aggression among children with varying day care experience. *Child Development* 56: 689–703.

Honig, A.S. 1982. Research in review. Prosocial development in children. *Young Children* 37 (5): 51–62.

Honig, A.S. 1985. Research in review. Compliance, control, and discipline. Part 1. *Young Children* 40 (2): 50–8.

Honig, A.S., & D.S. Wittmer. 1992. *Prosocial development in children: Caring, sharing, & cooperating: A bibliographic resource guide.* New York: Garland.

Howes, C., & J. Farber. 1987. Toddlers' responses to the distress of their peers. *Journal of Applied Developmental Psychology* 8: 441–52.

Krogh, S., & L. Lamme. 1983 (January–February). Learning to share: How literature can help. *Childhood Education* 59 (3): 188–92.

McGinnis, E., & A. Goldstein. 1984. *Skillstreaming the elementary school child: A guide to prosocial skills.* Champaign, IL: Research Press.

McGinnis, E., & A. Goldstein. 1990. *Skillstreaming in early childhood. Teaching prosocial skills to the preschool and kindergarten child.* Champaign, IL: Research Press.

Park, K., & E. Waters. 1989. Security of attachment and preschool friendships. *Child Development* 60: 1076–81.

Pines, M. 1979. Good Samaritans at age two? *Psychology Today* 13: 66–77.

Rushton, J.P., & G. Teachman. 1978. The effects of positive reinforcement, attributions, and punishment on model induced altruism in children. *Personality and Social Psychology Bulletin* 4: 322–5.

Rutherford, E., & P. Mussen. 1968. Generosity in nursery school boys. *Child Development* 39: 755–65.

Shure, M.B. 1992. *I can problem solve: An interpersonal cognitive problem-solving program.* Champaign, IL: Research Press.

Shure, M., & G. Spivack. 1978. *Problem-solving techniques in childrearing.* San Francisco: Jossey-Bass.

Trovato, C. 1987. Teaching today's kids to get along. *Early Childhood Teacher* 34: 43.

Vorrath, H. 1985. *Positive peer culture.* New York: Aldine.

Yarrow, M.R., & C.Z. Waxler. 1976. Dimensions and correlates of prosocial behavior in young children. *Child Development* 47: 118–25.

Zavitkovsky, D., K.R. Baker, J.R. Berlfein, & M. Almy. 1986. *Listen to the children.* Washington, DC: NAEYC.

Breaking the Cycle of Violence

Lorraine B. Wallach

Lorraine B. Wallach is a Distinguished Service Professor Emerita at the Erikson Institute in Chicago, Illinois.

Violence is epidemic in the United States today. The public at large and the media have finally taken notice of the brutality that has permeated our families and our communities. Of particular concern is the toll crime and violence are taking on the lives of our children (Kotlowitz (1991). In increasing numbers, children are the victims of violence both inside and outside their homes. They are the casualties of the chaos and destructiveness that have engulfed many neighborhoods.

Besides being the victims of violence, children are witnesses to the crime and brutality of the streets, and in their homes they see parents fighting and siblings being beaten. Research has shown that children suffer the consequences of witnessing violence as well as experiencing it directly (Pynoos & Eth, 1985, Tulsa World, August 4, 1994).

Perhaps the most alarming statistic is the increasing number of children who themselves engage in criminal acts. Adolescent gangs are the obvious wrongdoers in many communities, but increasingly younger children are guilty of many acts of brutality. We now have

children killing children (Illinois Criminal Justice Information Authority, 1992).

What can educators and child development professionals do to lessen the toll violence is taking on today's youngsters? Before seeking solutions, it is necessary to understand how living with violence penalizes healthy development.

The bonding of infants with care givers and the development of trust in the world are the major tasks of the early years (Erikson, 1950). These tasks are jeopardized when families live in stressful environments. When danger lurks outside and people are not safe in their own homes, families cannot provide the kind of consistent and predictable climate that is required for healthy child rearing. They do not have the emotional energy to meet the infants' needs in a warm, nurturing, and responsive manner.

At the toddler stage children are learning to walk and then to run and jump. In order to perfect these new skills they need safe space, which is found in parks, playgrounds, and community play areas. Toddlers have an inner push toward physical activity. They also have an inner push to do things their own way. This is the "no" and the "me do" stage (Brazelton, 1974). Toddlers who are confined to small, indoor quarters with

many restrictions on their activities can become difficult to manage. The combination of their drive toward physical exercise and the wish to do things their own way can cause friction with their caregivers. This interruption of the relationship between toddler and care giver is one more factor that can lead to physical punishment, and even abuse.

As children become preschoolers, their developmental goal is to reach out to people beyond their families (Erikson, 1950). They try to gain knowledge about how others live and relate to each other. They begin to know that there are different ways of doing things. When preschoolers cannot go out and there are restrictions on their activities, socialization can be jeopardized. Their understanding of the adult world is limited and children learn that outsiders are to be feared rather than trusted. Although such a lesson may be necessary in many communities, it interferes with learning how to get along with others.

School-age children must leave home to go to school, which means they must venture into the community each day. In school they are expected to gain the academic skills that will help them become capable workers, as well as the social skills that will make them effective members of society. Many children who grow up in households and communities

From *Children Today*, Vol. 23, No. 3, 1994-95. Reprinted by permission of *Children Today*, a publication of the Administration for Children and Families, U.S. Department of Health and Human Services.

beset by stress and violence have not learned the skills necessary to function well in school. They do not come prepared to learn and have difficulty meeting the demands of the school setting. If, in addition, they do not feel safe, academic and social learning are compromised. The strategies many children develop to protect themselves from fear of the outside world and from their inner tensions can include shutting out external stimuli, which interferes with learning the lessons school offers (A. Freud, 1937). Children are not open to learning to read, write, and to do arithmetic. In addition, they are not available to learn social skills and cooperative group behavior.

What can professionals do to break the cycle of violence that has overtaken us? There is no one simple answer, but those who care for and educate children on a daily basis can make a difference in the lives of those children. They can supplement what families can not, or do not, provide.

First, teachers and child care workers must be ready to deal with difficult children. They must be ready to start where the children are, and not expect them to be where the textbooks say they are (Donovan & McIntyre, 1990). If some children in third grade are reading at a first grade level, those children must be taught at that level. However, children must be approached with the expectation that they are capable of learning and the adults are there to help them. The same approach can be applied to children's behavior. If they do not have inner controls, they must be provided with firm, but benign, limits. It must be made clear, however, that children are expected to learn to control their own behavior.

The basis for all work with children who are at risk for pathological development is through relationships (Alexander, 1948). Adults must be ready to form meaningful relationships with children so that the children can alter their views of the world and of themselves. This is best done through identification with caring adults who provide models for behavior and learning, who communicate belief in the children's abilities, and who offer affection and respect. Most children get

these benefits from their families during their formative years. Those who are not so lucky have to get them later if they are to succeed in life. People who work with children are in the best position to compensate for such deficits.

This task is not an easy one because children who need extra help are the very ones who have difficulty forming meaningful relationships with adults. They have to be met more than half-way, and adults must be willing to spend the extra time and emotional energy necessary to succeed in this undertaking (Coopersmith, 1967).

In order to do this, those in responsible positions must redefine their roles. Professionals can no longer see themselves in the traditional roles of teachers,

Children who do not have adult models who express feelings in socially acceptable ways are in particular need of activities that encourage them to communicate their feelings.

social workers, nurses, or group workers. They must be ready to relate to children in a different way and on a deeper level. The first grade teacher must do more than teach children how to read and write, although those skills are essential. She must be ready to listen to the stories

children tell and to accept those stories, even when they are filled with violence and gore. In addition to teaching them the skills they need, the teacher who can accept children and their feelings will provide both a model for the children and an antidote to the hopelessness and despair offered by their communities.

Individual staff members can not do it alone. Programs must support their efforts by providing schedules that allow staff the extra time necessary to develop one-to-one relationships. Consistency of personnel must be a priority so that each child is encouraged and supported in getting close to one adult (Garbarino, Dubrow, Kostelny, Pardo, 1992).

Consistency and care are often lacking for children who live in stressful environments. Service programs can fill that gap in the children's lives by providing continuity in staff, stability in programs, and unvarying expectations. This does not mean that people and programs always have to be exactly the same. Of course, there will be changes, and there will be times when it is more important to be spontaneous than to rigidly adhere to a plan. However, it is essential for children to learn that they can count on some part of their world that will not change erratically, without warning.

Care is another ingredient that adults can give children. Children need to know that people care for them and about them (Cooperment, 1967). They need to know there are adults who are concerned enough to make efforts to help and support them. Care includes clear expectations and limits, which are most important for youngsters who live in chaos. All children need to know what is expected of them, but children who have not experienced consistency in their lives are in particular need of established rules of behavior. Even when they resist discipline, it is necessary to hold the line. If the expectations are appropriate to the children's stages of development and take into account individual differences, they provide a necessary structure. As children internalize the rules that are part of their daily lives, they begin to establish inner controls.

Discipline helps children learn what is right and what is wrong, but they need to learn constructive ways of expressing their feelings (Wallach, 1993). Children who do not have adult models who express feelings in socially acceptable ways are in particular need of activities that encourage them to communicate their feelings. They can benefit from dramatic play, a variety of art activities, and storytelling.

Play is very important for younger children. They can use stuffed animals and dolls as an outlet for their anger. If they are lonely, they can imagine that they have many friends. If they are frightened, they can pretend to be big and strong. Through play, they can transform bad experiences into scenarios with happy endings (Garbarino & Stott, 1990. Play also lets children relive the difficult times in their lives. The need to replay traumas occurs in children as well as adults (Terr, 1981). Grownups talk about traumatic events; children play them out. Sometimes they change the endings so that they are the winners and not the losers, or the transgressors and not the victims. In other words, they can pretend they are active instead of passive; they are in charge of things. Through play children can come to grips with the emotional residue of the difficulties they have experienced. Gradually, they learn to manage the anger, anxiety, and other feelings that are difficult to cope with by reenacting them time and again.

There is currently a controversy among child care and education professionals about whether or not to allow children to play with guns or to play war games. Each program has to decide for itself what is best for its children and families, and then convey that policy clearly to staff and parents. Consideration should be given to what guns and fighting mean in the community in which children live. The policy ought to spell out the difference between what staff provides for the children and what is produced by the children because of their own needs.

When programs offer guns to children, it may encourage aggressive play, and children may think aggression is sanctioned by adults. However, when children create their own aggressive games, they are seeking release of affect or are symbolically working out their own questions. If the adults who care for them accept their play while teaching them other ways of behaving, children will get the message that adults accept their feelings but do not approve of behavior that hurts others or destroys property. When there is a decision to

---

> *Those aspects of our society that breed violence must be changed, while the violence that presently exists must be restrained.*

---

restrict guns or aggressive play, alternative means for expressing hostility and anger must be provided so that children have an outlet for their emotions.

Dictating stories is an excellent way for young children to relive the difficulties in their lives and to come to grips with their feelings (Garbarino & Stott, 1990). Because the stories children invent are private and are not observed by other children, they allow great leeway for communicating the traumas they are experiencing—and they do not have negative effects on other children. If the adults who are sharing the storytelling with them accept what the children have to say, the children have an opportunity to work through their problems. Even if it makes adults uncomfortable, it is important for them to accept children's ideas and feelings. While adults may need to limit children's behavior, they should respect their feelings.

Older children can write their own stories. Putting ideas and feelings on paper offers each child the opportunity for emotional release. It also gives opportunities for children to take more objective views of what they are experiencing. It gives them a chance to stand aside and observe from the outside in. It gives them an observing ego.

Art activities can also be an outlet for children. The younger ones get a release from the sensory experience of playing with the materials. Paints, clay, crayons, sand, and water all offer ways for children to express feelings. Older children can use art materials to illustrate their stories or to spell out ideas and feelings through drawing, painting, or sculpting. What some children may find difficult to put into words may be expressed through the symbolism of their artwork (Garbarino) .

In addition to providing children with outlets for their feelings, programs can offer them social settings that are not filled with violence and hate. The social fabric of the children's group can be designed to promote cooperation, acceptance of individual differences, and non-violent ways of resolving conflicts. Starting with the youngest, children can be taught to get along with each other.

The first principle of teaching social skills is through modeling them. Adults should provide examples for the children. They have to demonstrate their acceptance of all the children, even those who cause difficulty or are aggressive with others. It does not mean letting unruly children run slipshod over everyone, but it does mean providing firm limits without being harsh or demeaning. Usually the children who have the most trouble accepting reasonable limits are the ones who suffer from poor self image. They do not value themselves, therefore they cannot value others. These children need to have their self esteem bolstered, not torn down.

Children also need to be taught the specific skills it takes to get along with one another. A recent book by Vivian Paley (1992) describes a method she used to help kindergarten children learn to function in a group without excluding anyone. The book is called *You Can't Say You Can't Play,* and describes her approach to encouraging children to learn new techniques for getting along with each other. The experiment was a great success, resulting in new social skills for both those children that excluded others and those who were excluded.

Professionals working in programs for children who are at risk have a most important task when it comes to helping parents and family members. In order to break the cycle of violence, teachers, child care workers, and social workers must give parents non-violent ways of disciplining their children. Harsh physical punishment has proven to be ineffective in helping children gain firm inner controls (Dorr, Zax, & Bonner lll, 1983). Physical abuse increases children's anger, making it harder for them to control themselves. It also provides a poor model of behavior. It has been demonstrated that violence begets violence.

Parents must be offered alternatives to physical punishment so they can provide firm controls without resorting to violence. Many parents think that beating children is the only way to make them behave. But children can be taught to behave without using violent means. !t is, of course, more difficult to set clear rules and hold to them in a consistent manner when there is no support from other families in the neighborhood. If families can get together and set standards of behavior and support each other in holding to those rules, parents will find it easier to relinquish physical punishment as their only means of discipline.But it is impossible to expect individual families or small programs to battle gangs and drug dealers alone. Curbing community violence requires a major effort on the part of every neighborhood. Programs for children and families can work together and with other community organizations, including local governmental agencies, to coordinate efforts to combat neighborhood violence.

Part of the effort to fight crime and violence on the neighborhood level must include letting politicians and policy makers know that educators and child care professionals support all attempts to reduce crime through gun control, the curbing of drugs, the restriction of gang activity, and any other means available. Policy makers must also be made aware of professional support for efforts to fight crime and violence through prevention: by providing jobs, decent housing, first rate education, and curbing discrimination.

Reducing violence in this country is going to take efforts in all directions. The cycle of violence must be broken at many points. Those aspects of our society that breed violence must be changed, while the violence that presently exists must be restrained. Children must be cared for so they do not perpetuate the cycle by growing into violent adults.

The task is a formidable one, but if crime can be reduced in one neighborhood, if one child or one family can be saved, the first battle in the war on violence will have been won.

References

Alexander, Franz (1948). Fundamentals of Psychoanalysis. New York: W.W. Norton.

American Bar Association Report finds child abuse root of major social problems. (1994, August 8). Tulsa World, p.7.

Brazelton, T. Berry (1974). Toddlers and Parents. New York: A Delta Book.

Coopersmith, Stanley (1967). The Antecedents of Self-esteem. San Francisco: W.H. Freeman Co.

Donovan, D.M., Mclntyre, D (1990). Healing the Hurt Child. New York: W.W. Norton.

Dorr, D, Zax, M., Bonner l l l, J.W. (1983). The Psychology of Discipline. New York: International University Press, Inc.

Erikson, Erik (1950). Childhood and Society. New York: W.W. Norton.

Freud, Anna (1937). The Ego and the Mechanisms of Defense. London: Hogarth Press.

Garbarino, J. & Stott, F. (eds.). (1990) What Children Can Tell Us. Chapter 8, San Francisco: Jossey-Bass Publishers.

Garbarino, J., Dubrow, N., Kostelny, K., Pardo, C. (1992) Children in Danger: Coping with the Consequences of Community Violence. San Francisco: Jossey-Bass Publishers.

Kotlowitz, A. (1991) There Are No Children Here. New York: Doubleday.

Paley, Vivian G. (1992). You Can't Say You Can't Play. Cambridge, MA: Harvard University Press.

Pynoos, R. & Eth, S. (1985). Children Traumatized by Witnessing Personal Violence: Homicide, Rape or Suicide Behavior. In S.Eth & R. Pynoos(Eds.), Posttraumatic Stress Disorder in Children (pp. 19-43). Washington, DC: Journal of American Psychiatric Press.

Terr, L. (1981). Forbidden Games: Posttraumatic Stress Disorder in Children. Journal of American Academy of Child Psychiatry, 20, 741—760.

Wallach, Lorraine B. (1993). Helping Children Cope with Violence. Young Children, 48(4), 4-11.

Additional Reading

The Friendly Classroom for a Small Planet by Priscilla Prutzman, Lee Stern, M. Leonard Burger, Gretchen Bodenhamer, New Society Publishers. A Handbook on Creative Approaches to Living and Problem Solving for Children.

Teaching Children to Care: Management in the Responsive Classroom by Ruth Sidney Charney.

Creating Conflict Resolution by William J. Kreidler. More Than 200 Activities for Keeping Peace in the Classroom.

Elementary Perspectives: Teaching Concepts of Peace and Conflict by William J. Kreidler.

Taking Positive Steps Toward Classroom Management in Preschool: Loosening Up without Letting It All Fall Apart

Cele M. McCloskey

W hen I graduated from college at the ripe old age of 21, I thought I had absorbed everything necessary to make me a dynamite classroom teacher. Classroom management was well within my command: after all, *I* was the *teacher,* *they* were the *students,* and *they* would do as *I* said because of that respected

Cele M. McCloskey is a special needs support teacher for the Community Progress Council in York, Pennsylvania. She also does educational consultant work and presents seminars. She has 20 years of experience with Head Start—18 years as a classroom teacher and two as a consultant. She says she has seen teachers transform "monsters" into "angels" by using these eight steps.

relationship. My view was distorted, and over the years the problems that I viewed as the *children's* were in fact due in part to my refusal to make necessary changes in *me.*

With 20 years of classroom experience now under my belt, I feel confident enough to offer my suggestions to others, in the hope that they will see that classroom management isn't as difficult as it seems (especially when a *positive approach* is taken). With this in mind, I would like to suggest eight steps toward a healthier environment for both preschoolers and their teachers.

1. Be committed to your role as a preschool teacher

Perhaps what I once heard is true, that "Preschool teachers are born not made." As adults, our first step toward improving the quality of our program is to make certain that we were meant to be preschool teachers. I have many friends—wonderful people, very intelligent, very talented—who cringe at the thought of 25 bouncy, verbally proficient, smiling four-year-olds tumbling through the door at 8:00 A.M. for a full day of fun. Teaching at the preschool level must be something that one almost feels destined to do; it's definitely not for everyone.

We need to be individuals that our students *want to please.* A situation that occurred about 12 years ago regularly reminds me of who and what I want to be. Ben, who had "graduated" from our program a few years earlier, was escorting his little sister Gwen into our child

care center for her big first day. As I approached them, I noted that Gwen's face was tear-stained, and that she was quietly sobbing. I asked her mother what the problem was, and received the shock of my career. "Oh," this mother responded, "Ben has been preparing her." "Preparing her for what?" I questioned. "For Mrs. M for Mean," came the matter-of-fact reply.

That was me! Good old Mrs. M, definitely in control of her classroom. That comment totally changed the teacher that I was. No longer did I want to be remembered as "Mrs. M for Mean." There had to be a better way, a way to control with love, so that children want to behave for the way it makes them feel, and for the praise they receive for doing it!

2. Remember Aretha Franklin's song about R-E-S-P-E-C-T?

In preschool, as in other areas of education, it must be a two-way street. Teachers *do* deserve respect; however, so do children. Rules must be designed so that both you and your children can

© Elisabeth Nichols

As adults, our first step toward improving the quality of our program is to make certain that we were meant to be preschool teachers. I have many friends—wonderful people, very intelligent, very talented—who cringe at the thought of 25 bouncy, verbally proficient, smiling four-year-olds tumbling through the door at 8:00 A.M. for a full day of fun. Teaching at the preschool level must be something that one almost feels destined to do; it's definitely not for everyone.

abide by them. Above all, mutual respect should prevail in all situations. When we are respected, we usually live up to the regard that another places upon us.

3. Develop a positive atmosphere in your classroom; build children up, instead of tearing them down

Noted author and teacher Haim Ginott wrote,

I have come to the frightening conclusion that I am the decisive element in the classroom. It's my personal approach that creates the climate. It's my daily mood that makes the weather. As a teacher, I possess a tremendous power to make a child's life miserable or joyous. I can be a tool of torture, or an instrument of inspiration. I can humiliate or humor, hurt or heal. In all situations, it is my response that decides whether a crisis will be escaJlated or de-escalated, and a child humanized or dehumanized. (*Teacher and Child* 1975, 13)

We need to catch our children being good, instead of relying on punitive measures when they misbehave. When I taught in the classroom, I had a technique I called the "buddy system" that worked quite well with the behaviorally challenging child. Either my coteacher or I would "buddy up" with the child from day one. We showered the child with praise throughout his/her first days. Even if we needed to start with "I love the way you're *breathing,*" we would find things to praise and compliment. After a few days, a child who had formerly been bombarded with negative attention usually warmed to the intrinsic satisfaction of praise and positive attention.

When a former student of mine was in kindergarten, he had problems with his behavior and wound up "in trouble" almost every day. It wasn't long before he had labeled himself as *bad.* When his mother asked him if there were any other children in the class who were *bad,* this child rattled off a list of four other troublesome classmates. His perceptive mother called a neighbor, whose son also attended the kindergarten class. When the neighbor asked her son who the *bad* children in his class were, he quickly listed the same five names (however, he placed my former student at the top of his list, instead of at the bottom!). What chance did that *bad* child have to be *good?* He had been labeled *bad* by his teacher and his classmates, and he had finally acknowledged it himself. He might as well have branded the word on his forehead.

Teach your children that your classroom is a place where everyone can have a positive experience. Look for the good and you'll reap the rewards of your efforts!

4. Let consistency, structure, and routine be your guides in setting up your program

Children feel secure and comforted when they have control over their lives. By choosing a routine, adding structure to it, and following it consistently, we allow our children to "settle in" and feel in control. I am not suggesting that we must be drill sergeants, ringing bells and flicking lights at precise moments. To offer a parallel, new clothes are fun, but nothing is quite as comfortable as an old pair of jeans! Try to set your routine for most times and offer some interruptions as your children show they can handle them.

Respect must be a two-way street. Teachers do deserve respect; however, so do children. Rules must be designed so that both you and your children can abide by them. Above all, mutual respect should prevail in all situations. When we are respected, we usually live up to the regard that another places upon us.

5. Mean what you say and say what you mean

As teachers, our word must be good. If we say a child may not go outside, we must be prepared to follow through with the consequence, even if it means having to keep the rest of the class inside because there is no staff person to sit with the child who is acting up.

Parents are often the most notorious abusers of this step. I was once shopping in the dead of winter and I observed a man dragging his misbehaving child through the aisles of a local department store. At one point he plopped the child down and boomed: "If you do not quit being a brat, I'm going to take you out to the car and lock you up with the snow chains in the trunk of our car!" I politely, but stupidly, marched up to the man and asked him if he would really do that. His look could've knocked me over! Needless to say, the child kept up his antics, and the snow chains probably never did come into play.

We must be do-ers, not just say-ers. It's better to say nothing, than to threaten a consequence and not follow through with it.

6. *Encourage choice*

To allow children the opportunity to make choices is to show them that you value what they think. However, learn the benefits of closed-ended versus open-ended choices. I remember the time a "whirling dynamo" child plowed through the manipulative toy area, leaving mayhem in his wake. I looked at him firmly and said, "You have just made a mess. You may not do that! What are you going to do now?" The child immediately shouted, "Wreck your school!" My question was an example of an open-ended choice! I quickly learned the benefits of closed-ended choices: "What are you going to do now— go to the block area, the art area, or play in the water tub?" By using closed-ended choice, you can allow choice yet still maintain control of the outcome.

7. *Never assume that a child knows how to do*

something or understands what you are talking about

A friend told me an amusing story about her son's teammate on a T-ball team. The five-year-old was relatively new to the game and every time he would advance to third base, he'd run off the field and over to his father. It took several practices to solve the riddle. The coaches had repeatedly instructed the new players to be sure to "run home" after they reached third base. The boy kept going to his father, since he wasn't allowed to "run home" by himself!

In preschool, we forget that our children may have never had "story time" or "circle time," or possibly never even have been expected to clean up toys. To give another example, what would you need if someone asked you to bake a batch of cookies? You would need the recipe, of course. Try

to remember to give your preschoolers the "recipes" needed to fit into your routine. Teach them how to transition, how to clean up toys, how to wash hands, and so on. Be a teacher, always.

8. *Any lesson plan or activity is worth sacrificing if it does not work*

If you find yourself using more control tactics than teaching tactics, calmly change your plans and keep it smoothly moving! Remember, we can't always predict what will be a success. Failure merely makes us wiser for the next situation.

*　　*　　*

By adopting these steps as part of the foundation of your program, it is my hope that you will have an easier time managing the children in your care. You could transform yourself from a "Mrs. M for Mean" to a "Mrs. M for Marvelous"!

The Caring Classroom's Academic Edge

Catherine C. Lewis, Eric Schaps, and Marilyn S. Watson

The Child Development Project has shown that when kids care about one another—and are motivated by important, challenging work—they're more apt to care about learning.

At Hazelwood School in Louisville, Kentucky, pairs of students are scattered around a 2nd–3rd grade classroom. Heads bent together, students brainstorm with their partners why Widower Muldie, of the book *Wagon Wheels*, left his three sons behind when he set off across the wilderness in search of a home site. Although this story of an African-American pioneer family is set in the rural America of more than 100 years ago, these inner-city students have little trouble diving into the assignment: Write a dialogue between Johnnie and Willie Muldie, ages 11 and 8, who are left in charge of their 3-year-old brother.

Teacher Laura Ecken sets the stage:

> Let's imagine that we're Johnny and Willie. It's the first night all alone without daddy. We've put little brother to bed, and we're just sitting up talking to each other.

Before students launch into their work, Ecken asks the class to discuss "ways we can help our partners." The children demonstrate remarkable forethought about how to work together: "Disagree without being mean." "If your partner says something that don't fit, then work it into another part." "Let your partner say all they want to say."

Over the next hour, students become intensely interested in figuring out what the Muldie boys might have said to each other. The teacher offers no grade or behavioral reward for this task, nor is any needed. Students are friendly, helpful, and tactful, but also determined to write the best dialogue they know how. In one partnership, John says, "We could talk about how much we miss daddy." Cynthia counters: "But daddy's only been gone for a day." After a few exchanges on this point, John and Cynthia agree to talk about "how much we're *going* to miss daddy." In another partnership, Barry makes use of a strategy suggested by a classmate in the preceding discussion: "How about if we use your idea to 'help me hunt for food' later, because right now we're talking about how the boys feel." Students seem remarkably comfortable questioning and expressing disagreement; the easy camaraderie extends to the many partnerships that cross racial and gender lines.

Fruits of Community

That children at Hazelwood School care about learning and about one another seems perfectly natural. But it didn't just happen. The school's staff has worked very hard over the past five years to create what they call "a caring community of learners"—a community whose members feel valued, personally connected to one another, and committed to everyone's growth and learning. Hazelwood's staff—and educators at other

A Salinas, California, student looks to her older "buddy" for help.

Do students view their classmates primarily as collaborators in learning, or as competitors in the quest for grades and recognition?

From *Educational Leadership*, September 1996, pp. 16-21. © 1996 by the Developmental Studies Center. Reprinted by permission.

© Blake McHugh/Developmental Studies Center

Child Development Project (CDP) schools across the country—believe that creating such a community is crucial to children's learning and citizenship. A growing body of research suggests they are right.

At schools high in "community"—measured by the degree of students' agreement with statements such as "My school is like a family" and "Students really care about each other"—students show a host of positive outcomes. These include higher educational expectations and academic performance, stronger motivation to learn, greater liking for school, less absenteeism, greater social competence, fewer conduct problems, reduced drug use and delinquency, and greater commitment to democratic values (Battistich et al., in press; Bryk and Driscoll 1988; Hom and Battistich 1995).

Our approach in the Child Development Project is to take research findings about how children learn and develop—ethically, socially, and intellectually—and translate them into a comprehensive, practical program with three facets: (1) a classroom program that concentrates on literature-based reading instruction, cooperative learning, and a problem-solving approach to discipline; (2) a school-wide program of community building and service activities; and (3) a family involvement program.

We originally developed these approaches in collaboration with teachers in California's San Ramon and Hayward school districts. We then extended them, beginning in 1991, to six additional districts nationwide (Cupertino, San Francisco, and Salinas in California; Dade County, Florida.; Jefferson County, Kentucky; and White Plains, New York). In both the original and extension sites, students in CDP schools were studied and compared with students in matched non-project schools (Solomon et al. 1992).

Everything about schooling—curriculum, teaching method, discipline, interpersonal relationships—teaches children about the human qualities that we value.

Five Principles to Practice

How exactly do Child Development Project schools become "caring communities of learners"? They adhere to five interdependent principles, striving for the following.

1. Warm, supportive, stable relationships. Do all members of a school community—students, teachers, staff, parents—know one another as people? Do students view their classmates primarily as collaborators in learning, or as competitors in the quest for grades and recognition? Teachers at our CDP schools carefully examine their approaches, asking, "What kind of human relationships are we fostering?" They recast many old activities.

For example, at one California elementary school, the competitive science fair has become a hands-on family science night that draws hundreds of parents. With awards eliminated, parents are free to focus on the pleasures of learning science with their children. A Dade County, Florida, elementary school removed the competitive costume contest from its Halloween celebration, so that children could enjoy the event without worrying about winners and losers. Other schools took the competition out of PTA membership drives, refocusing them to emphasize participation and celebration of the school's progress.

Teachers also added or redesigned many academic and nonacademic activities so that students could get to know one another and develop a feeling of unity and shared purpose as a class and school. "A big change for me is that on the first morning of school, the classroom walls are blank—no decorations, no rules," explains a teacher from California. Like many of her Child Development Project colleagues, she involves students in interviewing classmates and creating wall displays about "our class" that bring children closer together.

In the first class meetings of the year, students discuss "how we want to be treated by others," and "what kind of class we want to be." From these discussions emerge a few simple principles—"be kind," "show respect," "do

© Blake McKnight / Developmental Studies Center

Students work harder, achieve more, and attribute more importance to schoolwork in classes in which they feel liked, accepted, and respected by the teacher and fellow students.

our best"—that are remarkably similar across diverse schools.

Says one teacher,

> When you invest time up front in having the kids get to know one another, the picked-on child never has a chance to emerge. Kids find out that they share the same favorite food, hobby, or whatever; they see one another as human beings. The child who might have been the nerd in previous years never gets seen
>
> that way because classmates remember that that child's favorite food is McDonald's hamburgers, too.

2. Constructive learning. Children naturally try to make sense of the world—to figure out how magnets work or why friends help. Good teaching fosters these efforts to understand, but also hones them, helping children become ever more skillful, reflective, and self-critical in their pursuit of knowledge. How can teachers support and extend children's natural efforts to learn?

First, educators can provide a coherent curriculum, organized around important concepts, rather than a potpourri of isolated facts. Second, educators can connect the curriculum with children's own natural efforts to make sense of the world. Children should see mathematics, for example, as a powerful means for understanding the world, not as arbitrary principles that apply only within classroom walls. When children see how the ideas and skills of school help them understand and act upon the world—how they are genuinely useful—they begin to practice these academic skills throughout their home and school lives.

Third, lessons can be set up so that children must weigh new information against what they already know, work through discrepancies, and construct a new understanding. When children make discoveries, struggle to find explanations, and grapple with evidence and views that differ from their own, they are likely to reach more profound levels of understanding than they can achieve through simple rote learning. The students at Hazelwood School who wrote a dialogue between the Muldie boys were constructive learners in all these senses.

Like other books in our project's literature-based program, *Wagon Wheels* pursues important issues: What experiences have shaped the lives of diverse Americans? How have acts of principle, courage, and responsibility shaped history, and how do they shape our own daily lives? These issues are explored not just in literature and social studies, but in class meetings, problem solving, and in many other ways.

In addition, to make sense of an experience that happened long ago, Ecken's students needed to draw on both school learning and their own experiences. Would being left without parents and in charge of a younger brother feel any different in 1878 than in 1994? Finally, the task of writing a dialogue challenged students to take the perspective of the boys in the story and to reconcile their thinking with their partner's perspective.

3. An important, challenging curriculum. In an era of rapid techno-logical change, certain skills and habits are likely to remain important—thoughtful reading, self-critical reflection, clear communication, asking productive questions. But the de facto curriculum defined by commercial text-books and standardized tests often emphasizes something much less enduring—isolated subskills and piece-meal knowledge. Like Jere Brophy and Janet Alleman (1991), we believe that curriculum development must "be driven by major long-term goals, not just short-term coverage concerns." These goals should be broadly conceived to include children's devel-opment as principled, humane citizens.

Numerous critiques of the curriculum in this country argue that it sells chil-dren short by presenting material that is too simple and too easily mastered—for example, basal readers whose barren language and shallow ideas offer little reason to read. That a more challenging curriculum is more compelling to children, even so-called slow learners, is a tenet underlying some recent interventions (Hopfenberg 1993).

4. Intrinsic motivation. What kind of schooling produces eager, lifelong learners? Certainly not schooling that relies on the power of extrinsic rewards—prizes, honors, grades, and so forth. In fact, studies show that these can actually undermine children's interest in learning (Lepper and Greene 1978). Awarding prizes for creating science projects, reading books, running laps, or a host of other worthwhile ends can diminish interest in the activity itself by focusing children's

5. Attention to social and ethical dimensions of learning. Everything about schooling—curriculum, teaching method, discipline, interpersonal relationships—teaches children about the human qualities that we value. As students discuss the experiences of African-American families like the Muldies, they grow ethically and socially. This growth stems from the

promote children's responsible behavior in the long run. Teachers engage children in shaping the norms of their class and school, so that they see that these norms are not arbitrary standards set by powerful adults, but necessary standards for the well-being of everyone. Teachers also help children develop collaborative approaches to resolving conflicts, guiding them to think about the values needed for humane life in a group. Playground disputes become opportunities for students to learn about the needs and perspectives of other students, and to practice skills of nonviolent problem solving.

Faced with a competitive, skill-and-drill curriculum, educationally less-prepared children may preserve their self-esteem by reducing their efforts.

© Blake McHugh/Developmental Studies Center

Finally, teachers look at the many programs, special events, parent-supported activities, and policies of the school through the lens of social and ethical development. Do these activities help children understand the values that sustain democratic society? Do they give students many opportunities to develop and practice qualities that we want them to have as adults—responsibility, collaboration, tolerance, commitment to the common good, courage to stand up for their beliefs, and so on?

Synergy of Academic and Social Goals

It is common to think of the academic and social goals of schooling as a hydraulic—to imagine that fostering one undermines the other. But when schools attend to all five elements described above, they create environments where children care about one another and about learning.

For example, students work harder, achieve more, and attribute more importance to schoolwork in classes in which they feel liked, accepted, and respected by the teacher and fellow students. Warm, supportive relationships also enable students to risk the

attention on the reward, and by implying that the task is not inherently worthwhile (Kohn 1993). As one sage commentator quipped, "If we want children to read books, we should offer them books as a reward for eating pizzas, not pizzas for reading books."

To minimize extrinsic rewards, educators need a curriculum that is worth learning and a pedagogy that helps students see why it is worth learning. The students writing a dialogue between the Muldie boys were motivated by the task itself. *Wagon Wheels* raised issues of timeless importance, and the teacher took care to introduce the book in a way that piqued students' curiosity and helped them make personal connections to the book.

content they encounter, the experience of working with classmates, and the reflection following partner work on their difficulties and successes working with others.

Child Development Project teachers scrutinize disciplinary approaches not just for whether they help children behave in the short run, under an adult's surveillance, but whether they

To minimize extrinsic rewards, educators need a curriculum that is worth learning and a pedagogy that helps students see why it is worth learning.

new ideas and mistakes so critical to intellectual growth. It is no coincidence that, to create an environment in which students can discuss classmates' incorrect solutions to math problems, Japanese teachers spend a great deal of time building friendships among children and a feeling of classroom unity.

Schools that provide an important, challenging curriculum, and help children connect it to their own efforts to understand the world, become allies in children's quest for competence—and teachers in those schools have a head start in being seen as supportive, valued adults.

A shift away from competition, rewards, and punishments helps all students—not just the high-achievers—feel like valued members of the classroom community. Faced with a competitive, skill-and-drill curriculum, educationally less-prepared children may preserve their self-esteem by reducing their efforts. They may psychologically withdraw from the classroom or school community, leaving it powerless to influence their social, ethical, or intellectual development (Nicholls 1989).

The caring classroom is not one that avoids criticism, challenge, or mistakes. Parker J. Palmer (1983) has written:

> A learning space needs to be hospitable not to make learning painless but to make the painful things possible... things like exposing ignorance, testing tentative hypotheses, challenging false or partial information, and mutual criticism of thought. [None of these] can happen in an atmosphere where people feel threatened and judged.

Like a family, the caring classroom provides a sense of belonging that allows lively, critical discussions and risk-taking.

Countering Conventional Wisdom

We think relatively few American schools have managed to sustain a simultaneous focus on students' social, ethical, and intellectual development. What will it take to achieve this on a much broader scale? First, it will take changes in thinking; the agenda we have proposed runs counter to much

When children see how the ideas and skills of school help them understand and act upon the world—how they are genuinely useful—they begin to practice these skills throughout their home and school lives.

current conventional wisdom in education.

Such changes cannot be expected to come quickly or easily. Because adults, too, are constructive learners, they need the same five conditions that children do. School improvement hinges on a sense of community and collaboration among teachers, conditions that enable teachers to risk changing practice and to admit and learn from mistakes.

At the schools participating in the Child Development Project, teachers spend up to 30 days over three years in staff development. The schools have worked consciously to build strong personal connections among staff members. They do this through social events, shared planning and reflection, and often by meeting regularly in "learning partnerships" of two to four teachers to discuss their efforts to reshape practice. In an era of tight budgets, such time for adult learning is difficult to obtain.

Finally, we need to recognize that community and learning are interdependent and must be pursued in context. This means that it is not enough to ask whether a new science curriculum increases students' mastery of important scientific concepts; we must also ask whether it fosters their capacity to work with fellow students, their intrinsic interest in science, and their recognition that science depends upon both collaboration and honesty. This is a big picture to keep in focus. Educators who have traditionally worked in isolation from one another—specialists in subject matter, pedagogy, school climate, motivation—must help one another to keep it in perspective.

References

Battistich, V., D. Solomon, D. Kim, M. Watson, and E. Schaps. (In press). "Schools as Communities, Poverty Levels of Student Populations, and Students' Attitudes, Motives, and Performance." *American Education Research Journal.*

Brophy, J., and J. Alleman. (1991). "Activities as Instructional Tools: A Framework for Analysis and Evaluation." *Educational Researcher* 20, 4: 9–23.

Bryk, A. S., and M. E. Driscoll. (1988). *The School as Community: Theoretical Foundations, Contextual Influences, and Consequences for Students and Teachers.* Madison, Wisconsin: National Center on Effective Secondary Schools.

Hom, A., and V. Battistich. (April 1995). "Students' Sense of School Community as a Factor in Reducing Drug Use and Delinquency." Presentation to the 1995 American Educational Research Association Annual Meeting.

Hopfenberg, W. (1993). *The Accelerated Schools.* San Francisco: Jossey-Bass.

Kohn, A. (1993). *Punished by Rewards: The Trouble with Gold Stars, Incentive Plans, A's, Praise, and Other Bribes.* Boston: Houghton Mifflin.

Lepper, M. R., and D. Greene. (1978). *The Hidden Costs of Reward: New Perspectives on the Psychology of Human Motivation.* Hillsdale, N.J.: Lawrence Erlbaum Associates.

Nicholls, J. (1989). *The Competitive Ethos and Democratic Education.* Cambridge, Mass.: Harvard University Press.

Palmer, P. J. (1983). *To Know as We Are Known: A Spirituality of Education.* San Francisco: HarperCollins.

Solomon, D., M. Watson, V. Battistich, E. Schaps, and K. Delucchi. (1992). "Creating a Caring Community: A School-Based Program to Promote Children's Prosocial Development." In *Effective and Responsible Teaching: The New Synthesis,* edited by E. Oser, J. L. Patty, and A. Dick. San Francisco: Jossey-Bass.

Catherine C. Lewis is the Formative Research Director, **Eric Schaps** is President, and **Marilyn S. Watson** is Program Director, of the Developmental Studies Center, 2000 Embarcadero, Suite 305, Oakland, CA 94606-5300.

Misbehavior or
Mistaken Behavior?

Dan Gartrell

Dan Gartrell, *Ed.D., a former elementary teacher in Ohio and Head Start teacher for the Red Lake Ojibwe in northern Minnesota, is a professor in early childhood education and director of the Child Development Training Program at Bemidji State University in Minnesota and author of Delmar's* A Guidance Approach to Discipline.

A common situation in early childhood classrooms is when two children argue over use of a toy car. In this scenario two teachers handle the situation differently. **Teacher one** arrives, takes the car, and declares that because the children are not using it appropriately, they will have to find something else to do. One child sits on a chair and looks sad; the other child sticks up an index finger (wrong finger) at the teacher's back as she puts the car on the shelf (Gartrell 1994).

Teacher two arrives, gets down on the children's level and holds the car. She says, "We have a problem. Please use your words so we can solve this problem." With a bit of coaching, the two children determine that one child had the car first and the other wanted it. The teacher then helps the second child find "an almost new car that no one is using." The children play together using the two cars.

Traditional classroom discipline vs. conflict resolution and guidance

In their responses, the first teacher used traditional classroom discipline; the second used conflict resolution (Wichert 1989), an important technique in guidance. As commonly practiced, traditional discipline has failed to distinguish between nonpunitive teacher intervention and punishment (Gartrell 1987; Reynolds 1990). The effects of punishment—diminished self-esteem, loss of enjoyment of learning, negative feelings toward self and others—make its use inappropriate in the classroom setting (Bredekamp 1987).

The difference between these two approaches is that traditional discipline criticizes children—often publicly—for unacceptable behaviors, whereas guidance teaches children positive alternatives, "what they can do instead." Traditional discipline punishes children for having problems they cannot solve,

> **The difference between these two approaches is that traditional discipline criticizes children—often publicly—for unacceptable behaviors, whereas guidance teaches children positive alternatives, "what they can do instead."**

The teacher who uses guidance is not permissive; she does not let children struggle vis-a-vis boundaries that may not be there. Instead, she provides guidance and leadership so that children can interact successfully within the reasonable boundaries of the classroom community.

while guidance teaches children to solve their problems in socially acceptable ways (Gartrell 1994).

One of the joys of teaching young children, despite a continuing lack of resources in the early childhood field, is the capacity of the professional to be fully nurturing within the teaching role. The practice of guidance, the creation and maintenance of a positive learning environment for each child, supports the nurturing function. Guidance connotes activism on the teacher's part (Gartrell 1994). The teacher who uses guidance is not permissive; she does not let children struggle vis-a-vis boundaries that may not be there. Instead, she provides leadership so that children can interact successfully within the reasonable boundaries of the classroom community.

"Misbehavior" makes us think of punishing

As classroom guidance continues to displace a reliance on traditional discipline, it is important that educators reevaluate other widely used terms and practices. One such term is misbehavior. Traditionally, misbehavior implies willful wrongdoing for which a child must be disciplined (punished). The term invites moral labeling of the child. After all, what kind of children misbehave? Children who are "naughty," "rowdy," "mean," "willful," or "not nice." Although teachers who punish "misbehavior" believe they are "shaming children into being good," the result may be the opposite. Because of limited de-

velopment and experience, children tend to internalize negative labels, see themselves as they are labeled, and react accordingly (Ginott 1975).

Greenberg (1988) makes the point that informed early childhood teachers do not think in terms of good or bad children but good or bad forms of discipline. When children act out, there are more important things to do than criticize the supposed character flaws of the child or fuss about the specific method of discipline to use. The teacher needs to consider the reasons for the behavior—was it a mismatch of the child and the curriculum, for instance, or trouble in the child's life outside school?

Equally important, the teacher needs to think about how to teach the child acceptable alternatives during and after the intervention. Many teachers of young children try to follow the prescription of Ginott: address the behavior; protect the personality (1975). As long as the teacher views mistaken acts as misbehavior, however, the avoidance of punishment and labeling becomes difficult, because of the moralistic baggage that the term carries (Gartrell 1994).

Probably the roots of the term misbehavior go back to the Middle Ages and the view that children, by nature, were "wayward" and "tending toward evil" (Osborn 1980). Historically, "beating the devil" out of children for misbehavior has been an accepted teaching practice. Berger (1991) and especially deMause (1974) establish that strict discipline,

based on obedience and corporal punishment, was common in schools into the 20th century. With modern permutations, "obedience or consequences" discipline still persists in schools today—to control children's "misbehavior."

"Mistaken behavior" makes us think of guiding and educating

In European American education, a moralistic attitude about the nature of children has been common. Another viewpoint has coexisted, however, that children have worth in and of themselves and, with guidance, tend toward good (Osborn 1980). Since the middle of the last century, this more benevolent perspective has manifested itself in the work of such educators and psychologists as Froebel, Montessori, Dewey, Piaget, Purkey, Ginott, and all major modern early childhood educators (Gartrell 1994). Common in the writings of these progressives are the ideas that

• the child is in a state of development;

• the processes of learning and developing are complex;

• through methods and curriculum, educators need to accommodate the developmental and experiential circumstances of each child; and

• guiding behavior is a big part of every teacher's job.

Certainly, this is the premise of the well-known 1987 NAEYC position statement on developmentally appropriate practice.

In her article "Avoiding 'Me Against You' Discipline," Greenberg (1988) frames the issue of

Children's behavior poses higher emotional stakes for the teacher than most other teaching situations (Gartrell 1994). Matters of potential harm, disruption, and loss of control (by the adult as well as the child) are involved. This urgency factor makes accepting of the concept of mistaken behavior difficult for some teachers. The issue of intentionality also poses questions about the concept. If a child does something on purpose, is it still a mistaken behavior? The remainder of this article examines the concept of mistaken behavior.

Origins of the term "mistaken behavior"

Over the past 30 years, Rudolf Dreikurs (1968; Dreikurs, Grunwald, & Pepper 1982) has added much to our thinking about behavior management. Dreikurs's ideas, with which many readers are probably familiar, have been stepping stones to the concept "mistaken behavior." Dreikurs postulated that all behavior is

teacher–child relations from the developmental perspective:

Some adults see each individual child as being at this moment "good" and at that moment "bad." It all adds up to a view of a child as, overall, either a "good child" or a "bad child": She's a good girl; he's a hateful child, a really naughty boy.

Other adults, and certainly those of us well educated in child development, think differently about children. We consider all infants, toddlers, and young children *potentially* good people, naive little people with a very small amount of experience on Earth, who have much to learn, and *a great deal of motivation to please, to be accepted, to be approved, to be loved, to be cared for.* We see young children as generally receptive to guidance and usually eager to "do it right." (24–25)

as mistaken, the teacher is freed from the impediment of moral judgment about the child and empowered instead to meditate, problem-solve, and guide.

In the cognitive domain, a child who asks, "Is him going, too, teacher?" is not treated as

---

In the process of learning the complex life skills of cooperation, conflict resolution, and acceptable expression of strong feelings, children, like all of us, make mistakes. Guiding behavior is a big part of every teacher's job.

In the process of learning the complex life skills of cooperation, conflict resolution, and acceptable expression of strong feelings, children, like all of us, *make mistakes* (Gartrell 1987). The guidance tradition in early childhood education suggests that teachers who traditionally have considered problems in the classroom as misbehaviors think of them instead as mistaken behaviors (MnAEYC 1991). By considering behaviors

though she has misbehaved. In an affirming manner, the teacher models the conventional usage, "Yes, Carlita, he is going, too." In the realm of behavior, the teacher also uses a positive approach. Children are not punished for the mistakes of words or deeds; they are helped to learn from their mistaken behavior. The concept of mistaken behavior fits well with the guidance approach.

purposeful, and the purpose of behavior is to achieve social acceptance. Dreikurs derived four goals of misbehavior: attention getting, power seeking, revenge seeking, and displaying inadequacy (1968). Usually pursued by the child in order, the four goals represent inappropriate ways of seeking social acceptance. **Dreikurs's landmark contribution was that he suggested nonmoralizing intervention** strategies, such as "logical consequences," to correct children's behavior (1968). He spoke of the importance of democratic leadership in the classroom—the need for teachers to earn, rather than try to force, respect (Dreikurs 1968). For educators and parents alike, Dreikurs has done much to raise the discussion of behavior above the level of moralization.

As important as his contributions are, Dreikurs wrote before recent findings surfaced about child development. As well, his views differ, in part, from those of the "self" psychologists of the 1960s and 1970s—Maslow, Rogers, Combs, Purkey, etc. (Gartrell 1994). For Dreikurs, social acceptance was the primary motivation in children's behavior. In contrast, both developmental and self psychologists see social acceptance as a foundation for full, balanced personal development rather than as an end in itself.

The concept of mistaken behavior draws from Dreikurs's nonmoralizing approach but draws more directly from the developmental and self psychologists. The concept of *mistaken* behavior, rather than misbehavior is an extension of the work of Steven Harlow (1975). Harlow integrated the thinking of Piaget, Erikson, Holt, and Riesman in his construct of *relational patterns.* Harlow explains,

By relational patterns, I mean ways in which children relate to situations, persons, and things in the school environment. (1975, 28)

Harlow writes about three levels of relational patterns, "which differ in their openness to experi-

If a child does something on purpose, is it still a mistaken behavior?

ence, maturity, and their capacity to operate freely" (1975, 28). The three levels are **survival, adjustment, and encountering.** Children may show different relational patterns in different situations. Harlow cautions against using such behavioral constructs in order to label; instead, the purpose is to help children progress in their personal and social development.

Three levels of mistaken behavior

From almost 30 years of teaching and observing in early childhood classrooms, I have identified three levels of mistaken behavior, based on Harlow's writings (Gartrell 1987, 1994). As Figure 1 illustrates, the levels of mistaken behavior share motivational sources with the relational patterns. The levels of mistaken behavior identify the types of problems children in the various relational patterns are likely to experience.

Level three: Strong-needs mistaken behavior

Children showing the survival relational pattern likely have experienced their environment as a "dangerous and painful place" over which they have little control (Harlow 1975). The behavior patterns of these children tend

to be rigid and exaggerated. To protect themselves, they resist change and continue the same behaviors in new situations, even if their patterns are extreme and inappropriate.

The child at the survival level is difficult for teachers to accept because of the nonsocial, at times antisocial, character of the child's behavior. Yet it is necessary for the teacher to establish a productive relationship, built on trust, in order to empower the child to progress to a higher relational level.

Children at the survival relational pattern show *level-three, strong-needs mistaken behavior.* Wherever it occurs, this level of mistaken behavior is the most serious. A sure sign that the mistaken behavior is at level three is that it continues over time. (Anyone, including teachers, can have an occasional "level three" day.) As Harlow suggests, strong-needs mistaken behavior results from psychological and/or physical pain in the child's life that is beyond the child's ability to cope with and understand. Often children show strong-needs mistaken behavior in the classroom because it is a safe haven in their environment. Through withdrawal or acting out, these children are asking for help in the only way they can (Gartrell 1994).

As the most serious level of mistaken behavior, the teacher takes a comprehensive approach with the child that usually involves other adults, especially parents or caregivers. The teacher

- intervenes nonpunitively;
- works to build a positive relationship with the child;

Children's behavior poses higher emotional stakes for the teacher than most other teaching situations. Matters of potential harm, disruption, and loss of control (by the adult as well as the child) are involved.

147

• seeks more information through observation;

• seeks more information through conversation with the child, other adults who work with the child, and parents or caregivers;

• creates a coordinated "individual guidance plan" in consultation with the other adults; and

• implements, reviews, and modifies the plan as necessary. (Gartrell 1994)

Sometimes level-three mistaken behaviors are symptoms of such deep problems in the child's life that the comprehensive guidance approach is not completely successful. Even when working with parents, the teacher cannot necessarily change life circumstances for a child, but he can make life easier—in ways that may have lasting beneficial effects.

Level two: Socially influenced mistaken behavior

Children who show the adjustment relational pattern have an increased ability to adapt to situations. Their criteria for doing so, however, is the judgment of significant others. "New ways of thinking and behaving are first sanctioned by an individual or reference group representing authority, before they are considered by the adjuster" (Harlow 1975, 30). Children at the adjustment level seek high levels of teacher approval, put off completing tasks because "I can't do it right," and may involve adults or other children in doing their projects for them. They lack the self-esteem and individual strength necessary to respond to a situation on its own terms.

Some teachers find gratification in the obedience and dependence of a child at the adjustment level. They may be reinforcing long-term, other-directed response tendencies in the child, however, that inhibit full personal development (Har-

---

Motivational source	*Relational pattern*	*Level of mistaken behavior*
Desire to explore the environment and engage in relationships	Encountering	One: Experimentation
Desire to please and identify with significant others	Adjustment	Two: Socially influenced
Inability to cope with problems resulting from health conditions or the school or home environment	Survival	Three: Strong needs

Figure 1. **Common Sources of Motivation, Relational Patterns, and Levels of Mistaken Behavior**

Courtesy of Delmar Publishers Inc. (Gartrell 1994, 38).

---

low 1975). Deprived of confidence in his own values and judgment, the child may continue to be influenced by others—especially peers—including toward self-destructive or oppressive mistaken behaviors (Gartrell 1994). With a child at the adjustment level, the task of the teacher is to nudge him toward autonomy (the encountering relational pattern) by helping him build self-esteem and proactive social skills (Harlow 1975).

Children showing the adjustment relational pattern are subject to *level-two, socially influenced mistaken behavior.* Level-two mistaken behaviors are "learned behaviors," reinforced in the child, intentionally or unintentionally, by other people important in the child's life. A child who uses an expletive in a classroom exactly as an adult would is showing a socially influenced mistaken behavior. Likewise, children who join others in calling a child "poopy butt" or "dorky" have been influenced by peers into a level-two mistaken behavior.

In responding to level-two mistaken behaviors, the teacher notes whether one child or a group of children are involved. When a group of children are involved, an effective technique, even with preschoolers (Hendrick 1992), is the class meeting.

Respecting the dignity of all concerned, the teacher points out the problem and, with the children, works out a solution. The teacher monitors progress and calls additional meetings, if necessary. If one child is involved, the teacher handles the situation privately; in a firm but friendly manner, explains what is unacceptable; and provides a guideline for an acceptable alternative. In either individual or group situations, the teacher follows up with encouragement and "compliment sandwiches"—two or three acknowledgments of progress along with one reminder of the agreed-to guideline (Gartrell 1994) (it is easier for us to change behaviors when others acknowledge our efforts).

By assisting children to learn alternatives to socially influenced mistaken behavior, the teacher helps them to understand that they have the capacity to evaluate, choose, and interact for themselves—essential life skills for a democracy (Wittmer & Honig 1994).

Level one: Experimentation mistaken behavior

Harlow's construct of relational patterns is built around the importance of autonomy—Piaget's term for the ability of the individual to make intelligent, ethical decisions

(Kamii 1984). Autonomy is the social relation pattern shown by children at the highest level, *encountering* (Harlow 1975).

Children at the encountering level are learning most effectively about themselves and the world; yet, because they are so open to new experience and because they are young, they are susceptible to mistaken behavior—and vulnerable to teacher criticism. About children at the encountering level, Harlow states,

In contrast with the adjustor and survivor, the encounterer is less concerned with security and certainty and much more occupied with what Erikson referred to as the inner mechanism that permits the individual to turn "passive into active" and to maintain and regain in this world of contending forces an individual sense of centrality, of wholeness, and of initiative. (1975, 30–31)

Children at the encountering relational pattern show *level-one, experimentation mistaken behavior.* The term *experimentation* is used because the child is learning through full engagement in the experiment of life. To cite previous illustrations, the two children who argued over use of a toy car were totally involved in that situation; they were demonstrating level-one mistaken behavior. Interestingly, perhaps in progressing from level three, the child who swore rather then hit also was showing level-one mistaken behavior. The experimentation can be "natural," through full involvement in the affairs of the classroom, or it can be "controlled," as in the case of a young child who, with a smile, uses an expletive in order to see the teacher's reaction.

The teacher responds in different ways to different situations. Sometimes he may step back and allow a child to learn from the experience; other times, he will reiterate a guideline and, in a friendly tone, teach a more appropriate alternative behavior. With children at level one, as with those at two and three, the teacher uses guidance and avoids the use of traditional discipline.

Understanding mistaken behaviors

An occasional misunderstanding about mistaken behavior is that some mistaken behaviors occur at only level one, others at level two, and still others at level three (Gartrell 1994). At each level, mistaken behaviors have distinct motivational sources. Behaviors that appear similar can be a result of differing motivations, and so be at different levels. The teacher must observe carefully to infer the motivation and the level of mistaken behavior in order to respond effectively. Figure 2 illustrates how similar mistaken behaviors can be at different levels.

At any relational level, the cause of mistaken behavior is insufficient understanding about how to act maturely in the complex situations of life. With a child's internal need to go forward and to learn—but limited ability to balance her own needs with those of others—mistaken behavior will occur. Knowledge of the relational patterns and the levels of mistaken behavior assists the teacher to understand and work with children when they make mistakes (Gartrell 1994).

The issue of intentionality

When people think about behavior, they may associate mistaken behavior with "accidents" and misbehavior with acts "done on purpose" (Gartrell 1994). Mistaken behavior includes both accidents and intentional behaviors. A young child on a trike who runs over the toe of another child by accident has shown level-one mistaken behavior. The accident was unintentional but was level one because it was a mistake that arose from involvement.

A child may run over another's foot for a second reason related to level one (Gartrell 1994). As a part of encountering social relations, the trike rider hits the other's foot "accidentally on purpose" to see what will happen. The lack of development of young children results in their difficulty understanding how another child would feel under such circumstances. The act was intentional but was done without full awareness of the consequences and so is level-one mistaken behavior. The importance of the term *mistaken behavior* is that it reminds the adult that the trike rider needs guidance about human feelings and the consequences of actions, not punishment for making a mistake.

Of course, hitting another child's foot might also be a level-two or level-three mistaken behavior (Gartrell 1994). At level two, one child follows another on a trike. The second rider sees the first swing close to a bystander and follows suit but strikes the bystander's foot. At level three, a trike rider who is harboring feelings of hostility acts out against an innocent child. When the teacher hypothesizes that level two or level three is involved, she reacts with increasing degrees of firmness, although she retains the element of friendliness, which is at the heart of guidance. If the trike rider's motives indicate that strong-needs mistaken behavior is present, the teacher should follow up as suggested for level three. The additional step is important because serious mistaken behaviors occur when children are the victims of life circumstances that are beyond their control. Even the mistaken behavior of aggression is a nonverbal request for assistance, not a situation requiring punishment.

It should be noted that whatever the level of mistaken behavior, the teacher reacts to the immediate situation by using guidance. She first gives attention to the victim, who deserves it. This action shows support for the wronged child (and also may help the teacher calm down). The teacher then speaks with the trike rider. She does some empathy building by pointing out that the trike hurt the other child and she cannot let anyone (including the trike rider) be hurt at school. She discusses with the trike rider how he could avoid having this problem next time. Although the teacher does not force an apology, she perhaps asks how the trike rider could help the child who was hurt feel better. The teacher then assists the trike rider back into positive activity, which often includes helping him to make amends. In guidance practice the teacher avoids the traditional discipline reaction. She does not lecture about how naughty the behavior was or automatically put the child in a time-out. The goal is to help the child learn from the mistake, not punish him for making it.

Again, the value of the term *mistaken behavior* is that it has different implications than the conventional term, *misbehavior*. Misbehavior tends to connote a judgment of character that leads to punishment rather than guidance. Mistaken behavior precludes character assessment and asks that the child be accepted as a person of worth (by virtue of being alive). The person may need to face consequences, but at the base of those consequences is guidance, so the possibility of change is maximized (Gartrell 1994).

A premise in the use of guidance is that even willful acts that are done "on purpose" still constitute mistaken behavior. A child who deliberately bites or intentionally

Figure 2. Classifying Similar Mistaken Behaviors by Level

Incident of mistaken behavior	Motivational source	Level of mistaken behavior
Child uses expletive	Wants to see the teacher's reaction	One
	Wants to emulate important others	Two
	Expresses deeply felt hostility	Three
Child pushes another off the trike	Wants trike; has not learned to ask in words	One
	Follows aggrandizement practices modeled by other children	Two
	Feels the need to act out against the world by asserting power	Three
Child refuses to join in group activity	Does not understand teacher's expectations	One
	Has "gotten away" with not joining in	Two
	Is not feeling well or feels strong anxiety about participating	Three

Courtesy of Delmar Publishers Inc. (Gartrell 1994, 49).

disobeys has made a mistake. The adult who is able to approach children as worthwhile individuals who make mistakes is in a philosophically strong position to assist them with healthy personal and social development.

References

Berger, S.K. 1991. *The developing person through childhood and adolescence.* New York: Worth.

Bredekamp, S., ed. 1987. *Developmentally appropriate practice in early childhood programs serving children from birth through age 8.* Exp. ed. Washington, DC: NAEYC.

deMause, L., ed. 1974. *The history of childhood.* New York: Peter Benrick Books.

Dreikurs, R. 1968. *Psychology in the classroom.* 2nd ed. New York: Harper and Row.

Dreikurs, R., B. Grunwald, & F. Pepper. 1982. *Maintaining sanity in the classroom.* New York: Harper and Brothers.

Gartrell, D.J. 1987. More thoughts... Punishment or guidance? *Young Children* 42 (3): 55–61.

Gartrell, D.J. 1994. *A guidance approach to discipline.* Albany: Delmar.

Ginott, H.G. 1975. *Teacher and child.* New York: Avon Books.

Greenberg, P. 1988. Ideas that work with young children. Avoiding "me against you" discipline. *Young Children* 44 (1): 24–29.

Harlow, S.D. 1975. *Special education: The meeting of differences.* Grand Forks, ND: University of North Dakota.

Hendrick, J. 1992. Where does it all begin? Teaching the principles of democracy in the early years. *Young Children* 47 (3): 51–53.

Kamii, C. 1984. Autonomy: The aim of education envisioned by Piaget. *Phi Delta Kappan* 65(6): 410–15.

Minnesota Association for the Education of Young Children (MnAEYC). 1991. *Developmentally appropriate guidance of children birth to eight.* Rev. ed. St. Paul: Author.

Osborn, D.K. 1980. *Early childhood education in historical perspective.* Athens, GA: Education Associates.

Reynolds, E. 1990. *Guiding young children: A child-centered approach.* Mountain View, CA: Mayfield.

Wichert, S. 1989. *Keeping the peace: Practicing cooperation and conflict resolution with preschoolers.* Philadelphia, PA: New Society.

Wittmer, D.S., & A.S. Honig. 1994. Encouraging positive social development in young children. *Young Children* 49 (5): 61–75.

Building Successful Home/School Partnerships

Strategies for Parent Support and Involvement

David M. Rosenthal and
Julanne Young Sawyers

*David M. Rosenthal is Associate Professor, Department of Family Practice, and
Director, Family Stress Clinic, and Julanne Young Sawyers is a doctoral student,
Division of Counselor Education, College of Education, The University of Iowa, Iowa City.*

Over the last two generations, the delineation of "informal" and "formal" education has become a boundary between family and school. As a society, we believe a world of difference exists between teaching a child to hold a spoon and teaching that same child to hold a pencil. With the acceptance of this boundary, we have created two separate, sometimes adversarial, worlds— home and school—and have populated them with separate, sometimes adversarial, adults— parents and teachers. Children must live in both worlds, moving back and forth at the beginning and end of each school day. While both parents and teachers strive toward a goal of well-educated and well-loved children, various problems appear to hinder achievement of this goal.

Many individuals in both the popular press (Dodge, 1991; Foster, 1994; Rubenstein, 1988; Shea, 1993; Singal, 1991; Vogel, 1994) and academic publications (Edelman, 1992; Kozol, 1991; O'Callaghan, 1993) have addressed the conditions in America's public schools and the seeming inability of these institutions to educate many children. Teachers claim that a whole variety of social problems prevent them from teaching. Many children come to school undernourished, in poor physical health and with their basic needs for safety and security unmet. Some children may come to school under the influence of drugs or alcohol and / or may be armed. These conditions undoubtedly make learning in school difficult, if not impossible, for children. Children must feel safe before they will be able to learn (Garbarino, Kostelny & Dubrow, 1991). On the other hand, many parents claim that teachers are failing to teach their children critical academic skills and values, and schools have become places where children can easily find drugs, alcohol and weapons. Thus, some parents perceive school to be an introduction to trouble rather than a way to stay out of it.

Data currently indicate that fewer than 70 percent of the young people in the United States will graduate from high school; minority children have even lower graduation rates (Garbarino, Dubrow, Kostelny & Pardo, 1992). Furthermore, according to Kozol (1991), many children who *do* graduate may not be reading at an 8th-grade level. While the reasons for such outcomes are varied, and, in fact, difficult to pin down, it is certain that parents and teachers, working separately, will not be able to solve the problems.

Teamwork and collaboration are more likely to achieve positive results than when school systems and families work alone. The teacher bears the responsibility for developing and fostering this collaboration (Rotter, Robinson & Fey, 1987). Recognizing the classroom as the accepted site of a child's education and the home as the site of a child's nurturance, support and socialization (Lightfoot, 1978), classroom teachers can use several strategies to enlist parents' collaboration.

Effective schools share a number of basic features: strong leadership, an emphasis on academics, ongoing evaluation, a safe school climate and positive teacher-pupil relationships (Garbarino, Dubrow,

From *Childhood Education*, Summer 1996, pp. 194-200. © 1996 by the Association for Childhood Education International, 11501 Georgia Avenue, Suite 315, Wheaton, MD. Reprinted by permission.

Kostelny & Pardo, 1992). In addition, a high level of parental involvement appears to have a direct impact on student achievement (Henderson, 1987; Marcon, 1993; Rotter, Robinson & Fey, 1987; Seldin, 1991). Teachers recently named greater parental involvement as their number one priority for improving education (Chira, 1993). Thus, in light of research findings showing the benefits of parental involvement *and* teacher support for such involvement, an obvious solution to some of the problems becomes apparent. Before a truly effective parental involvement program can be implemented, administrators must understand the nature of change within a system (in this case, a school) and the roles and culture within the school. Then, the interface of the home and school systems and strategies teachers can use when dealing with family and classroom situations can be discussed.

Change

The structure of many organizations makes it difficult to implement change. Long-standing rules must be followed, and resistance to change is inherent to many of the rules. Often, organizations respond to requests for change by only appearing to do something different, while the same basic rules or methods are still used. This is called "first order change" (Watzlawick, Weakland & Fisch, 1974). Real, or "second order," change requires alteration of the rules or methods of doing things (the structure).

Consider the school principal who wishes to increase the number of parents attending school functions and so asks the teachers to send out an invitation and two reminder notes, rather than just an invitation alone. If the turnout remains poor, the principal may conclude that the parents are just apathetic and continue to rely on the same strategy. The reminder notes, while a deviation from previous actions, are merely elements of first order change. If, however, the principal changed the function from the usual weekday evening to a Saturday morning, provided child care and encouraged a buddy system in which each parent brings another parent, attendance might increase. These actions constitute second order change because the structure of the activity has changed. Such second order change required the principal to cease viewing parents as having many faults, and instead to recognize parents' strengths that can be tapped simply by being flexible with rules and methods.

Roles and Culture Within a School

Schools and families have many structural similarities (Fisher, 1986). Both have different individuals performing complementary behaviors defined by their roles within the system. A degree of flexibility in those roles and behaviors marks well-functioning systems. Flexibility allows individuals to perform tasks according to their strengths rather than simply according to the role they occupy. The roles in school, however, often do not appear to be negotiable. Parents' roles in school settings are rarely discussed, making their responsibilities unclear and making it likely that they will only be called upon when their child is having a problem.

A school culture built on the idea of collaboration leaves teachers free to discuss parents' interests and responsibilities for participation and to incorporate them into the classroom without feeling threatened by their presence. This strategy allows parents to define their participation and involves them in determining the boundaries between home and school, rather than being told where that boundary ought to be. Moving toward a system that encourages inclusion, participation and collaboration is the ultimate goal.

Strategies for Improving the Home-School Relationship

Building upon Strengths. Reframing is a strategy that family therapists use to shift from a deficit perspective, in which faults are highlighted, to one that recognizes strengths. In order to reframe something, one must consider what useful purpose a seemingly negative behavior might serve and then shift to that frame of reference. For too long, many professionals have taken a custodial view toward families they perceived to be dysfunctional. As a result of this deficit model perspective, professionals often believed that parents were incapable of being allies and simply needed to be tolerated and avoided. Educators, without ever meeting many parents, would often blame them for their children's difficulties. Whatever level of

*M*oving toward a system that encourages inclusion, participation and collaboration is the ultimate goal.

truth lies in that assessment, it makes it difficult, if not impossible, to develop a positive bond between family and educator. It would be much more helpful to "think of parents as professional child-rearers with considerable on-the-job experience" (Hayes, 1987).

Reframing behaviors that have been negatively labeled in the past can also promote collaboration. When attending a teacher's conference, I once heard a parent describe their child as being very active and often out of control. The wise teacher looked at the parents and said that the child was "spirited"—giving the parents a new label they found acceptable and helpful. After all, what parent would ever want to break a child's spirit? While the child's behaviors did not change dramatically, the parents now looked upon their child in a new way and worked to channel that spirit rather than quell it.

By digging a little deeper beneath the surface, one can view multi-problem families as also being multi-resource (Walker 1991). These families often have support from extended family and almost always are strongly motivated to help their children succeed. Walker suggests that many of these multi-resource families are better able to deal with a crisis since they live in an often chaotic world in which their resources are constantly challenged. When professionals recognize all that these families have been able to conquer, rather than focusing on what they have failed at, they will find it easier to appreciate the families' strengths.

Making Schools Family-Friendly. Families sometimes bring their own unique concerns into the schools. These concerns can, and should, be acknowledged in a helpful manner, as long as the child's school issues remain the focus. "The child is the family-school connection. It is he or she who must traverse the worlds of home and school each day and it is he or she who brings the worlds in juxtaposition" (Eno, 1985, p. 161). Any program developed to enhance home-school collaboration must improve students' classroom achievement. Both home and school affect a child's academic performance. By focusing on school issues, parents and teachers can discuss just about anything in a non-threatening, collaborative manner (e.g., How does that situation affect your child's school performance? What can we do to help your child handle this in a better way?). In such a climate, parents are more likely to participate as most parents will do almost anything "for the good of their children."

Understanding that parental participation is critical, school personnel should assess families' comfort levels when participating in school activities. Drawing up a needs assessment of all the parents, focusing on their current levels of involvement and seeking suggestions they might have for increased participation are all strategies for moving toward a more collaborative home-school relationship. In the meantime, educators could ask themselves a few simple questions in order to assess the "family-friendliness" of their schools:

- Are all school meetings with parents problem-focused?
- How easy is it for a parent to find out what is going on in a classroom?
- Are parents a source of information? Is parental input valuable and can you name a few specific instances when parental input had an impact on outcome?
- Do parents typically come to the school to discuss positive activities?
- Are meetings only held during the school day?
- Do school personnel usually discuss parents in a negative fashion?
- Are parents informed when their children are doing well?
- What percentage of parents were at the last school function?
- Do teachers and parents describe their relationship in an adversarial fashion?
- Did most of the parents struggle with school themselves?

If the answers to these questions

PARENTAL INVOLVEMENT PROGRAMS AND STRATEGIES

1. Educational support and drop-out prevention programs.
2. Parenting skills training.
3. Workshops where parents can judge their schools' quality.
4. Adult literacy programs.
5. Parent tutoring programs for their own children.
6. Random meetings with the principal.
7. Potluck meals in the classroom.
8. Field trips with invited parents.
9. Invitations for parents to visit and participate.
10. Invitations for parents to make presentations.
11. Assignment of parents to committees.
12. Recognition of parents at school assemblies.
13. Fathers' night out.
14. Evening conferences.

Table 1

PARENT-TEACHER CONFERENCES
Joining

1. Speak the language of the family; use their words and definitions.
2. Understand the family's rules and rituals.
3. Try to keep jargon to a minimum—especially at first.
4. Monitor your own level of discomfort; do you resort to "the facts" when you become uncomfortable?
5. Try to build a collaborative, rather than an adversarial, system.
6. Ask the family to suggest solutions.
7. Recognize signs of a power struggle.

Table 2

---

suggest that parents are not comfortable in school settings or simply cannot find the time to participate, then specific strategies can be developed to meet those concerns. Since so many parents were uncomfortable with school when they were children, they may now be reluctant to participate. Parents may feel intimidated by education jargon and the system and may, as a result, distance themselves from involvement.

Sometimes educators feel too much is demanded of them. A strength-focused, collaborative perspective turns parents into partners, thus lightening educators' load.

Joining with Families. The parent-teacher relationship is the most important interaction between home and school. Such alliances might even reduce the number of children referred for therapeutic intervention. While teachers and parents may meet for a variety of reasons, the overriding goal should be for the teacher to "join" with as many families as possible. Joining means "letting the family know" that the teacher "understands them and is working with and for them" (Minuchin & Fishman, 1981, pp. 31-32). The following strategies, if implemented at the beginning of the school year, may help teachers join with their students' families and thus create a family-friendly school (see also Table 1).

■ Parents can be invited to meet their children's teachers before the year begins at an orientation, or the teachers could invite parents to a potluck dinner. These activities provide opportunities for teachers to solicit parental input and ask what educational methods the parents have found to be effective in the past. They also provide an opportunity for teachers to build a positive relationship with parents, rather than one based on problems.

■ In another successful strategy, teachers send home children's work each week with a letter. The letter can include a review of the week's activities and suggestions for reinforcing school-learned knowledge at home. Parents can be encouraged to respond with "Monday Messages." This strategy establishes a two-way dialogue rather than a one-way evaluation directed to parents.

■ In schools with computerized telephone systems and resources for multiple answering machines, teachers can record messages concerning study units and homework assignments so that parents can call at their convenience to gather information. This allows parents to be involved and to reinforce at home what their child has

done during the day (Minner, Prater & Beane, 1989).

■ Principals can set the tone by having lunch meetings with parents to discuss their concerns and ask for suggestions.

■ Principals can actively seek parents' input by asking them to sit with teachers on certain committees.

Principals also need to support teachers' efforts to "join" with families by granting time off or compensating teachers for extra time spent with families. Teachers will feel supported and appreciated.

The Parent-Teacher Conference As an Opportunity for Connection. Goals for the parent-teacher conference can include "the exchange of feelings, beliefs and knowledge between parent and teacher about a particular student. This exchange should facilitate cooperation between home and school for the benefit of the student" (Manning, 1985). Since the parent-teacher conference is often the sole contact between parents and teachers, it presents the primary opportunity to facilitate this cooperation. Consequently, what happens during this time is critical. Several counseling techniques, including active listening and developing a trusting relationship with parents, are particularly suited to the conference process. Table 2 lists many of the techniques that can be used to build such relationships. In addition, by scheduling conferences during the first few weeks of school, teachers will allow parental participation early on in the planning of the academic year and thus avoid many potential problems from the outset (Neilsen & Finkelstein, 1993).

This first meeting is a good time for teachers to gather information about the family's rules, roles and learning style (Green, 1992). Teachers should seek answers to the following questions:

SOLUTION-FOCUSED QUESTIONS

1. When do you not experience_____?
2. What is different at those times?
3. What are you doing differently when_____ is not happening?
4. How will you know when the problem is solved?
5. If you woke up tomorrow and your problem was miraculously solved, what would be different?
6. If a person had all of the skills you believe necessary to solve this issue what might he or she do?
7. What is a sequence around the issue?
8. How do you stop things from getting worse? (Emphasize that things *could* be worse and preventing further deterioration requires some competence.)
9. How have you resolved this problem in the past?
10. Has there ever been a time when this was not happening?

For a more complete listing see:
O'Hanlon, W. H., & Weiner-Davis, M. (1989). *In search of solutions.* New York: W. W. Norton.

Table 3

- Who has the primary responsibility for child rearing (and, consequently, monitoring school work)?
- What is the child-rearing style in this family? Parents usually exhibit one of three styles (Baumrind 1967, 1968):
  - Authoritarian (behavior is controlled according to absolute standards)
  - Authoritative (behavior is controlled according to developmental needs)
  - Permissive (no control is attempted; instead, a non-punishing, affirming manner is used).
- How is the family defined (who are its members)?
- How does the family describe their style of problem solving?
- Who speaks for the family and is it the same person who has primary child-rearing responsibilities?

This information will allow the teacher to assess the family structure and identify points of entry into the family system. Family structure and family learning styles have an enormous impact on a child's school adjustment (Green, 1992). Teachers would also benefit from knowing if parents are involved with other professionals (e.g., social workers). Too often, different groups of professionals work with the same family without any coordination.

The Solution-Focused Conference. Teachers should consider using a solution-focused approach during conferences. Borrowing from the work of Kral (1989), O'Hanlon & Weiner-Davis (1989) and de Shazer (1985), the solution-focused conference has several features. After joining with the family, the teacher works to clearly define the concern, redefine it as a *solvable* problem, agree on a specific, clearly defined goal and gather information from parents about whether a similar situation exists at home and what has been done to correct it. If the parents have successfully handled the problem at home, the teacher can enlist their help in forming a strategy for the classroom. A list of questions that may be used in a solution-focused conference can be found in Table 3.

Assigning specific tasks and establishing follow-up plans provides support for the changes discussed dur-

PARENT-TEACHER CONFERENCES
Making Plans: Strategies for Change

1. Write up behavior contracts.
2. Offer advice.
3. Ask solution-focused questions.
4. Gather more information and plan for follow-up.
5. Design tasks for the parents, particularly to observe something.
6. Create a task for family members whereby they look for their strengths.
7. Ensure that any assigned task is possible; build on success.
8. Think about direct skill training.
9. Practice during the meeting.
10. Avoid detours or being overwhelmed.
11. Contract for mutually agreed-upon goals.
12. Decide if a referral is necessary.
13. Ask yourself, Am I stuck?

Table 4

MAKING REFERRALS

1. Know the agencies in your area.
2. Know competent people with whom you can work at these organizations.
3. Refer to specific people, not just an organization.
4. Get agreement from the family that they will participate.
5. Ask the family to predict what might prevent them from participating and ask for solutions.
6. Check on families' ideas about solutions and possible referrals.
7. Make sure you provide for a follow-up meeting.

Table 5

ing conferences. These may also be used to strengthen any past successes. Table 4 lists a number of options that can be used to plan change strategies. If the conference leads only to an impasse, the group should consider involving other people, including other family members or consultants working with the family.

Referral. There will be times when both parties conclude that a referral for services outside the school system is appropriate. Teachers should know about the agencies in their area and develop contacts there. Table 5 lists a few specific steps that are important when making a referral. The goal is to find an appropriate fit between the family's needs and the referral's services. Such compatibility is more likely if the teacher is well-joined with the family, has knowledge of agency services and makes a referral to a specific person (Braden & Sherrard, 1987).

Conclusions

The authors have presented a collaborative, solution-focused approach that teachers can use to enlist parents' cooperation in creating effective, family-friendly schools. Lack of teacher training in systemic interpersonal skills, lack of family-friendly school programs and difficulties of focusing on family and educational strengths act as barriers to effective collaborative systems. The specific strategies reviewed in this article can help remove those barriers. Lightfoot (1982) argued that threats of physical illnesses (e.g., diphtheria, tuberculosis, typhoid, rheumatic fever) have been replaced by the psychosocial "illnesses" of drugs, alcoholism, juvenile suicide, adolescent pregnancy, abusive parenting and educational failure. Viewing these concerns in the context of the family and working to improve family-school collaboration might, at last, result in the reduction or alleviation of many of these long-standing problems.

References

Baumrind, D. (1967). Child care practices anteceding three patterns of preschool behavior. *Genetic Psychology Monographs, 75,* 43-83.

Baumrind, D. (1968). Authoritarian versus authoritative parental control. *Adolescence, 3,* 255-272.

Braden, J. P., & Sherrard, P. A. (1987). Referring families to nonschool agencies: A family systems approach. *School Psychology Review, 16*(4), 513-518.

Chira, S. (1993, June 23). What do teachers want most? Help from parents. *The New York Times,* p. 7.

de Shazer, S. (1985). *Keys to solution in brief therapy.* New York: W. W. Norton.

Dodge, S. (1991, September 4). Average score on SAT verbal section falls to all-time low: Math score declines for first time in more than 10 years. *The Chronicle of Higher Education,* pp. A45-A48.

Edelman, M. W. (1992). *The measure of our success.* Boston: Beacon Press.

Eno, M. M. (1985). Children with school problems: A family therapy perspective. In R. L. Ziffer (Ed.), *Adjunctive techniques in family therapy* (pp. 151-180). New York: Grune & Stratton.

Fisher, L. (1986). Systems-based consultation with schools. In L. C. Wynne, S. H. McDaniel, & T. T. Weber (Eds.), *Systems consultation: A new perspective for family therapy* (pp. 342-356). New York: The Guilford Press.

Foster, D. (1994, July/August). The disease is adolescence. *Utne Reader, 64,* 50-56.

Garbarino, J., Dubrow, N., Kostelny, K., & Pardo, C. (1992). *Children in danger.* San Francisco, CA: Jossey-Bass.

Garbarino, J., Kostelny, K., & Dubrow, N. (1991). *No place to be a child: Growing up in a war zone.* Lexington, MA: Lexington Books.

Green, R. (1992). "Learning to learn" and the family system: New perspectives on underachievement and learning disorders. In M. J. Fine & C. Carlson (Eds.), *Family-school intervention* (pp. 157-174). Boston: Allyn and Bacon.

Hayes, R. L. (1987). The reconstruction of educational experience: The parent conference. *Education, 107*(3), 305-309.

Henderson, A. T. (1987). *The evidence continues to grow: Parent involvement improves student achievement. An annotated bibliography.* (Report No. ISBN-0-934460-28-0). Columbia, MD: National Committee for Citizens in Education. (ERIC Document Reproduction Service No. ED 315 199)

Kral, R. (1989). *Strategies that work.* Milwaukee, WI: Brief Family Therapy Center.

Kozol, J. (1991). *Savage inequalities: Children in America's schools.* New York: Crown.

Lightfoot, S. L. (1978). *Worlds apart: Relationships between families and schools.* New York: Basic Books.

Lightfoot, S. L. (1982). Toward conflict and resolution: Relationships between families and schools. *Theory into Practice, 20*(2), 97-104.

Manning, B. H. (1985). Conducting a worthwhile parent-teacher conference. *Education, 105*(4), 342-348.

Marcon, R. A. (1993, March). *Parental involvement and early school success: Following the "Class of 2000" at year five.* Paper presented at the Biennial Meeting of the Society for Research in Child Development, New Orleans, LA. (ERIC Document Reproduction Service No. ED 357 881)

Minner, S., Prater, G., & Beane, A. (1989). Alternative methods of communicating with parents. *Academic Therapy, 24*(5), 619-624.

Minuchin, S., & Fishman, H. C. (1981). *Family therapy techniques.* Cambridge, MA: Harvard University Press.

Neilsen, L. E., & Finkelstein, J. M. (1993). A new approach to parent conferences. *Teaching K-8, 24*(1), 90-92.

O'Callaghan, J. B. (1993). *School-based collaboration with families.* San Francisco, CA: Jossey-Bass.

O'Hanlon, W. H., & Weiner-Davis, M. (1989). *In search of solutions.* New York: W. W. Norton.

Rotter, J. C., Robinson, E. H., & Fey, M. A. (1987). *Parent-teacher conferences: What research says to the teacher* (2nd ed.). (Report No. ISBN-0-8106-1075-2). Washington, DC: National Education Association. (ERIC Document Reproduction Service No. ED 312 058)

Rubenstein, E. (1988, October 28). They never learn. *National Review,* p. 42.

Seldin, C. A. (1991). *Parent/teacher conferencing: A three-year study to enrich communication.* (Report No. 140). (ERIC Document Reproduction Service No. ED 338 597)

Shea, C. (1993, January 13). Fewer test takers get top scores on the verbal SAT. *The Chronicle of Higher Education,* pp. A29-A33.

Singal, D. J. (1991, November). The other crisis in American education. *The Atlantic Monthly,* pp. 59-74.

Vogel, J. (1994, July/August). Throw away the key. *Utne Reader, 64,* 56-60.

Walker, G. (1991). Pediatric AIDS: Toward an ecosystemic treatment model. *Family Systems Medicine, 9,* 211-227.

Watzlawick, P., Weakland, J., & Fisch, R. (1974). *Change.* New York: W. W. Norton.

Curricular Issues

The ten articles in this unit make it the largest ever on curricular issues. Education will be very different as we move into the twenty-first century. The amount of information children are required to learn has increased over the past generation, and more is available every day. Children cannot possibly be responsible for knowing all this new information, but they will be required to know how they can access it. Where would be the best place to look? What Web site should they check? What information have they gathered, and what conclusions can they draw?

These are the types of questions our young children will be asking themselves in the not too distant future.

At the end of a busy day, most teachers would relish the thought of walking into a restaurant where they would not have to make any choices about what to eat or do any of the shopping and cooking. All the food would be prepared by others and set before the hungry teachers to consume. Sounds wonderful! Maybe for two or even three nights the idea would be appealing, but come the fourth night, some teachers really would not like what was being served, or would cook it differently. In this restaurant, there are no opportunities for customer suggestions.

Does this sound like some classrooms? The adults choose the topic of study and spend frantic weeks preparing the materials and activities. The teachers then lay everything out in front of the children and wait for them to eagerly lap up the information and activities prepared by the teacher. Unfortunately, this is how many classrooms operate.

Teachers in these classrooms do all the work, with no input from the children, their families, or their environment. Topics of study are often decided months in advance. A strict schedule is adhered to so that all the teacher-chosen topics can be covered in a particular time frame. Each year, themes are covered at the same time, and little, if any, deviation from the master calendar occurs. Unknowingly, teachers are making more work for themselves by ignoring the ideas and expertise that children and their families could contribute. The skills children acquire, such as investigating, predicting, and hypothesizing, can be more useful in future learning than knowing specific facts about a particular topic. Every teacher cannot teach the same information about every possible topic of study. What every teacher can do, however, is ensure that all children have equal opportunities to develop the learning skills they will need as they move through their formal education and into their chosen professions. It is not important if a particular preschool teacher does an in-depth investigation of boats and her friend who teaches in another part of the country does not. What is important is that the children in both classrooms have opportunities to develop and use skills, such as exploring, expression, and investigating, that extend their learning. These are the skills they will need in the future, more so than specific information on boats or any other topic of study.

This unit deals with developing a child-centered, hands-on curriculum. Just as teachers want a say in what they eat and how it is prepared, so children want a chance to investigate topics about which they are curious and to gather some of the information. A child-centered curriculum offers possibilities for investigating, exploring, predicting, and collaborating, among other skills that are the benchmarks of a successful school experience. In "Project Work with Diverse Students: Adopting Curriculum Based on the Reggio Emilia Approach," Shareen Abramson, Roxanne Robinson, and Katie Ankenman describe a project-based approach to learning. Children living in an area where it snows can do many experiments with the snow inside and outside to answer questions.

In "A Framework for Literacy" and "Read Me a Story: 101 Good Books Kids Will Love," the reader is presented with valuable information on the benefits of a quality literacy program. Many of the books on the list will be recognized as classics we remember from childhood. Reread a favorite, or check out an unknown title and enjoy it with a child. Make reading to and with children a ritual both in and out of the classroom.

A truly child-centered curriculum in a developmentally appropriate program is constantly changing, just like the children who attend that program. It is the job of the teachers and caregivers to keep pace with the children's needs and interests as they grow and learn.

Looking Ahead: Challenge Questions

What changes can teachers make to their theme-based planning to make the learning more meaningful to the children?

How can math, science, and technology be an integral part of classroom learning?

How are the processes of learning to read and write connected? What can facilitate these processes in the classroom?

What role do the diverse lifestyles of the children in a classroom play in the development of the curriculum?

What are the negative effects of using worksheets with young children? What types of learning experiences should be offered instead?

How can curriculum webs be built with input from the children?

What should teachers or parents consider when choosing literature for children?

What are the benefits of an inquiry approach to curriculum development?

Voice of Inquiry: Possibilities and Perspectives

Clint Wills

Clint Wills is an education consultant.

"You could count their claws and teeth," Michael said when asked to think like a mathematician about dinosaurs. Twenty-three more 1st-graders nodded their approval at this suggestion. I wondered aloud, "How would you do that?" Michael took some time to think about it.

"Well, when they roar you would just look real quick!"

As I noted this answer, Michael's classmates offered their solutions. The discussion and debate picked up momentum.

"When they roar, you might not have time to count, so you could jam a stick in their mouth."

"Uh-uh, it might break!"

"Not if it's a big stick, like a little tree."

This line of thinking diverged when Kelly offered, "You could tie their mouth open with a rope." The moment of silence that ensued while the children considered the possibility was short-lived.

"They might cut through it with their teeth."

"Wait! You could use some wire, like some *big* wire!"

The discussion diverged again when Vanessa said, "You could count the teeth in the skull of a dead dinosaur."

"Yeah!" exclaimed Michael, "and we could really do that, too."

"Even with a picture," David added.

Others voiced support for Vanessa's strategy and I wrote it on the chart tablet, adding to the growing list of mathematical ways to think about dinosaurs.

This lively conversation took place as my 1st-graders helped plan a dinosaur study we had undertaken. It is significant to note that the students played a role in creating a curriculum in which we operated as a group of researchers. In fact, it was the inclusion of students' voices in the curriculum that caused me to take my first serious look at the use of inquiry in my classroom.

Beginning with my first day of undergraduate classes, countless teachers, mentors and friends urged me to make my classroom a democracy by planning my curriculum with the help of my students. Intuitively, I agreed with these exhortations; I left each exchange filled with enthusiasm, eager to achieve democracy in my classroom. I always fell short of these goals.

While I had become very good at knowing what I should be doing, I still had very little understanding of *how* to do it. In other words, I was long on belief and short on practice.

During my third year as a 1st-grade teacher, my fifth year in the classroom, I heard Carolyn Burke explain inquiry-driven curriculum (Burke, 1991) and something important dropped into place for me. Now I could see a practical, sensible way to collaborate with my students.

Curricular Structures: Four Models

Inquiry is sometimes referred to as the newest version of thematic teaching, and in some ways this is true. A comparison of four curricular models (Prescriptive, Thematic, KWHL and Inquiry) reveals some logical relationships, and a progressive pattern emerges.

The characteristic unifying these (and other) curricular models is this: learning progresses from the known to the unknown. Once we have acknowledged this basic similarity, however, a more pronounced division emerges. A strong connection exists between the prescriptive and thematic models and between the KWHL and inquiry models, but these two subsets are fundamentally different.

A close look reveals that most thematic models have evolved from a linear view of learning, which identifies knowledge as a static, immutable, quantifiable entity. The inquiry model has evolved from a

It was the inclusion of students' voices in the curriculum that caused me to take my first serious look at the use of inquiry in my classroom.

From *Childhood Education*, Annual Theme Issue, 1995, pp. 261-265. © 1995 by the Association for Childhood Education International, 11501 Georgia Avenue, Suite 315, Wheaton, MD. Reprinted by permission.

circular or recursive perspective that presupposes the tentative, dynamic nature of knowledge. In order to better understand Inquiry as curriculum, it is helpful to examine its evolution and its relationship to the three other curricular structures.

The Prescriptive Model

The original prescriptive model (see Figure 1), one still widely used, is found in countless programs and the common denominator is the DPTT continuum (i.e., **D**iagnose, **P**rescribe, **T**each and **T**est). Ideally, this continuum allows for learning programs that fit the needs of individual students, with little or no wasted instructional time for the teacher and little or no "busy work" for the student. The teacher administers a pretest to determine student ability, prescribes a course of study, teaches these skills, then administers a retest to determine progress.

Even when used correctly, however, this model casts the teacher as the active transmitter of knowledge and the child as the passive receiver (Weaver, 1990). Furthermore, the knowledge being transmitted is often lifted verbatim from an outside source, such as a teacher's manual. This practice effectively keeps the expertise in the hands of the "program" from which the manual came.

The prescriptive model views learning from a very linear perspective, much like a train racing along a railroad track. The course is predetermined and no detours are allowed. The only variable is the speed with which the journey is made. An unusually quick trip denotes a child whose learning ability is above grade level; an on-time arrival denotes a child at grade level. All educators are familiar with the many labels for those who arrive late. Of course, many of those late arrivals never complete the trip, eventually choosing to jump from the train.

This linear nature frequently prevents teachers from implementing the DPTT curriculum as a collection of individually tailored learning programs. The school year takes on the characteristics of a race; teachers feel intense pressure to hurry the students along toward the finish line. It seems there is not enough time in the school year to test, teach, retest and reteach. In such a classroom, Vanessa's brilliant strategy for exploring dinosaurs would be left unspoken, because if I invited such seemingly random conversations, our train would be derailed and the race could be lost.

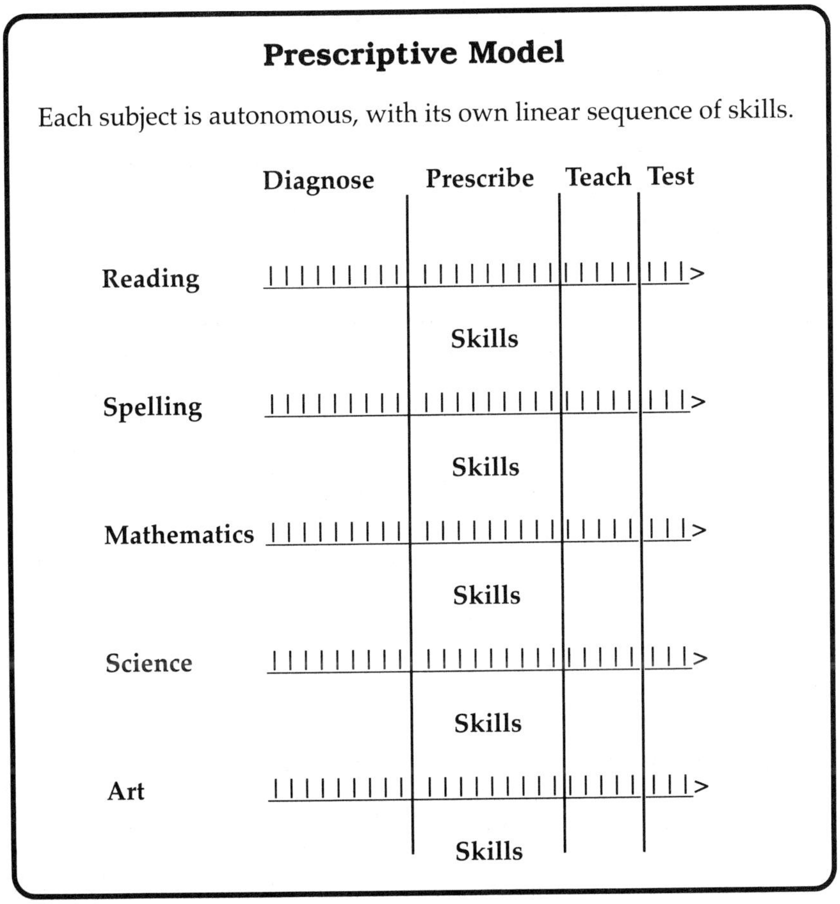

The Thematic Model

Ironically, most "thematic approaches" are closely tied to the prescriptive model. While thematic models (see Figure 2) attempt to make learning more authentic by drawing connections between the disciplines, these connections are usually in the form of prescribed activities designed to teach the same predetermined skills as the prescriptive model. Progress is still essentially linear: the sequence, duration and composition of the themes are predetermined by the teacher or grade level.

Themes may be independent of the children's interests (and, often, the teacher's as well) and they frequently have no connection to each other. As in the prescriptive model, curriculum (knowledge) is viewed as predetermined and finite and thus is transmitted to the child. Because the school year still frames a curricular race, little or no provision is made for the transaction of new questions or insights generated by the child (Weaver, 1990). Yet a cursory glance appears to show a curriculum that is more integrated, and therefore more authentic.

Figure 1

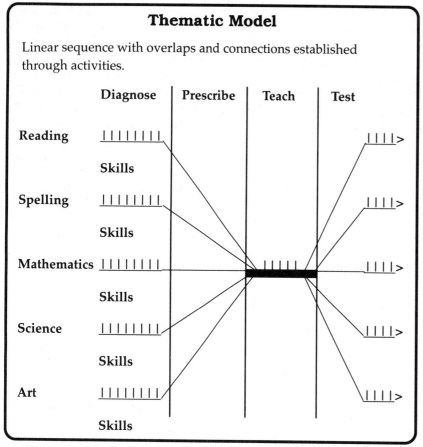

Thematic Model

Linear sequence with overlaps and connections established through activities.

Figure 2

More simply, prescriptive models tell the student what to learn, while KWHL models ask the student what he or she would like to learn.

The Inquiry Model

To understand how KWHL differs from inquiry, it is helpful to look at the general structure of a unit from an inquiry perspective (see Figure 4).

I begin the school year by asking the children what they would like to know more about. The questions and topics we generate are displayed on a bulletin board and serve as a curricular guide for the rest of the year. This strategy gives me access to two of the three primary influences on my curriculum, which are the children's interests, my own interests and the units I am required to teach.

My curriculum is a negotiation, a balance that I achieve among these three sources of input. Part of my job is to streamline the topics we will cover, combining and unifying when possible. This unification process, which often begins by simply observing, "Hey, that's kind of like . . . ," is an authentic means of connecting knowledge. All that is required is an open forum for discussion and a teacher who is willing to listen to the children and

The KWHL Model

The third model is called KWL or KWHL (see Figure 3), which is an acronym for: What do you already **Know**? What would you like to know? **How** will you find out? What did you **Learn**? While this process utilizes inquiry techniques, KWHL is used primarily as a means for guiding student research. Inquiry addresses student research, but also includes dimensions of curricular construction and professional growth.

Like the prescriptive and thematic models, KWHL progresses from what is known to the unknown, and has a means of accounting for new learning. Prescriptive models, however, progress from pre-test to post-test while KWHL models progress from "What do you already know?" to "What did you learn?"

This critical difference puts the responsibility for learning on the student, allowing for the value of experience, self-directed questioning, familiarity with research procedures and self-evaluation or reflection.

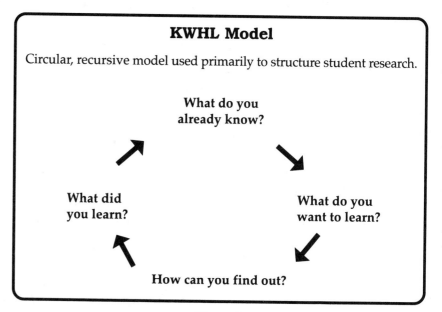

KWHL Model

Circular, recursive model used primarily to structure student research.

What do you already know?

What do you want to learn?

How can you find out?

What did you learn?

Figure 3

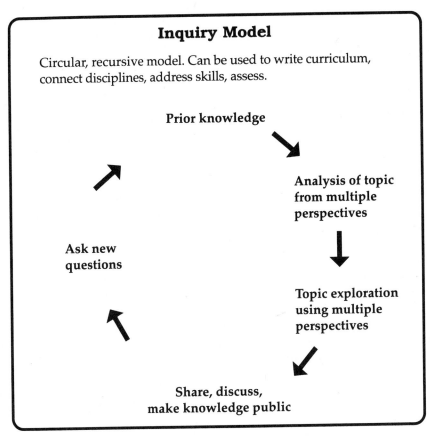

Inquiry Model

Circular, recursive model. Can be used to write curriculum, connect disciplines, address skills, assess.

Prior knowledge

Analysis of topic from multiple perspectives

Ask new questions

Topic exploration using multiple perspectives

Share, discuss, make knowledge public

Figure 4

learn from them. After establishing the areas of interest, we begin our studies. I have found that our questions most often fit into the curricular definitions of science, social studies and health.

Most of our units progress according to the following plan, which is very closely based on ideas presented by Carolyn Burke (1991):

- *Organize a text set.* I assemble all resources available from the library, my own collections, students, other teachers, etc. I gather any and all artifacts related to the topic, including, but not limited to, books.
- *Hold a book browse.* When most or all of my resources are in the classroom, I place them on the four tables where the children sit. The children then spend about 15 minutes looking at the resources, discussing them, playing with them, etc. After 15 minutes, the groups move to new tables and the

process is repeated until, at the end of an hour, each group has visited each table and is back "home."

- *Create graffiti boards.* Upon returning to their original seats, students help to clear the desktops. Each group is then given one large sheet of bulletin board paper (large enough to cover the entire table) and each child writes and/or draws everything he or she knows about the topic. In this alternative to webbing and mapping, the students are responsible for their own efforts and do not need the teacher as a mediator. The exercise is usually fairly noisy as comments, questions and small group discussions accompany the drawing and writing. These discussions can be illustrated on the graffiti board. A child whose idea stems from the drawing or writing of another child can draw lines connecting the two ideas. The finished product should be covered with words, pictures and lines.

- *Share graffiti boards.* When the graffiti boards are completed, each student explains his or her contribution. During this process, I usually record the key points on a chart tablet. A good title for this chart is "What We Think We Know," which gives the document the characteristics of a rough draft and avoids possible conflicts over "facts." This also gives me the chance to cull the information, eliminating repetition and creating a reference source that will be posted for the duration of the study.

- *Hold a sign system/knowledge domain discussion.* This terminology, which seems complex at first glance, represents a very basic and simple premise that is central to the Inquiry model. It is simply another way of saying that sign systems are how we communicate and knowledge domains are what we communicate. There are five main sign systems: language, art, music, drama and mathematics. Each system is non-redundant; that is, each system, when used to convey knowledge of a topic, could yield different information. Knowledge domains are a bit more complex and there are many more of them. Philosophy, biology, geography, nutrition, quantum physics—all of these are knowledge domains. Every subject area, every discipline and every school of thought can be a knowledge domain, each offering a different perspective.

The opening dialogue is an example of 1st-graders using the mathematic sign system to think about dinosaurs. While seated at the chart tablet, I had asked the students to talk about things a mathematician might do to show others what he or she knows about dinosaurs. As they responded, I recorded their ideas. Eventually, we had a set of math activities to pursue in large groups, small groups or individually. Repeating this process while considering art, music, language and movement gave us activities in those curricular areas. Expanding this process to include some basic knowledge domains would give us science, social studies or health activities. The net result is a unit planned by, and with, the children.

I ask the children to consider three types of questions for each sign system or knowledge domain:

■ What would an artist say about this topic (or a picture depicting the topic)? This question generates a list of things the children already know (prior knowledge, or the "K" of KWHL).

■ What would an artist ask about this topic? This generates a list of questions or things we want to know (the "W" of KWHL).

■ What would an artist do to show others what he or she knows about the topic? This generates a list of activities for us to do (part of the "H" of KWHL).

Conduct explorations (large group, small group and individual). I post the lists we create and incorporate them into my lesson plans. They serve as jumping-off points for discussions, field trips, guest speakers, class-made books, research projects and so on. Some of the questions lend themselves to individual research projects, while some are better suited to be answered by a field trip. Some activities demand that we walk outside for a whole-class experience; some are perfect for a small-group response. I trust my own judgment, with input from my students, in making these decisions.

Share insights, discuss, ask new questions. This step, which sounds like a final procedure, actually occurs throughout the study. It is the evaluative component that offers the student a chance to self-evaluate while giving the observant teacher insight into the child's use of skills and strategies. The key to realizing the full potential of this process is the teacher's ability to fa-

cilitate sharing in a way that is naturally respectful of the children's ideas. This single element may be the most elusive and difficult aspect of an inquiry (or indeed any) curriculum. It requires teachers to be listeners and learners in a profession that has trained them to be talkers and authority figures.

Teachers need to believe that the class absolutely cannot function effectively without sharing ideas and asking new questions. This process is so fundamental that, if used properly, students' observations and questions will connect the curriculum in ways far more subtle, sophisticated and authentic than our own clumsy, agenda-laden efforts to force a vestige of each discipline into every activity. The sophisticated connections that students make are part of a process known as reflexivity (Watson, Burke & Harste, 1989). This process occurs when we apply our knowledge in one area to other areas, making new connections and increasing our understanding of the relationships between knowledge.

Reflexivity differs from reflection. For instance, a child who has studied dinosaurs might reflectively say, "Tyrannosaurus ate Triceratops." The same child might then reflexively say, "Hey, that's like how lions eat zebras." The child has applied a knowledge of one predator/prey relationship to another, making a reflexive connection. For the observant teacher, this is an event to be documented. It is also a wonderful springboard into other questions and research.

Conclusions

My purpose in this article was not to elevate the status of one curricular model at the expense of others; the realities of teaching today often necessitate finding a balance among these and other models. We should, however, have a clear understanding of the implications, applications and characteristics of the curricular models we choose to utilize.

After so much talk of inquiry and other models, it would be appropriate to conclude by mentioning whole language, a model to which inquiry is quite closely related (Harste & Leland, 1994). A fundamental trust in children as capable decision-makers drives the philosophy and practices we call whole language. This same trust also drives inquiry. Belief that children make sense, make connections and seek literacy forms the foundation of whole language, as well as inquiry. Whole language trusts teachers to be autonomous experts capable of valid, authentic assessment and insightful evaluation of developing language strategies. Inquiry demonstrates a trust in teachers to be expert researchers, learners and leaders. So close are these connections and so prevalent are the principles of whole language in other disciplines that many contend it is time for a change to the term whole literacy.

By any name, what I strive for is a democratically constructed curriculum that respects all voices of the learning community; values questions, ideas and opinions; treats assessment and evaluation as a natural part of the learning process; and enables children to feel happy and secure. I am quite certain that the struggle to achieve this matters far more than the achievement itself.

References

Burke, C. (1991, October). *Keynote address.* Paper presented at the Eisenhower Grant Meeting, Columbia, SC.

Harste, J., & Leland, C. (1994). Multiple ways of knowing: Curriculum in a new key. *Journal of Language Arts, 71*(5).

Watson, D., Burke, C., & Harste, J. (1989). *Whole language: Inquiring voices.* New York: Scholastic.

Weaver, C. (1990). *Understanding whole language.* Portsmouth, NH: Heinemann.

Project Work with Diverse Students

Adapting Curriculum Based on the Reggio Emilia Approach

Shareen Abramson, Roxanne Robinson, and Katie Ankenman

Shareen Abramson is Professor, Early Childhood Education Program, Department of Literacy and Early Education and Director of the Early Education Center, California State University, Fresno. Roxanne Robinson and Katie Ankenman are student teachers, Early Education Program, California State University, Fresno.

The preschools of Reggio Emilia, Italy, have generated excitement among early childhood educators in the U.S. and throughout the rest of the world. Presentations at professional conferences concerning these Italian schools draw standing-room-only crowds (Weissman, Saltz & Saltz, 1993). Visitors to Reggio Emilia schools marvel at the exceptional quality of the programs; the dedication, sensitivity and intelligence of the teachers and staff; the depth and sophistication of the project work; and the remarkable evidence of learning that is taking place (Bredekamp, 1993; Katz, 1990; New, 1990; Rankin, 1992).

Some educators in the United States are now attempting to adapt the Reggio Emilia approach (Forman, Moonja, Wrisley & Langley, 1993; Fyfe & Caldwell, 1993; LeeKeenan & Nimmo, 1993). The community of Reggio, however, tends to be culturally homogeneous. Although all socioeconomic levels exist in the area, the compre-

hensive social services limit the effects of poverty. Could Reggio Emilia principles and practices be translated into a community that, like so many in the U.S., is culturally, economically and linguistically diverse? Could it be implemented successfully with older elementary students as a means for promoting their development? Could student teachers apply the Reggio Emilia approach as they develop curriculum for diverse students?

These are the questions that the authors sought to address during a course on integrated curriculum in the Early Childhood Education Program at California State University, Fresno.

Reggio Emilia Approach

Preschools in Reggio Emilia demonstrate a number of exemplary and innovative education practices. The approach is discussed in detail in *The Hundred Languages of Children* (Edwards, Gandini & Forman, 1993). Key features of this approach include:

Community Commitment. Over the last 30 years, Reggio Emilia has created a publicly supported system of early childhood education centers that serve 35 percent of infants/toddlers and 47 percent of preschoolers in the community (Gandini, 1993b).

Supportive Relationships. Parents founded the Reggio Emilia schools at the end of World War II

(Gandini, 1993b). Loris Malaguzzi, the director of these schools for 40 years, engaged staff, parents, children and the community in the continuing development and management of programs (Malaguzzi, 1993b; Rinaldi, 1993; Spaggiari, 1993). Reciprocity and interaction characterize relationships among these participants. "Our goal is to create an amiable school—that is, a school that is active, inventive, livable, documentable and communicative . . . a place of research, learning, revisiting, reconsideration and reflection . . . where children, teachers and families feel a sense of well-being . . ." (Malaguzzi, 1993c, p. 9). Staff members collectively participate in decision-making and teachers work in pairs. In addition, schools have an "atelierista" (artist) and a "pedagogista" (curriculum specialist) who work with teachers on curriculum development. A parent advisory council at each school helps facilitate an active home-school partnership. Because children stay with the same teacher for three years, these relationships are further enhanced.

A Unique Philosophy. The Reggio Emilia philosophy draws upon a number of constructivist theories, including those of Vygotsky and Piaget, but is most often described in terms of the "image of the child" (Gandini, 1993b; Malaguzzi, 1993b; Rinaldi, 1993). Reggio educators view each child as an individual with rights and potentials. They reject a portrayal of children as dependent or needy.

The authors are grateful for the suggestions of Lella Gandini, the U.S. liaison for Reggio Emilia schools, in the preparation of this manuscript.

5. CURRICULAR ISSUES

Preparation of the Environment. Reggio teachers recognize that the environment has teaching functions. The environment can be both a "container" for experiences and "content" for study and exploration (Gandini, 1993a). Teachers pay careful attention to all aspects of the environment, looking for ways to increase children's educational, aesthetic and social opportunities (Gandini, 1993b). All of the schools have unusual, open-ended, creative play structures and spaces that are often related to projects. School interiors and grounds are beautiful and a source of pride for children, teachers, parents and the community.

Atelier (Studio/Resource Room). Each school has a large atelier staffed by an artist who works with teachers and parents in planning, implementing and documenting project work (Vecchi, 1993). The atelier offers an incredible variety of supplies for children's use. Each classroom has a "mini-atelier" for additional experiences.

Project-based Curriculum. Much of the curriculum in Reggio Emilia schools centers around projects, which are unique in several important ways. Their distinguishing aspects include:

- the teacher role of both facilitator and partner in learning
- topic selection based on student interests and experiences
- collaboration among students, teachers and parents
- project content emerging from students' evolving understanding and not from a set of prepackaged activities
- multiple experiences with media to represent understandings
- repetition of activities for different purposes
- extended period of time devoted to a project
- small-group rather than whole-class projects

- project documentation (Edwards, 1993; Gandini, 1993b; Katz, 1993; New, 1990; Rankin, 1993).

Rather than "covering" the curriculum or a project, teachers and children together "uncover" a project (LeeKeenan & Nimmo, 1993). This project work helps all children develop their language, literacy, scientific, mathematical and social knowledge.

Collaboration. Educators in Reggio Emilia prefer using small groups because they provide a social context that fosters meaningful dialogue, collaborative problem solving and productive cognitive conflict (Malaguzzi, 1993c). Working together as a group takes precedence over individual efforts when children collaborate on large-scale projects such as creating murals or building a dinosaur. Parents interact frequently with teachers, formally and informally, and are involved in curriculum development activities, discussion groups and special events.

Multiple Languages. Echoing Howard Gardner's (1985) theory of "multiple intelligences," Reggio educators believe that children have the capacity for representing ideas in a wide variety of symbolic and graphic modes, what Malaguzzi called the "hundred languages of children" (Malaguzzi, 1993a). Gardner identified seven sources of intelligence: linguistic, musical, logico-mathematical, spatial-aesthetic, bodily kinesthetic, interpersonal and intrapersonal. An approach that recognizes multiple paths of expression and intellectual performance is especially effective with students whom the standard curriculum often fails to reach. Reggio educators believe the visual arts are not "a separate part of the curriculum but . . . [are] inseparable from the whole cognitive-symbolic expression of the developing child" (Gandini & Edwards, 1988, p. 15). Pretend play is another manifestation of the symbolic functioning es-

sential to children's development (Malaguzzi, 1993c). Children's expression of knowledge through musical performance, drama and manipulative constructions provides adults with a potent means for accessing children's perception and understanding of their world.

Documentation. Children's conceptual development can be documented over time, creating a basis for evaluating and planning future activities (Vecchi, 1993). Teachers can combine photographs, audiotape transcripts, videotapes, notes and products of children's project work to create a detailed, visual display of learning. This documentation serves as an individual and collective "memory" of activities, a method for reflecting on learning that leads to new experiences, a way to share learning with parents and others and a mechanism for capturing growth and development (Vecchi, 1993). Documentation displays are everywhere in Reggio Emilia schools. While many are of current project work, other displays are historical in nature—in effect, the collective "memory" of former students and their families.

All of the above principles have profound implications for educational practice. The use of projects and recognition of multiple languages seem to be especially relevant to the needs of diverse learners.

Projects as a Teaching Strategy for Diverse Students

Teaching strategies for linguistically diverse learners are undergoing dramatic changes. While earlier methods emphasized rote learning and drill, newer approaches to teaching a second language are based on a holistic view that gives primacy to both language as meaningful communication and to students' own experiences as the source for language development (Abramson, Seda & Johnson, 1990; Enright, 1986; Enright & McCloskey, 1985; Hudelson, 1984).

Projects that relate to students' experiences and interests, as in the Reggio Emilia approach, can be ideal ways to encourage language and conceptual development.

Allen (1986), for example, describes how an extended project began with a reading of *Strega Nona* (De Paola, 1975). Linguistically diverse children, ages 8 to 10, tested "magic" objects and powders, examined different types of pasta, and planned and prepared a pasta lunch. As Allen notes, these related experiences help children develop vocabulary, acquire scientific and mathematical ideas and refine their literary skills.

Melvin and Stout (1987) urge teachers of the linguistically diverse to rely more heavily on authentic materials. In the project "Discover a City," for example, students view an introductory slide show or videotape of city scenes, locate sights of interest on a map, contact the tourist bureau for additional information, create an itinerary for a four-day visit to the city and calculate costs for transportation, meals and other activities. Such activities provide a real and motivating context for language use.

Crawford (1993) believes that diverse learners are greatly interested in themes with multicultural dimensions. She describes an investigation of folktales that begins by introducing students to new concepts through bulletin board displays, audiovisual and community resources and dramatic experiences. Subsequent activities develop direction and organization for the study and include techniques such as brainstorming, semantic maps and prediction guides. Finally, students explore the theme or topic through various learning activities, develop generalizations and culminate the study. This project approach demonstrates the power of projects as a teaching strategy for diverse students and the value of adapting the Reggio Emilia approach.

Multiple Languages and Diverse Students

Reggio schools give prominence to the visual languages. Educators there view creative production as a nonverbal and alternative mode of expression that affords insights to an individual's level of understanding, perceptions and feelings. For linguistically diverse learners, such activities free them from the need to express ideas in a language that may be new and unfamiliar. Moreover, expressive activities give linguistically diverse students equity and a common ground with others.

According to Clay (1986), talking, reading, writing, thinking, drawing and making are all constructive processes in which the learner attempts to make sense of experience. She distinguishes "constructive" learning activities that involve relating, thinking and problem solving from those involving rote learning and repetitive tasks. She argues that "when instruction requires each child to shift to a constructive mode of thinking, to link the current task with personal knowledge, then any competency that the child has is allowed to contribute to the output" (p. 768).

Drawing on the work of Howard Gardner (1985), Shier (1990) makes a case for the importance of the visual arts for teaching linguistically diverse learners. According to Shier, both Project Zero and Arts Propel, initiatives begun at Harvard University and based on Gardner's theory of multiple intelligences, are examples of programs that successfully utilize creative expression and demonstrate the interrelatedness of cognitive and affective processes. Shier finds that such a curriculum promotes language development, enhances an appreciation of cultural differences and increases creative and thinking skills. Visual arts, literary arts, video and theater, as well as visits by guest artists and trips to art museums, have enormous potential for expanding the learning horizons of linguistically diverse children.

Seely and Hurwitz (1983) reviewed a summer program serving Asian, Mexican, Caribbean and European immigrant children ranging in age from 6 to 17. An art teacher, drama teacher and language specialist worked together to use visual arts and drama as a means for developing language. The students' use of creative expression not only supported their English language development, but also affirmed their sense of themselves as productive, inventive and active learners. The teachers believed that creative endeavors enhanced students' attitudes of risk-taking, spontaneity and self-confidence that then carried over into their language learning.

Student Teachers Learn About the Reggio Emilia Approach

The Early Childhood Education Program at the authors' university includes a course on "Integrated Curriculum." The course examines research and uses projects based on an adaptation of the Reggio Emilia approach. Instead of turning in an elaborate final project, student teachers work in the practicum classroom, representing the progress of the project over the semester with photo-documentation, examples of student work, observational notes and reflections, as well as lesson plans.

In the practicum, student teachers are assigned to a public elementary school that has a highly diverse student population. Approximately 70 percent of the students are classified as limited-English-proficient. Student teachers are placed in groups of three to encourage collaborative learning and create a support system during the practicum.

After observing in their classrooms and talking with students and their cooperating teacher, the student teachers think about broad topic areas that might interest the students. They introduce these topics to the whole class, sharing ideas, books and materials and exploring related questions. Children sign up for projects, ranking the topics in order of their interest. Working individually, with their class group and with one another, student teachers identify some of the topic's conceptual dimensions through brainstorming and "webbing" sessions (Workman & Anziano, 1993).

It is important to note that these first student teacher projects are not yet of the same caliber as ones seen in Reggio Emilia schools. Beginning student teachers in the United States are, however, making use of insights from the work of Reggio educators, as well as other information sources, in developing curriculum for diverse students.

Projects in Diverse Classrooms

The student teachers' projects covered a broad range of topics and activities. The teachers and children, for example, of a 1st-grade class decided to pursue a project on sand. As part of the project, the group played in the sand box. Before and after this activity, the children drew pictures of sand. After the sandbox visit, Pavi, who was only beginning to learn English, drew an elaborate picture showing one child building a sand castle and another child with a bucket and shovel digging nearby. While Pavi could say only "sand, sand" when asked to tell about it, his picture graphically demonstrated a great deal more knowledge than he was able to verbalize.

As project activities developed, student teachers adapted to the Reggio Emilia approach by listening to students' conversations, looking at their pictures and generating questions. Some of these activities included: examining rocks, shells and sand through a magnifying glass; counting and grouping rocks into various categories; identifying the rocks that were collected; comparing sand to other similar sub-

Students can create sand in a jar by combining rocks, shells, and water.

Photo courtesy of the authors

stances such as sugar, flour, salt, cornmeal, popcorn kernels, oatmeal, baking powder and birdseed; studying the effects of mixing water with sand and other substances; reading the story *Sand Cake* (Asch, 1979) and making an edible "sand" cake; and finally, building a sand castle. During these activities, students often conversed with others in their native language, thereby promoting their conceptual development (Abramson, Seda & Johnson, 1990; Enright & McCloskey, 1985).

Initially, many students appeared confused about the nature and origin of sand. The children's questions about sand inspired a sand-making activity. After trying a number of different methods, the children discovered that they could create sand if they combined rocks and shells in containers filled with water and then shook them.

The teachers gave students unlimited time to explore and digress, providing invaluable opportunities for collaborative problem solving and scientific inquiry. Students were concerned when some of the containers in the sand-making experiment leaked at the lid after a hard shake. The student teacher recorded their discussion on tape:

Outhay: We need to put tape around the lid so it doesn't leak.

Vue: We need to hold paper towels around it.

Tasha: I'm not going to shake mine at the top. If you don't make the water go to the top, it won't leak out.

Leticia: We need to make the lids tighter.

The students were allowed to try all the solutions. The tape worked until it became too wet to adhere. The children closely examined one of the containers that did not leak, discovering that the lid had an interior rubber seal. The student teacher and children discussed how to make a better seal for the other containers, eventually deciding upon putting a rubber band at the screw top. This technique worked very well, and the children experienced a strong sense of accomplishment. Working on this problem was closer to the children's interests and more rich than a teacher-initiated lesson might have been.

Keeping written records and photographic documentation, as Reggio educators do, helped the student teachers follow the children's progress, reflect on the learning and plan future activities. The children enjoyed looking at their photographs and sharing them with their classmates. They often conversed in their native language about the activities captured by the photographs.

In a 4th-grade classroom, a study of "Homes" led to a different type of project. While such a project might not be especially interesting to young children (LeeKeenan & Nimmo, 1993), the older students soon immersed themselves in home studies. When asked about their interest, several students explained that they already knew something about the topic, which made them confident. The student teachers developed a "KWL" (Know/ Want to learn/ Learned) chart (Tompkins & Hoskisson, 1991) to find out what the students knew. The resulting list mainly included things that are found in homes, such as bedrooms, bathrooms, sinks and doors.

A graphic representation activity also revealed students' knowledge of homes. Asked to draw a home or to make one with clay, the students drew very similar pictures: a classic, "flat" drawing of a box with a triangle on top, two square windows and a door in the middle. Clay representations also were similar, as most students flattened the clay and used a pencil to draw a house, suggesting perhaps a limited familiarity with this media.

To help students gain a three-dimensional understanding of how a home is constructed, the student teacher suggested that the students try to create a "standing" home from available materials, including drinking straws and pipe cleaners. Although most students began by working on their own, they were soon discussing construction strategies with one another, explaining how they had connected the walls or added the ceiling. They tried a large number of different ways to create house frames. Some students twisted pipe cleaners around

the end of the straws to connect them. Others inserted the pipe cleaners into the straws and bent them to create joints. Through collaboration and demonstration, they identified the most effective ways for constructing their models.

As the project continued, the students discussed different types of homes, especially homes in other cultures. Before going to the library to research cultures, the teachers paired strong readers with less proficient students who shared the same interest. The students recorded the information they found on a data chart (Tompkins & Hoskisson, 1991). They were excited by many of their discoveries. The students studying the Navajos, for example, could not believe that *hogans* were made from mud and grass. Two students who chose to study the Southeast Asian culture were surprised by the many different styles of homes found in that culture. Cooperation was high among the students as they gathered information for each other and shared books that could help other groups. Ultimately, the students used the completed data charts to write research reports.

After the research was done, the students were eager to build models. Model building, like some of the earlier activities, required problem solving, creativity and collaboration. The students expanded upon their learning from the earlier home-building activity. Concerned with the accuracy of their model, students who built a Navajo *hogan* with wood sticks reexamined the photograph of a modern-day *hogan*. One of the group members said, "It's not quite right. Look, they have grass covering their walls." The group then collected dried grass and twigs to glue on the walls, and dirt to create the surrounding environment.

On the final day of the project, the students set up a "Home Exhibit" that included their models, a name card identifying the culture each house represented, the names

of the students who worked on the model and the written reports. Parents were invited to the exhibit, where they had a chance to join students in viewing the different homes, reading about the cultures and asking questions.

Conclusion

The above examples prove the benefits of adapting Reggio Emilia principles to teaching culturally diverse elementary-age students. These students responded enthusiastically to projects that were interesting and meaningful. Project experiences that encouraged expression in multiple modes or "languages" helped to build concepts and bridge language differences. The projects enabled the students to achieve curriculum objectives in ways that were far more meaningful than using a textbook. Students learned to collaborate, conduct research and create representations of their learning. Their thinking was extended and deepened by having more time to explore and solve problems. Documentation allowed them to examine their own progress.

Student teachers were successful in utilizing strategies from Reggio Emilia schools to design an enriching curriculum. In doing so, they discovered the power of the Reggio Emilia approach to reach all children, especially the culturally and linguistically diverse.

References

Abramson, S., Seda, I., & Johnson, C. (1990). Literacy development in a multilingual kindergarten classroom. *Childhood Education, 67*, 68-72.

Allen, V. G. (1986). Developing contexts to support second language acquisition. *Language Arts, 63*, 61-66.

Asch, F. (1979). *Sand cake.* New York: Parents Magazine Press.

Bredekamp, S. (1993). Reflections on Reggio Emilia. *Young Children, 49*(1), 13-17.

Clay, M. M. (1986). Constructive processes: Talking, reading, writing, art, and craft. *Reading Teacher, 39,* 764-770.

Crawford, L. W. (1993). *Language and literacy learning in multicultural classrooms.* Boston: Allyn & Bacon.

De Paola, T. (1975). *Strega nona.* Englewood Cliffs, NJ: Prentice Hall.

Edwards, C. (1993). Partner, nurturer and guide: The roles of the Reggio teacher in action. In C. Edwards, L. Gandini, & G. Forman (Eds.), *The hundred languages of children: The Reggio Emilia approach to early childhood education* (pp. 151-169). Norwood, NJ: Ablex.

Edwards, C., Gandini, L., & Forman, G. (Eds.). (1993). *The hundred languages of children: The Reggio Emilia approach to early childhood education.* Norwood, NJ: Ablex.

Enright, D. S. (1986). "Use everything you have to teach English": Providing useful input to young language learners. In P. Rigg & D. S. Enright (Eds.), *Children and ESL: Integrating perspectives* (pp. 113-162). Washington, DC: TESOL Publications.

Enright, D. S., & McCloskey, M. L. (1985). Yes, talking! Organizing the classroom to promote second language acquisition. *TESOL Quarterly, 15,* 431-453.

Forman, G., Moonja, L., Wrisley, L., & Langley, J. (1993). The city in the snow: Applying the multisymbolic approach in Massachusetts. In C. Edwards, L. Gandini, & G. Forman (Eds.), *The hundred languages of children: The Reggio Emilia approach to early childhood education* (pp. 233-250). Norwood, NJ: Ablex.

Fyfe, B., & Caldwell, L. (1993). In P. Weissman, R. Saltz, & E. Saltz (Eds.), *Innovations in Early Education: The International Reggio Exchange, 1*(2) (p. 6-7). Detroit, MI: Merrill-Palmer Institute.

Gandini, L. (1993a). Educational and caring spaces. In C. Edwards, L. Gandini, & G. Forman (Eds.), *The hundred languages of children: The Reggio Emilia approach to early childhood education* (pp. 135-149). Norwood, NJ: Ablex.

Gandini, L. (1993b). Fundamentals of the Reggio Emilia approach to early childhood education. *Young Children, 49*(1), 4-8.

Gandini, L., & Edwards, C. P. (1988). Early childhood integration of the visual arts. *Gifted International, 5*(2), 14-17.

Gardner, H. (1985). *Frames of mind: The theory of multiple intelligences.* New York: Basic Books.

Hudelson, S. (1984). Kan yu ret an rayt en Ingles: Children become literate in English as a second language. *TESOL Quarterly, 18,* 221-238.

Katz, L. G. (1990). Impressions of Reggio Emilia preschools. *Young Children, 45*(6), 11-12.

Katz, L. G. (1993). What can we learn from Reggio Emilia? In C. Edwards, L. Gandini, & G. Forman (Eds.), *The hundred languages of children: The Reggio Emilia approach to early childhood education* (pp. 19-37). Norwood, NJ: Ablex.

LeeKeenan, D., & Nimmo, J. (1993). Connections: Using the project approach with 2- and 3-year-olds in a university laboratory school. In C. Edwards, L. Gandini, & G. Forman (Eds.), *The hundred languages of children: The Reggio Emilia approach to early childhood education* (pp. 251-267). Norwood, NJ: Ablex.

Malaguzzi, L. (1993a). No way. The hundred is there. In C. Edwards, L. Gandini, & G. Forman (Eds.), *The hundred languages of children: The Reggio Emilia approach to early childhood education* (pp. vi). Norwood, NJ: Ablex.

Malaguzzi, L. (1993b). History, ideas and basic philosophy. In C. Edwards, L. Gandini, & G. Forman (Eds.), *The hundred languages of children: The Reggio Emilia approach to early childhood education* (pp. 41-89). Norwood, NJ: Ablex.

Malaguzzi, L. (1993c). For an education based on relationships. *Young Children, 49*(1), 9-12.

Melvin, B. S., & Stout, D. F. (1987). Motivating language learners through authentic materials. In W. M. Rivers (Ed.), *Interactive language teaching* (pp. 44-56). Cambridge: Cambridge University Press.

New, R. (1990). Excellent early education: A city in Italy has it. *Young Children, 45*(6), 4-10.

Rankin, B. (1992). Inviting children's creativity—A story of Reggio Emilia, Italy. *Child Care Information Exchange, 85,* 30-35.

Rankin, B. (1993). Curriculum development in Reggio Emilia: A long-term curriculum project about dinosaurs. In C. Edwards, L. Gandini, & G. Forman (Eds.), *The hundred languages of children: The Reggio Emilia approach to early childhood education* (pp. 189-211). Norwood, NJ: Ablex.

Rinaldi, C. (1993). The emergent curriculum and social constructivism. In C. Edwards, L. Gandini, & G. Forman (Eds.), *The hundred languages of children: The Reggio Emilia approach to early childhood education* (pp. 101-111). Norwood, NJ: Ablex.

Seely, C., & Hurwitz, A. (1983). Developing language through art. *School Arts, 82*(9), 20-22.

Shier, J. H. (1990). Integrating the arts in the foreign/second language curriculum: Fusing the affective with the cognitive. *Foreign Language Annals, 23,* 301-314.

Spaggiari, S. (1993). The community-teacher partnership in the governance of the schools. In C. Edwards, L. Gandini, & G. Forman (Eds.), *The hundred languages of children: The Reggio Emilia approach to early childhood education* (pp. 91-99). Norwood, NJ: Ablex.

Tompkins, G. E., & Hoskisson, K. (1991). *Language arts: Content and teaching strategies.* New York: Macmillan.

Vecchi, V. (1993). The role of the atelierista. In C. Edwards, L. Gandini, & G. Forman (Eds.), *The hundred languages of children: The Reggio Emilia approach to early childhood education* (pp. 119-127). Norwood, NJ: Ablex.

Weissman, P., Saltz, R., & Saltz, E. (Eds.). (1993). *Innovations in Early Education: The International Reggio Exchange, 1*(2). Detroit, MI: Merrill-Palmer Institute.

Workman, S., & Anziano, M. C. (1993). Curriculum webs: Weaving connections from children to teachers. *Young Children, 48*(2), 4-9.

To Build a House: Designing Curriculum for Primary-Grade Children

**Teresa T. Harris
and J. Diane Fuqua**

Teresa Harris, *Ph.D., is associate professor in early childhood education at James Madison University, Harrisonburg, Virginia. A former classroom teacher and an early childhood supervisor for the Virginia Department of Education, Teresa was the lead teacher for this project.*

Diane Fuqua, *Ph.D., is associate professor in early childhood education at James Madison University. She has taught four-year-olds through fourth graders and now focuses on kindergarten and primary curriculum teacher education.*

Designing experiences that are interesting and meaningful to children in the primary grades requires an understanding of the learners as well as an understanding of how to organize the curriculum to meet their needs. Using a curriculum-planning strategy that is based on an understanding of a constructivist model of learning, a group of teachers planned, implemented, and assessed a social studies unit, building a house, with a multiage group of children. In this article, we share our process for developing a six-week unit and the experiences in which the children engaged.

Getting ready

It was a new term and a new group of children. It was time to get to know the children and their parents. It was time to plan new experiences that the children would find interesting and challenging. It was time to think about how we could grow into a community of learners. The new class of five- to seven-year-olds reflected our community's growing diversity in terms of culture, language, and socioeconomic status. Within our heterogeneous groups we wanted the children to see themselves as competent learners. How could we plan curriculum to meet the diverse needs of all these children? This was the challenge we faced as teachers of children in the primary grades.

In getting to know our children and in preparing the learning environment for them, we considered many possibilities for organizing curriculum. A project approach offered the most flexibility for responding to the interests of the children while allowing graduate students who do their practice with us opportunities to study children as active participants in creating curriculum. According to Katz and Chard, a project refers to a "way of teaching and learning that emphasizes the teacher's role in encouraging children to interact with people, objects, and the environment in ways that have personal meaning to them. It emphasizes children's active participation in their own studies of the world that is family to them" (1991, 3).

Selecting a familiar topic was important because we could build on children's previous knowledge and understandings and allow them opportunities to ask their own questions and pose their own problems about the topic. The idea that was most appealing to us was a project based on construction. Construction activities were all around us. The hospital, located next door to our school, was building a covered walkway to join the main hospital to the new oncology center. Our university's student center, located in our back-

From *Young Children*, November 1996, pp. 77-83. © 1996 by the National Association for the Education of Young Children.
Reprinted by permission.

Figure 1. An Outline of the Unit "Build a House"

1. Construction

Impression

visits to sites
materials
    rubbings
    prints

Extension

maps
Building a House by Byron
    Barton
A House Is a House for Me
    by Mary Ann Hoberman

Expression

clay — free play
     — potter's wheel
woodworking
dollhouses

blocks — hollow
       — unit
       — modular
       — Legos

Build a House

2. Hardware

Impression

hardware store visit

Extension

Toolbox by Ann & Harlow
    Rockwell
Tools by Ann Morris

Expression

hardware store prop
    box
woodworking

3. Plumbing

Impression

plumbing-supply com-
pany visit

Extension

chart

Expression

water table—add filters
    and pumps
plastic pipes and joints—
    add to water/hose play
plumbing store prop box

down the sink

Impression

water treatment plant visit

Extension

filtering experiments
aerators—blender, Jell-O
*The Magic School Bus at the
    Waterworks* by Joanna Cole

Expression

water pump play
woodworking

6. Neighborhood

next step of unit

4. Decorating

Impression

visit to paint and wallaper store
paint mixing

Extension

Oh! Were They Ever Happy! by
    Peter Spier
Mr. Rumphius by Barbara Cooney

Expression

painting the
    playhouse   dropper art
crayon melt   wallpaper collage
decorator's shop
stenciling

5. Landscaping

Impression

class garden
walk to see/talk with
    ground crew

Expression

fruit snacks
designing yard
edible dirt

nature
walk

ANIMAL HOMES: turtle

Impression   crayfish

bug hunt   *class pets:*
classroom guests: fish
goats   guinea pig
chicks   hermit crab
dog   crab
cat
class finds: **Extension**
bird's nest
                     *A House for Hermit
                         Crab* by Eric Carle

*Box Turtle at Long
    Pond* by William
    George
*Have You Seen My
    Cat?* by Eric Carle

Expression

building bug cages
naming the hermit
    crab

yard, was laying the foundation for a new wing. And in a nearby neighborhood, several houses were in various stages of construction. With the physical environment so busy with building, the topic seemed a logical place to start. In identifying subtopics for the construction theme, we webbed possible related topics we might want to explore with the children (Katz & Chard 1991; Katz 1994; Stone 1995/96). With housebuilding at the center of the web, we brainstormed the many directions the topic might take. From the web we selected a beginning focus for our study. Next, we created an outline (see Figure 1) in which we identified concepts and planned initial activities and experiences to support concept construction.

Planning curriculum to appropriately meet the needs and interests of a multiage group of children is a challenging task. As teachers, we identify learning goals and concepts that reflect our understanding of child development and the content to be studied, locate materials and develop activities that will lead to concept construction, create a learning environment that encourages children to explore and ask questions, and interact with children as they use what we have provided and pose their own problems to pursue (Bredekamp & Rosegrant 1992; Short et al. 1992).

Like the learning cycle described by Bredekamp and Rosegrant (1992) and the inquiry cycle presented by Short and colleagues (1996), the curriculum planning strategy (CPS) builds on children's prior experiences and provides a framework for thinking about curriculum (see Figure 2). CPS is based on the understanding that through concrete experiences with real objects and materials (Piaget 1969; Kamii & DeVries 1978) and through interaction with people and the environment (Kamii 1985, 1989), children construct understandings about the world in which they live and begin to represent and use symbols as tools for thinking (Piaget & Inhelder 1969). The three components of CPS are impression, extension, and expression experiences (Dickerson & Leonard 1986; Fuqua 1991; Van Scoy 1995).

1. Impression or intake activities. Real, firsthand experiences with things, situations, and people serve as the raw materials for thinking. Children construct physical and logical mathematical knowledge through their direct experiences in and with the environment (Wadsworth 1996).

2. Extension activities. Promoting a greater depth of understanding and supporting the construction of social knowledge, these activities involve the child with symbols through reading and listening about their experiences. Books, magazines, charts, and pictures are used to extend the impression experiences and provide additional information that cannot be gained through firsthand exploration.

3. Expression activities. Acting on their developing understandings about construction, children engage in activities that permit the outward expression of their thinking about their experiences using words and symbols. Children play out experiences and situations through dramatic play. They draw, write, talk, build with blocks, and construct using a variety of materials. Expression

---

As they explored the topic, children were able to learn and use reading, writing, mathematics, science, and social science skills where the skills were useful and meaningful.

Figure 2. The Curriculum Planning Strategy

Name	IMPRESSION	EXTENSION	EXPRESSION
Definition	Real experiences that provide the "raw material" for thinking	Symbolic experiences that go beyond the experience to promote communication, understanding, and recall	Representational experiences in which children express their understanding and thinking using the symbolic mode
Examples	Firsthand experience with people, materials, community, nature in the classroom or in the field	Secondary experience with stories, books, poems, fingerplays, models, photographs, pictures, movies, filmstrips, graphs, charts, maps, games	Representational experiences include dramatic play, block play, woodworking, sand and water play, art, conversations, language experiences, writing, graphing, recording

New areas of the theme were based on the interests that the children expressed during field trips and activity time.

activities, both teacher initiated and child initiated, form the basis for assessment, as these activities reflect what children understand.

Getting going

Following the CPS, we began the house-building theme and its sub-topics with impression activities and extensions. The first impression experience centered around the children's own homes. Extending this experience, the children brought in photographs of their homes and created class charts of the materials from which their houses were made. This experience was followed by another impression activity—visits to two houses in a nearby neighborhood under different stages of completion to see the workers, their tools, and the processes involved in building a house. Children gathered scrap building materials from each site to bring into the classroom.

We added fiction and nonfiction literature on houses and building to the reading area and used it to extend children's understanding of the theme. We also talked about our trips to the construction sites and made charts that listed things children had seen and reinforced the vocabulary they had heard. To express their developing understanding of the construction theme, children used the materials they had found at the sites in woodworking projects and cardboard constructions. They drew and painted pictures of what they had seen. They built buildings with blocks, to which they added drain pipe. They stacked cardboard boxes and decorated their own "dream" houses.

Water, water, everywhere

Because plumbing was being installed in one of the houses visited and because the children already enjoyed playing with water, the teachers decided that a trip to the plumbing supply company would be an appropriate follow-up trip to provide additional impression experiences.

To extend children's understanding of water in relation to plumbing and water treatment, the teachers identified a variety of print and nonprint resources that could be used with the children in preparation for the trip and in follow-up upon our return. Children referred to pictures we had taken of the houses under construction to see where pipes were being placed. We displayed a chart of where the water travels and placed in the reading area an issue of *Ranger Rick* that had a section about water.

As the project moved from plumbing to waste water treatment, the teachers decided that *The Magic School Bus at the Waterworks* would be the literature to help the children make the transition from water entering the house to water leaving the house. Additional extension resources included two teacher-made books that we created with the children following our trip—one based on the plumbing supply company

and the other to accompany our trip to the treatment plant. After the trip to the treatment plant, one of the teachers made a new book, *Do Not Drink the Water,* based on the many signs we saw at each step of the treatment process.

We also included models and simulations in our plans. Children conducted experiments to determine which materials most effectively filtered our dirty water. They also conducted experiments to simulate aspects of water treatment that could not be directly observed on the field trip.

Children show their interests by what they choose to do, the conversations they have, and the questions they ask. We knew that the children were interested in exploring water based on their water play, dramatic play, and

Based on children's interests and explorations, some initial aspects of the theme were omitted and new ones were introduced.

constructions. To support this interest, we placed a variety of strainers and spray bottles in the water table to see how children would use them. Buckets were everywhere so that children could fill up the water table or move water from one place to another. We hooked up the hose almost every day so that children could create rivers and pools on the playground. We carried lengths of PVC pipe that had been available as gutters for houses built in the block area to the playground to channel water on the ground. These expression activities allowed children to show what they were interested in and what they understood about water.

The children take over

Children actively participated in teacher-led discussions and experiments related to water and the purification process, but two distinct interest groups arose in response to the materials we had provided in the environment and the experiences we were having in the community.

One group of children decided to build a swimming pool on the playground

The play equipment was located on a gentle slope and built on a base of sand. The children dug a trench from the base of the slide at the top of the incline to the bottom of the hill, where there was ample room to create their pool. The children spent several days digging, with some children assuming responsibility for the trench and others assuming responsibility for the pool. By midweek the children were ready to turn on the hose to fill their pool.

Starting at the top of the hill, the children turned on the hose and watched as the water soaked into the sandy bottom of the trench. As the water was absorbed into the ground, the children were amazed! With the water still running, they gathered buckets, filled them with water, and poured the water into the trench. They kept adding more and more water until finally the water ran down toward their pool and filled it.

With the pool filled and children eager to splash, the builders began looking for new challenges. The children routed water through the playground's climbing structure via plastic guttering until it cascaded down the slide and into the trench. Leaks that occurred between sections of guttering presented new problems to be solved as children constructed new understandings about the fluid nature of water. In the days that followed, the children applied the lessons they learned in new situations that they created. For example, based on their earlier experience with water absorption in the first trench and their recent experience with guttering, when a new trench was started, the children experimented with wax paper and aluminum foil as "liner" to prevent additional absorption.

While the builders were digging out the trench and the pool, another group of children was involved in dramatic play

A plumbing store had been set up outside as a place for children to gather supplies that they might need for water play. The children had equipped the store, an old wooden climbing structure that resembled a house, with telephones, calculators, paper and markers, and wooden signs. Hoses, pipes, and buckets were "for sale" to interested customers.

One day, two of the regular shopkeepers became frustrated about their lack of customers. They had worked hard at preparing their shop and were eager to sell their supplies. Finally, one of the girls went to a teacher and said, "No one will come to our store!" The teacher asked what they had done to encourage customers to come by, and the child's response was that the other children were doing other things and didn't want to play with them. The teacher sat with the children and asked how stores got people to come in to buy things. The two shopkeepers were puzzled and said they didn't know.

"Sometimes stores have contests to get people to come into the store," one child pointed out.

"We can't have a contest. We don't know how," responded the girls.

Knowing that watermelon was for snack that day, the teacher suggested, "Well, you could have the children guess how many seeds will be in their watermelon at snack today. Then the person who guesses closest to the right number can win a prize."

"But we don't have any prizes."

"Well, let's look in the office to see if there is something you can use, " offered the teacher. The girls went with the teacher and found a small blank tablet and a pen.

"How's this?" asked the teacher. The girls agreed that the paper and pen would be a worthy prize and then began to prepare their chart for guessing the seeds in the watermelon. The chart was posted on the plumbing store wall, and the girls spent the rest of activity time going from child to child to obtain and record their guesses. While the girls were completing their chart, the teacher was busy preparing small cups for contestants to use in saving their seeds. At the end of the day, the two shopkeepers held up their chart and asked each person to tell how many seeds they actually had in their watermelon. Although guesses ranged from a few to 100 seeds, some children were close in their estimates, and one child actually guessed the exact number of seeds in her watermelon. The shopkeepers proudly awarded their prize to the winner.

In these two child-initiated activities children selected the mate-

---

Community businesses were responsive when we asked to visit, and they provided materials for woodworking, construction activities, and dramatic play.

---

rials and the peers with whom they wanted to work. They posed problems and looked for solutions to questions that were most meaningful and interesting to them. We believed that our role was to prepare the environment and supply appropriate materials and then let the children take the lead in how to use them (Dewey 1938). We observed children using what was available and, based on their questions and comments, provided additional materials or helped them design new materials to meet their particular needs. Katz (1994) pointed out that

> if the topic of a project is exotic and outside of the children's direct experience they are dependent upon the teacher for most of the questions, ideas, information, thinking, and planning. Young children are dependent on adults for many aspects of their lives and their learning experiences; however, project work is that part of the curriculum in which their own interests, ideas, preferences, and choices can be given relatively free rein. (Katz 1994, 23)

Dewey (1938) stated that teachers are responsible for creating learning environments and choosing experiences that maximize the likelihood that learners will raise questions, seek solutions, and construct understanding. CPS provides the framework for selecting activities and materials that lead to concept construction. However, the teachers maintain the flexibility to modify curriculum decisions based on the needs and interests of the children. This flexibility allows children to pursue their own interests, pose problems that are important to them, and search for their own solutions.

Assessment

Consistent with the NAEYC guidelines for appropriate assessment (NAEYC 1992), we see assessment as a continuous process of observing, recording, and documenting the work and behaviors of the children to guide our curriculum decisions. As the unit was planned, teachers identified the goals, objectives, concepts, and skills that would be addressed, based on their knowledge of child development and individual children's interests and needs. Then teachers observed the behaviors and products of the children—their "expressions"—recording observations through anecdotal records, photographs of children's constructions, work samples, and videotapes of children's interactions and activities. These sources of observational information were analyzed, interpreted, and reported as teachers met to review the day's activities, to discuss children's progress toward individual and program goals and objectives, and to plan for additional activities and experiences.

As they explored the topic, children were able to learn and use reading, writing, mathematics, science, and social science skills where the skills were useful and meaningful. New areas of the theme were based on interests that the children expressed during field trips and activity time. Based on children's interests and explorations, some initial aspects of the theme were omitted and new ones were introduced.

Children's Books

Aardema, V. *Who's In Rabbit's House?*
Adkins, J. *How a House Happens.*
Asch, F. *Goodbye House.*
Baker, L. *The Third-Story Cat.*
Barton, B. *Machines at Work.*
Bolian, P., & M. Schima. *I Know a House Builder.*
Burton, V.L. *The Little House.*
Cole, J. *The Magic School Bus at the Waterworks.*
Frasconi, A. *The House that Jack Built.*
Fyleman, R. Wanted. In *Springboards*, ed. J. Tuinman.
Gauch, P.L. *Christina Katerina and the Box.*
Gibbons, G. *How a House is Built.*
Hoberman, M.A. *A House Is a House for Me.*
Keats, E.J. *Apt. 3.*
LeSieg, T. *Come Over to My House.*
Miller, M., & M. Miller. *Oscar Mouse Finds a Home.*
Pope, B.N., & R.W. Emmons. *Your World: Let's Build a House.*
Ramos, G. *Careers in Construction.*
Shay, A. *What Happens When You Build a House?*
Sobol, H.l. *Pete's House.*
Waber, B. *The House on East 88th Street.*
Walker, L. *Housebuilding for Children: Step-by-Step Plans for Houses Children Can Build Themselves.*
Williams, R. *Our Tree House.*
Wood, A. *The Napping House.*

miles of our classroom. We had a sufficient budget to support the program, so consumable supplies

Parents were available to drive to field trips, most of which were within five miles of our classroom.

Teachers made resources available to support the theme. Community businesses were responsive when we asked to visit, and they provided materials for woodworking, contruction activities, and dramatic play. Parents were available to drive to field trips, most of which were within five

could be purchased as needed by the teachers and children.

Conclusion

As teachers, it is our responsibility to provide children a variety of experiences with people and with the real materials that are part of the children's community. In recognizing that children can and will make good decisions about using materials to "express" or represent their experiences and further explore their world, we then provide an array of resources and materials from which they may choose. To support good choices, we also organize space so that children can assume responsibility for selecting, using, and cleaning up the materials that are available to them. We schedule large blocks of time so that children can plan, implement, and reflect on the activities and projects in which they choose to become involved. Finally, we continually observe children's interactions with the materials, their peers, and adults to gain clues to what they know, what they need to know, and what they want to know.

This approach to planning, the curriculum planning strategy, supports children's need for autonomy, their need for "real" experiences, their innate interest in the world around them, and their need to learn and use skills in real and meaningful contexts. It supports what we know about the primary-age child.

References

Bredekamp, S., & T. Rosegrant. 1992. Reaching potentials through appropriate curriculum: Conceptual frameworks for applying the guidelines. In *Reaching potentials: Appropriate curriculum and assessment for young children,* Vol. 1, eds. S. Bredekamp & T. Rosegrant, 28–42. Washington, DC: NAEYC.

Dewey, J. 1938. *Experience and education.* New York: Collier.

Dickerson, M., & A.M. Leonard. 1986. "Suggestions for curriculum implementation from knowledge of levels of representational functioning and modes of learning." School of Education, James Madison University, Harrisonburg, VA. Photocopy.

Fuqua, J.D. 1991. *Whole learning: A model for planning.* Paper presented at the annual meeting of the Association for Childhood Education International, April, San Diego, California.

Harris, T. 1994. The snack shop: Block play in a primary classroom. *Dimensions of Early Childhood* 22 (4): 22–23.

Kamii, C. 1985. *Young children reinvent arithmetic: Implications of Piaget's theory.* New York: Teachers College Press.

Kamii, C. 1989. *Young children continue to reinvent arithmetic—2nd grade: Implications of Piaget's theory.* New York: Teachers College Press.

Kamii, C., & R. DeVries. 1978. *Physical knowledge in preschool education: Implications of Piaget's theory.* Englewood Cliffs, NJ: Prentice-Hall.

Katz, L.G. 1994. What can we learn from Reggio Emilia? In *The hundred languages of children: The Reggio Emilia approach to early childhood education,* eds. C. Edwards, L. Gandini, & G. Forman. Norwood, NJ: Ablex.

Katz, L.G., & S.C. Chard. 1991. *Engaging children's minds: The project approach.* Norwood, NJ: Ablex.

National Association for the Education of Young Children. 1992. Guidelines for appropriate curriculum content and assessment in programs serving children ages 3 through 8. In *Reaching potentials: Appropriate curriculum and assessment for young children,* Vol 1, eds. S. Bredekamp & T. Rosegrant, 9–27. Washington, DC: NAEYC.

Piaget, J. 1969. *Science of education and the psychology of the child.* New York: Viking.

Piaget, J., & B. Inhelder. 1969. *The psychology of the child.* New York: Basic Books.

Short, K.G., J. Schroeder, J. Laird, G. Kauff-man, M.J. Ferguson, & K.M. Crawford. 1996. *Learning together through inquiry: From Columbus to integrated curriculum.* York, ME: Stenhouse.

Stone, S.J. 1995–96. Integrating play into the curriculum. *Childhood Education* 72 (1): 104–07.

Van Scoy, I.J. 1995. Trading the three R's for the four E's: Transforming curriculum. *Childhood Education* 72 (1): 19–23.

Wadsworth, B.J. 1996. *Piaget's theory of cognitive and affective development.* 5th ed. White Plains, NY: Longman.

Teachers and Children Together: Constructing New Learning

by Lella Gandini

*Lella Gandini is an author of children's books, books for parents and teachers, and a correspondent for the Italian early education magazine, **Bambini**. She serves as official liaison in the United States for the dissemination of the Reggio Emila approach for children. She is adjunct professor in the School of Education at the University of Massachusetts, Amherst.*

A Story

We find two teachers intent on placing on a large table many samples of different papers they had been collecting. They are trying to divide them according to weight from lightest to heaviest.

Now they realize that it is difficult to ignore the differences in color, which gets in the way of their first attempt to categorize by weight. As a solution, they decide to work at first just with white paper.

Immediately, as they proceed to touch and handle their selections, they notice how the pieces of white paper — tissue, rice paper, parchment, tracing paper, typing paper, newsprint, packing paper — are distinct and differ not only in weight, of course, but also in texture, pliability, and feel. As they move them around, some seem to catch the breeze, while others remain flat and rigid. "Look, they also have different ways to show the light if you hold the pieces up to it." Now they start to place the white papers on the windowpanes. "Oh, look at the shadow of that tree on the paper; it's working as a screen."

This selection and exploration takes a long time and gives much pleasure. The teachers learn about the properties of paper in general and of those different pieces that are making an attractive design on the table. Paper has become more and more a material full of surprises. The two teachers, as they continue to work, realize that tearing and crumpling paper makes interesting sounds, that collages can have an infinite palette of colors and textures, and that adding the design of letters and words and cut-out images opens up many possibilities for beautiful pictures and intense narratives.

Later, they start a list of verbs that communicate the different actions that working with paper implies, such as crumpling, folding, tearing, cutting, gluing. . . .

At a certain point, they stop to reflect about their experience. They go over the sequence of their decisions to learn more about the possibilities of paper as a material to use with the young children in their classroom.

They had given themselves the following tasks:

• We will look independently for as much variety of paper samples as we can find.

• We will make notes about where we found each kind of paper, about its availability, size, weight (and eventually cost).

• We will collect it neatly in a box, and then we will meet and we will surprise each other with what we found.

• Together, we will divide the paper in categories; we will experiment and make a list of what could be done with each or with the combination of various kinds of paper.

Now, thinking back, they reflect: "Are we learning all these secrets to teach them directly to our children? We gave ourselves trust and time, and we gave ourselves a chance to pursue unknown paths in order to make discoveries. We should offer the children the same chance. But we have also learned a great deal from our experience; now we can offer a good selection of paper, and we know how to display it to enhance specific aspects. We helped each other with our uncertainties, with our questions, and with what we learned; now we can support children with questions and offer them skills when they need them. Other discoveries and other questions will be suggested by the children themselves, and together with them we will continue to learn about this."

Materials can be used to enhance the learning experience of young children (and their teachers) by opening new avenues for discovering, creating, and constructing. There are many materials that have that potential all

Photograph by Lella Gandini

around us; they can be brought inside the classroom together with the usual crayons, markers, scissors, paper, and glue. And even the variety and the use of crayons, markers, scissors, paper, and glue can be expanded and transformed into a powerful mine of ideas, as our first story tells us.

It is helpful to look around and observe what is available or search for things that can be used, combined, or transformed. It is not obvious or easy at first — but when we start to pay attention, our eyes gradually will see better and detect more paths to potential materials that our environment offers for our work and pleasure.

If we go on a walk in the woods, we will begin to see interesting leaves, twigs, chips of bark, acorns, pine cones, grasses. Let us just observe the leaves we found. How can we put side by side combining or contrasting shape, size, colors, texture, the fresh and the dried ones? Is the skeleton visible or not? From what tree do they come?

If we are near a beach or a river, we could find shells, pebbles, or splinters of wood bleached by the sun. What about on the environment closer to our daily chores, like a supermarket? Let us look at the variety of fruit displayed there. Could we take some to school to observe, touch, cut open, and taste? Could we keep the peel to dry and use for our collages? Could we explore the seeds of these fruits, plant them, and keep track to see if they sprout and how?

Another Story

A teacher in a classroom of five year olds decided to try out clay with the children. She thought the children could shape a small bowl to give to their parents as a gift. There was a kiln available in the school; therefore, she thought, the bowls could be fired and then painted.

When I visited the classroom, this teacher was disappointed and frustrated. The children had not become involved as she hoped; they had hurriedly shaped approximate, tentative bowls; and now that it was time to paint them, they did so with a few dabs of color and rushed back to other things available in the room. "I guess these children are not artistically inclined when it comes to clay, or else I am not able to give life to this experience" was her comment.

We turned to look at the children who had left the table with the abandoned, sad bowls. Some of those children were building with blocks. I noticed right away how complex the block structure was and how eagerly the children were adding and modifying parts, discussing and negotiating the next steps in their building within the group.

The teacher saw my interest, smiled, and with enthusiasm began to explain: the children were working on the cityscape, and they had discussed with her some of the buildings they knew. As their interest grew, they had decided together to place the silhouette drawing of the city skyline behind the block area. They had discussed the problems of building bridges and highways and had made drawings as plans. They had selected the different shapes of blocks to make ramps and had become aware of the fact that small blocks placed together became as big as the larger blocks.

As she went on, her narrative and her observations about the children's discoveries and learning showed competence and pleasure. At a certain point, she stopped to breathe, and I asked: "Do you like clay?" She was surprised, but just for a few seconds. "I see," she said, "You noticed how much I like blocks. I realize I know very little about clay and its properties; I feel a little uneasy about it; and I never used it myself. I wanted to give the children an artistic experience, and now you help me realize the difference in the way I approached this experience and the one with blocks." The experience of that teacher and those children working with blocks had been a co-construction; their learning was constructed together.

It happens often that the continuous availability, abundance, and variety of blocks — as well as of special space set-ups and of time available for block play, plus the extended experience of teachers with that material — make block play into a very developed, constructive, and creative language. Other materials, that is, other potential languages, have less space, time, and variety. Often teachers have not had a chance to observe or experiment with them; therefore, there is less attention given to the way they are offered to children.

Another problem frequently encountered is the notion that *art* or *art activities* are something separate from the learning experiences of children; the same is true of the thought than an exploration of harmony and beauty can be done only with a limited range of materials, called *art materials*, only in a specific corner of the classroom, and only at a set time of day. There is also a tendency to think that an experience for children, in order to be creative and *artistic*, can only be spontaneous, open ended, and perhaps messy.

The fear of focusing too much on the product rather than the process makes teachers afraid to offer the children the chance to improve and feel successful and pleased with what they want to make. To give that possibility to children requires offering them occasions to learn skills at the moment they feel that they need them, or when it is clear that without them they could get stuck or become discouraged. What is called for is that delicate and observant way of being with children, sustaining them, and encouraging them to go forward when they are about ready to do so. To construct new learning with them is a way to respect their potential. And, by the way, they do not need to be considered artists; that is an adult notion.

Co-Exploration of Materials in Reggio Emilia

We turn to the schools of Reggio Emilia to reflect with those teachers on ways to support the explorations of very young children with materials in such a way that those explorations become meaningful experiences. The educators here feel that it is useful to be close to the children, especially when they begin to explore new materials, in order to sustain their discovery and to enjoy it with them, but also to open the way to constructing communication through the materials.

The teachers strongly believe that children desire to learn and have potentially many ways to communicate their feelings, their interests, and their questions about themselves and the world around them. The goal of the teachers is to give, gradually and remaining respectful of the children's own time, a repertoire of many media and materials. These media and materials they consider to be languages because they make communication possible and open the door to learning.

With that in mind, the teachers organize the space of the classroom in such a way that many engaging activities that children can do by themselves are available. Several of these are set up so that children can gather in small, autonomous groups. When a new material or a new project is presented to one group, one of the teachers will stay with that group while the other will be available to the rest of the children.

When children are three or younger, the range of materials should be presented gradually, but the occasions to explore and construct with them should be many. These occasions become part of the ongoing daily activities, to create continuity and familiarity, while at the same time offering the pleasure of discovering and being surprised.

There are many different materials that are developmentally appropriate for very young children. Some of the materials we have seen in the Reggio infant-toddler centers or schools are familiar to all of us, but the teachers, working together, have found ways to extend and enrich some apparently simple objects.

kamp, 1987; Stone, 1995). Reading requires a child to look at symbols or representations (i.e., letters and words) and extract meaning from them. A play-based curriculum offers children opportunities throughout the day to develop the ability to think abstractly by experiencing real objects using their senses (Bredekamp, 1987; Kostelnik, Soderman, & Whiren, 1993). Blocks can represent an airplane or a train. High heels can transform a preschooler into a mother or princess. Blocks and high heels are three dimensional, tangible objects. Sufficient practice using concrete objects as symbols is a necessary prerequisite to the use and comprehension of print (Stone, 1995).

Mathematical understanding is more than recognition of numerals and amounts. Sorting, categorizing, putting items in a series, and problem solving are all important math concepts (Raines & Canady, 1990). The teacher may believe that Jamaica understands the concept of "four" if she circles four flowers on the worksheet. But until Jamaica can transfer that learning to other situations, such as the number of places at the table for four people, Jamaica does not truly understand what "four" means. Similarly, Jamaica may be able to print the letters "R," "U," and "N" on a worksheet, but be unable to read the word "run" when she sees it in a book. The mere accomplishment of the worksheet task does not signify the child's ability to read or comprehend.

Emotional Development

In any group of young children asked to do a paper-pencil task, some will succeed and some will be less successful. The successful children may truly comprehend the task—or may simply have guessed correctly. The less successful ones often learn to think of themselves as failures, and ultimately may give up on school and on themselves (Katz & Chard, 1989). These children may react to the stress created by fear of giving the wrong answers by acting out their frustrations and becoming behavior problems, or by with-

drawing and becoming reclusive (Charlesworth, 1996). Parents may report school phobic behaviors such as stomach aches in the morning or refusal to get into the car to go to preschool. These children have learned, at an early age, that school can be an emotionally painful place.

School should be a welcoming, peaceful place for children—an environment to which children come eager to see what challenging, stimulating, and fun activities are in store. Children know they may not succeed at everything they try, but also know they will be valued for who they are. Children's efforts should be rewarded, so that they will persevere and they will see themselves as learners (Kostelnik, Stein, Whiren, & Soderman, 1993).

Physical Development

Children are born with a need to move (Kostelnik, Soderman, & Whiren, 1993). They wiggle, toddle, run, and climb as naturally as they breathe. When we insist that children sit still and do what for them may be a meaningless task, such as completing a workbook page, we force children into a situation incompatible with their developmental needs and abilities. When children cannot or will not do such a task, we may label them "immature" or "hyperactive." We may complain about their short attention span, or as in Jamaica's case, criticize her efforts. On the other hand, if we allow children to choose their own task from among appropriate offerings, we may see children as young as three and four years old spend 30 to 45 minutes completely engrossed in building with unit blocks, painting at the easel, or listening to stories. When we plan developmentally appropriate activities for children, they will attend to them, work hard, and learn (Bredekamp & Rosegrant, 1992).

Before a child can hold a pencil and make an accurate mark on paper, he must have a great deal of small motor control. He needs practice with various materials and objects that require grasping, holding, pinching, and squeezing. He must have

ample opportunity to make his own marks with objects such as paint brushes, chalk, fat crayons, and felt-tip markers. Only later, when he has achieved the necessary finger and hand control, should he be asked to write words or numerals with a pencil. The timing of this accomplishment will vary among children. Some four-year-olds and most five-year-olds are ready to write a few things, notably their own names. But, we must remember that each child develops on his or her own schedule, and some six-year-olds may be just starting this task. If they are encouraged, rather than criticized, they will continue to learn and grow and feel confident.

Social Development

Teachers who require young children to perform passive tasks like worksheets may be heard exhorting them, "Do your own work. Eyes on your own paper." There are few situations in the adult world in which we cannot ask a friend or colleague for help with a task, or for their ideas about a problem. In fact, leaders in business and industry say they need employees who can work in teams to solve problems. Yet we ask children to do what are often impossible tasks, and insist that they suffer through them alone.

The foundations for our social relationships are laid in the early years (Kostelnik, Stein, Whiren, & Soderman, 1993). This is the time when we discover the roles we may play, the rules for getting along in society, the consequences for not following rules, and how to make friends. The only way to learn these concepts is to engage actively with others. When we do not allow children enough time to accomplish fundamental social tasks, we set the stage for social problems later on. Middle and high schools cope daily with antisocial behaviors that in some cases reach the point of violence. If we expect adolescents to know how to work and live with others, and solve problems peacefully, we would do well to begin the process when children are young.

Developmentally Appropriate Activities

There are many active, and far more interesting, ways for children to begin understanding words and numbers than via worksheets (Mason, 1986). A classroom with a developmentally appropriate curriculum is a print-rich environment. The walls are covered with signs naming objects, stories children have dictated, lists of words they have generated, pictures they have painted and labeled, and charts of classroom jobs (such as feeding the pet and passing out napkins for snack). At the small motor activities table there may be sandpaper letters to feel and puzzles to complete. Creative activities may include squirting shaving cream onto the table and having children make designs and write their names. And always there are many books to explore, examine, wonder about, listen to, and love as they are read aloud. In these ways, children learn that reading and writing are useful skills, not simply tedious activities adults invent to make school boring. It takes a lot of experience with words and print for children to understand why it is good to be able to read.

Demonstrating Progress

If we cannot demonstrate children's progress with worksheets, how do we provide evidence of learning? Here are several ways:

Portfolios—A portfolio is a collection of a child's work. Portfolios can include the following:

Work Samples: Keep samples of each child's drawings and writing, including invented spelling. Photographs of creations of clay, wood, and other materials can also be included. Children should have a say in what is included in their own portfolio. Date each piece so that progress throughout the school year can be noted.

Observations: Keep observational records of what children do in the class. There are many efficient methods of recording children's behavior. Audio and video tape can capture them in action. Occasional anecdotal notes also help.

Checklists: Record children's skill development on checklists. Progress in beginning letter recognition, name writing, and self-help skills, for example, can be listed and checked off as children master them.

Appropriate worksheets: For example, children experimenting with objects to discover if they sink or float can record their observations on paper divided into a float column and a sink column. This shows that they are doing actual scientific experimentation and recording the data.

For more information on portfolios, see "Why Portfolio-Based Assessment Works" on page 20 of the January/ February 1996 issue of Early Childhood News.

Parent Newsletters—Teachers can send home periodic parent newsletters which explain the activities children are doing at school and the teacher's goals and objectives. When parents understand the value of developmentally appropriate activities they will feel confident that their children are learning and growing, not "just playing."

Center Labels—Signs in the classroom describing what children learn in the various learning centers help adults understand the value of children's work in that area. In the block corner, for example, children learn about weight, length, balance, volume, and shape, as well as problem solving, social role playing, and cooperation. At the art center children learn to express themselves on paper and with other media, to solve problems, and to communicate with others. Signs help skeptics see what is really happening as children work at play.

Photographs—Photographs of daily activities in the classroom can be displayed around the room and in hallways. They provide graphic evidence to parents, administrators, and other teachers of children working and learning in a rich, exciting atmosphere.

Conclusion

There are two fundamental problems with worksheets. First, young children do not learn from them what teachers and par-

What Can Blocks Teach?
by Nancy Thomas

Block building offers opportunities to grapple with concepts such as comparing, sorting, and categorizing (Hirsch, 1984). When children are storing blocks, it should be clear where each shape belongs. Putting blocks away is like putting together a puzzle and is a learning experience in its own right. This task becomes increasingly complicated when you add to the number of shapes.

Blocks are best stored in low, open shelving with the place for each shape block designated by a silhouette. Cut block silhouettes out of contact paper and stick them to the shelf. Church & Miller (1990) suggest that you store blocks in a "top-down, left-right, small-large pattern" as a prereading (sorting and classifying) activity.

References
Hirsch, E.S. (Ed.). (1984). *The block book.* Washington, DC: Natl. Assn. for the Education of Young Children.

Church, E.B. and Miller, K. (1990). *Learning through play blocks.* New York, NY: Scholastic.

Worksheets and workbooks should be used in schools only when children are older and developmentally ready to profit from them (Bredekamp, S. & Rosegrant, T., 1992).

R E S O U R C E S

The following resources will support your efforts to create a developmentally appropriate curriculum.

Blake, S.; Hurley, S.; Arenz, B. (Winter 1995). **Mathematical problem solving and young children.** *Early Childhood Education Journal.* (23) 2, 81-88.

Diffily, D. (January 1996). **The project approach: A museum exhibit created by kindergartners.** *Young Children.* 51(2), 72-75.

Freeman, E.B. (May 1990). **Issues in kindergarten policy and practice.** *Young Children.* (42) 4, 29-39.

Gandini, L. (March/April 1996). **Teachers and children together: Constructing new learning.** *Child Care Information Exchange.* 108, 43-46.

Isenberg, J.P. & Jalongo, M.R. (1993). *Creative expression and play in early childhood curriculum.* Englewood Cliffs, NJ: Prentice-Hall.

Raines, S.C. & Canady, R.J. (1990). *The whole language kindergarten.* New York: Teachers College, Columbia University.

Stone, S.J. (September 1995). **Wanted: Advocates for play in the primary grades.** *Young Children.* (50) 6, 45-54.

Stroud, J.E. (Fall 1995). **Block play: Building a foundation for literacy.** *Early Childhood Education Journal.* (23) 1, 9-13.

VanHoorn, J.; Nourot, P.; Scales, B; & Alward, K. (1993). *Play at the center of the curriculum.* Englewood Cliffs, NJ: Prentice-Hall.

Wasserman, S. (1990). *Serious players in the primary classroom: Empowering children through active learning experiences.* New York: Teachers College Press.

ents believe they do (Kostelnik, Soderman, & Whiren, 1993). Second, children's time should be spent in more beneficial endeavors (Willis, 1995). The use of abstract numerals and letters, rather than concrete materials, puts too many young children at risk of school failure. This has implications for years to come. Worksheets and workbooks should be used in schools only when children are older and developmentally ready to profit from them (Bredekamp, S. & Rosegrant, T., 1992). Our challenge is to convince parents and others that in a play-based, developmentally appropriate curriculum children are learning important knowledge, skills, and attitudes that will help them be successful in school and later life.

References

Bee, H. (1992). *The developing child,* 6th Edition. New York: Harper Collins.

Bodrova, E. & Leong, D.J. (1996). *Tools of the mind: The Vygotskian approach to early childhood education.* Columbus, OH: Prentice Hall/Merrill.

Bredekamp, S. (Ed.). (1987). *Developmentally appropriate practice in early childhood programs serving children from birth through age eight.* Washington, DC: Natl. Assn. for the Education of Young Children.

Bredekamp, S. & Rosegrant, T. (Eds.). (1992). *Reaching potential: Appropriate curriculum and assessment for young children.* Washington, DC: Natl. Assn. for the Education of Young Children.

Charlesworth, R. (1996). *Understanding child development: For adults who work with young children,* 4th ed. Albany, NY: Delmar.

Fordham, A.E. & Anderson, W.W. (1992). Play, risk-taking, and the emergence of literacy. In *Play's place in public education for young children,* edited by V.J. Dimidjian, 105-114. Washington, DC: National Education Association.

Katz, L. (1989). What should children be doing? In Paciorek, K.M. & Munro, J.H. (Eds.). *Annual Editions: Early Childhood Education,* 10th Edition. Guilford, CT: Dushkin.

Katz, L.G. & Chard, S.C. (1989). *Engaging children's minds: The project approach.* Norwood, NJ: Ablex.

Kostelnik, M.J.; Soderman, A.K.; & Whiren, A.P. (1993). *Developmentally appropriate programs in early childhood education.* New York: Merrill.

Kostelnik, M.J.; Stein, L.C.; Whiren, A.P.; & Soderman, A.K. (1993). *Guiding children's social development,* 2nd edition. Albany, NY: Delmar.

Mason, J.M. (1988). In Spodek, B., *Today's kindergarten: Exploring the knowledge base, expanding the curriculum.* New York: Teachers College Press.

Raines, S. & Canady, R.J. (1990). *The whole language kindergarten.* New York: Teachers College, Columbia Univeristy.

Stone, S.J. (1995, September). *Wanted: Advocates for play in the primary grades.* Young Children. 50 (6), 45-54.

Willis, S. (1995). *Teaching young children: Educators seek developmental appropriateness.* In Paciorek, K.M., & Munro, J.H. Guilford, CT: Dushkin.

A Framework for Literacy

Don't try to <u>tell</u> them – <u>show</u> them just exactly what whole language really is

MARY HOPKIN

Mary Hopkin teaches at the Saudi Arabia International Schools, Dhahran, Saudi Arabia.

In the May 1995 issue of *Teaching K-8*, Maryann and Gary Manning highlighted the most difficult obstacle to whole language implementation: the education of parents and other concerned stakeholders as to just what whole language is and what it's not.

> On pages 193–194, there are two reproducible pages you can use that will show your children and their parents how specific learning tasks evolve into literacy.

Parents, as well as some educators, are confused by whole language because they can't quite grasp how it fits into the existing structure to which they've grown accustomed. They hear so many conflicting defin-

itions and criticisms that they're hesitant to accept this common-sense approach to teaching literacy, no matter how strongly enthusiastic teachers advocate it.

No easy task. As the Mannings point out, the task of whole language advocates is to articulate the whole language philosophy in user-friendly terms within the context of a reasoned and logical instructional framework. This is no easy task.

After many attempts to discuss the merits of whole language with colleagues and parents, a group of my comrades-in-arms and I put our heads together and developed a schematic framework to present the philosophy in a clear, succinct format. The framework has become a practical, functional tool for use throughout the curriculum implementation process. The more we use it, the more uses we find for it. It is presently:

1. a process-productive instrument kept in the student's portfolio and used by the students themselves to observe and document their learning in process;

2. a tool used in conferencing to focus participants on the student's learning occurring within the context of our specified expectations;

Schematic A – The Flow

Belief Statement — Program Outcomes — Integrated Topics — Specific Objectives — Exhibitions of Literacy

Schematic B – Translating Beliefs into Expected Program Outcomes

Belief statement: "We believe that literacy enhances personal career achievement and provides a source of enrichment and joy in life."

The Language Arts Curriculum Overview: Early Stages Through Elementary Fluency

The central focus of our elementary literacy program is the broad curricular area which we call language arts. The language arts consist of the development of reading, speaking, listening and writing skills, and are integrated with all other curricular subjects. A variety of resources are utilized in the process of learning to construct meaning from language, including periodicals, textbooks, reference books, children's experiences and thoughts, technology and a large collection of children's literature.

READING OUTCOMES: EARLY STAGES THROUGH ELEMENTARY FLUENCY

Language Development

As a result of our language arts program, we expect our students to:
> enjoy shared reading experiences
> acquire adequate vocabulary
> relate sounds to letters
> use contextual clues
> construct meaning from text

Emergent Reading

As a result of our language arts program, we expect our students to:
> enjoy shared reading experiences
> decode new words
> read orally with consequence
> detect sequences
> predict outcomes
> experience the making of books
> understand the relationship of reading to writing and thinking

Reading Fluency

As a result of our language arts program, we expect our students to:
> share reading for pleasure
> enjoy a variety of literature
> read with expression/clarity
> draw logical conclusions
> identify main ideas
> locate/research data
> read for both information gathering and pleasure

WRITING OUTCOMES: EARLY STAGES THROUGH ELEMENTARY FLUENCY

Pre-Writing Skills

As a result of our language arts program, we expect our students to:
> develop fine motor coordination
> form letters in conventional ways
> relate sounds to letters
> experience thoughts written down
> experience teacher model-writing

Emergent Writing

As a result of our language arts program, we expect our students to:
> use sight words appropriately
> use spelling approximations
> space words correctly
> write legibly
> write short sentences
> sequence written ideas logically

Writing Fluency

As a result of our language arts program, we expect our students to:
> generate ideas to communicate
> write first draft
> revise/edit first draft
> use conventional spelling, grammar and punctuation
> publish final draft
> write for particular audiences

LISTENING AND SPEAKING OUTCOMES: EARLY STAGES THROUGH ELEMENTARY FLUENCY

Sharing Information

As a result of our language arts program, we expect our students to:
> participate in group discussions
> communicate ideas with clarity
> respond appropriately in discussions
> follow and relay oral directions
> enjoy sharing in the group process

Critical Listening

As a result of our language arts program, we expect our students to:
> follow oral directions
> draw logical conclusions
> distinguish facts
> analyze oral information
> evaluate oral information
> listen selectively for main ideas

Speaking Fluency

As a result of our language arts program, we expect our students to:
> use expressive words
> articulate words and thoughts
> present information with clarity
> communicate effectively
> demonstrate self-confidence and poise in group speaking

3. a tool to orient new members quickly to our mission, values and instructional goals, and the direction we are moving in order to get there;

4. a documentation tool which ensures that our transferring students have a clear and accurate record of their achievements within our specified curricular framework.

More of the same. The first time we sat down with a group of parents and presented our process tool, the sense of reassurance and understanding on their faces brought us an enormous sense of pride and satisfaction. And when we presented the framework to our colleagues, their predictable reaction was, "Well, what else is new? We've been doing this for years." Exactly. Of course we

---

Schematic C – Grade 3 Integrated Curriculums

The theme for the year is *Voyages from Past to Present*. The theme was chosen for its flexibility in allowing maximum integration across the curriculum. After reviewing the instructional topics offered in grades 2 and 4, the grade 3 team identified the following thematic topics for the 1995-96 school year. The chosen topics provide continuity from grade 2 and preparation for grade 4. The five boldfaced headings below represent the major topics for the year; the activities and content listed below the headings relate to the curriculum outcomes specified for grade 3 (*Schematic D*).

Traveling Through Time
Our Planet
The oceans
Land forms
Rocks/fossils/minerals
Making a timeline
Weather
Matter and composition
Civilization
Early communities
Needs of people
Ancient civilizations
Simple machines
Explorations
Keeping a journal
Bartering and money
Telling time
Great explorers
The Mayflower voyage
Settling in the New Regions
Getting along
Historical fiction
Remembering the past
Early schools

Folktales Around the World
Historical Perspectives
Origins of folktales
Fun and fanciful tales
Folklore
International communities
Geographical Perspectives
Locating countries on maps
and globes
Seasons
Winter diorama
A snow day
Writing short stories
Human Needs
Families and friends
Giving and receiving
Expressions of thought
 writing poetry
 writing short stories
 reading for pleasure
 telling stories
Celebrations and holidays
 international feast

Fact or Fiction
Shared Inquiry
Research skills
Making timelines
Measurement
Geometric shapes
Multiplication/division
True-to-life fiction
Sharing novels
Problem solving
Collaborative projects
Independent Research
Locating information
Information Processing
Drawing conclusions
Critical Thinking
Analyzing oral information
Evaluating information
Identifying facts
Developing strategies for
 solving problems
Listening selectively
Presenting ideas
Revisiting Fantasy

Our World Today
Research Projects
Using reference tools
Collecting data
Organizing data
Recording data
Writing essays
Reading non-fiction
Reading statistics
Using decimals/fractions
Using graphs/tables
Applying critical thinking
Sharing information
Making observations
Recording observations
Global Responsibility
Eco-systems
Endangered species
Habitats

Adaptation
Climate
Problem-solving
Map-making
Earth Day

Planning for Our Future
Being a person
Body systems
Health and nutrition
Emotions and stress
Adaptation
People We Admire
Autobiographies
Biographies
Our Personal Best
Presentations/exhibitions
Personal responsibility
Making choices
 literature
 writing
 presentations
Assessing the Year
Taking achievement tests
Portfolio review

---

have! Now let's do more of the same and document that we're doing it.

Although the framework has evolved into a more refined and functional tool through the years, it remains my most trusted strategy in convincing skeptics that whole language isn't just a frivolous waste of valuable instructional time, but is instead a way of looking at our curriculum and what we do in terms of our literacy goals and just what our expectations are for the students as a result of our interaction with them.

Schematics A, B, C and D are parts of the framework I share with parents and new teachers. We begin by defining the framework in terms of observable program expectations (*Schematic A*). In other words, what do we expect our students to be able to do in this broad area we call literacy (*Schematic B*)? Only after we have defined what it is can we integrate our beliefs into our instructional program (*Schematic C*). Finally, we want parents and students to see specific learning tasks evolving into literacy through practical applications of language experiences (*Schematic D*).

The schematics clearly and succinctly define our beliefs, our program outcome

Schematic D – Specific Learning Objectives

We believe that literacy enhances personal and career achievement, and provides a source of enrichment and joy in life.

Language Arts Curricular Outcomes
This Is What I Can Do in Grade Three

My Name

My Class

The Day I Began   The Day I Finished

On the Way to Reading Fluency

R 1 Specific Reading Outcomes	Date	I Can Do It!	I Saw You Do It!
R 1.1 I enjoy listening to chapter stories.			
R 1.2 I choose to read independently.			
R 1.3 I choose to explore unfamiliar resources.			
R 1.4 I share creatively about books I have read.			
R 1.5 I share my feelings about books.			
R 1.6 I can re-tell stories in sequence.			
R 1.7 I can recall facts from informational books.			
R 1.8 I can re-read for details.			
R 1.9 My English language experience is OK for reading.			
R1.10 I recognize the basic sight words.			
R1.11 I enjoy reading a variety of literature.			
R 2 Oral Reading Fluency			
R 2.1 When I read aloud, I observe punctuation.			
R 2.2 I read with confidence and expression.			
R 3 Reading Attitudes			
R 3.1 I choose to read because I enjoy reading.			
R 3.2 I can select books that I enjoy and can read.			
R 3.3 I like to share reading materials with others.			

On the Way to Writing Fluency

W1 The Conventions of Handwriting	Date	I Can Do It!	I Saw You Do It!
W 1.1 I can form letters correctly.			
W 1.2 I can join letters correctly in cursive writing.			
W 1.3 I can space my words correctly.			
W 1.4 I write so others can read what I have to say.			
W 2 The Conventions of Punctuation in Writing			
W 2.1 I can use capital letters at the right times.			
W 2.2 I can use periods at the right times.			
W 3.3 I can use commas at the right times.			

(Continued on next page)

expectations, how we integrate our topics and the way we involve our learners in their own learning.

The final products are the student's personal exhibitions of learning, the portfolio of achievement. Our whole language framework shows an obvious link between our mission and beliefs and the processes in place to provide the opportunities for our students to achieve literacy competence and fluency.

Writing Fluency continued from previous page

The Conventions of Punctuation (continued)	Date	I Can Do It!	I Saw You Do It!
W 2.4 I can use question marks at the right times.			
W 2.5 I can use exclamation marks when I need to.			
W 2.6 I can use quotation marks at the right times.			
W 3 The Conventions of Spelling in Writing			
W 3.1 I follow phonetic rules when they work.			
W 3.2 I can use basic sight words.			
W 3.3 I can use a dictionary or spell check to check.			
W 4 Creative Writing			
W 4.1 I can pre-plan my writing tasks.			
W 4.2 I can sequence my ideas logically.			
W 4.3 I can form paragraphs with main ideas.			
W 4.4 I can use interesting and colorful words.			
W 4.5 I can proofread and edit my first drafts.			
W 4.6 I can write short stories.			

On the Way to Listening Competency

L. 1 Specific Listening Skills	Date	I Can Do It!	I Saw You Do It!
L 1.1 I enjoy listening to my teacher read.			
L 1.2 I enjoy listening to my classmates read.			
L 1.3 I listen attentively when my teacher talks.			
L 1.4 I listen attentively when my classmates talk.			
L 1.5 I follow instructions.			
L 1.6 I enjoy talking in a small group.			
L 1.7 I enjoy participating in large group discussions.			
L 1.8 I enjoy a variety of listening activities.			

On the Way to Speaking Fluency

S 1 Specific Speaking Skills	Date	I Can Do It!	I Saw You Do It!
S 1.1 I like to give information to others.			
S 1.2 I like to talk to my teacher.			
S 1.3 I like to talk with other students.			
S 1.4 I speak with appropriate grammar.			
S 1.5 I can speak my thoughts fluently and confidently.			

General Observations and Comments

Read me a story:
101 good books kids will love

Experts agree that there are many benefits to reading to children. One important one: It takes time to read a book. What better gift can we give a child than time?

By **Joan Garvey Hermes**, *the mother of six and a freelance writer who also teaches English at Bishop McNamara High School in Kankakee, Illinois.*

We've made many mistakes raising our children—on a family vacation several years ago we left two of them behind in a Pizza Hut in Minocqua, Wisconsin, a fact that is still the subject of many a guilt trip. But I know we've done one thing right. We read to them.

Goodnight Moon, The Fuzzy Duckling—the list of books we read would be familiar to many young parents; so would our motives for reading: We love books, and we wanted to share this love with our children. We enjoyed the quiet time a book provided, and, at day's end, we liked the ritual of bath, books, prayers, and bed for them—followed by some time alone for us.

As time passed and our son and daughters grew and changed, our reasons for reading to them did the same. We still enjoyed the quiet time, but something else was added. The books we read often enhanced Tom's or Maggie's pleasure in the things he or she had seen that day. Sometimes the very titles Annie or Kate would choose would give us, as parents, a clue to something that had been important to them that day. Martha and Molly, as did their older siblings before them, would often find, in books, a certain comfort to soothe a worry or hurt that had been part of their day.

Much has been written about the value of books. Reading books and being read to at an early age develops literacy, enhances vocabulary and grammar skills, instructs the reader about the world close at hand and far away, and encourages creativity and imagination. Being read to establishes a never-to-be-forgotten sense of security in providing a ritual, a period of time during which a child and reader sit together and attend to a story.

As I look back over the years of reading, being read to, and reading to, I remember many of the books that are part of me as a result of these experiences. It gives me pleasure to think of the many books that are also part of our children's histories.

Most of us read to our children for the sheer fun of it. It gives us pleasure to pass on to our children the stories we loved when we were their age. We enjoy discovering with them stories that are new to us and them. Often, too, a story can say for us the things we feel inadequate to express in our own words. Even those who are not big readers themselves choose to read to their children because educators stress the benefits of reading, particularly early reading, to children. There are also subtle reasons to read to our children, and these are perhaps the most important of all.

When we read, we have to slow down. We gather our child or children to ourselves, and we spend time with them. We give, they receive. Sometimes they give as they make their own observations about the story being read. We establish a ritual, and rituals provide security. We establish a tradition, and this leads to another important reason to read to our children.

Parents pass a culture to their children. As parents we do this whether we want to or

From *U.S. Catholic*, October 1995, pp. 6-15. © 1995 by Claretian Publications. Reprinted by permission.

not. What we choose to do, or not to do, conveys a message to our children. When we read to our children, we teach them that they are important to us. Books are a relatively inexpensive treat, and public libraries provide them for free. But we do spend time when we read. It takes time to sit down to read a book. What better gift can we give our child than the gift of time?

Because books teach as they are enjoyed, they provide a near perfect way to say what is important to us. Children might soon lose interest in a lecture about the importance of honesty or kindness, yet they will spend hours listening to stories.

Reading provides an oasis in a world too busy and too active at times to stop and take note of what really matters. This, too, is why it continues to be of value to read to our children long after they have learned to read themselves. Two years ago when one daughter in our house was making her way through Ray Bradbury's *Fahrenheit 451*, I read the book to her. As an honors English student, she was more than capable of reading the book herself, but we enjoyed moving through it together and talking about the ideas. I hope that experience remains for her as pleasant as it does for me. And I am sure there are older parents who continue, as mine do when we talk on the phone or visit, to say, "What are you reading?" or "Have you read . . . ?" While we can no longer curl up on the couch together, we can still share our love of books and the ideas they hold.

Perhaps the best reason for reading to children is the reason that motivates our own reading as well: We read because it is good for the soul. . . . Reading can remind us that we are not alone in thinking certain values are important. They can put us in the presence of families who are working to be good people. Books can remind us that it is important to be kind, accepting, and to stand up for what is right.

Feel free to browse

What follows is a look at books for children. . . . Books are subtle. They can teach without preaching. The titles have been chosen in a less-than-scientific manner. I began and ended my research at my children's bookshelves. I also spent time in the juvenile sections of Stuart Brent and Waterstone's bookstores in Chicago, and I spoke with lovers of books—adult friends of mine and the high-school students I teach.

One thing to bear in mind: I hold a prejudice so deeply seated that it feels like a universal truth that books and television are mutually exclusive. Period. A family that truly enjoys books will keep television viewing to such a minimum that it will be virtually nonexistent. It's difficult to maintain the attention of a toddler who has been raised on a diet of images that change every few seconds. It is virtually impossible to expect a child of early school age to settle in with a book and adapt to the challenge of following the words if that child has grown accustomed to receiving his or her entertainment in a passive manner. Turn off the television.

A second point. Children's books come with a recommended reading level. While this idea is well intentioned, it can be a mistake. Author Robertson Davies said it best in his speech "The Conscience of a Writer." "There are," Davies says, "no absolutes in literature that can be applied without reference to personal taste and judgment. The great book for you is the book that has the most to say to you at the moment when you are reading. I do not mean the book that is the most instructive, but the book that feeds your spirit. And that depends on your age, your experience, your psychological and spiritual need."

Taking this into account, then, the books that follow have been loosely grouped into even looser categories, and these categories overlap. Books have been listed from younger to older readers, starting with books that are often read aloud to children, continuing to the junior-high-school level, after which point we can assume that the child is making almost all reading choices fairly autonomously.

Listen, my children

It is possible to read to a very small child. Children old enough to sit in a lap can look at pictures as the pages of a book are turned for them. This establishes a ritual and teaches the skill of sitting while looking at brightly colored pictures. While the littlest readers may not understand the actual words themselves, the ritual of words and their rhythm is a wonderful introduction to reading. Little children love the idea of ritual. Equally important to them is security.

Children also have an early aesthetic sense and can enjoy the feel, texture, and color of a book at a very young age. Anyone who has observed a baby playing endlessly with his or her fingers and toes knows that this person has a developing capacity for enjoying intellectual stimulation. The following books are colorful, pleasant to look at, repetitive in tone, and provide a chance to look at the world inside and out of the house.

Goodnight Moon by Margaret Wise Brown: A little bunny says goodnight to the familiar objects in his room. *Pat the Bunny*, a tactile "look" at the child's world by Dorothy Kunhardt. *Each Peach, Pear, Plum* by Janet and Allan Ahlberg, with its charming illus-trations and rhymes, invites a baby to play a game of "I Spy." *Are You My Mother?* by Philip D. Eastman and *A House Is a House for Me* by Mary Ann Hoberman: repetition promotes a sense of security. *Peter's Chair* (which also deals with the arrival of a new baby), *The Snowy Day*, and almost any book by Ezra Jack Keats use colorful yet gentle illustrations that put a child in a world of people doing pleasant things together and on their own. *The Baby* by John Burningham and *Grandmother and I* by Helen E. Buckley give a look at family members young and old. . . .

Once upon a time

THE FOLLOWING STORIES are timeless and appealing because they are both comforting and empowering. Good is rewarded and evil punished; size and age mean nothing if one is clever; magic is possible. These stories come in many forms, with varied text and illustrations. A subtle benefit of folk tales is the window they provide into different cultures.

Paul Galdone:
The Three Bears
The Three Little Pigs
Peter Asbjornsen:
The Three Billy Goats Gruff
Marcia Brown:
Stone Soup
Robert McCloskey:
Andy and the Lion (an updated version of the traditional *Androcles and the Lion*).
Wanda Gag:
Millions of Cats
Esphyr Slobodkina:
Caps for Sale
The Brothers Grimm:
Bremen Town Musicians
Rumpelstiltskin
Shoemaker and the Elves

Charles Perrault:
Little Red Riding Hood
Cinderella
Ezra Jack Keats:
Over in the Meadow
Jacob Grimm:
Frog Prince
Hans Christian Anderson:
The Ugly Duckling
The Princess and the Pea
The Emperor's New Clothes
Thumbelina
Arlene Mosel:
Tikki Tikki Tembo
Oscar Wilde:
The Selfish Giant
Peter Parnall:
The Great Fish
Arthur Ransome:
The Fool of the World and the Flying Ship
Margot Zemach:
It Could Always Be Worse
Harve Zemach:
Salt: A Russian Tale
William Steig:
Caleb and Katie
The Amazing Bone
Brave Irene
Tiffky Doofky
Gerald McDermott:
Anansi the Spider: A Tale from Ashanti
Tomie de Paola:
The Legend of the Indian Paintbrush
The Legend of the Bluebonnet
The Legend of Old Befana

Finally, the following classics need little description. Their longevity is testimony enough to the fact that they answer a need in the children to whom they are read: *Scuffy the Tugboat* by Gertrude Crampton (Scuffy is also brave and resourceful), *Tawny, Scrawny Lion* by Kathryn Jackson and *Saggy, Baggy Elephant, Poky Little Puppy* by Janet S. Lowrey, *The Little Engine That Could* by Watty Piper ("I think I can, I think I can . . ."), *Carrot Seed* by Ruth Krauss, and *Harold and the Purple Crayon* by Crockett Johnson.

The Runaway Bunny by Margaret Wise Brown should be in a category all by itself because this one does it all. A little bunny asks what his mother would do were he to run away. With beautiful words and even more beautiful illustrations, she convinces him that there is no place on earth he could go that she would not be there to protect him. An all time favorite. Brown has also given us the ultrasatisfying *Home for a Bunny*. Another type of book that can be included in a selection of books for babies is any Mother Goose book. Children love the security of repetition and the humor inherent in these rhymes. These books act as a child's first introduction to poetry. Choose your own favorites—two from this house are *Classic Mother Goose* and an edition illustrated by Tomie de Paola.

Very first reading experiences will include titles that will change depending on the child being read to. Parents are advised not to discount books that have some story line. Many times the pleasure of the rhythm of the words means as much to a child as would knowing their literal meaning. Books without words can be enjoyed by a child who enjoys time alone with books. The following books provide a way for a child to "read" on his or her own, but can be enjoyed with an adult as well: *Babies* by Gyo Fujikawa, *The Snowman* by Raymond Briggs, *Seasons* by

John Burningham, *Ah-Choo* by Mercer Mayer (and also by Mayer, *Four Frogs in a Box* and *A Boy, a Dog, a Frog, and a Friend*), *Deep in the Forest* by Brinton Turkle (a twist on the story of the three bears), *Blackboard Bear* by Martha Alexander, and *Moonlight* by Jan Ormerod, a delightful look at a family putting a reluctant child to bed.

Relative adjustments

The following books present young children with loving and sometimes imperfect families. In *Go and Hush the Baby* by Betsy Byars, Will hushes the baby with a cookie and a story among other things, before the baby finally falls asleep. *Jeremy Isn't Hungry* by Barbara Williams shows how a big brother "helps" his harried mother by looking after baby brother Jeremy. *A Birthday for Frances* and *Bedtime for Frances* by Russell Hoban—time spent in the company of this very human little-girl badger is time well spent and never to be forgotten. In these two favorites, Frances prepares for her sister's birthday and for bed respectively. *Big Brother* by Charlotte Zolotow is dependably satisfying, as are all Zolotow's books. *And My Mean Old Mother Will Be Sorry, Blackboard Bear* by Martha Alexander and *Someday, Said Mitchell* by Barbara Williams give us children who are angry, but know they are loved. Maurice Sendak's classic *Where the Wild Things Are* does the same, and perhaps the paradigm of this type is William Steig's *Spinky Sulks*. When Spinky gets teased one time too often, he takes to his hammock until his family's love is proved to his satisfaction.

Papa Small is a classic Lois Lenski look at a father. *Lyle, Lyle Crocodile* by Bernard Waber continues the adventures of Lyle and his adopted human family from *The House on East Eighty-Eighth Street* and *Lyle Finds His Mother*, which reunites this fetching crocodile with his biological mother. Beverly Cleary's *Two Dog Biscuits* gives us ordinary children and an ordinary day, and the beauty of *Owl Moon* by Jane Yolen lies in its ability to take us with an ordinary parent and child as they experience the extraordinary beauty of a perfect night for "owling."

Sylvester and the Magic Pebble by William Steig gives us a donkey whose parents are reunited with him even though he has been transformed into a rock, and Rosemary Well's *Hazel's Amazing Mother* gives us a mother who acts for mothers everywhere

> While the littlest readers may not understand the actual words themselves, the ritual of words and their rhythm is a wonderful introduction to reading.

when she swoops down on some nasty little children who are tormenting her beloved Hazel. Finally *Fay and Delores* by Barbara Samuels are two appealingly human sisters.

Hey, what about me?

All children need acceptance. The following books introduce the reader to families and friends who come to accept someone. Perhaps the classic case of the need for acceptance can be seen in sibling rivalry. In *A Baby Sister for Frances*, Russell Hoban, lets us watch Frances as she comes to love baby sister Gloria. *Alexander and the Terrible, Horrible, No Good, Very Bad Day* and *I'll Fix Anthony* are two Judith Viorst tales to which any siblings can relate. *I'll Be the Horse If You'll Play With Me* and *Nobody Asked Me If I Wanted a Baby Sister* by Martha Alexander show older and younger-aged children respectively as they adjust to the problems and pleasures of living with a sibling. And no look at sibling rivalry would be complete without (my favorite) Rosemary Well's *Noisy Norah*. You simply must meet Norah, an absolutely gorgeous little spitfire of a mouse who does what it takes to get the familial attention she needs.

Other kinds of acceptance within the family can be seen in *Poinsettia and Her Family* by Felicia Bond, wherein a little pig from an overcrowded house comes to see her family is not so bad to have around; *Dinner at Alberta's* by Russell Hoban, with a funny family who accommodate one another, as do family members at William's House in Charlotte Zolotow's *William's Doll*.

Leo the Late Bloomer by Robert Kraus and *Gregory the Terrible Eater* by Mitchell Sharmat give us a lion whose parents love him enough to accept him as he is and a goat who reaches a compromise with his loving parents. In *Fish Is Fish*, Leo Lionni advises self-acceptance as a fish learns this important truth. *Thy Friend Obadiah* by Brinton Turkle has Obadiah, the charming little Nantucket Quaker who reluctantly befriends a ubiquitous seagull, just as Molly's friend in Kay Charao's *Molly's Lies* befriends the little kindergartner and thus inspires her to stop fibbing. *Ferdinand* by Munro Lief is the sweet, classic story of a gentle bull, and *Oliver Button Is a Sissy* by Tomie de Paola gives us Oliver who, having been teased for taking dance lessons, shows his schoolmates that those lessons can be impressive.

Acceptance can sometimes take the form of forgiveness. Kevin Henkes' *Chrysanthemum* is a sweet little mouse who loves her name, until classmates make fun of it. They get their comeuppance, though, and Chrysanthemum is gracious about it. Again, Maurice Sendak's *Where the Wild Things Are* features Max, who, while wearing his wolf suit, is sent to bed by his mother, yet it all works out in the end. I hope Richard Scarry's book *The Naughty Bunny* is still in print. It tells the story of a bunny who puts his mother through a harrowing day. Of course she forgives him. And the paradigm for all of us who need forgiveness is the beloved *Curious George*.

Though there are some pallid later versions, the original H. A. Rey books—*Curious George Rides a Bike* and the first title above—must be on every child's bookshelf. There is nothing this adventuresome little monkey will not try, and the man in the yellow hat forgives him unconditionally. You'll also want to make the acquaintance of Oliver and Amanda pig in Jan Van Leeuwen's *Oliver Pig at School*. Children can read Else Holmeskund Minarick's *Little Bear* books to themselves or enjoy them with an adult. *No Fighting! No Biting!* by the same author encourages a gentler approach to living. Wendell, in Kevin Henkes' *A Weekend With Wendell*, isn't easy to love as he teases and torments his hosts for the weekend, but his hostess comes to find him endearing. You will, too.

Mole and Troll by Tony Johnston and *Frog and Toad* by Arnold Lobel are great friends, as are *George and Martha*, a hippopotamus couple from James Marshall. Tomie de Paola's *Bill and Pete*, a crocodile and his little bird friend, are not to be missed; neither are *Strega Nona*, de Paola's little "grandma witch" and Big Anthony, her helper, who is in constant need of forgiveness. . . .

And they all lived happily . . .

As children grow and move a bit away from the protective circle of home and family, they have a need to feel competent. Children like to be reminded that things usually turn out just fine in the long run. . . . Here are some books that place our children in the presence of people, things, and animals who are making their way successfully through the world. *Frederick* is Leo Lionni's little mouse who provides for his fellow mice by giving

them something they didn't know they needed. *Swimmy* by the same author tells the story of one tiny black fish, who, united with his fellow fish, finds strength and protection.

Virginia Lee Burton gives us *Katy and the Big Snow*, wherein a valiant little snowplow digs an entire town out after a blizzard. I have memorized the words to Burton's *Mike Mulligan and His Steam Shovel*, having read it almost daily to a parade of children eager to hear one more time how Mike and his machine dug the cellar of the new town hall in record time. Ivan Sherman's *I Am Giant* reminds the reader of just how powerful a little girl giant can be. William Steig's *Brave Irene* delivers a dress for her ailing seamstress mother despite the obstacle of a raging blizzard. *Lentil* saves the day for Robert McCloskey's town filled with people waiting to welcome home a local hero.

McCloskey has given us so many unforgettable books. The mallard family in his *Make Way for Ducklings* has become so famous that Boston's Public Gardens have a statue of them. *Blueberries for Sal* ends happily despite the crisis of mistaken identities that happens when a mother bear and Sal's mother unknowingly swap offspring. *One Morning in Maine* features this same family. A tooth has been lost, then lost again, but all works for the best in the end.

Parents will love *Oh Were They Ever Happy!* by Peter Spier, which tells the tale of thoughtful children painting the house while the parents are gone for the day. Mercer Mayer's Little Critter runs into a little trouble himself when he tries to help out in *Just For You*. Don Freeman gives us a little bear who solves a problem in *A Pocket for Corduroy*.

Marjorie Flack's classic *The Story About Ping* takes us to China, where we meet Ping as he is separated from, and reunited with, his family. In *A Bargain for Frances*, Hoban brings Frances back again, this time to solve the problem of a friend who has tricked Frances out of her favorite tea set. Shel Silverstein's *The Missing Piece* finds its soul mate. The little boy in his book *The Giving Tree* finds wisdom. And James Marshall's Miss Nelson, from several titles beginning with *Miss Nelson is Missing*, finds a way to discipline her unruly class of school children when she must be away from school.

The illustrations in Lore Segal's *Tell Me a Mitzi* are unusual yet captivating in this series of stories, the first one following Mitzi

> Children like to be reminded that things usually turn out just fine in the long run.

In times of trouble

SOME THINGS ARE TOO PAINFUL TO TALK ABOUT. Watching others move through similar situations can provide comfort.

DEATH:
Nana Upstairs, Nana Downstairs by Tomie de Paola
The Tenth Good Thing about Barney by Judith Viorst
The Dead Bird by Margaret Wise Brown

LIVING WITH A SINGLE PARENT:
Mushy Eggs Adrienne Adams
I Love My Mother by Paul Zindel

A Father Like That by Charlotte Zolotow

ILLNESS:
The Sick Story by Linda Hirsch
A Visit to the Hospital by Francine Chase
Just Awful by Alma Whitney

WAR:
Potatoes, Potatoes by Anita Lobel
War and Peas by Michael Foreman
Millions of Cats by Wanda Gag. The best of the best—not to be missed.
Brave Soldier Janosh by Victor Ambrus
Drummer Hoff by Barbara Emberley

---

as she puts in a full day's work before her parents are even out of bed. *Mr. Popper's Penguins* by Richard and Florence Atwater has captivated children for ages as it follows the ups and downs of Mr. Popper as he tends to these creatures. The idea of caring for something or someone is beautifully realized in Lynn Reid Bank's series featuring *The Indian in the Cupboard.* Omri discovers that a cabinet he has received is magic as the plastic toy he has placed inside it comes to life. The three books that follow Omri and his magic cupboard are not to be missed.

Perfect the Pig by Susan Jeschke provides magic of another sort as we watch Perfect, a lovely little winged pig, get stolen and reunited with his friend Opal. *Lost in the Storm* reunites a boy and his dog after an island storm. *Left Behind* by Carol Carrick reunites a boy with his classmates after they become separated on a class trip. Well before its time is Marjorie Flack's *The Easter Bunny and the Little Gold Shoes.* Not only is this feminine Easter Bunny able to provide a kindness for a sick little boy, but she has filled her position only after overcoming social prejudice and managing to get her household of numerous little bunnies in order by giving them all household chores to tend to.

Another wonderful role model with a slightly older reading level is Carol Ryrie Brink's *Caddie Woodlawn.* Caddie is brave, resourceful, and compassionate as she grows up in her native Wisconsin. Like Laura Ingalls Wilder's wonderful *Little House* books, Brink's book is based on family history. . . .

The end never comes

Books take us out of ourselves to a world we might not otherwise see. They introduce us to people worth meeting. They put us in the presence of virtues worth imitating. The youngest child can enjoy a book, and that very book, enjoyed before even the first day of school, may speak to the child on such a profound level that it comes to mind years later when it is needed. Children will lead us, and later lead themselves, to the books that speak to them. These will stay with them forever.

Kathryn Button
Margaret J. Johnson
Paige Furgerson

Interactive writing in a primary classroom

Interactive writing provides a means for teachers to engage in effective literacy instruction, not through isolated skills lessons, but within the framework of constructing texts filled with personal and collective meaning.

"We're going to finish up our list for our story map," Paige Furgerson explains to her kindergarten students. "Let's read what we have so far."

As Ali points to the words written on the paper attached to the easel, her classmates read along with her: "Trees, 3 bowls, 3 spoons, 3 chairs, house, 3 beds, 3 bears."

"I know that there are some other things that we need. Can you think about the story of 'Goldilocks and the Three Bears'? What else do we need to write on our list?" Miss Furgerson asks.

Brody suggests, "A window."

Joey requests, "Three bathrooms. One for each bear."

Katelin volunteers, "Goldilocks."

"Oh, you know what?" Furgerson says. "I think we really do need her. Did you hear what Katelin said, that we needed Goldilocks?"

"Goldilocks," the children repeat in unison.

"Goldilocks," Furgerson replies. "We need a Goldilocks. We're almost out of room

right here." Furgerson points to the bottom of the list of items needed for the class story map. "So where should we write *Goldilocks*?" After the children decide that a new column needs to be started, they help Furgerson hear the sounds in the word *Goldilocks* and proceed to write the word.

"Let's say the word together, slowly," Furgerson reminds the children.

"Goldilocks. *O*, I hear an *o*," Adam states.

"I hear a *d*," Quang suggests.

"A *g*, a *g*," repeats Katelin.

After observing her children and listening to them encode *Goldilocks*, Furgerson explains. "There is an *o* and a *d* and a *g*. The *g* is at the beginning, Katelin. You come up and write the *g*, and then we'll let Adam write the *o* that he heard. Do you know what? This is a person's name, *Goldilocks*. Do you know what kind of a *g* we have to use?"

Rosa replies, "A capital."

"A capital *g* because it's somebody's name." Furgerson then leads the class forward in their task. "That's a good capital *g*. Now, Adam, you come up and write the *o*. Class, let's say the word again to see if we hear any other sounds. Help me."

This scene took place in a kindergarten classroom at Ramirez Elementary School in Lubbock, Texas, USA. Of the 17 students in the class, 2 were Asian, 8 Hispanic, 6 non-Hispanic White, and one African American. Fifteen of the children received free or reduced-price lunch, and 6 had attended a prekindergarten program. The teacher, Paige Furgerson, and the children spent their days engaged in a variety of literacy activities, including interactive writing lessons like the one described above.

Roots of interactive writing

Interactive writing has its roots in the language experience approach developed by Ashton-Warner (1963) in which children dictated a text and the teacher acted as scribe. The text was then used as reading material for the youngsters. McKenzie (1985), working with British teachers, developed a process she called "shared writing" in which the teacher and children collaborated on a text to be written. The focus of the writing could come from a children's literature selection, an event experienced by the children in the class, or a topic under study in social studies or science. In McKenzie's model, the teacher served as scribe and usually used chart paper to create a text that then served as the students' reading text. As the charts accumulated, they were displayed around the room, surrounding the children with meaningful print.

Interactive writing, a form of shared writing, is part of the early literacy lesson framework (see Figure 1) developed by educators at The Ohio State University (Pinnell & McCarrier, 1994) to provide rich, educative experiences for young children, particularly those considered to be educationally at risk. The framework draws on the concept of emergent literacy, a term coined by Clay (1966), and is explicated by other early childhood educators (see Strickland & Morrow, 1989; Teale & Sulzby, 1986).

In the early literacy framework, the use of quality literature (Huck & Kerstetter, 1987) scaffolds the development and integration of all literacy processes (reading, writing, speaking, listening, thinking). Three to five trade books, which represent various genres, are read aloud to children each day. Prior to the construction of the students' list for their story map of "Goldilocks and the Three Bears," Miss Furgerson had read aloud Galdone's (1972) version several times. The repeated readings helped students reconstruct the story line and recall characters and story sequence, the information necessary to generate their lists and construct the actual map. Often the focus of the daily interactive writing lesson was an extension of a book read aloud to the class.

Clay (1991) explained that children are active constructors of their own language and literacy. Their competence grows as they gain inner control over constructing meaning from print. This growth does not take place without environmental support. Rather, with supportive instruction, children develop in language and literacy competence (Vygotsky, 1962). The early literacy framework is a balanced program of instruction and independent exploration. Interactive writing provides opportunities for teachers to engage in instruction precisely at the point of student need.

Interactive writing provides opportunities for teachers to engage in instruction precisely at the point of student need.

Interactive writing differs from shared writing in two important ways. First, children take an active role in the writing process by actually holding the pen and doing the writing. Second, the teacher's role changes as she scaffolds and explicates the children's emerging knowledge about print (Button, 1992). Through questioning and direct instruction, the teacher focuses the children's attention on the conventions of print such as spaces between words, left-to-right and top-to-bottom directionality, capital letters, and punctuation. Clay (1979) reminds teachers to utilize the child's strengths and not to do for the child "anything that she can teach him to do for himself" (p. 4).

Interactive writing in practice

To guide the interactive writing process and make children's knowledge about print explicit, the teacher might ask questions such as these:

"How many words are there in our sentence?"

"Where do we begin writing?"

Figure 1
The Ohio State University Early Literacy Learning Initiative
A framework for early literacy lessons

Element	Values
1. Reading aloud to children (rereading favorite selections)	Motivates children to read (shows purpose). Provides an adult demonstration. Develops sense of story. Develops knowledge of written language syntax and of how texts are structured. Increases vocabulary and linguistic repertoire. Supports intertextual ties through enjoyment and shared knowledge; creates community of readers.
2. Shared reading Rereading big books Rereading retellings Rereading alternative texts Rereading the products of interactive writing	Demonstrates early strategies. Builds sense of story and ability to predict. Demonstrates process of reading. Provides social support from the group. Provides opportunity to participate, behave like a reader.
3. Guided reading	Provides opportunity to problem solve while reading for meaning. Provides opportunity to use strategies on extended text. Challenges the reader and creates context for successful processing on novel texts. Provides opportunity for teacher guidance, demonstration, and explanation.
4. Independent reading	Children read on their own or with partners from a wide range of materials.
5. Shared writing	Children compose messages and stories; teacher supports process as scribe. Demonstrates how writing works.
6. Interactive writing	Demonstrates concepts of print, early strategies, and how words work. Provides opportunities to hear sounds in words and connect with letters. Helps children understand "building up" and "breaking down" processes in reading and writing. Provides opportunities to plan and construct texts.
7. Guided writing and writers' workshop Teacher guides the process and provides instruction	Demonstrates the process of writing. Provides opportunity for explicit teaching of various aspects of writing. Gives students the guidance they need to learn writing processes and produce high-quality products.
8. Independent writing Individual retellings Labeling "Speech balloons" Books and other pieces	Provides opportunity for independence. Provides chance to write for different purposes. Increases writers' ability to use different forms. Builds ability to write words and use punctuation. Fosters creativity and the ability to compose.
9. Letters, words, and how they work	Helps children learn to use visual aspects of print.

Extensions and themes: Drama, murals, story maps, innovations on text, surveys, science experiments, and others.
• Provides opportunities to interpret texts in different ways.
• Provides a way of revisiting a story.
• Fosters collaboration and enjoyment.
• Creates a community of readers.
• Provides efficient instruction through integration of content areas.

(continued)

Figure 1
The Ohio State University Early Literacy Learning Initiative (cont'd.)

Documentation of progress
- Provides information to guide daily teaching.
- Provides a way to track the progress of individual children.
- Provides a basis for reporting to parents.
- Helps a school staff assess the effectiveness of the instructional program.

Home and community involvement
- Brings reading and writing materials and new learning into children's homes.
- Gives children more opportunities to show their families what they are learning.
- Increases reading and writing opportunities for children.
- Demonstrates value and respect for children's homes.

Oral language is the foundation for all elements of the framework.

"After writing one word, what do we have to remember to do? Why?"

"What word are we writing next?"

"Say the word slowly. What sounds do you hear?"

"Can you write the letter that stands for that sound?"

"Can you find the letter on our alphabet chart that we need to write?"

"What comes at the end of the sentence?"

"Would that make sense?"

"Does that look right?"

"Would you point and read what we have written so far?"

These questions and the instruction they represent vary according to the knowledge and needs of the children (see Figure 2). For children beginning the process, the teacher may need to attend more to letter formation. At times the teacher may show a child a model or assist the child with the formation of the needed letter. As children gain competence, attention may shift to punctuation, capitalization, prefixes, suffixes, and phonetic structures such as digraphs, consonant blends, and vowel patterns.

An interactive writing lesson need not be lengthy. On the first day of kindergarten, Furgerson and her students engaged in interactive writing for 15 minutes. As the year progressed, lessons lasted from 20 to 30 minutes. The power of the lesson lies not in the length of the text constructed but in the quality of the interaction. Typically the children are seated on a carpet facing an easel holding unlined chart paper, a marking pen, correction tape,

and a pointer. The teacher usually sits within easy reach of the easel, facing the children. Teachers have found interactive writing to be successful with classes that range in size from 15 to 32 children.

The environment the teacher creates during this process should support risk taking. Children are encouraged to take an active role in negotiating the text. The teacher assumes that the children are in the process of learning about print and that some of their responses will be approximations. The teacher explains to the children that because they and other people will be reading the story, it is important that the words be conventionally constructed. The teacher uses correction tape to mask preconventional attempts (the child's approximations) and helps the child to write the word, letter, or punctuation mark conventionally. Teacher sensitivity is needed to value the knowledge reflected in the attempt yet also to teach the standard conventions of print used in books such as the ones the children read.

For example, during the construction of a class big book about the incubation of eggs, a classroom experience that occurred late in the school year, the children decided to write the sentence: "When the chicks get bigger, we will send the chicks to the farm." After everyone repeated the sentence aloud, Furgerson asked the class what word needed to be written first. They agreed that the first word should be *when*. Rosa stepped up to the easel and wrote *wen*. Furgerson said, "It does sound like *w-e-n*, but we need an *h* before the *e*." She then cov-

---

Figure 2
Interactive writing expectations and guidelines in primary classrooms over a school year

Beginning of the year ⟶   Later in the year ⟶

Establish routine
Negotiate simple text (a label)
Construction of text may be completed in one
    day (news)
Repeat orally word or line to be written

The teacher will
Model hearing sounds in words
Model sound/symbol relationships
Support letter recognition (using alphabet chart
    or chart listing class members' names)
Model and question for Concepts About Print
    (CAP): spacing, left-to-right directionality,
    top-to-bottom directionality, word-by-word
    matching during shared reading
Link words to be written with names of children
    in the class

The teacher may
Write more of the text
Write challenging parts of word/text
Assist with letter formation

Routine established
Negotiate a more complex text
Construction of text continues over several days
Count the words to be written before starting to
    write

Students will
Hear dominant sounds in words
Represent sounds with symbols (letters)
Write letters without copy
Have control of core words
Begin linking known words to unknown words
Leave spaces between words
Use familiar chunks (-*ed*; -*ing*)
Control word-by-word matching during shared
    reading
Punctuate sentences on the run
Write text with little support
Make generalizations about print

---

ered the letters *en* with a piece of correction tape and asked Rosa to write an *h* and then the *en* that she initially had written. During the writing of the word *the* Simon wrote *teh*. For some of the children *the* was a known word, but Simon could not yet spell it conventionally. Xuchen responded, "You have the right letters but in *the* the *h* comes before the *e*." One of the children tore off a piece of correction tape and handed it to Simon to place over the letters *eh*. He then wrote *he*. Jane asked Furgerson, "What did it say?" After the teacher pronounced *teh*, Jane commented that it didn't make sense. The children agreed that *the* looked right and that *teh* neither made sense nor looked like a word they knew. This information confirmed for Furgerson that some of her students knew that what they wrote needed to make sense (semantics).

Texts for interactive writing represent many forms of writing. Children might want to create a list of characters from a story as part of the process of forming a story map. Survey questions might be used as a basis for interactive writing. For example, after reading the books written by their visiting author, Rafe

Martin, the children created a survey chart to display their favorite book title. Children might retell a story they have read or write an alternative text. After students read *The Farm Concert* (Cowley, 1990), they wrote their own variant entitled "The Classroom Concert." Children might compose an invitation to a class party or write a letter to pen pals in another city. Recipes, a review of a trip, class news, and many other forms of communication can also serve as topics for interactive writing.

What interactive writing looks like in one classroom

At the beginning of the school year, Furgerson used informal assessments, including Clay's Observation Survey (Clay, 1993a), to determine the strengths and knowledge of her students. She found about half her children could write their names. Only two of the children could name all the letters of the alphabet. All of the children could identify the front of a book, distinguish between illustrations and print, and indicate where they would begin to read. They all knew print carried a message.

On the first day of kindergarten, Furgerson began with an interactive writing experience based on the focus book of their first thematic unit. After reading Galdone's (1975) *The Gingerbread Boy*, the class took a walking tour of the school to find gingerbread boys hidden in certain spots throughout the building. When they returned to the classroom, they created a list of the spots where the gingerbread boys were found. After explaining the purpose of the writing, Furgerson asked the students what word they wanted to write first on their list.

They decided to begin with the word *lab*. She asked the children where they should start writing. One child stepped forward to point to the upper left-hand corner of the chart paper. Furgerson asked the students to say the word aloud—*lab*—listening for the sounds they heard. Some of the students heard a *b* and some an *l*. At this initial point in the process, Furgerson took the responsibility of seriating the sounds. "Yes," she told the children, "we do hear a *b* and an *l*. When we write the word *lab*, the *l* comes first."

Furgerson knew Larry could write his name. "Larry," she said, "you come and write the *l*. You have an *l* in your name." After Larry wrote the letter *l*, the children said the word again, listening for additional sounds. Brody heard the sound represented by the letter *b*. While Brody came up to write the *b*, Furgerson explained to the class that Brody's name began with a *b*. Before he wrote the *b*, however, she explained that the letter *a* came before the *b* although it was hard to hear. Brody wrote the *a* and then the *b*.

Furgerson then called another child to come up to the chart and, using the pointer, point under the word they had just written for the class to read. She then asked where else they found gingerbread boys. They followed a similar process with other items on their list. Furgerson chose to write three words at this sitting and to add to the list on subsequent days. Interactive writing was a daily event in her classroom.

Furgerson built on the knowledge students had about the sounds represented by letters in their names. She used everything the children appeared to know at the time of the lesson and then, through demonstration and explanation, extended their knowledge by providing the letters representing unfamiliar sounds. Clay (1993b) states, "At the beginning of the school year what the child can write is a good indicator of what the child knows in detail about written language" (p. 11). As the children finished writing a word, a list, or a sentence, they read it. One child pointed under each word to help the others to track the print while reading. This process demonstrates in a powerful and immediate way the reciprocal nature of reading and writing.

Later in the year, the children were thoroughly familiar with the routine of interactive writing and much more sophisticated in their knowledge about the conventions of print. They were able to analyze the phonological features of the message to be written (hear sounds in words), sequence the sounds heard, represent the sounds they heard with letters, and discern many different patterns. The children were also aware that their purpose for writing dictated the type of writing they would undertake. When the class decided to reply to their Ohio pen pals, they knew their letter would begin with the line, "Dear Miss Patacca's Class," and what followed would be written from left to right across the page.

On the first day of kindergarten, Furgerson began with an interactive writing experience based on the focus book of their first thematic unit.

In the spring the children decided to retell the story of Michael Rosen's (1989) *We're Going on a Bear Hunt*. They had spent several days listening to repeated readings of the book. Using interactive writing, they had made lists of the characters and the different settings from the story, which then served as references for an elaborate story map. To accompany the map, the children spent several days writing a retelling of the story.

Furgerson and the children negotiated the first line of the retelling. Borrowing in part from the text of the story, they decided to write: "The children walked through the forest, stumble trip, stumble trip." They repeated the sentence several times to fix the message clearly in their minds and to give them something against which to monitor their writing. Furgerson then asked the children to count the words as they said the sentence. She asked them what word they would write first. At this point in the school year, *the* was a known word for all the children in the room. Miss Furgerson asked the children what they needed to remember. Most knew that they start writing in the upper left-hand corner of the page, begin the first word of the sentence with a capital letter, and leave a "hand space" between the words.

Although the focus of Furgerson's curriculum was not to teach her children to read, but to immerse them in meaningful print rich activities, most of them were reading by spring of their kindergarten year.

After writing and reading *the*, the children told Furgerson that the next word they needed to work on was *children*. This was not a known word for most of them. Following a routine well established at this point, the students said the word together slowly, yet naturally, thinking about the order of the sounds in the spoken word. One child commented that the word had two parts—*chil* and *dren*. Furgerson turned the child's observation into a teaching moment, explaining that, indeed, *children* had two syllables and showing the class how to clap as they said the word, one clap for each syllable. Capitalizing further on the observation, she told the students they would be listening for the sounds in the first syllable. They heard the first sound easily and all knew the digraph *ch*. Furgerson asked Chaz to come up to the easel and write the first two letters while the class said the first syllable again, listening for additional sounds.

Rosa said she heard an *i* like in *him*. At this point, most of the children were beginning to connect known words and new words. Rosa came up, took the marker from Chaz, and wrote the *i*. As Rosa repeated the word aloud while writing, she said she also could hear an *l*. Furgerson said, "You are right. You may write the *l*." She then asked the children to say the word again, listening for the sounds in the last syllable. Quang said he heard a *tr*. Furgerson said, "Yes. It does sound like a *tr*, but in this word it is a *dr*. TR and *dr* do sound almost alike." Quang came up to the easel and wrote the *dr*. After saying the word one more time, Joshua said he heard an *n*. Furgerson said, "Yes, you are right, there is an *n*. But before the *n*, there is an *e* which is harder to hear. Would you like to come up and write *en* for us?"

Throughout the school year the children also had 20 to 30 minutes every day to write independently either in their journals or at the writing center. This gave students time to use the knowledge gained from interactive writing instruction and time to take further risks as writers. They made independent choices about what to write about and how to organize their texts. They were encouraged to use invented spelling, copy from environmental print, and make use of their growing core of known words. Furgerson's observations of what the students wrote and how they wrote independently informed her teaching for future interactive writing sessions.

Literacy assessment

Assessment in the early literacy framework is ongoing as the teacher documents the children's growth over time. Furgerson used a checklist she developed to monitor the growth children exhibited through their journal writing. Although the children varied in their control of the conventions of print, they all thought of themselves as readers and writers. Although the focus of Furgerson's curriculum was not to teach her children to read but to immerse them in meaningful print-rich activities, most of them were reading by spring of their kindergarten year.

To document the growth her students made during the year and to provide information for next year's first-grade teacher, Furgerson and a class of trained undergraduate language/literacy students administered the Observation Survey (Clay, 1993a) in May to all of the children. She analyzed the children's scores on each of the six tasks assessed and then compared the May scores with the September scores.

The children exhibited growth in all areas measured by the Observation Survey. In the spring of the year, 13 of 17 children were able to read with 90% or better accuracy books like *The Chick and the Duckling* (Ginsburg, 1972) and *Mary Wore Her Red Dress and Henry Wore His Green Sneakers* (Peek, 1985). These books have illustrations that provide moderate support for the reader and stories that tell about familiar objects. The stories contain varied, often repetitive, simple sentence patterns that include action such as, "'I am taking a walk,' said the Duckling." (See Peterson, 1991, for characteristics of texts to support beginning readers.)

The children improved the most in their ability to hear sounds in words as measured by the Dictation Task. In this task, children are asked to record a dictated sentence containing a possible 37 phonemes. Each child's attempt is scored by counting the number of letters (graphemes) written by the child that represent the sounds (phonemes) analyzed by the child. In the fall the children had a mean dictation score of 9.8 (maximum score = 37). The children represented primarily initial consonants. In the spring, the children's mean dictation score was 29 (almost three times higher than in the fall). The children's ability to hear sounds in words, practiced daily during interactive writing, enabled them to represent initial and final sounds heard in each word. In addition, they could accurately spell high-frequency words like *the*, *is*, and *it*. This growth in the Dictation Task is particularly significant given the importance of phonemic awareness as a predictor of success in learning to read (see Adams, 1990).

On the Writing Vocabulary Task of the Observation Survey children were asked to write as many words as they could in a 10-minute period. In the fall, the children's scores ranged from 0 to 20 with a mean score of 4.8. Many children were able to write their first name and names of family members like *mom* and *dad*. In the spring, the Writing Vocabulary scores ranged from 1 to 56 words written in a 10-minute period with a mean score of 23.9. In addition to writing names of family members and friends, the children wrote high-frequency words like *on*, *the*, *in*, *go*, and *to* and favorite words like *pizza* and *dog*.

Meeting individual students' needs

Furgerson used information from the Observation Survey, anecdotal notes, and writing checklists to help her meet the needs of each of her students. Valerie's fall Observation Survey summary indicated that she could recognize 14 of 54 letters, no high-frequency words, and 7 out of 24 concepts about print; could represent no phonemes on the Dictation Task; and could write no words during the Writing Vocabulary Task. During the interactive writing lesson, Furgerson built on Valerie's strengths, asking her to write the *l* and *a* when they were needed in words the class was writing, as these were 2 of the 14 letters Valerie knew. Valerie delighted everyone one day when she announced that the particular sentence the class was writing needed a question mark at the end. She quickly became in charge of question marks. As the year progressed, Furgerson also worked individually with Valerie at the teacher table during center time and guided her during journal writing. At the end of kindergarten Valerie recognized 46 of the 54 letters, no high-frequency words, and 14 of the 24 concepts about print; she could represent 3 phonemes on the Dictation Task, and on the Writing Vocabulary Task she could write her name. Furgerson stated that Valerie's spring scores exhibited growth even though the growth was atypical for children her age. Valerie also showed marked growth in other areas such as art and oral language. Even with the most supportive literacy framework, some children require more intensive instruction. Valerie would be a prime candidate for Reading Recovery (see Pinnell, Fried, & Estice, 1990).

Concluding remarks

Interactive writing provides an authentic means for instruction in phonics and other linguistic patterns within the context of meaningful text. Children learn the conventions of spelling, syntax, and semantics as they engage in the construction of letters, lists, and stories. Interactive writing is a tool that puts reading and learning about conventions into a dynamic relationship. As children attend to meaningful text, they develop their knowledge of the conventions embedded in that text. As they gain more knowledge of conventions, they are able to construct and interpret more sophisticated messages.

Interactive writing is an important part of the early literacy lesson framework (see Figure 1) because it provides so many opportunities to teach directly about language conventions, sense of story, types of writing, and concepts about print. These teaching moments do not follow a specified sequence but evolve from the teacher's understanding of the students' needs. The early literacy lesson framework blends independent problem solving, shared literacy experiences, and teacher instruction within a literacy-rich classroom.

Too often teachers feel they must choose between using holistic literacy experiences and teaching basic skills. In interactive writing sessions, teachers do both at the same time. Interactive writing provides a means for teachers to engage in effective literacy instruction, not through isolated skills lessons, but within the framework of constructing texts filled with personal and collective meaning.

Button teaches early literacy courses and Johnson teaches language and literacy courses at Texas Tech University. Furgerson teaches kindergarten in the Lubbock Independent School District. Button may be contacted at Texas Tech University, Box 41071, Lubbock, TX 79409-1071, USA.

References

Adams, M.J. (1990). *Beginning to read: Thinking and learning about print*. Cambridge, MA: MIT Press.

Ashton-Warner, S. (1963). *Teacher*. New York: Simon & Schuster.

Button, K.A. (1992). *A longitudinal case study examination of the theoretical and practical changes made by three urban kindergarten teachers during participation in early literacy training*. Unpublished doctoral dissertation, The Ohio State University, Columbus.

Clay, M.M. (1966). *Emergent reading behavior*. Unpublished doctoral dissertation, University of Aukland, New Zealand.

Clay, M.M. (1979). *The early detection of reading difficulties: A diagnostic survey with recovery procedures*. Portsmouth, NH: Heinemann.

Clay, M.M. (1991). *Becoming literate: The construction of inner control*. Portsmouth, NH: Heinemann.

Clay, M.M. (1993a). *An observation survey of early literacy achievement*. Portsmouth, NH: Heinemann.

Clay, M.M. (1993b). *Reading Recovery: A guidebook for teachers in training*. Portsmouth, NH: Heinemann.

Huck, C.S., & Kerstetter, K.J. (1987). Developing readers. In B. Cullinan (Ed.), *Children's literature in the reading program* (pp. 30-40). Newark, DE: International Reading Association.

McKenzie, M.G., (1985). Shared writing: Apprenticeship in writing. *Language Matters, 1-2*, 1-5.

Peterson, B. (1991). Selecting books for beginning readers. In D.E. DeFord, C.A. Lyons, & G.S. Pinnell (Eds.), *Bridges to literacy: Learning from Reading Recovery* (pp. 119-147). Portsmouth, NH: Heinemann.

Pinnell, G.S., Fried, M.D., & Estice, R.M. (1990). Reading Recovery: Learning how to make a difference. *The Reading Teacher, 43*, 282-295.

Pinnell, G.S., & McCarrier, A. (1994). Interactive writing: A transition tool for assisting children in learning to read and write. In E. Hiebert & B. Taylor (Eds.), *Getting reading right from the start: Effective early literacy interventions* (pp. 149-170). Needham, MA: Allyn & Bacon.

Strickland, D.S., & Morrow, L.M. (1989). *Emerging literacy: Young children learn to read and write*. Newark, DE: International Reading Association.

Teale, W.H., & Sulzby, E. (Eds.). (1986). *Emergent literacy: Writing and reading*. Norwood, NJ: Ablex.

Vygotsky, L. (1962). *Thought and language*. Cambridge, MA: MIT Press.

Children's books cited

Cowley, J. (1990). *The farm concert*. Bothell, WA: The Wright Group.

Galdone, P. (1972). *The three bears*. New York: Clarion.

Galdone, P. (1975). *The gingerbread boy*. New York: Clarion.

Ginsburg, M. (1972). *The chick and the duckling*. New York: Macmillan.

Peek, M. (1985). *Mary wore her red dress and Henry wore his green sneakers*. New York: Clarion.

Rosen, M. (1989). *We're going on a bear hunt*. New York: McElderry.

How Good Is Your Early Childhood Science, Mathematics, and Technology Program?

Strategies for Extending Your Curriculum

Mary Martin Patton and Teresa M. Kokoski

Science, mathematics, and technology are the cornerstones of the schools of the future, described by David Campbell as "a combination of EPCOT Center, The Smithsonian Institution, a first-rate zoo or premier science museum, a television studio, and a media center complete with satellite communications systems and extensive computer networks" (1991, 20).

Science, math, and technology are everywhere in children's environment! Science and technology museums where children are playing laser tag and building circuits have popped up around the country in the last 10 years. Consumer-oriented businesses like computer and nature stores are in every mall. Television programs, such as *Mathnet, Newton's Apple, Challenges of the Unknown, Spaceship Earth, Square One,* and *Beakman's World,* have joined nature programs like *National Geographic Explorer.* To some extent, all of these programs reflect essential components and concepts related to science, mathematics, and technology. In elementary schools, technology is perhaps the least recognized and attended to of the three disciplines. Yet, elementary-school children use technology every day. Most have VCRs and can whip up a snack in the microwave while holding a hand-held computer game! In school they need to be inventing simple machines and taking apart old ones to see how they work as well as using computers, microscopes, and calculators.

If you are a reader of *Young Children,* perhaps you are already doing a lot of hands-on science, mathematics, and technology in your early childhood classroom (pre-K to grade 3). Yet, when we ask early childhood educators about their confidence in providing learning opportunities in science, mathematics, and technology, we've found that many are not as confident about their preparation in these disciplines as in other areas of the curriculum (Patton & Kokoski 1993). This article puts forth some ideas for you to consider that should be natural extensions to what you are already doing and gives some new ideas to incorporate into your classroom, the outdoor environment, and your parent-involvement program.

How good is your science/mathematics/technology curriculum?

Are you confident about your science, mathematics, and technology curriculum? Do your children explode into the room on Monday expecting to "do" investigations and constructions? Do you recognize and explain to parents how the children are developing process and problem-solving skills, constructing their own meanings,

Mary Martin Patton, *Ph.D., is an assistant professor in early childhood education at Texas Christian University in Fort Worth. She was a teacher and principal for 17 years prior to becoming a teacher educator. Her interests focus on children's play, early childhood curriculum, and homeless children.*

Teresa M. Kokoski, *Ph.D., is an assistant professor of science education in the Division of Educational Specialties, University of New Mexico in Albuquerque. She has worked on statewide systemic efforts for improving science, mathematics, and technology elementary education in New Mexico.*

From *Young Children,* July 1996, pp. 38-44. © 1996 by the National Association for the Education of Young Children. Reprinted by permission.

and acquiring positive attitudes toward science, mathematics, and technology? In the past decade these disciplines have taken a front seat when school programs are rated for excellence.

The discussion that follows is meant to help you feel good about what you are already doing and inspire you to try some new things. We discuss four areas of your early childhood program: environment, curriculum, the classroom outside your door, and parent involvement; we suggest ways to extend science, mathematics, and technology experiences in each area.

The environment for learning

If the science coordinator from your school district walked into your classroom, would she immediately see evidence of science, mathematics, and technology?

Do a quick visual check. Does your environment have

- a science/mathematics center;
- a clearly defined library/resource center rich with science, mathematics, and technology information and literature;
- live plants and animals;
- a variety of manipulatives for hands-on/minds-on explorations;
- construction materials and supplies accessible to your children and in sufficient quantities (i.e., wood chips, fabric scraps, boxes, paint, glue);
- computers, calculators, microscopes, hand lenses and multimedia available and in use throughout the day;
- student projects, inventions, and constructions displayed;
- running water, sinks, and sufficient electrical outlets; and
- a productive hum and children planning, negotiating, and moving about the room in purposeful engagement?

If you answered "yes" to all of the above, the stage is set and you are ready to examine your curriculum! If you answered "no" to some of the above, you can begin to think about ways to provide more opportunities for your children to explore, compute, construct, investigate, and manipulate.

Once you establish your environment, consider the *time* the children have to use it and the opportunities they have to *explore* it. Research indicates that young children require 30 to 50 minutes of free play/independent exploration time in order to fully engage in these types of environments (Johnson, Christie, & Yawkey 1987). The National Association for the Education of Young Children (Bredekamp 1987) and the National Council for Teachers of Mathematics (NCTM 1989) support the strategy of providing large blocks of time for children to engage in meaningful learning, which includes play and exploration of materials as well as structured learning experiences. Allowing children to move freely about the classroom, initiating learning experiences in a variety of ways, requires a movement away from rigid scheduling of discrete, subject-driven activities to an integrated, holistic view of curriculum, development, and learning.

Defining the curriculum

Do you use an integrated curriculum that is developed around an in-depth study of a particular theme or project? Do science, mathematics, and technology figure prominently in your themes? Science is everywhere. Appropriate early childhood themes include life and the environment; water and air, energy and change (Blackwell & Hohmann 1991); the human body and senses; bouyancy (Butzow & Butzow 1989); and pillbugs and insects (Burnett 1992). Mathematics is imbedded in the themes as children sort, count, classify, measure, estimate, problem solve, commu-

nicate, and construct projects (NCTM 1989). Technology for children is often thought of as computers, video games, and tape players, but technology in the early childhood classroom should be broadly defined as any tool that extends the senses, such as hand lenses, magnifying bug boxes, string telephones, thermometers, and compasses. Look through your planning book! Do you

- emphasize in-depth study of a theme rather than a theme-a-week;
- specify daily blocks of time for hands-on science, mathematics, and technology-related experiences;
- include science, mathematics, and technology as central components of the integrated curriculum;
- include district, state, and national standards/competencies for science, mathematics, and technology;
- emphasize conceptual understanding rather than memorization of facts; and
- include each child's culture, language, and experiences?

Do children in your classroom

- participate in the planning process;
- demonstrate what they know through a variety of authentic assessment strategies (exhibitions, demonstrations, journals, group projects); and
- participate fully in science, mathematics, and technology experiences, with every child getting to go to centers and computers, not just the "accelerated" children who finish first?

Examining your curriculum with the above criteria should help to ensure that the disciplines of science, mathematics, and technology are fully integrated. Generating curriculum is perhaps the most time-consuming process of teaching. It is critical to remember when planning an integrated curriculum for young children that *less is more,* meaning that we want to teach fewer concepts/ themes but in greater depth. A first step to achieving greater depth is moving away from the theme-of-the-week practice that has been the mainstay of many early childhood programs.

Also critical to the planning process is the input of children. Curriculum has little meaning for children unless it connects them to real-world experiences and their culture. Since children don't view their world as discrete disciplines but as an interactive, dynamic system, the interdisciplinary curriculum is a natural forum for their explorations. Young children have an innate interest in the natural aspects of their world, a fascination with technology and how things work, and they bring a huge store of these experiences to school with them. Unfortunately, these experiences are often overlooked in the defining of the curriculum. A strategy for ensuring that every child has access to science, mathematics, and technology disciplines is for teachers to use an inclusive planning process (Nelson & Frederick 1994).

The teachers we work with have found the shared-web process that we teach in our courses to be a very effective way to engage children in the planning process. The first step is for the teacher to decide on a theme (based on teacher interest and confidence about teaching the topic and on children's interests) and develop a thematic web guided by district, state, and national standards. The teacher then conducts a brainstorming session with the children to create a web that reflects what the students already know and what they are interested in knowing more about (Figure 1). The final product is a web that aligns children's prior knowledge, shared interests, teacher goals, and mandated competencies, integrated across the curriculum (Figure 2).

A final critical component is a sensitivity to the cultures of the school population. Culture provides the infrastructure through which children make sense of their world and bring meaning to their environment. A culturally insensitive curriculum risks the possibility of placing children in conflict with the home and school environment. In New Mexico, for example, it is critical to understand the community of the school since many of the cultural mores and practices vary among Pueblo, Navaho, and Apache communities and often are unfamiliar to the nonnative person. For example, many plants and animals carry a symbolic representation within the Native American communities. A teacher from a Navaho community pointed out to our class that putting cornmeal in the sand/water table would be offensive in her community. While a study of corn is acceptable, playing with it is not. Overall, a good interdisciplinary science, mathematics, and technology curriculum will include a planning process that incorporates child interests, collaborative planning, and community consideration.

Taking the curriculum beyond the classroom

The classroom outside your door can be the most valuable and inexpensive resource available to you and is often the least used. The value of extending learning beyond the boundaries of the classroom is to facilitate the connections children make to their real-world experiences. Do you

• use your schoolyard for daily explorations (i.e., sand, water, simple machines, colors, plant life);

• plan structured activities for your field experiences to help children focus on specific events (i.e., trip boards, nature hunts, sketchbooks, journals) and extend the learning with pre- and

postactivities; and

• take weekly walking field trips to bridge what children are learning in school to what they are learning in the community?

We must push ourselves to think about learning outside the four walls of the classroom. The outdoors is a natural extension and basic bridge connecting the child's real world with the school environment. When children are "doing science" by coloring a ditto of a plant or animal that exists naturally outside the classroom, they miss a great opportunity for authentic learning. Children will make stronger connections to their own backyards and territories of exploration when they are touching, etching, coloring, and constructing with real models. This connection enables children to recognize and initiate the learning opportunities that exist even between the cracks in the sidewalk.

Whether the settings for your outdoor experiences are formal (i.e., museum, zoo) or informal (i.e., nature center, city park, neighborhood walk), the connections to the curriculum can be made explicit through preactivities, by engagement at the setting, and in follow-through activities. For example, to extend a study of color, plan a colors-in-nature neighborhood walk. Before going on the trip, provide many opportunities for the children to "read" nature books, such as the Eyewitness Book *Plants* (Burne 1989) and *Nature Walk* (Florian 1989); cut pictures from magazines of flowers, plants, and trees; and sort them by color and make posters of Reds in Nature, Blues in Nature, Greens in Nature, and so on. Read to the children a variety of books that explore colors in nature, such as *Red Leaf, Yellow Leaf* and *Planting a Rainbow* (Ehlert 1991, 1989).

On the day of the nature walk, have a clipboard with paper, glue stick, and a baggie full of color chips (small squares of paper in a

Figure 1. Children's Web: What Do They Know? What Are Their Interests?

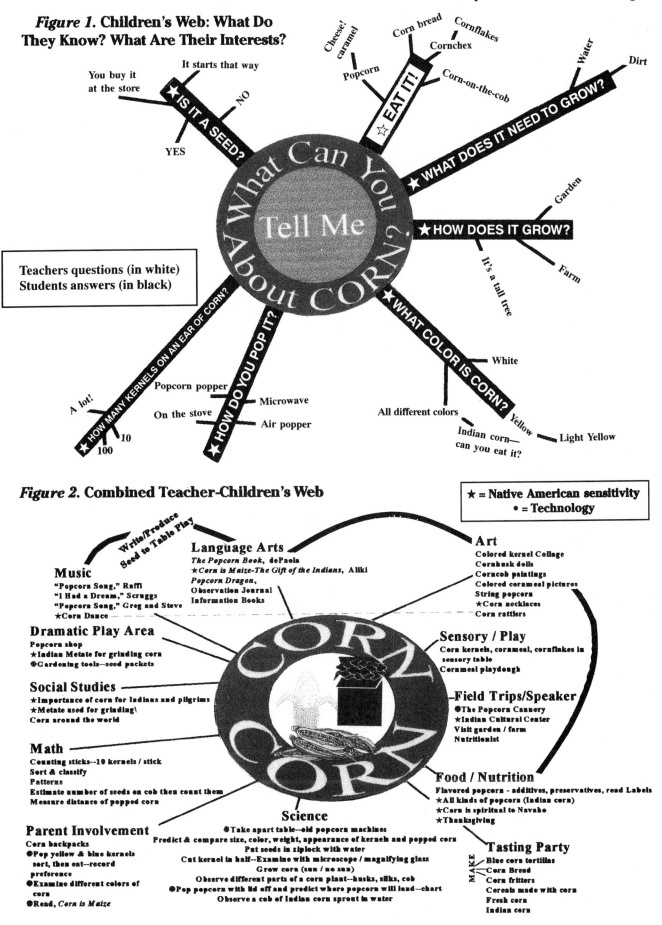

Teachers questions (in white)
Students answers (in black)

What Can You Tell Me About CORN?

IS IT A SEED?
It starts that way
You buy it at the store
NO
YES

EAT IT!
Cheese! caramel
Popcorn
Corn bread
Cornchex
Cornflakes
Corn-on-the-cob

WHAT DOES IT NEED TO GROW?
Water
Dirt

HOW DOES IT GROW?
Garden
Farm
It's a tall tree

WHAT COLOR IS CORN?
White
All different colors
Indian corn— can you eat it?
Yellow
Light Yellow

HOW MANY KERNELS ON AN EAR OF CORN?
A lot!
10
100

HOW DO YOU POP IT?
Popcorn popper
On the stove
Microwave
Air popper

Figure 2. Combined Teacher-Children's Web

★ = Native American sensitivity
• = Technology

Music
"Popcorn Song," Raffi
"I Had a Dream," Scruggs
"Popcorn Song," Greg and Steve
★Corn Dance

Write/Produce Seed to Table Play

Language Arts
The Popcorn Book, dePaola
★*Corn is Maize-The Gift of the Indians*, Aliki
Popcorn Dragon,
Observation Journal
Information Books

Art
Colored kernel Collage
Cornhusk dolls
Corncob paintings
Colored cornmeal pictures
String popcorn
★Corn necklaces
Corn rattlers

Dramatic Play Area
Popcorn shop
★Indian Metate for grinding corn
•Gardening tools--seed packets

Social Studies
★Importance of corn for Indians and pilgrims
★Metate used for grinding\
Corn around the world

Math
Counting sticks--10 kernels / stick
Sort & classify
Patterns
Estimate number of seeds on cob then count them
Measure distance of popped corn

Sensory / Play
Corn kernels, cornmeal, cornflakes in sensory table
Cornmeal playdough

Field Trips/Speaker
•The Popcorn Cannery
★Indian Cultural Center
Visit garden / farm
Nutritionist

Food / Nutrition
Flavored popcorn - additives, preservatives, read Labels
★All kinds of popcorn (Indian corn)
★Corn is spiritual to Navaho
★Thanksgiving

Parent Involvement
Corn backpacks
•Pop yellow & blue kernels sort, then eat--record preference
•Examine different colors of corn
•Read, *Corn is Maize*

Science
•Take apart table--old popcorn machines
Predict & compare size, color, weight, appearance of kernels and popped corn
Put seeds in ziplock with water
Cut kernel in half--Examine with microscope / magnifying glass
Grow corn (sun / no sun)
Observe different parts of a corn plant--husks, silks, cob
•Pop popcorn with lid off and predict where popcorn will land--chart
Observe a cob of Indian corn sprout in water

Tasting Party
MAKE:
Blue corn tortillas
Corn Bread
Corn fritters
Cereals made with corn
Fresh corn
Indian corn

CORN CORN

213

wide variety of colors) for every two children. Each "color detective team" matches color chips to natural objects the twosome finds on the walk. Then the children glue the color chips to the paper and sketch the plant, flower, leaf, rock, worm, and so on next to each. When you return to the classroom, the children will be delighted with their findings! Follow-up activities might include making natural dye from red onion peels, beets, and blueberries; planting seeds for your garden; or returning to the outdoors with watercolors to paint with a keener eye the variety of colors in nature.

Connecting with parents

The ways to involve and inform parents are numerous; the time commitment is overwhelming. You think: "Can I do one more thing?" Ask yourself if these strategies will work for you and within your time constraints.

• Schedule exhibition times for children to share their science, mathematics, and technology projects with parents.

• Extend science/mathematics/ technology learning experiences to the home through hands-on/ minds-on, take-home backpacks.

• Provide varied opportunities for parents to support school activities through a variety of roles during and after school hours.

• Engage in frequent, two-way communication through a variety of technologies (interactive newsletters, telephone, electronic mail, voice mail).

• Get your administrator to support your parent-involvement efforts with resources (time, money, and moral support)!

The influence of parents and the home environment on learning is recognized by professionals as a significant component of a child's education (McIntyre 1984; NCIS 1989). More and more schools are reaching out to include parents

through programs to enhance the child's success in school. A recent review of effective parent-involvement programs identified specific elements to successful programs and illuminated a variety of roles that parents assume in supporting their child's education and the school's program (Williams & Chavkin 1989). Whether it be as home tutor, audience, program supporter, or colearner, the parent's involvement supports and conveys the value of an education to the child. Also, the manner in which schools legitimize parent roles, train parents, communicate and network with parents, and support involvement programs is crucial to the success of the program and ultimately the child's education. Research has established that children show increased achievement in school and better self-esteem when parents are involved in the learning process (Rasinki & Fredericks 1989; Goldenberg, Reese, & Gallimore 1992).

A particularly useful strategy for involving parents is the use of science/mathematics backpacks. These backpacks provide meaningful, relevant learning experiences in the home and also serve to inform parents of the nature of learning in the classroom. The backpack is a type of mobile learning center that contains a parent letter explaining the purpose of the backpack activities, an information book and children's literature book on the theme, directions for the activity, and all the materials necessary to complete the activity (Kokoski & Patton 1994). Children and parents actively engage in learning at home by measuring, sorting, graphing, and conducting experiments and investigations. These backpack experiences have been implemented by several teachers in New Mexico and Texas with student populations whose parents tend not to be involved with the school life of their children. These teachers report that the response from both children and parents has been en-

thusiastic and translates into more positive student attitudes toward science and mathematics learning in school.

Final thoughts

Developmentally appropriate practice (Bredekamp 1987) encourages planning interactively with the children, providing a variety of materials and utilizing a variety of teaching strategies and assessments; adult-child interactions that promote trial-and-error learning; self-regulation through many opportunities to inquire, question, make decisions, and problem solve; and partnerships with families. National reform movements mandate that schools improve all areas of teaching and learning for children but have specifically targeted science, mathematics, and technology— areas in which we lag behind many of the industrialized nations. Early childhood/primary programs are critical for grounding young children in the skills and knowledge base they will need to be successful citizens and productive workers in the information age. As you extend your program to include the attributes described above, you can feel confident that your program is on the cutting edge of sound practices in science, mathematics, and technology.

References

Blackwell, F.F., & C. Hohmann. 1991. *High Scope K-3 curriculum series: Science.* Ypsilanti, MI: High/Scope.

Bredekamp, S., ed. 1987. *Developmentally appropriate practice in early childhood programs serving children from birth through age 8.* Rev. ed. Washington, DC: NAEYC.

Burne, D. 1989. *Plant.* New York: Random House.

Burnett, R. 1992. *The pillbug project: A guide to investigation.* Washington, DC: National Science Teachers Association.

Butzow, C.M., & J.W. Butzow. 1989. *Science through children's literature.* Englewood, CO: Teacher Ideas.

Campbell, D.N. 1991. Shaking off inertia. *The American School Board Journal* 178 (6): 20–21.

Ehlert, L. 1988. *Planting a rainbow.* New York: Harcourt Brace.

Ehlert, L. 1991. *Red leaf, yellow leaf.* New York: Harcourt Brace.

Florian, D. 1989. *Nature walk.* New York: Greenwillow.

Goldenberg, C., L. Reese, & R. Gallimore. 1992. Effects of literacy materials from school on Latino children's home experiences and early reading achievement. *American Journal of Education* 100 (4): 497–536.

Johnson, J.E., J.F. Christie, & T.D. Yawkey. 1987. *Play and early childhood development.* Glenview, IL: Scott, Foresman.

Kokoski, T.M., & M.M. Patton. 1994. *Beyond homework: Science and mathematics backpacks.* Unpublished manuscript.

McIntyre, M. 1984. Involving parents in science. In *Early childhood and science,* ed. M. McIntyre, 134–35. Washington, DC: National Science Teachers Association.

National Center for Improving Science (NCIS). 1989. *Science and technology education for the elementary years: Frameworks for curriculum and instruction.* Andover, MA: Author.

National Council for Teachers of Mathematics (NCTM). 1989. *Curriculum and evaluation standards for school mathematics.* Reston, VA: Author.

Nelson, L., & L. Frederick. 1994. Can children design curriculum? *Educational Leadership* 51 (5): 71–74.

Patton, M.M., & T.M. Kokoski. 1993. Promoting science and mathematics in early childhood education. Presentation at the National Science Teachers Association national convention, 1–4 April, Kansas City, Missouri.

Rasinski, T., & A.D. Fredericks. 1989. Can parents make a difference? (Working with parents). *The Reading Teacher* 42 (1): 84–85.

Williams, D.L., & N.F. Chavkin. 1989. Essential elements of strong parent involvement programs. *Educational Leadership* 47 (2): 18–20.

Other resources

Helm, J. 1994. Family theme bags: An innovative approach to family involvement in the school. *Young Children* 49 (4): 48–52.

Hohmann, C. 1991. *High Scope K-3 curriculum series: Mathematics.* Ypsilanti, MI: High/Scope.

Roth, C.E., C. Cervoni, T. Wellnitz, & E. Arms. 1988. *Beyond the classroom: Exploration of schoolground & backyard.* Lincoln, MA: Massachusetts Audubon Society.

Russell, H.R. 1990. *Ten minute field trips.* Washington, DC: National Science Teachers Association.

For further reading

Science

Clemens, J.B. 1996. Gardening with children. *Young Children* 51 (4): 22–27.

Fenton, G.M. 1996. Back to our roots in nature's classroom. *Young Children* 51 (3): 8

Goldhaber, J. 1992. Sticky to dry; red to purple: Exploring transformation with play dough. *Young Children* 48 (1): 26–28.

Holt, B. 1989. *Science with young children.* Washington, DC: NAEYC.

Jaelitza. 1996. Insect love: A field journal. *Young Children* 51 (4): 31–32.

Klein, A. 1991. All about ants: Discovery learning in the primary grades. *Young Children* 46 (5): 23–27.

Kokoski, T.M. & N. Downing-Leffler. 1995. Boosting your science and math programs in early childhood education: Making the home-school connection. *Young Children* 50 (5): 35–39.

National Association for the Education of Young Children. 1987. Outstanding science trade books for children. *Young Children* 42 (6): 52–56.

National Science Teachers Association. 1992. Outstanding science books for young children in 1991. *Young Children* 47 (4): 73–75.

Perry, G., & M. Rivkin. 1992. Teachers and science. *Young Children* 47 (4): 9–16.

Rivkin, M., ed. 1992. Science is a way of life. *Young Children* 47 (4): 4–8.

Tomich, K. 1996. Hundreds of ladybugs, thousands of ladybugs, millions and billions of ladybugs—and a couple of roaches. *Young Children* 51 (4): 28–30.

Ziemer, M. 1987. Science and the early childhood curriculum: One thing leads to another. *Young Children* 42 (6): 44–51.

Math

Greenberg, P. 1993. Ideas that work with young children. How and why to teach all aspects of preschool and kindergarten math naturally, democratically, and effectively (for teachers who don't believe in academic programs, who do believe in educational excellence, and who find math boring to the max)—Part 1. *Young Children* 48 (4): 75–84.

Greenberg, P. 1994. Ideas that work with young children. How and why to teach all aspects of preschool and kindergarten math naturally, democratically, and effectively (for teachers who don't believe in academic programs, who do believe in educational excellence, and who find math boring to the max)—Part 2. *Young Children* 49 (2): 12–18, 88.

Harsh, A. 1987. Teach mathematics with children's literature. *Young Children* 42 (6): 24–29.

Jones, G.A., & C.A. Thornton. 1993. Research in review. Children's understanding of place value: A framework for curriculum development and assessment. *Young Children* 48 (5): 12–18.

Kamii, C. 1982. *Number in preschool and kindergarten: Educational implications of Piaget's theory.* Washington, DC: NAEYC.

Mills, H., D.J. Whitin, & T. O'Keefe. 1993. Teaching math concepts in a K–1 class doesn't have to be like pulling teeth—but maybe it should be! *Young Children* 48 (2): 17–20.

Price, G.G. 1989. Research in review. Mathematics in early childhood. *Young Children* 44 (4): 53–58.

Stone, J.I. 1987. Early childhood math: Make it manipulative! *Young Children* 42 (6): 16–23.

Van Scoy, I.J., & S.H. Fairchild. 1993. It's about time! Helping preschool and primary children understand time concepts. *Young Children* 48 (2): 21–24.

Whitin, D.J. 1994. Literature and mathematics in preschool and primary: The right connection. *Young Children* 49 (2): 4–11.

Technology

Anselmo, S., & R.A. Zinck. 1987. Computers for young children? Perhaps. *Young Children* 42 (3): 22–27.

Burns, M.S., L. Goin, & J.T. Donlon. 1990. A computer in my room. *Young Children* 45 (2): 62–67.

Clements, D.H. 1987. Research in review. Computers and young children: A review of research. *Young Children* 43 (1): 34–44.

Clements, D.H., B.K. Nastasi, & S. Swaminathan. 1993. Research in review. Young children and computers: Crossroads and directions from research. *Young Children* 48 (2): 56–64.

Haugland, S.W., & D.D. Shade. 1988. Developmentally appropriate software for young children. *Young Children* 43 (4): 37–43.

Hyson, M.C., & A. Eyman. 1986. Approaches to computer literacy in early childhood teacher education. *Young Children* 41 (6): 54–59.

Wright, J.L., & Shade, D.D. 1994. *Young children: Active learners in a technological age.* Washington, DC: NAEYC.

Reflections

The American family of the 1830s is not so different from families of today. Diversity and ethnicity have always characterized families. So says Stephanie Coontz in "Where Are the Good Old Days?" For people who long to return to the good old days when fathers went to work and mothers cared for young children in the home, this is a wake-up call. Families have continually been affected by extremes of war and peace and poverty and wealth. Care for children outside the home is not a new trend but an old tradition in America.

Dorothy W. Hewes, a prominent historian of early childhood education, points out in her essay the long-standing connection between child care and sponsorship of centers outside the home. Kindergartens began to spread in an era when people were concerned about social policies to improve the nation. This fortunate timing ensured child care as a factor in reform through the decades. To Hewes, kindergarten has never been sentimental, for it has made a strong impact on our nation.

"The Movers and Shapers of Early Childhood Education" continues our theme of reflecting on heritage to understand the present. In concise form, Roger Neugebauer presents vignettes of 30 people who have contributed to the profession and influenced its direction into the future. They are researchers, educators, gurus, and bureaucrats—the movers and shapers of early childhood education. Some are prolific writers or leading speakers, while others are community activists or hard-working practitioners. It is important to know who has shaped the profession, for all their expertise has made it strong and influential.

An important addition to this unit is not an article, but a list of addresses. "Child Advocacy Directory" is a comprehensive listing of national organizations that advocate for young children. A concise mission statement is included for each of the 24 organizations. A valuable learning project might be to contact these organizations for more information on their early childhood involvement.

One kindergarten teacher who has made an impact on her students and on innumerable teachers-in-training is Vivian Paley. For 24 years, she taught at the historic University of Chicago Lab School, the experimental school begun by John Dewey. Barbara Mahany's report, "Mrs. Paley's Lessons," is a rich, full portrait of a teacher who truly respects children.

The United States has a rich heritage of early care and kindergartens. It has produced many wonderful early childhood educators and leaders. We close with the words of one of them—Mrs. Paley—about the importance of our field: "You in your classrooms are far more powerful to achieve moral changes than you think you are. You don't even need a new curriculum to do it. We have more of an opportunity to change the moral landscape of our little universe than the doctor does in the hospital, than the lawyer does in the court, than the reporter does on the newspaper, than the engineer does in the field. Think about it. Twenty, thirty children. What a bonanza we have!"

Class dismissed.

Looking Ahead: Challenge Questions

What was the status of children in colonial families, in post–Civil War era families, and in 1950s families?

What teachers or writers or researchers in early childhood education have influenced you?

Name three national organizations that advocate for young children. Where are they located?

What do you think of the idea that schools need to be surrogate parents?

UNIT 6

In Search of the American Family

WHERE ARE THE GOOD OLD DAYS?

Raising a family is hard enough without having to live up to myths. In fact, the American family is as strong—and as fragile—as it ever was.

Stephanie Coontz

Family historian Stephanie Coontz is the author of The Way We Never Were: American Families and the Nostalgia Trap *(Basic Books, 1992) and* The Way We Really Are: Coming to Terms with America's Changing Families *(Basic Books, 1997). A recipient of the Dale Richmond award from the American Academy of Pediatrics, Coontz teaches history and family studies at The Evergreen State College, Olympia, WA.*

THE AMERICAN FAMILY IS UNDER SIEGE. To listen to the rhetoric of recent months, we have all fallen down on the job. We're selfish; too preoccupied with our own gratification to raise our children properly. We are ungrateful; we want a handout, not a hand.

If only we'd buckle down, stay on the straight and narrow, keep our feet on the ground, our shoulder to the wheel, our eye on the ball, our nose to the grindstone. Then everything would be all right, just as it was in the family-friendly '50s, when we could settle down in front of the television after an honest day's work and see our lives reflected in shows like *Ozzie and Harriet* and *Father Knows Best*.

But American families have been under siege more often than not during the past 300 years. Moreover, they have always been diverse, both in structure and ethnicity. No family type has been able to protect its members from the roller-coaster rides of economic setbacks or social change. Changes that improved the lives and fortunes of one family type or individual often resulted in losses for another.

A man employed in the auto industry, for example, would have been better off financially in the

---

EARLY DAYS

In 1745 in Massachusetts, any child age 6 who did not know the alphabet was removed from the home and placed with another family.

During the Civil War, the number of orphans in almshouses increased by 300 percent. In 1825, there were two orphanages in New York State; by 1866, there were 60, but still not enough to meet the need. Homeless children swarmed in the cities' streets and "menaced the gentry."

1950s than now, but his retired parents would be better off today. If he had a strong taste for power, he might prefer Colonial times, when a man was the undisputed monarch of the household and any disobedience by wife, child, or servant was punishable by whipping. But woe betide that man if he wasn't born to property. In those days, men without estates could be told what to wear, where to live, and whom to associate with.

His wife, on the other hand, might have been happier in the 1850s, when she might have afforded two or three servants. We can be pretty sure, though, that the black or Irish servants of that day would not have found the times so agreeable. And today's children, even those scarred by divorce, might well want to stay put rather than live in the late 19th century, when nearly half of them died before they reached their late teens.

THE AMERICAN FAMILY HAS ALWAYS BEEN VULNERABLE TO SOCIAL AND ECONOMIC CHANGE

A History of Tradeoffs

These kinds of tradeoffs have characterized American family life from the beginning. Several distinctly different types of families already coexisted in Colonial times: On the East Coast, the Iroquois lived in longhouses with large extended families. Small families were more common among the nomadic Indian groups, where marital separation, though frequent, caused no social stigma or loss of access to group resources. African-American slaves, whose nuclear families had been torn apart, built extended family networks through ritual co-parenting, the adoption of orphans, and complex naming patterns designed to preserve links among families across space and time.

White Colonial families were also diverse: High death rates meant that a majority spent some time in a stepfamily. Even in intact families, membership ebbed and flowed; many children left their parents' home well before puberty to work as servants or apprentices to other households. Colonial family values didn't sentimentalize childhood. Mothers were far less involved in caring for their children than modern working women, typically delegating the task to servants or older siblings. Children living away from home usually wrote to their fathers, sometimes adding a postscript asking him to "give my regards to my mother, your wife."

A Revolution of Sorts

Patriarchal authority started to collapse at the beginning of the Revolutionary War: The rate of premarital conception soared and children began to marry out of birth order. Small family farms and shops flourished and, as in Colonial days, a wife's work was valued as highly as her husband's. The revolutionary ferment also produced the first stirrings of feminism and civil rights. A popular 1773 Massachusetts almanac declared: "Then equal Laws let custom find, and neither Sex oppress: More Freedom give to Womankind or to Mankind give less." New Jersey women had the right to vote after the Revolution. In several states slaves won their freedom when they sued, citing the Declaration of Independence.

But commercial progress undermined these movements. The spread of international trade networks

and the invention of the cotton gin in 1793 increased slavery's profits. Ironically, when revolutionary commitment to basic human equality went head-to-head with economic dependence on slavery, the result was an increase in racism: Apologists now justified slavery on the grounds that blacks were *less* than human. This attitude spilled over to free blacks, who gradually lost both their foothold in the artisan trades and the legal rights they'd enjoyed in early Colonial times. The subsequent deterioration in their status worked to the advantage of Irish immigrants, previously considered nonwhite and an immoral underclass.

Feminist ideals also faded as industrialization and wage labor took work away from the small family farms and businesses, excluding middle-class wives from their former economic partnerships. For the first time, men became known as breadwinners. By the post-Civil War era of 1870–90, the participation of married women in the labor force was at an all-time low; social commentators labeled those wives who took part in political or economic life sexual degenerates or "semi-hermaphrodites."

Women Lose; Children Lose More

As women left the workforce children entered it by the thousands, often laboring in abysmal conditions up to ten hours a day. In the North, they worked in factories or tenement workshops. As late as 1900, 120,000 children worked in Pennsylvania's mines and factories. In the South, states passed "apprentice" laws binding black children out as unpaid laborers, often under the pretext that

---

. . . OTHERS DO NOT

Between 1890 and 1915, 18 million immigrants entered the country; then tenement homes often doubled as sweatshops for child labor.

By 1900, the U.S. had the highest divorce rate in the world. Birthrates among the educated had plummeted to an alarming degree, prompting Teddy Roosevelt to call it "race suicide" in 1903. Some state legislatures passed laws prohibiting abortions in order to boost the nation's birthrate.

---

their parents neglected them. Plantation owners (whose wives and daughters encased themselves in corsets and grew their fingernails long) accused their former female slaves of "loaferism" when they resisted field labor in order to stay closer to home with their children.

So for every 19th-century middle-class family that was able to nurture its women and children comfortably inside the family circle, there was an Irish or German girl scrubbing floors, a Welsh boy mining coal, a black girl doing laundry, a black mother and child picking cotton, and a Jewish or Italian daughter making dresses, cigars, or artificial flowers in a sweatshop.

Meanwhile, self-styled "child-saver" charity workers, whose definition of an unfit parent had more to do with religion, ethnicity, or poverty than behavior, removed other children from their families. They sent these "orphans" to live with Western farmers who needed extra hands—or merely dumped them in a farm town with a dollar and an earnest lecture about escaping the evils of city life.

The Outer Family Circle

Even in the comfortable middle-class households of the late 19th century, norms and values were far different from those we ascribe to "traditional" families. Many households took in boarders, lodgers, or unmarried relatives. The nuclear family wasn't the primary focus of emotional life. The Victorian insistence on separate spheres for men and women made male-female relations extremely stilted, so women commonly turned to other women for their most intimate relationships. A woman's diary would rhapsodize for pages about a female friend, explaining how they carved their initials on a tree, and then remark, "Accepted the

marriage proposal of Mr. R. last night" without further comment. Romantic friendships were also common among young middle-class men, who often recorded that they missed sleeping with a college roommate and laying an arm across his bosom. No one considered such relationships a sign of homosexuality; indeed, the term wasn't even invented until the late 19th century.

Not that 19th-century Americans were asexual: By midcentury New York City had one prostitute for every 64 men; the mayor of Savannah estimated his city had one for every 39. Perhaps prostitution's spread was inevitable at a time when the middle class referred to the "white meat" and "dark meat" of chicken to spare ladies the embarrassment of hearing the terms "breast" or "thigh."

The Advent of the Couple

The early 20th century brought more changes. Now the emotional focus shifted to the husband and wife. World War I combined with a resurgence of feminism to hasten the collapse of Victorian values, but we can't underestimate the role the emergence of a mass consumer market played: Advertisers quickly found that romance and sexual titillation worked wonders for the bottom line.

Marriage experts and the clergy, concerned that longer lifespans would put a strain on marriages, denounced same-sex friendships as competitors to love; people were expected to direct all their emotional, altruistic and sensual impulses into marriage. While this brought new intimacy and sexual satisfaction to married life, it also introduced two trends that disturbed observers. One was an increased dissatisfaction with what used to be considered adequate relationships. Great expectations, social historian Elaine Tyler May points out in her book of the same name, could generate great disappointments. It's no surprise that the U.S. has had both the highest consumption of romance novels and the highest divorce rates in the world since the early part of the 20th century.

The second consequence of this new cult of married bliss was the emergence of an independent and increasingly sexualized youth culture. In the late 19th century, middle-class courtship revolved around the institution of "calling." A boy was invited to call by the girl or her parents. It was as inappropriate then for a boy to hint he'd like to be asked over as it was in the 1950s for a girl to hint she'd like to be asked out. By the mid-1920s, calling had been almost totally replaced by dating, which took young people away from parental control but made a girl far more dependent on the

EVEN IN THE LATE 1800s FAMILY VALUES VARIED A GREAT DEAL FROM THOSE OF THE 1950s

boy's initiative. Parents especially worried about the moral dangers the automobile posed—and with reason: A middle-class boy was increasingly likely to have his first sexual encounter with a girlfriend rather than a prostitute.

The early part of the century brought a different set of changes to America's working class. In the 1920s, for the first time, a majority of children were born to male-breadwinner, female-homemaker families. Child labor laws and the spread of mass education allowed more parents to keep their children out of the workforce. Numerous immigrant families, however, continued to pull their offspring out of school so they could help support the family, often arousing intense generational conflicts. African-American families kept their children in school longer than other families in those groups, but their wives were much more likely to work outside the home.

There Goes the Family

In all sectors of society, these changes created a sense of foreboding. *Is Marriage on the Skids?* asked one magazine article of the times; *What Is the Family Still Good For?* fretted another. Popular commentators harkened back to the "good old days," bemoaning the sexual revolution, the fragility of nuclear-family ties, the cult of youthful romance, and the threat of the "emancipated woman."

The stock market crash, the Great Depression, and the advent of World War II moved such fears to the back burner. During the '30s and '40s, family trends fluctuated from one extreme to another. Depression hardship—contrary to its television portrayal on *The Waltons*—usually failed to make family and community life stronger. Divorce rates fell, but desertion and domestic violence rose sharply; economic stress often translated into punitive parenting that left children with emotional scars still apparent to social researchers decades later. Murder rates in the '30s were as high as in the 1980s; rates of marriages and births plummeted.

WWII started a marriage boom, but by 1946 the number of divorces was double that in 1941. This time the social commentators blamed working women, interfering in-laws and, above all, inadequate mothers. In 1946, psychiatrist Edward Strecker published *Their Mothers' Sons: The Psychiatrist Examines an American Problem,* which argued that women who were old-fashioned "moms"

THE DAWN BEFORE . . .

The clock has struck "sex o'clock" shrieked a tabloid headline in 1913. The 1920s brought flappers, short skirts, and "necking parties."

In the '20s, the average annual income was about $1,000; only middle-class families earning $3,000 or more could afford domestic help. By 1927, 60 percent of homes had electricity and some of the new-fangled labor-saving appliances were showing up (the electric iron was a big hit).

instead of modern "mothers" were emasculating American boys.

Moms, he said disapprovingly, were immature and unstable and sought emotional recompense for the disappointments of their own lives. They took care of aging parents and tried to exert too much control over their children. Mothers, on the other hand, put their parents in nursing homes and derived all their satisfaction from the nuclear family while cheerfully urging independence on their children. Without motherhood, said the experts, a woman's life meant nothing. Too much mothering, though, would destroy her own marriage and her son's life. These new values put women in an emotional double-bind, and it's hardly surprising that tranquilizers, which came on the scene in the '50s, were marketed and prescribed almost exclusively to housewives.

The '50s: Paradise Lost?

Such were the economic and cultural ups and downs that created the 1950s. If that single decade had actually represented the "tradition" it would be reasonable to argue that the family has indeed collapsed. By the mid 1950s, the age of marriage and parenthood had dropped dramatically, divorce rates bottomed out and the birthrate, one sociologist has recently noted, "approached that of India." The proportion of children in Ozzie-and-Harriet type families reached an all-time high of 60 percent.

Today, in contrast, a majority of mothers, including those with preschool children, work outside the home. Fifty percent of children live with both bio-

> ## . . . THE DARK YEARS
>
> During the Depression, divorce rates dropped; desertion soared. Half of all births were in families on relief or making under $1,000 a year.
>
> *World War II years: The GNP soared: from $90 billion in 1939 to $213 billion in 1945. So did divorces: from 264,000 in 1940 to 610,000 in 1946. Women and teenager built aircraft, ships, tanks, weapons. Fewer than half the teenagers who entered high school graduated.*

logical parents, almost one quarter live with single parents and more than 21 percent are in step-families. Three quarters of today's 18–24-year-olds have never been married, while almost 50 percent of all first marriages—and 60 percent of remarriages—will end in divorce. Married couples wait longer to bear children and have fewer of them. For the first time there are more married couples without children than with them. Less than one quarter of contemporary marriages are supported by one wage earner.

Taking the 1950s as the traditional norm, however, overstates both the novelty of modern family life and the continuity of tradition. The 1950s was the most atypical decade in the entire history of American marriage and family life. In some ways, today's families are closer to older patterns than were '50s families. The median age at first marriage today is about the same as it was at the beginning of the century, while the proportion of never-married people is actually lower. The number of women who are coproviders and the proportion of children living in stepfamilies are both closer to that of Colonial days than the 1950s. Even the ethnic diversity among modern families is closer to the patterns of the early part of this century than to the demographics of the 1950s. And the time a modern working mother devotes to childcare is higher than in Colonial or Revolutionary days.

The 1950s family, in other words, was not at all traditional; nor was it always idyllic. Though many people found satisfactions in family life during that period, we now know the experiences of many groups and individuals were denied. Problems such as alcoholism, battering, and incest were swept under the rug. So was discrimination against ethnic groups, political dissidents, women, elders, gays, lesbians, religious minorities and the handicapped. Rates of divorce and unwed motherhood were low, but that did not prevent 30 percent of American children from living in poverty, a higher figure than at present.

It's All Relative

Why then, do many people remember the 1950s as so much easier than today? One reason is that after the hardships of the Depression and WWII, things *were* improving on many fronts. Though poverty rates were higher than today, they were falling. Economic inequality was also decreasing. The teenage birthrate was almost twice as high in 1957 as today, but most young men could afford to marry. Violence against African-Americans was appallingly widespread, yet many blacks got jobs in the expanding manufacturing industries and for the first time found an alternative to Southern agriculture's peonage.

What we forget when politicians tell us we should revive the 1950s family is that the social stability of that period was due less to its distinctive family forms than to its unique socioeconomic and political climate. High rates of unionization, heavy corporate investment in manufacturing, and generous government assistance in the form of public-works projects, veterans' benefits, student loans and housing subsidies gave young families a tremendous jump start, created predictable paths out of poverty, and led to unprecedented increases in real wages. By the time the "traditional male breadwinner" reached age 30, in both the 1950s and '60s, he could pay the principal and interest on a median-priced home on only 15–18 percent of his income. Social Security promised a much-needed safety net for the elderly, formerly the poorest segment of the population. These economic carrots combined with the sticks of McCarthyism and segregation to keep social dissent on the back burner.

The New Trends

Because the '60s were a time of social protest, many people forget that families still made economic gains throughout the decade. Older workers and homeowners continued to build security for their retirement years. The postwar boom and government subsidies cut child poverty in half from 1949 to 1959. It was halved again, to its lowest levels ever, from 1959 to 1969. The high point of health and nutrition for poor children came in 1970, a period that coincided with the peak years of the Great Society, not the high point of the '50s family.

Since 1973, however, a new phase has emerged. Some things have continued to improve: High school graduation rates are at an all-time high; minority test scores rose steadily from 1970 to 1990; poverty rates among the elderly have continued to fall while life expectancy has risen.

GENEROUS FEDERAL PROGRAMS GAVE YOUNG 1950s FAMILIES A TREMENDOUS JUMP START

Other trends show mixed results: The easy availability of divorce has freed individuals from oppressive or even abusive marriages, but many divorces have caused emotional and economic suffering for both children and adults. Women have found new satisfaction at work, and there's considerable evidence that children can benefit from having a working mother, but the failure of businesses—and some husbands—to adjust to working mothers' needs has caused much family stress and discord.

In still other areas, the news is quite bleak. Children have now replaced seniors as the poorest segment of the population; the depth and concentration of child poverty has increased over the past 20 years so it's now at 1965 levels. Many of the gains ethnic groups made in the 1960s and '70s have been eroded.

History suggests that most of these setbacks originate in social and economic forces rather than in the collapse of some largely mythical traditional family. Perhaps the most powerful of these sources is the breakdown of America's implicit postwar wage bargain with the working class, where corporations ensured labor stability by increasing employment, rewarding increased productivity with higher wages, and investing in jobs and community infrastructure. At the same time, the federal government subsidized home ownership and higher education.

Since 1973, however, real wages have fallen for most families. It increasingly requires the work of two earners to achieve the modest upward mobility one could provide in the 1950s and '60s. Unemployment rates have risen steadily as corporations have abandoned the communities that grew up around them, seeking cheap labor overseas or in nonunionized sectors of the South. Involuntary part-time work has soared. As *Time* magazine noted in 1993, the predictable job ladders of the '50s and '60s have been sawed off: "Companies are portable, workers are throwaway." A different article in the same issue found, "Long-term commitments . . . are anathema to the modern corporation."

During the 1980s the gap between the rich and middle-class widened in 46 states, and each year since 1986 has set a new postwar record for the gap between rich and poor. In 1980 a CEO earned 30 to 40 times as much as the average worker; by 1994 he earned 187 times as much. Meanwhile, the real wages of a young male high school graduate are lower today than those earned by his 1963 counterpart.

A MIXED BAG

The 1950s: Father knew best; mother stayed home; wages grew; divorces dropped; teen pregnancies peaked (so did teen marriages).

Many black families moved north, leaving the agricultural South to share in the postwar industrial boom. But racism was rampant. In 1957, Life *magazine noted that of the 10,000 blacks working at the Ford Motor Company's Dearborn plant, not one was allowed to live in Dearborn.*

These economic changes are not driven by the rise in divorce and unwed motherhood. Decaying wage and job structures—not changing family structures—have caused the overwhelming bulk of income redistribution. And contrary to what has been called a new bipartisan consensus, marriage is not the solution to poverty. According to sociologist Donald J. Hernandez, Ph.D., formerly with the U.S. Census Bureau, even if every child in America were reunited with both biological parents, two thirds of those who are poor today would still be poor.

Our Uncertain Future

History's lessons are both positive and negative. We can take comfort from the fact that American families have always been in flux and that a wide variety of family forms and values have worked well for different groups at different times. There's no reason to assume that recent changes are entirely destructive. Families have always been vulnerable to rapid economic change and have always needed economic and emotional support from beyond their own small boundaries. Our challenge is to grapple with the sweeping transformations we're currently undergoing. History demonstrates it's not as simple as returning to one or another family form from the past. Though there are many precedents for successfully reorganizing family life, there are no clear answers to the issues facing us as we enter the 21st century.

A bit of history clarifies the present

Sisterhood and Sentimentality— America's Earliest Preschool Centers

Dorothy W. Hewes, Ph.D.

Dorothy Hewes, professor emeritus of the Department of Child and Family Development at San Diego State University, has been involved with varied aspects of early education over the past half century. She coordinates the History Seminar at the NAEYC annual conference and is currently finishing a history of parent participation preschools.

America's "oldest child care centers" were started during a period of economic growth and intellectual turbulence. Although there were a few wealthy families during the 18th century, someone described the nation as having "pyramids of money in a desert of want." By the mid-1800s, however, professional and business men began to prosper. As the morally superior gentler sex, middle-class wives improved their minds and discharged obligations to the unfortunates of society through church, club, and literary groups. There was no unifying sense of sisterhood, no mutual faith or endeavor.

When the German kindergarten of Friedrich Froebel became known to English-speaking Americans during the 1870s, women became energized by his idea that within each child lies the potential for self-realization and self-learning, a potential developed not through stern discipline but by "learning by doing" in a joyous play school. Parents abandoned old beliefs in children's innate depravity to promote development of their innate goodness through the kindergarten system. Three to six year olds could learn morality and citizenship while they enjoyed educational games and songs or busied themselves with bead stringing, block building, paper folding, and the construction of "forms of beauty" with wooden slats or parquetry blocks. Mothers could extend their domestic role by assisting the teachers in the classroom, learning new methods to apply at home.

There were less than a dozen kindergartens in 1870, all dependent upon parent fees. Ten years later, when there were about 400 in 30 states, most of them had some form of outside financial support. Early sponsors included the New England Women's Club, Sorosis, and the Women's Christian Temperance Union (with its motto of "Prevention, Not Reform—the Kindergarten Not the Prison is True Philanthropy").

Women of all social classes, religious denominations, and political orientations banded together to promote both charity and fee-paid kindergartens. Affluent matrons gave generously to the cause. Jane Stanford contributed $30,000 to San Francisco's Golden Gate Kindergarten Association by 1887 and a later endowment of $100,000. . . . Pauline Agassiz Shaw, who used some of the profits from her husband's copper mining interests to underwrite 31 Boston kindergartens by 1882, objected to the term "charity" because it was demeaning to the recipients. Names like Armour, Vanderbilt, and Hearst are also on the donor lists, but some kindergarten association members pledged 50¢ a month, saved penny by penny.

Whatever their financial status, these women shared more than a faith in Froebel's system; they shared inferior status in a society that was controlled by men. Even in the National Education Association, the Kindergarten Department represented a chasm between genders that was greater than any distinctions based upon professional training.

The expansion of charity kindergartens, many of them in churches, supplemented or replaced some of the custodial day nurseries for poor working mothers. In her history of kindergartens, Nina Vandewalker wrote that "the new institution became recognized as the most valuable of child-saving agencies, with mission kindergarten work so valuable among wealthy young women as to be almost a fad."

Although about half of the country's 4,000 kindergartens were philanthropic when the 1893 depression began, mere numbers cannot capture the evangelical fervor contained in letters and publications of the period; Ross aptly called it "The Kindergarten Crusade."

Kindergarten advocates were often considered to be "sentimental," but this term can mean the use of sensitivity and emotions rather than logical processes. It was a feminine strategy that made a strong impact during an era when people were concerned with the moral, social, and political aspects of good citizenship; a clearly rational approach would never have gained momentum. However, extravagant claims were often made—as when Mary Mann wrote that entire neighborhoods were transformed if "little minds" were "fertilized" by the kindergarten. "Fathers found entertainment in the children's singing to keep them home from the grog shop" and the beer money went into a savings fund.

American enthusiasts also added their own interpretations to the original German writings. For example, Froebel devised the "Snail Game" as a transition from active outdoor play to indoor activities. Children were to join hands with the teacher, who slowly turned so that the line formed a spiral and then uncoiled to become a circle. The American translation ended with the mystical interpretation that this symbolized the wholeness of humanity but missed its practical intention.

Critics could easily point to writings like these to condemn the whole system—and to provide a basis for their own *advanced* ideas. But to children in the urban missions, on the Indian reservations, at places like the Colorado Fuel and Iron Company where there were 27 home languages, or in countless parlors where mothers presided over a cluster of young neighbors, the hours in kindergarten were filled with delightful activities.

Our list of oldest child care organizations includes a substantial number that originated in settlement houses that were established as multipurpose service centers in urban poverty areas. One of the first was in Detroit, opening in 1881; but the best known was Jane Addams' Hull House in Chicago. Its kindergarten, opened in 1889 as a model of beauty and convenience, had competent staff assisted by students from Alice Putnam's training classes. Many others were equally excellent, but some were so horrible that the first child care licensing laws were developed as an attempt to control the worst of them.

In the early kindergartens, teachers conducted a morning class for about 15 children and made social calls on families during the afternoon. The children were taught to address the teachers as "Auntie" to emphasize her sisterly relationship with their mothers.

By the late 1890s, men with advanced degrees in the "new sciences" like psychology and sociology began to propound a logical and unsentimental approach to education and the problems of poverty. Organizations like the National Conference of Charities and Corrections professionalized and systematized philanthropy, thus creating paid administrative positions and promoting "Friendly Visitors" to make certain that their funds were well spent. The resulting philanthropic kindergartens often had larger classes and a more structured program than the more informal groups of the early years. In the public school kindergartens, also efficiently administered, teachers not only had large classes but were expected to teach double sessions.

OUR HERITAGE FROM THE PAST CENTURY

Much of today's equipment and methodology has been an outgrowth of those early kindergartens. We may schedule *circle time* with finger plays and action games just as Froebel did in 1837. We have plastics and play dough instead of wood and natural clay, but we still believe that "what a child imitates, he begins to understand." This didn't just happen. After kindergartens became public school classes for five year olds, Progressive Froebelians maintained the philosophy of learning through play by developing nursery schools for the younger children and by organizing the Committee on Nursery Schools,

now the National Association for the Education of Young Children (NAEYC), in the 1920s.

Our heritage goes beyond methods and materials. The United States has always had some sort of other-than-mother care, as Geraldine Youcha and other writers have pointed out; but the first public concern about standards and salaries began in the kindergarten era. By 1908, when there were about 400 settlement house and mission kindergartens, Vandewalker reflected popular opinion when she criticized those "whose purpose is served if the children are kept clean, happy, and off the streets. . . . The large number of children enrolled, the economy exercised in the use of material, the low salaries paid, these and other conditions that too frequently prevail in philanthropic work have done much to obscure the real educational value of the kindergarten. . . . The teacher often undertook her work as a labor of love and asked for no remuneration. If salaries were paid, they were wholly out of proportion to the services rendered (p. 126)."

The negative inheritance from those early kindergarten enthusiasts persists in the expectation that psychic rewards are adequate compensation, that work with young children and their parents is so fulfilling that any mention of higher salaries or public funding somehow defiles its sentimental sanctity. As we prepare to enter the 21st century, it is time to move beyond charity, sentimentality, and sisterhood with evidence that child care is a worthwhile public investment.

SUGGESTIONS FOR FURTHER READING

Addams, Jane. *Twenty Years at Hull House.* New York: Macmillan, 1920.

Braun, S. J., and E. P. Edwards. *History and Theory of Early Childhood Education.* Belmont, CA: Wadsworth, 1972.

Hewes, Dorothy W. "Patty Smith Hill." *Young Children* (May) and ERIC EJ148709 PS505187, 1976.

Hewes, Dorothy W. "NAEYC's First Half Century." *Young Children* (September) and ERIC EJ148709 PS505187, 1976. (This publication is scheduled to be reprinted later this year.)

Hewes, Dorothy W. "Compensatory Early Childhood Education: Froebelian Origins and Outcomes." ERIC ED264980 PS015596, 1985.

Hewes, Dorothy W. "Early Childhood Exhibit Controversies: 1890 and 1990." ERIC ED330431 PS019280, 1990.

Kelley, Mary. *Woman's Being, Woman's Place: Female Identity and Vocation in American History.* Boston: G. K. Hall, 1979.

Ross, Elizabeth. *The Kindergarten Crusade: The Establishment of Preschool Education in the United States.* Athens, OH: Ohio University Press, 1976.

Rothman, David J. *Poverty, USA: The Charitable Impulse in Eighteenth Century America.* New York: Arno, 1971.

Vandewalker, Nina C. *The Kindergarten in American Education.* New York: Macmillan, 1908.

Weber, Evelyn. *The Kindergarten: Its Encounter with Educational Thought in America.* New York: Teachers College Press, 1969.

Williams, Leslie R., and Doris Fromberg. *Encyclopedia of Early Childhood Education.* New York: Garland, 1992.

Youcha, Geraldine. *Minding the Children—Child Care in America from Colonial Times to the Present.* New York: Scribner, 1995.

A tribute to some of the many VIPs of child care

The Movers and Shapers of Early Childhood Education

Roger Neugebauer

We recently invited a random selection of our readers to tell us who they see as the key people who have shaped our profession. Their response was overwhelming — they chronicled the contributions of over 200 individuals. We have selected 30 of these individuals to represent the rich diversity of very important people in our profession.

These people have much in common — most began their careers as preschool teachers, many were active in the early days of Head Start, many have served in leadership roles in NAEYC, and all have remained steadfast advocates for children for more than three decades. However, they followed many paths and bring diverse talents and interests to the profession. This mix of common interests and varied contributions represents the norm in this profession and is what makes it so strong and vibrant....

— Scholars —

Most veterans in the early childhood profession cut their teeth on the works of **Urie Bronfenbrenner**, professor of child development at Cornell University. He not only has influenced generations of adults with his teaching and writing, but he also has influenced millions of children by actively participating in the launching of Head Start.

Constance Kamii, an internationally renowned proponent of Piagetian theory, now teaches at the University of Alabama where she is actively experimenting with Piagetian approaches to math education. Her career includes studying and teaching under Jean Piaget at the University of Geneva, as well as participating in the landmark Perry Preschool Project.

For over three decades, **Bernard Spodek**, as professor of early childhood education at the University of Illinois, has worked tirelessly to promote an understanding of how children develop. He has lectured extensively throughout the world. His writings include the popular *Foundations of Early Childhood Education* (Prentice Hall, 1991), co-authored with Olivia Saracho.

— Researchers —

When the demand for child care was poised to explode in the mid-1960s, research of **Bettye Caldwell** at Syracuse University on the effects of child care was instrumental in shaping the direction of Head Start,

as well as the direction of most professionally oriented child care. She continues to be a strong child advocate at the University of Arkansas.

Alice Sterling Honig was a partner in research with Bettye Caldwell at Syracuse University and has remained there to focus her attention on the youngest children. Through her prolific writing and her engaging presentations, she has become the leading authority on caring for infants in group settings.

In 1960, **David Weikart** launched the Perry Preschool Project to demonstrate the impact of a carefully designed curriculum. Over three decades later, this project is still influencing our profession as advocates promote its positive research results, and as practitioners shape their programs around the High/Scope curriculum which evolved from this research.

When Head Start was launched, many of our profession's top thinkers were tapped to give it direction. **Edward Zigler** was a key player among these. His continuing research on child development as sterling professor of psychology at Yale University has kept him in the forefront of the profession. He remains an active advisor to Head Start as it grows and evolves.

— Translators —

No single instrument has had more impact on the early childhood centers than the *Early Childhood Environment Rating Scale* (Teachers College Press, 1980) of which **Thelma Harmes** is the first author. This tool is accepted by researchers as a standard for evaluation and is widely employed by centers as a guide to improving service delivery.

Joanne Hendrick has educated early childhood teachers both as a professor, currently at the University of Oklahoma, and as the author of popular texts on early childhood education which concisely translate current thinking on child development into principles and practices to apply in the classroom.

A mentor for generations of early childhood teachers, **James L. Hymes, Jr.** began his career as head of two Kaiser Child Service Centers in Portland, Oregon, during World War II. He has influenced the direction of our field as an educator, a writer, a lecturer, and as president of NAEYC. He now serves as a chronicler of the profession with his *Year In Review* publications.

There is no more effective explicator of early childhood teaching practices than **Lilian Katz**. She is respected worldwide for her writing and speaking on teacher training and curriculum development. Currently, she serves as director of the ERIC Clearinghouse on Elementary and Early Childhood Education and as professor of early

childhood education at the University of Illinois.

— Educators —

Anyone who has heard **Barbara Bowman** speak soon recognizes that she combines an uncommon grasp of child development and learning theory with an extraordinary eloquence. She was one of three founders of the Erikson Institute for the Advanced Study in Child Development, a leading early childhood teacher training institution. Now, three decades later, she serves as its president.

Countless early childhood professionals have had their careers enriched and inspired by **Elizabeth Brady**. Her influence has been felt in the classrooms of the University of California, in countless AEYC workshops and retreats, as well as in individual program consultations. She touches students of all ages with a quick wit and a deep commitment to quality education.

Shirley Moore's first day as an early childhood teacher was nearly her last as she was assigned to supervise nap time and chaos ensued. Fortunately for the profession, she persevered, and 50 years later she is still educating and inspiring new teachers. The past 30 years she has worked at the University of Minnesota, first at the lab school and currently as professor emeritus at the Institute of Child Development.

Over half a century ago, **Joan Swift** studied at the Iowa Welfare Station where pioneering research on child development was taking place. In this pioneering spirit, she authored one of the earliest literature reviews on the effects of early childhood education programs, established one of the first paraprofessional training programs, and provided impetus to the establishment of six laboratory preschools in Chicago.

— Practitioners —

For decades, **Mozelle Core** operated high quality child care centers, including the Donner Belmont Demonstration Child Care Center in Nashville, Tennessee. She inspired generations of early childhood professionals in Tennessee as a mentor and model in her center as well as through her active involvement in professional organizations.

When **Grace Mitchell** had her first child, she also gave birth to Mrs. Bailey's Nursery School in Waltham, Massachusetts. Sixty years later, she is still working hard on behalf of children and early childhood professionals. Today, she keeps active by sharing her insights in books and by traveling to visit centers and give inspirational keynotes.

Winona Sample, like James Hymes, began her career during World War II providing child care for Army wives. She continued her career as a preschool teacher and director, and later became active in providing services for migrant workers and later for Native Americans in Head Start. Currently, she shares her expertise as a Head Start trainer and consultant.

Docia Zavitkovsky is known as the storyteller of the early childhood community. She uses her endless collection of classroom stories not only to entertain but, more importantly, to educate and to inspire. Her wealth of stories flows from her decades of work as a teacher and director — most recently as director of Santa Monica's child development programs.

— Bureaucrats —

When **Bertha Campbell** had her first child, she realized she didn't know enough about young children and pursued a masters degree in child development. Years later, having earned two more masters degrees as well as a doctorate in education, she was hired by the state of New York as a program and staff development specialist. She recently retired as chief of the Bureau of Child Development.

Not many of us think of **Polly Greenberg**, the editor of *Young Children*, as a bureaucrat. However, during the Kennedy years, she was one of "Bobby's Guerrillas." She wrote an early position paper on Head Start for Sargent Shriver. When Head Start was launched, she was appointed to head the southeast region where she worked aggressively to recruit Head Start providers and to support parent participation in these programs.

Jenni Klein began her career as a preschool teacher in the 1950s. When Head Start was launched, she was appointed educational specialist in the Head Start Bureau. For over a decade, she rose steadily in the Bureau, all the while remaining active and influential in NAEYC and other professional organizations.

Jeannette Watson is known as "Mrs. Early Childhood Education of Texas." For 17 years, starting in the late 1940s, she directed a child care center in Austin. In 1971, she was appointed director of early childhood development for the state of Texas. In this position, and through professional associations, she has implemented many innovative programs for children and families.

— Advocates —

T. Berry Brazelton has been called the "pediatric guru of the 1980s."

He is well known for his insights on child development and parenting. In addition, he has given countless hours traveling across the country promoting the value of properly funded early childhood programs.

Asa Hilliard, III, a moving lecturer and an articulate writer, has used these talents to deliver hundreds of papers and keynotes on the nature of diversity education, the validity of current testing practices for black children and teachers, quality teaching of black children, and the historical roots of black Americans. The huge success of National Black Child Development Institute (NBCDI), which recently celebrated its 25th anniversary, can be attributed to the dedication of its founder and current executive director, **Evelyn K. Moore**. NBCDI serves as a gathering place for all those concerned about the future of African American children; it regularly informs the American public on the status of these children, and it advocates actively for legislation meeting the needs of all poor and disadvantaged children.

— Gurus —

Millie Almy began her career as a teacher and director of nursery schools in the late 1930s. For the past 50 years, she has inspired thousands as a professor, most recently at the University of California. Not only is she a great teacher of teachers, she also helps professionals see the key role the director plays in supporting the development and performance of teachers.

In 1943, **Dorothy Hewes** received a

degree in institution management. Throughout her career, she has built on this training, first as a center director and currently as a professor at San Diego State University, to professionalize center administration. Her books and articles were among the first to focus in-depth attention on the work of the center director.

Gwen Morgan is the Jacqueline of all trades in early childhood education. She has been a vocal advocate for federal funding, has promoted coordination efforts at the state level, and has focused attention on improving state licensing laws. In addition, in providing summer seminars for directors at Wheelock College for 25 years, she has personally trained many of the current leaders in the field.

Day Care as a Child-Rearing Environment (NAEYC, 1972), by **Elizabeth Prescott**, was a landmark publication. It looked at centers not as a collection of classrooms but as self-standing organizations influenced by leadership styles and structural patterns. This publication and subsequent creative work by Prescott and her peers at Pacific Oaks College inspired an entire generation of directors to look at their work in a new light.

These are but a few of the many individuals who have shaped, and continue to impact, the early childhood profession. In communities across the world, countless individuals with a wide range of talents, resources, and interests have supported the development of much needed early childhood services.

Child Advocacy Directory

The following national organizations engage in advocacy in the early childhood arena. The person listed as CEO is in most cases the organization's executive director. When a separate person is listed after ECE, this person leads the organization's early childhood division.

Alliance of Work/Life Professionals
465 Carlisle Drive
Herndon, VA 22070
(800) 874-9393
CEO: Brad Googins, Mary Ellen Gornick

Mission: The Alliance of Work/Life Professionals is a membership organization with the vision of promoting work/family and personal life balance. Through sharing cutting edge thinking, promising practices, and helpful resources, the Alliance strives both to improve the professionalism of those working in the work/life arena and to influence the better integration of work and family life.

American Academy of Pediatrics
141 Northwest Point Boulevard
Elk Grove Village, IL 60007
(800) 433-9016
Fax: (847) 228-1281
CEO: Joe M. Sanders, Jr., MD
ECE: Kathleen Sanabria

Mission: The American Academy of Pediatrics is committed to the attainment of optimal physical, mental, and social health for all infants, children, adolescents, and young adults.

Association for Childhood Education International
11501 Georgia Avenue, Suite 315
Wheaton, MD 20902
(301) 942-2443/(800) 423-3563
Fax: (301) 942-3012
CEO: Gerald C. Odland

Mission: ACEI's mission is to promote the inherent rights, education, and well-being of all children to bring into active cooperation all individuals and groups concerned with children; to raise the standard of preparation for those actively involved with the care and development of children; and to focus the public's attention on the rights and needs of children.

Board on Children, Youth, and Families
(of the National Research Council and the Institute of Medicine)
2101 Constitution Avenue NW, HA 156
Washington, DC 20418
(202) 334-2998
Fax: (202) 334-3829
CEO: Deborah Phillips
ECE: Anne Bridgman

Mission: The Board on Children, Youth, and Families was created in 1993 to provide a national focal point for authoritative, nonpartisan analysis of child, youth, and family issues relevant to policy decisions. It does so primarily by establishing committees to synthesize and evaluate research from scientific disciplines that are relevant to critical national issues, including child care.

Center on Effective Services for Children
PO Box 27412
Washington, DC 20038-7412
(202) 785-9524
Fax: (202) 833-4454
CEO: Jule M. Sugarman

Mission: The Center on Effective Services for Children is dedicated to improving the efficiency and effectiveness of child and family services. Its current focus has been preparing states and localities to take advantage of impending federal changes to improve services and offering guidance on how multiple programs and funding sources can be combined.

Child Care Action Campaign
330 7th Avenue, 17th Floor
New York, NY 10001-5010
(212) 239-0138
Fax: (212) 268-6515
CEO: Barbara Reisman

Mission: The Child Care Action Campaign (CCAC) is a national non-profit coalition of individuals and organizations whose goal is to improve the lives of children and their families by expanding the supply of good quality, affordable child care. CCAC uses its information resources and strategic skills to engage parents, policymakers, business leaders, and child care providers in improving child care and early education.

Child Welfare League of America
440 First Street NW, Suite 310
Washington, DC 20001
(202) 638-2952
Fax: (202) 638-4004
CEO: David Liederman
ECE: Bruce Hershfield

Mission: CWLA believes that every child is entitled to live in a loving, stable, and protective family, free from abuse and neglect. CWLA is the nation's oldest and largest organization devoted entirely to the well-being of America's vulnerable children. CWLA's almost 1,000 members provide a wide range of services to strengthen and support families for children.

Children's Defense Fund
25 E Street NW
Washington, DC 20001
(202) 628-8787
Fax: (202) 662-3560
CEO: Marian Wright Edelman
ECE: Helen Blank

Mission: CDF exists to provide a voice for all American children. Our staff includes

From *Child Care Information Exchange*, September/October 1996, pp. 25, 27-28. © 1996 by Exchange Press, Inc. Reprinted by permission of *Child Care Information Exchange*, P.O. Box 2890, Redmond, WA 98073. (800) 221-2864.

specialists in children's issues, including child care. CDF gathers data and disseminates information on key children's issues involving child care and Head Start. We monitor the development and implementation of federal and state policies.

Children's Foundation
725 15th Street NW, #505
Washington, DC 20005
Voice/Fax: (202) 347-3300
CEO: Kay Hollestelle
ECE: Sandra Gellert

Mission: The Children's Foundation is a national educational non-profit organization striving to improve the lives of children and those who care for them. Our mission is to provide a voice for caregivers, children, and their families on issues of critical concern. We conduct research and provide information and training.

National Association for the Education of Young Children
1509 16th Street NW
Washington, DC 20036-1426
(202) 232-8777/(800) 424-2460
Fax: (202) 328-1846
CEO: Marilyn M. Smith
ECE: Barbara Willer, M. Therese Gnezda

Mission: NAEYC exists for achieving healthy development and high quality education for all young children. To accomplish its mission, NAEYC promotes improvements in professional practice and working conditions in all family child care homes, early childhood programs, and centers. Building and maintaining a strong, diverse, and inclusive organization enables NAEYC to achieve these goals.

National Association for Family Child Care
206 6th Avenue, Suite 900
Des Moines, IA 50309
(515) 282-8192
Fax: (515) 282-9117
CEO: Deborah E. Eaton

Mission: NAFCC is the national membership organization dedicated to strengthening and expanding the more than 400 local and state family child care provider associations. NAFCC facilitates the professional development of the field in identifying and developing existing and emerging leaders; administering a provider accreditation program; and producing and disseminating informational materials.

National Association of Child Care Resource and Referral Agencies
1319 F Street NW
Washington, DC 20004
(202) 393-5501
Fax: (202) 393-1109
CEO: Yasmina S. Vinci
ECE: Rachel Bly

Mission: NACCRRA's mission is to promote the growth and development of quality child care resource and referral services and to exercise national policy leadership to build a diverse, quality child care system with parental choice and equal access for all families.

National Black Child Development Institute
1023 15th Street NW, #600
Washington, DC 20005
(202) 387-1281
Fax: (202) 234-1738
CEO: Evelyn Moore

Mission: NBCDI is dedicated to improving the quality of life for Black children and families through services and advocacy. As a national, membership organization, NBCDI keeps its members informed about critical issues in child care, education, child welfare, and health that face Black children and families. NBCDI's affiliate network is composed of dedicated volunteers who help to educate their communities about national, state, and local issues facing Black children and families.

National Center for Children in Poverty
154 Haven Avenue
New York, NY 10032
(212) 927-8793
Fax: (212) 927-9162
CEO: J. Lawrence Aber
ECE: Ann Collins

Mission: The National Center for Children in Poverty (NCCP) uses demographic research and program and policy analyses to identify and communicate strategies that reduce the incidence of young child poverty and improve the lives of poor young children.

National Center for the Early Childhood Work Force
733 15th Street NW
Washington, DC 20005
(202) 737-7700
Fax: (202) 737-0370
CEO: Claudia E. Wayne

Mission: NCECW is a policy, research, and advocacy organization dedicated to enhancing the compensation, working conditions, and training of child care staff and providers. It coordinates the Worthy Wage Campaign, a grassroots initiative empowering the work force itself to press for staffing solutions, and the Early Childhood Mentoring Alliance, a network for mentors and mentoring programs nationwide.

National Child Care Association, Inc.
1029 Railroad Street
Conyers, GA 30207
(800) 543-7161
Fax: (770) 388-7772

CEO: Lynn White
ECE: Nancy Granese

Mission: The purpose of NCCA is to promote the growth of quality child care focusing on licensed, proprietary, tax-paying providers with emphasis on efforts to (1) provide the public with information concerning the benefits of licensed, center-based child care services; (2) assist legislative, regulatory, standard-setting bodies in the development of policies affecting child care services; and (3) expand the availability of professionally managed, licensed, proprietary child care centers.

National Coalition for Campus Child Care
PO Box 258
Cascade, WI 53011
(414) 528-7080/(800) 813-8207
Fax: (414) 528-8753
CEO: Michael Kalinowski
ECE: Todd Boressoff

Mission: NCCCC is a non-profit educational membership organization. NCCCC supports research and activities affecting college and university early childhood education and service settings, family and work issues, and the field of early childhood education in general. NCCCC expresses this mission through its newsletters, publications, conferences, and grants.

National Head Start Association
1651 Prince Street
Alexandria, VA 22314
(703) 739-0875
Fax: (703) 739-0878
CEO: Sarah M. Greene
ECE: James A. Delaney

Mission: The National Head Start Association (NHSA) strives to (1) define and implement strategies for funding the Head Start program; (2) be a direct provider of training and professional development services; (3) advocate for the provision of quality services to the Head Start community; (4) advocate for measures that support the development of children; (5) advocate for measures that assist parents to meet the needs of their children and families; (6) advocate for professional development for Head Start staff; and (7) develop and disseminate research, information, and resources.

National Women's Law Center
11 Dupont Circle NW, #800
Washington, DC 20036
(202) 588-5180
Fax: (202) 588-5185
CEO: Nancy Duff Campbell
ECE: Elisabeth Donahue

Mission: The National Women's Law Center is a national organization that has been working since 1972 to advance and protect women's legal rights. The center focuses on major policy issues of importance to women and their families, including employment, education, family support, income security, and reproductive rights and health.

Southern Early Childhood Association

7107 West 12th, Suite 102
Little Rock, AR 72215
(800) 305-7322
Fax: (501) 663-2114
CEO: Dr. Clarissa Leister-Willis

Mission: For almost 50 years, the Southern Early Childhood Association (SECA) has provided teachers and caregivers of young children with practitioner-oriented publications, opportunities for professional growth and development, and has become a regional organization dedicated to providing for all children.

USA Child Care

2104 East 18th Street
Kansas City, MO 64127
(816) 474-3751, ext. 603
Fax: (816) 474-1818
CEO: Shirley Stubbs Gillette
ECE: Cliff Marcussen

Mission: The mission of USA Child Care is to provide a national voice for direct service providers to ensure quality, comprehensive childhood care, and education that is affordable and accessible for all families. The primary focus of the organization is the provision of quality childhood care and education for low- and moderate-income families.

YMCA of the USA

101 North Wacker Drive
Chicago, IL 60606
(312) 977-0031
Fax: (312) 977-9063
CEO: David Mercer
ECE: John Brooks

Mission: The YMCA, one of the nation's largest providers of child care, is a not-for-profit agency which puts Christian principles into practice through programs that build healthy spirit, mind, and body for all. YMCA child care centers are family centered with an emphasis on building self-esteem and character.

YWCA of the USA

624 9th Street NW, 3rd Floor
Washington, DC 20001
(202) 628-3636
Fax: (202) 783-7123

CEO: Dr. Prema Mathai-Davis
ECE: Rhea Staff

Mission: The YWCA is a women's membership movement to empower women and girls and eliminate racism.

Zero to Three/National Center for Infants, Toddlers, and Families

734 15th Street NW, Suite 1000
Washington, DC 20005
(202) 638-1144
Fax: (202) 638-0875
CEO: Matthew Melmed, JD
ECE: Beverly Roberson Jackson, Ed.D.

Mission: Zero to Three's urgent mission is to advance the healthy development of America's young children, by: (1) increasing public awareness of the critical importance of the first three years of life; (2) fostering professional excellence through training and related activities; (3) inspiring tomorrow's leaders by identifying and engaging promising young professionals; (4) promoting the discovery and application of new knowledge; (5) stimulating effective service approaches and responsive policies; and (6) educating parents and other caregivers.

Mrs. Paley's Lessons

The only kindergarten teacher to receive a MacArthur grant has a message for you from her pupils

Barbara Mahany

Boiled down, a day in one particular kindergarten amounts to this:

Two tummyaches of undetermined origin. A bunny that breakfasts on pink paper hearts and a teacher's brown shoelace after that. A breathless report of a wiggly tooth surrendered to the tooth fairy the night before, and, offered as proof, a curled-up dribbling tongue poking through the now vacant space. A broken piggy bank to tape back together, and a little boy's broken heart with it. Twenty-one heads to count, milk cartons to fetch and, on the playground, two sets of tears, first to wipe, then to referee. A 5-year-old curled up in a ball, refusing to come out from the cubby hole. A squeaky old heating vent that must be slapped and slapped, and still it won't stop its whine.

At lunchtime, it's a little boy who won't eat what's packed: bored, he protests, with peanut butter-and-jelly day after day after day. After lunch, it's a little girl who says she feels sick to her stomach and then proves it.

And just about 2 o'clock, when the chief arbiter, healer and repairwoman in this classroom is seated at the very edge of her teeny-tiny chair turning the teeny-tiny pages of a child's hand-drawn storybook, called an "Eensy Book" around here and narrated publicly by its young illustrator, someone from the back of the story circle yells, "I can't hear!" "If you concentrate you can hear even if there's a hurricane outside," calls back the one turning the pages, prompting this: "What's a hurricane?" "It's like a tornado," offers a more learned little someone, who then provides a fairly convincing imitation of a twister at full-throttle.

So goes the cacophony of kindergarten.

All that and in between, oh, somewhere around 100 or so yankings at one rolled-up oxford cloth sleeve, followed every time by the insistent and unrelenting "Teacher! Teacher!", a refrain that not once all day, all week, in Room 284 of the University of Chicago Laboratory Schools went unheard, unanswered, unexplored.

You see, until the final school bell rang three weeks ago Wednesday, ending a 36-year teaching career—two dozen of those years at the grand old Lab Schools, the last six in that very classroom—Room 284 was that of Vivian Gussin Paley.

And long ago in those kindergartens, Paley, 66, taught herself to hear not what some would call the noise, the nonsense, of 5- and 6-year-olds at the work of play. No, Paley has heard beyond all that. Far, far beyond.

She has learned the essential lesson, and from her little schoolroom in Hyde Park she's taught it to a generation of teachers and parents and caretakers of children around the globe. It is this: Take very seriously the things that children say, and take equally seriously the things you say to children.

What's coming from the mouths of kindergartners is often the truest truth, the uncluttered voice of the soul, and none of us can afford not to listen. Likewise, what's seeded in those nascent souls, through the words we choose to speak to them, may well take root and change forever the way the next and the next generations see and shape the world.

Nothing less is at stake in the kindergarten, what Paley calls "the official start of public life," and where the classroom, in the end, is the moral laboratory and the social experiments done there the most everlasting. For, if you begin at the beginning—when consciousness and conscience are taking form—with a curriculum that soars beyond reading and writing and counting to 99 and seeks to draw the best from human nature, creating in kindergartners a sense of fairness and rightness for life, then the "children's garden" is not some romping ground for ring-around-the-rosy but the crucible for hope. And teaching there, says Paley, is every bit a "moral act."

What she hears from kindergartners slips by most of us. Some can only wish to hear it. Some can't imagine it's there.

But it is, this magic, this poetry, what Paley calls "literature in every sense; the simplicity of their stories nonetheless miraculously reveals the deepest of human emotions."

Twenty years ago, not long after moving back to the city where she'd grown up and not long after accepting a position at the Lab Schools, which just happened to be hiring that first summer and just happened to be walking distance from the

Hyde Park tri-level she'd moved into with her husband, Irving, and two nearly grown sons, David and Bobby, Paley picked up a borrowed tape recorder and marched back into her classroom.

She was determined, after years of not really hearing the dialogue all around her, to absorb every last word of the scripts being unspooled by these young dramatists, philosophers and, oh yes, theologians in her care.

She'd gotten an inkling that these were "the genuine intellectual people," the ones building block cities and cradling baby dolls all around her. She set out to prove it—first, to herself; later, to anyone who cared to turn an ear.

Immersed in this gathering of child thought, Paley came upon a novel means of eliciting even more storytelling, that is, letting the children spin aloud their own dramas and mysteries and fairy tales. She began every day taking dictation from the little story weavers, taking down two-sentence, three-sentence, sometimes notebook-page-long narratives. And then she made it a practice to have the young thespians act out their works in the daily story circle.

So grew the volume of the dialogue, and so too the wisdom of the children's transcriber, stage director and master of ceremonies.

Since then Paley has poured what she's heard onto the pages of eight remarkable books, the latest, "Kwanzaa and Me: A Teacher's Story," published in February by Harvard University Press. Each book tackles a single central question of classroom life—the racism, the stories, the gender differences, the children's development, the outsider and the struggle to belong, the ethics, and the ways in which classrooms dismiss the differences, and thus the heart, of the children who make up their rosters. With each, Paley probes the question as it unfolds among a community of children over the course of a school year. (In "Kwanzaa," though, Paley takes her question cross-country to the lectures and workshops that fill her weekends' calendar.)

Each book reads in part like passages from a teacher's journal, the source from which the musings and commentaries and self-analyses are drawn. And, too, each volume gives the reader the sense that he or she, like Paley, is perched at the doll corner door, listening in—hearing about and seeing the world, not for the first time, of course, from the mouths and through the eyes of a 3- or 4- or 5- or 6-year-old child.

Along the way, and probably a good bit of the reason she was awarded a MacArthur Foundation "genius" award in 1989—the only elementary teacher and one of only two classroom teachers so honored—Paley has given all of us not just snapshots of the minds and souls of preschoolers and kindergartners but full-blown portraits of how they think, what they feel and the ways in which they imagine, complete with all the shadings and brush strokes that can be born only of a child's most intimate, unguarded revelations.

Listen in:

Wally: I know all about Jonas. He got swallowed by the whale.
Fred: How?
Wally: God sent him. But the whale was asleep so he just walked out.
Fred: How did he fly up to God? I mean how did he get back to shore if it was so deep?

Wally: He didn't come from the sky. But he could have because there's an ocean in the sky. For the rain to come down.
Fred: Oh yeah. That's for the gods. When they go deep they never drown, do they?
Wally: Of course not. They're just going nearer to Earth.
Jill: How does the ocean stay up?
Fred: They patch it up. They. . . .
Wally: They take a big, big, big bag and put it around the ocean.
Fred: It's a very, very, very big bag.
Eddie: Which reminds me. Do you know how many Christmas trees God gets? Infinity.
Teacher: Who gives him Christmas trees?
Eddie: He makes them.
Wally: When people burn them. . . . You see he's invisible. He takes up the burned parts and puts them together.
Rose: Are there decorations?
Wally: Invisible decorations. He can see them because he's invisible. If you tell him there's an invisible person here, he believes it.
Eddie: You can't fool God.
Wally: Sure you can. It's a good trick. You can say, "I'm here," and you're really not, but he can't see you. You can fool him.
Eddie: But he hears you.
Wally: Right. He hears you talk. He talks, too. But you have to ask him. He talks very soft. I heard him.
Eddie: You know, 353 years ago everyone could see God. He wasn't invisible then. He was young, so he could stay down on Earth. He's so old now he floats up in the sky. He lived in Uganda and Egypt.
Fred: That's good, because everyone in Egypt keeps. They turn into mummies.

Paley and her players keep at it, page after page, explaining away in kindergarten terms the mysteries of the universe.

There's Wally, again, who observes in one of his wiser moments: "You can never take a picture of thinking." And there's Rose, who suddenly wonders as the class readies a pile of vegetables for a dramatization of the children's classic "Stone Soup." "Do stones melt?" "They will if you cook them," informs Lisa. "If you *boil* them," corrects Eddie, who soon presides over the lowering of three stones into a pot of boiling water as the class decides to test his hypothesis.

There's Deana, who swears she bumped into the tooth fairy at the bank, and has this to report: "She has purple shoes and red hair." And flying to the Man in the Moon, there's Wally again letting us in on a celestial secret: "The moon is right next to God so he could talk to God." And when the subject is Martin Luther King, the little historians clarify one civil rights issue: "Martin changed all the rules," says Wally. "All the *bad* rules," says Lisa. "But not the one for the bathroom," says Fred. "The girls have to separate from the boys."

There's more to be learned from the Land of Paley's Little People, and it's not all dialogue and not all earth-shattering, though it does suggest how keenly someone is keeping watch over her kingdom.

Paley tells you, almost in passing, that she's noticed these things: Kindergartners draw people from the feet up. They don't color in the faces on their drawings. And they almost always leave a big blank space between the blue sky at the top of the page and the green grass at the bottom. The most vulnerable hero in a kindergartner's story is the one who gets lost in the woods. And you can tell the end of the kindergarten year is nearing, not by some quantitative developmental scale, but when the wall paintings have fewer drips, the labels are in the children's handwriting, and their letters sit more comfortably side by side.

And this, from the gender gap: Boys fly, leap, crash, and dive. Girls have picnics and brush their teeth. The meanest, ugliest character in a girl's story goes on picnics and keeps his teeth clean. Boys animate their drawings of volcanoes and space wars with exploding noises, as if they had jumped inside the pictures—if they sit down to draw at all. Girls sit for hours at the drawing table; flowers, houses and families, three favorite motifs. Boys thrive on blood and mayhem, girls avoid the subject; a character in a girls' story simply dies, no details given. In one particular class, Paley discerned this: You hop to get your milk if you are a boy and skip to the paper shelf if you are a girl. All evidence, she writes, of the "five-year-old's passion for segregation by sex."

Child psychologist Jerome Bruner, himself a master in the domain of deep thought, calls Paley's work "a miracle," and "a rich journey into the mind of a child."

"Blessed Vivian," he calls her, and goes on to say: "She's one of those marvelous characters who has this intuitive gift for knowing how to get into the domain of children. Where did that gift come from? It came from God. But she's not some naive angel. She brings to it a reasoned moral stance that's astonishing. I keep thinking I wish she had taught my children; then I think, I wish she had taught me!"

Dr. Robert Coles, the Harvard child psychiatrist who won a 1973 Pulitzer Prize for two volumes of his "Children of Crisis" series, puts Paley in the company of poets and novelists, "experts on nothing save life itself," and, in particular, says she "belongs in the company of those specially talented novelists who can evoke childhood in all its contradictions and inconsistencies, its never-ending thickness and complexity."

In his foreword to Paley's 1990 book, "The Boy Who Would Be a Helicopter: The Uses of Storytelling in the Classroom," Coles writes: "In an age when ambitious theorists strut across any stage they can find, assaulting us with pronouncements meant to advance careers, here is a teacher who lets life's complexities have their full dignity, who moves ever so gently and thoughtfully from observed life to carefully qualified comment."

Paley has been compared to and, by some, put on the same plane as Jean Piaget, the Swiss cognitive psychologist who broke ground with his studies of how children think at four clearly-defined stages, and Lev Vygotsky, the developmental psychologist referred to as "the Russian Piaget," who took so seriously children's play.

But, of course, this being academia, Paley has her share of critics.

Judith Wells Lindfors, professor of curriculum and instruction at the University of Texas at Austin, remembers being at an academic conference shortly after the publication in a professional journal of her glowing review of Paley's 1984 "Boys & Girls: Superheroes in the Doll Corner," a somewhat controversial examination of the natural separation of the sexes as observed in the nursery school classroom. A "very, very ardent feminist" cornered Lindfors, she recalls, "practically screaming, 'What have you done?' She was absolutely overwhelmed that I'd reviewed it positively. [Paley] really hit an exposed nerve with that one."

And then there is what several academics referred to as, "a wonderful dilemma for researchers," who knot themselves up pondering: "Do you let her in?" As in into the club called Significant Clinical Data Gathering. "Researchers," says Lindfors, "don't know what to do with her."

Lindfors, who is amused by the whole quandary, continues: "There's a funny sort of discomfort. We know she's terribly important, but there's some discomfort with conventions."

It is this bone that they pick: Usually research tapes are transcribed with all the "hmming and hawing and disfluency," says Lindfors. "The sidetracks, overlaps and disciplinary asides are all there." Paley, though, follows the idea of the child, cuts out some of the interruptions, and does not see fit to squib in every last 'Hmm.'

"A researcher gets it down like a photograph; hers is like a painting," says Lindfors, asserting there's nothing dishonest about Paley's "cleaned-up versions" of the script.

And just who is this schoolteacher who has been likened to an anthropologist, armed with her trusty tape recorder (its red "record" button pushed so many times it now dangles from its case), hunkering down with a tribe called Kindergartners, sending out jottings on the heretofore uncharted rites, rituals and beliefs of this naive and as yet unharnessed civilization?

If you'd wanted to catch Paley on her way into the classroom, you'd better have climbed the stairs and rounded the corner by 7:30 a.m. sharp in the Lab Schools' Emmons Blain Hall, a graceful Gothic building looking down on the Midway Plaisance. That's the precise time you'd have bumped into Paley, her beloved husband, Irving, and their yellow Labrador, Cass, bustling in from the daily constitutional that took them first past the neighborhood newsstand and then straight toward Room 284.

Ever since Irving, 70, retired six years ago from the Museum of Science and Industry, where he lived out his "p.r. dream" as head of its public relations department, he had insisted on walking Paley to school each morning and being the one to take down the classroom chairs, worried that his wife of 47 years might wrench her back with all that lifting.

Huffing behind Paley as she cranked into full classroom gear—she'd darted to the sand table, the cubby holes and back to the bookshelves before you could get to the sand table—you wouldn't guess that chiropractic concerns ever crossed her mind.

Nor would you guess that this was the schoolteacher called to Capitol Hill in June of 1994, invited by Sen. Paul Simon to testify at a Senate subcommittee hearing on hate crimes. Paley's name was on a short list that included Hollywood's Steven Spielberg. ("Spielberg had the cameras, she had the credibility," said Sara Bullard of the Southern Poverty Law Center, in Montgomery, Ala., who also was among those testifying in the Senate chambers.)

Paley, known among educators world-wide for her work on the subject, laid out for the senators the social experiment she undertook in her kindergarten to abolish that human foible she says is "older than the Bible"—life's first hate crime, perhaps—the inclination to taunt: "You can't play with us, sit with us, walk with us or join our teams."

The schoolteacher told the senators: "The habit of believing one has the right to demean another classmate publicly can be replaced by an equally powerful notion that everyone owns the classroom in exactly the same way—if we begin early enough without ambivalence."

Paley in person couldn't be more unpretentious. She slops through playground puddles wearing see-through galoshes she calls her "old lady rubbers." She writes in a left-handed scrawl that could be mistaken for a child's. She lays out her lunch—cellophane-wrapped cheese on little rye rolls, a Granny Smith apple, skim milk poured from its little carton into an even littler plastic cup—on a brown paper towel, just like the little people unloading their Lion King lunch boxes all around her. She is forever chasing Snowball, the mischievous white rabbit, lunging boldly for the scruff of his neck, in hopes of staving off his final great escape. And she can't help but chuckle sometimes at the silly rabbit's tricks.

This, the class that would be Paley's last, is a polyglot group from China, Cuba, India, Italy, Mexico, Russia and Scotland, as well as Chicago's Hyde Park—the sons and daughters of a used-car parts salesman, a jeweler, three doctors, a court reporter, a nurse, a recycler, a couple of social workers and the usual smattering of attorneys and academics (this being a neighborhood thick with Ph.D.'s). And many of those parents had to fork over the kindergarten's eye-popping tuition of $7,278 per year (scholarships and tuition breaks for university faculty and staff bring down some bills.)

But, when Paley is talking to the children, no notice is taken of any ethnic or economic difference. There is on her face only the seriousness that heralds her regard for each and every child. She is really, really listening, straining to hear even what they do not say and how they say it all.

It is as in her writing. "Once you've seen the children through her eyes, once you've been given glimpses of the richness of their lives," says Becky New, education professor and coordinator of the graduate program in early childhood education at the University of New Hampshire, "they can't ever again be reduced to ciphers on a screen. They're not just cute or problematic."

To the mother of one of the 21 children in this, Paley's last class, that is the blessing that made it not quite so wrenching to leave her little girl at the kindergarten door. "My daughter is learning how to navigate life outside the home with this extraordinary navigator and friend."

A nd this is how that navigator, that friend, that scribe of the kindergarten class, has come to map the mind of the 5- or the 6-year-old child:

"Well," she begins in her gravelly voice one spring afternoon, sitting in the sun-drenched den that doubles as her home office, a thermos of decaf coffee within easy reach, "the kindergarten child is first of all filled with lots and lots of stories. There's a continually running internal monologue, which then goes public and has to learn to accommodate to a lot of other people's internal monologues that have gone public. Because, beginning around the kindergarten year, the need to make a friend is so strong that the closer you come to joining your internal stories to their internal stories, you are learning how to create social play.

"The young child wants to play. He wants to play because intuitively he understands that through play he will understand more about who he is than in any other format.

"What else is on a child's mind? Loneliness for his family. The pangs of separation are there, but he is quick to accept a substitute adult who is there for him. The child must really have adults who care about him, are glad to see him, listen to his ideas, give him a hug, make him feel school is a good second place to home.

"What else? Of growing importance, the growing need to feel, 'I am an interesting person. I have interesting ideas. I can pretend things.'

"All of that. I mean this is a very, very lively mind," she says, pausing only for a second before rushing forth with another stream of thought.

"And of course, you have the child-the-philosopher. He's wondering about everything. All the while he's learning to sit in a group and have a discussion and listen to a story and all these things that are important as you begin kindergarten, first grade.

"Yes, this is a very, very busy person."

Time and again in talking to Paley's colleagues—the director of the Lab Schools, the lower school principal, the teachers who work by her side and the ones whose classrooms are down the hall—even to the students, now grown, who've been "Mrs. Paley's kindergarten kids," you hear this about how she comes to know so wholly the children's inner lives: Respect, profound respect, the kind a kid can tell is genuine right away and always.

"Everybody felt they were the greatest kids in the world," remembers Jason Tyler, now 24, and a credit analyst at the American National Bank after graduating from the Lab Schools and Princeton University.

For Tyler, an African-American from the far South Side who was stepping into the predominantly white, middle-class world of the Lab Schools, it was a particularly scary climb up the stairs that first morning of kindergarten, a day he still remembers in vivid detail. Paley swept him in from the start, he says, never batted an eye when there were rough spots. She made him feel proud of his skin color and his neighborhood, first of all simply acknowledging his differences, calling his blackness beautiful and nonchalantly asking about where he lived and wasn't it great that he lived outside Hyde Park.

"You don't necessarily want to have your greatest teachers in high school," Tyler says. "The most important thing is the second they walk in the door to have someone who will really impact the kids. She's the perfect person to have."

Beverly Biggs is now the lower school principal at the Lab

6. REFLECTIONS

Schools, but 15 years ago she was Paley's teaching assistant in a nursery school classroom. (Paley had asked to be transferred there for a year so she could learn the ways of the pre-kindergarten thinker. She stayed six years.)

Biggs offers this on her colleague: "She always has the most profound respect for kids. You can see it in every single exchange between her and the kids. When she is talking to them she is talking to just [one] child. Somehow she has antennae that know what the rest of the kids are doing. But she really is focusing on that one child most earnestly.

"That child knows from the way she's looking and listening and attending to him or her that what they're saying is very important. And that whatever they have expressed, she will respond, whether she needs to do something, talk to them, reassure them or empower them."

Watching Paley in her classroom, you see what Biggs is talking about a dozen different ways each day.

You see it when she won't let a music class begin because, en route down the stairs, someone pushed a little girl who then erupts in tears. "Mrs. Wang, excuse me, we have a very serious problem," she says, marching into the room where all but the little girl, who is sobbing at Paley's side, are gearing up to sing. "We can't have any happy singing," Paley says, because the little girl "feels terrible, and I just want to give her a moment to feel better."

And you see it on the way back from music class when, yet again, someone is pushed out of line. There is no scolding (unheard of in Paley's world view, where there is no punishment, only discussion, and certainly not a time-out chair, that latter-day incarnation of the old-fashioned "stand in the corner"). Instead, Paley stops the line and announces that the child pushed out "feels something very unfair has taken place." That's followed by an airing from both sides on what actually has occurred and then a most civilized discourse on what is fair.

Even the simplest infraction inside Paley's four walls becomes fodder for a fairness talk. Nothing is labeled good or bad, only fair or unfair, the lens through which Paley sees all.

Says Paley: "Any classroom—I know the kindergarten best—should develop into a close-knit community of people who care deeply about each other and show it in dozens of ways, who feel free to complain and argue about each other because there is no punishment. It is dialogue. We are attempting to understand why we do the things we do, what we enjoy doing, what other people do not enjoy when we do it. It is a place where ideas, learning how to communicate ideas and listen to the ideas of others, should be among the most exciting activities going on.

"And of course the teacher, above all, models all of this."

Above a dusty blue vinyl phonograph in the corner of Room 284 hangs a sign written in black marker: "You Can't Say You Can't Play." It's the No. 1 rule in Paley's classroom as well as the title of her seventh book, one in which she reported on the year she spent exploring the pain and loneliness of the child who's never asked to play, repeatedly pushed away from the group. That was the year, after much debate with children all the way up to 6th grade, she set down the rule she considers possibly her most lasting contribution to children's lives.

Here is some of that kindergarten debate:

Teacher: Should one child be allowed to keep another child from joining a group? A good rule might be: "You can't say you can't play."

Ben: If you cry people should let you in.

Teacher: What if someone is not crying but feels sad? Should the teacher force children to say yes?

Many voices: No, no.

Sheila: If they don't want you to play they should just go their own way and you should say, "Clara, let's find someone who likes you better."

Angelo: Lisa and her should let Clara in because they like Clara sometimes but not all the time so they should let her in.

A little later in the same debate:

Angelo: Let anybody play if someone asks.

Lisa: Then what's the whole point of playing?

Nelson: You just want Cynthia.

Lisa: I could play alone. Why can't Clare play alone?

Angelo: I think that's pretty sad. People that is alone they has water in their eyes.

Still stinging from the pain of all the children who ever "has water in their eyes," including the one she remembered from her own school days—an overweight girl who always wore the same dress, and was ridiculed by the teacher—Paley set down the rule. She concluded: "Each time a cause for sadness is removed for even one child, the classroom seems nicer. And, by association, we all rise in stature." And the results, even shortly after. "The children are learning that it is far easier to open the doors than to keep people out."

Four years after instituting the anti-rejection rule, Paley is more convinced than ever that the classroom is the laboratory for the moral life of the child: "This is the first place where the morality of life is examined by children, by the teacher, where one can begin to imagine a world that has more fairness, equality and compassion in it. You can do this in a classroom in a way that you really can't do it in the outside society."

As Paley writes and talks abut the "essential loneliness of the child," paying such painstaking attention to the child left out of play, you get the palpable sense she's been there. You're right.

It is stunning to come upon one particular disclosure while reading the works of the woman whose self is so consumed by kindergarten:

"To be accurate," she writes in the opening pages of "You Can't Say," "I didn't really attend kindergarten. Miss Estelle, the teacher, advised my mother to take me out and keep me at home until first grade. 'Your daughter just sits outside the circle and watches,' she said. Much later, when I asked my mother why she didn't insist that I remain and learn how to enter the magic circle, she shrugged. 'But that was the teacher telling me.' "

Paley never mentions that piece of her story in all the hours talk about kindergarten.

In fact, when asked about her first school memory she responds: "first, last and always, though I myself was not directly affected because I was always very well behaved, to the point of being somewhat shy and quiet, my memories of school were of teachers who were not very nice to a lot of children.

"I never discussed it with anyone—not even at home—but I can remember thinking that there were unnecessarily mean things that were done."

Home for Paley was on Division Street in Humboldt Park where she was one of three children born to Jewish immigrant parents, her father a proctologist—"the doctor in a prayer shawl," she recalls—her mother, now 94, a factory bookkeeper early on.

Theirs was a strictly observant Jewish home, and even today Paley and her husband keep a kosher kitchen, following a strict code of dietary laws. And now, as then, hers is a house filled with books. Shelves and shelves of them. Whole walls, in fact.

Paley remembers being drawn to the stories by Yiddish writers. "I read those stories at an early age and very, very often it was the odd person, the poor person, the cast-aside person who ends up in the role [of] 'best loved by God.' "

In her own growing-up story, Paley's natural-born introspection shadows every page. "I can remember at a very young age, a *very* young age, beginning to wonder if there was really a God. I'd never heard anyone ask that question. I wondered about it all the time and never asked anyone because I knew that it was not a question that was appropriate to ask.

"And I certainly did a lot of wondering about why teachers did what they did, why they behaved so unfairly in so many situations. I'd never talked to anyone about that either.

"I wondered everywhere. Sitting in the classroom, I did a lot of daydreaming."

Any wonder then that she should have found herself back in the classroom daydreaming in the late 1960s?

'This is the first place where the morality of life is examined by children, by the teacher, where one can begin to imagine a world that has more fairness, equality and compassion in it.'—Vivian Paley

---

She'd gotten into teaching she candidly admits because, "Ohhh, I couldn't think of anything else. Sad to say, I hadn't considered anything else either." And for the first 13 years that a bunch of kids called her "Teacher," she did her job the easy way. "I wanted to get through the day as quietly and quickly as possible." She followed the teacher's guides, passed out the mimeographed sheets, even had a time-out chair when it came into vogue.

But then, working on her master's degree in New York, Paley met Professor Piaget, first in textbooks, and once, in person, at a lecture. She was hooked. Here was this guy who didn't just look at kids through a glass wall, scribbling down mysterious notes. He actually talked to children, questioned them, listened to their thoughts, got them doing all sorts of experiments that showed how they processed ideas. And he didn't jump to conclusions.

Paley tried out Piaget's experiments in her own Long Island classroom. "I was generally beginning to find out what children are like. And little by little I began to listen to conversations that seemed so incredible, so fanciful, that it never occurred to me that children really believed in them."

Not long after that, Irving, who'd graduated from the U. of C., got an offer he wouldn't refuse from his alma mater's public information office. Back to Hyde Park moved the Paleys.

And the schoolteacher in the family settled into one of the kindergartens in the cavernous limestone edifice that houses the Lab Schools' lower school. Still longing for more meaning in her classroom, and beginning what she calls her "awakening," Paley audited a class, "Analysis of Teaching," taught by the esteemed educator Philip W. Jackson, who was then both director of the Lab Schools and dean of the university's graduate school of education.

Paley recalls: "I had *never* thought of myself as a writer. I never wrote so much as an interesting letter. I don't remember the assignment exactly, but I was to think back on the first time I *felt* like a teacher. Now I had been a teacher 13 years and for the very first time I sat myself down and went back in my memory—way, way back—to how I felt the very first time I somehow said to myself, 'I am a teacher.' " She turned in three or four pages.

"I got it back with a note, 'Vivian, see me after school.' He said, 'Look, you didn't follow the assignment, but you have a very interesting voice when you talk about yourself as a teacher.'

"I went home that night—[discovering that voice] had a magical effect—I started writing. It turned out to be 'White Teacher,' " Paley's first and still best selling book. Published in 1979, "White Teacher" examines the ways in which a child's differences—race, religion, even a stutter—are washed over, ignored, never addressed, leaving the child only to feel outcast for that which makes him or her unlike the others.

There've been seven books and some 640 children since then, the moment Paley realized she had, right there before her on the story rug, "an assemblage of truth-tellers" and that the "stuff of children's play is the original Great Books."

She quickly took the role of the ancient Greek chorus, repeating the children's words and phrases, keeping their plots on track. And whenever the Great Ideas of preschool or kindergarten—"birthdays, cooking and eating, going to bed, watching for bad guys, caring for babies," her partial list—were discussed, she would be their Socrates.

That is all over now, now that Paley has packed up her tape recorder and taken it home for the very last time.

But she promised to waste no time transcribing the last classroom voices on the solitary tape she allows herself. (A measure of her discipline: She'd buy only one tape at a time, forcing herself to play back, write down and ponder the previous day's recordings every morning at 4:30, putting in a good two hours' desk work before dawn.)

She would be at her desk the very next morning after the very last day, she vowed, penning the first pages of her ninth book, the one that will tie together all her years in the classroom, one that she "must do, emotionally, before I can go on."

And then, on this fine spring afternoon that was losing its light, the schoolroom philosopher drained the very bottom of her flowered-china coffee cup. She offered one last morsel, delivered with full Paley punch:

"I think about the classroom. I figure, 'What the heck, I don't have to think about everything.' How can I? I'll assume other people think about the other things."

"You in your classrooms," she says, her valedictory to the teachers she leaves behind, "are far more powerful to achieve moral changes than you think you are. You don't even need a new curriculum to do it. We have more of an opportunity to change the moral landscape of our little universe than the doctor does in the hospital, than the lawyer does in the court, than the reporter does on the newspaper, than the engineer does in the field.

"I mean, think about it. Twenty, thirty children. What a bonanza we have!"

She paused, only to gather gusto. "I'll miss it. I will miss the kinds of opportunities that come only in the classroom, I swear, and no place else on Earth. I feel sorry for people who work in offices."

And then the teacher rose. Class dismissed.

IT TAKES A SCHOOL

A new approach to elementary education starts at birth and doesn't stop when the bell rings

MARGOT HORNBLOWER NORFOLK

THE SIGN ON THE SQUAT BRICK schoolhouse in the midst of crime-ridden public-housing projects in Norfolk, Virginia, reads BOWLING PARK ELEMENTARY: A CARING COMMUNITY. Principal Herman Clark is one of those who does the caring, which is why every year he takes the parents of his pupils on a field trip to local attractions. One year it was to Greensville Correctional Center in Jarratt. "We got the chance to see the electric chair," he says. There have been visits to a prison in Chesapeake and a women's penal institution in Goochland. Two months ago, it was a walk through Death Row at Mecklenburg Correctional Center.

"The parents are subjected to a shakedown body search" for weapons or drugs, Clark says. "They hear the door slam. They look at the inmates and see the way the inmates look back at them. We ask the prisoners, 'Was there something that led you to this life?' They say, 'Yes, my parents were not there when I was a kid. There was nothing to do, so I did this or that [crime].' It is frightening. It makes our parents realize: this is where their child is heading." Every three years, Clark puts his pupils through a similar ordeal. "We target students who have the potential to get in trouble," he says. When a group of 26 returned from Deerfield Correctional Center, Clark says, "I was glad to see the bullies crying."

The shock treatment of the field trips is just one of many innovative therapies that Clark, a Ph.D. in education, has brought to

> **"Schools are being called on to be those 'surrogate parents' that can increase 'teachability.'"**

his school. Bowling Park is where the rhetoric of "standing for children" moves beyond talk. If children are to be rescued, the reasoning goes, who is better equipped to do so than the elementary school, a solid institution already in the business? Yet to rescue children, one must start early—even before birth. And to rescue children, whole families must be rescued along with them—hence the transformation of the neighborhood school into a "caring community." It may sound like a platitude, but it is in fact a revolution, one that is spreading through the country, from inner-city ghettos to prosperous suburbs and rural enclaves, as fast as you can say *ABC*.

One of the most far-reaching programs, which began in Missouri and has spread to 47 states, hires "parent educators" who offer parenting skills and developmental screening to families with young

children, beginning in the third trimester of pregnancy. Bowling Park's Michael Bailey, a soft-spoken Mister Rogers type, hands out flyers in food-stamp lines to encourage new mothers to sign up. Each day he drives out to visit one of the 35 families who have joined the program. "Hello, teacher!" shrieks Tonesha Sims, 2½, running out of her house to hug him on a recent morning. Bailey spends an hour reviewing colors and numbers with the pigtailed toddler. As Bailey leaves, Tonesha begs, "Teacher, can I play with you next week?" Lottie Holloman, 68, her great-grandmother—and her guardian since Tonesha's mother, a drug addict, abandoned the girl to foster care—credits Bailey with inspiring her to buy books and read to the child. Children in the program get priority for slots in Bowling Park's preschool.

By delving into the critical first three years of life, schools such as Bowling Park are expanding far beyond traditional academics. But to many educators it is a logical evolution. Moving away from a narrow focus on curriculum reform, some schools are assuming responsibility for the foundations of learning—the emotional and social well-being of the child from birth to age 12. Thus anything that affects a child is the school's business—from nutrition to drug-abuse prevention to health care and psychological counseling. "Schools are being called on to be those 'surrogate parents' that can increase the 'teachability' of children who arrive on their doorsteps in poor shape," according to Joy G.

Dryfoos, author of the 1994 book *Full-Service Schools.*

Bowling Park was chosen in 1992 as the site of the first CoZi school, a model that combines the education programs of two Yale professors, James P. Comer and Edward Zigler. Over the past three decades, Comer, a psychiatrist, has helped convert 600 mostly inner-city schools to a cooperative management in which parents, teachers and mental-health counselors jointly decide policy and focus on building close-knit relationships with children. Zigler, one of the founders of Head Start, designed "The School of the 21st Century," a program operating on 400 campuses, offering year-round, all-day preschool beginning at three, as well as before- and after-school and vacation programs. Bowling Park combines both approaches in what may be the nation's most comprehensive effort, as Zigler puts it, "[to] make the success of the child in every aspect of development our constant focus." Other CoZi schools are operating in Bridgeport, Connecticut, and in Mehlville, Missouri.

At Bowling Park staff members "adopt" a child; many take on several at a time. Often the child is one whose parent has died or gone to prison, or whose siblings are dealing drugs, or whose single mother neglects him. "We take these kids home with us for the weekend or out to eat or to get a haircut," says principal Clark. "School has to be about more than reading, writing and arithmetic. These kids need so much—and sometimes what they really need is a good hug."

In Clark's office the other day, Rashid Holbrook, 11, fidgeted with his wraparound shades and sought to explain why he had gone after a boy with an ax and spray painted a family's front steps. "I got a bad temper," he says. "When I get home at night, I pile up feelings." Rashid lives with an aunt who, Clark says, takes little interest in him. "My daddy's in prison," the boy says, showing little emotion. "He hit my momma. He went for breaking and entering and a hundred other charges." Interjects Clark: "But you're going in a different direction."

Rashid volunteers that he might be an engineer or a policeman. Why a policeman? "I don't like people doing things to other people," he says. And then after a long pause, "But I do it."

Rashid has been "adopted" by Clayton Singleton, 25, an art teacher. "We've been to art museums and shopping at the mall," says Singleton, pausing during a drawing class that sprawls over the floor of a corridor. "He was getting curious about the man-woman thing, so we had The Talk. Whatever questions he asked, he got the real answer." The talk was timely: only a few weeks before, Rashid had asked the

> **"We have fine buildings. Why let them sit vacant 14 hours a day and three months of the year?"**

daughter of another teacher if she wanted "to make a baby."

The key to Bowling Park's success, which has shown up in higher test scores and a 97% attendance rate, is getting parents into the school. Many of them had never bothered even to walk their first-graders to class. CoZi offers "parent technicians"—two in Bowling Park's case—to visit parents at home, ask them what they need and spur them to form committees and organize projects. Responding to parent feedback, Bowling Park now offers adult-education courses, adult-exercise classes, a once-a-month Family Breakfast Club at which parents talk about children's books, a singing group and a "room moms" program that puts parents into the classroom to help teachers. Parents also pressed the principal for school uniforms—and now help launder them. Bowling Park's programs are funded through a combination of federal funds set aside for inner-city schools, parent fees, private grants and school-district money.

"This is a holistic approach," says CoZi coordinator Lorraine Flood. "If parents are not sitting at the table, we don't find out the underlying reasons for children's academic or behavioral problems." When a mother of children at the school lost her husband to cancer recently, leaving her with six sons, parent technicians set up a workshop on grief. A welfare mother, who had put her child in foster care, found her self-confidence so built up by parenting and adult-education classes and her service in the PTA that she recovered her daughter and got a secretarial job. Recently parent techs held a wedding reception at the school for a mother who finally got married. A grandfather, inspired by a writing workshop, reads his poems at school functions.

But the lessons of Bowling Park, where the student body is overwhelmingly black and low income, are not just for schools that serve the poor. In fact, Zigler's concept of expanding school into a full-day, year-round enterprise is equally crucial to middle-class parents at Sycamore Hills Elementary School in Independence,

Missouri, where students are mostly white.

In Independence all 13 elementary schools work on the 21st Century model. Thirty-five percent of new parents take advantage of the state-funded home-visit program for children younger than age three. "We have fine buildings. Why let them sit vacant 14 hours a day and three months of the year?" says superintendent Robert Watkins. "Now we can see a child with a speech impediment at age three and get started on remediation."

Once start-up costs were absorbed for remodeling school basements or buying modular units, the preschool and after-school day care became mostly self-supporting: 85% of the $2 million program comes from parents' fees. "Schools should be a community hub," says fourth-grade teacher Darlene Shaw. In three decades at Sycamore Hills, she has witnessed profound change. "Out of my 23 students today, only one has a stay-at-home mom," she said. "Without consistent, quality day care, kids flounder. And for kids dealing with divorce and single-parent families, school is their stability when things are going crazy at home."

Nicole Argo, one of Shaw's fourth-graders, has tried riding the bus home after school at 3:15 p.m. But she found she would rather stay in Sycamore's after-school program. "It's boring to watch TV at home," she says. "At 21st Century you do projects and go places." So Nicole's parents—an engineer and a human-resources officer—pick her up after work at 4:30—along with her five-year-old sister Amanda—and drop them both off each morning at 6:30, more than an hour before school begins. Nearly a third of Independence's students have a similar 10-hour day on campus. "It's Bobby's second home," says Laurie French, the divorced mother of a nine-year-old with muscular dystrophy. "The staff is like family, and since Bobby was three, we've done a pretty good job raising him together." Although he walks with difficulty, Bobby takes karate lessons in the program. And lately his favorite activity has been crochet, taught at the day-care center by a volunteer grandmother.

Independence and Norfolk have not experienced opposition to their reforms, but that does not mean every school district is ready for change. Overcrowded classrooms, pinched budgets and teachers set in their ways are only a few of the obstacles. Julia Denes, assistant director of Yale's Bush Center of Child Development and Social Policy, warns, however, that not adopting CoZi-like programs will ultimately cost more. "We must invest in children at an early age to prevent special needs and delinquency," she says. That's the message too of principal Clark's field trips.

Index

Credits/Acknowledgments

Cover design by Charles Vitelli

1. Perspectives
Facing overview—United Nations photo by Jan Corash.

2. Child Development and Families
Facing overview—Photo courtesy of Louis P. Raucci.

3. Educational Practices
Facing overview—Photo courtesy of Sally Morrison.

4. Guiding and Supporting Young Children
Facing overview—EPA Documerica photo.

5. Curricular Issues
Facing overview—United Nations photo by John Isaac.

6. Reflections
Facing overview—New York Times Pictures photo by Steve Miller.

ANNUAL EDITIONS ARTICLE REVIEW FORM

■ NAME: _____ DATE: _____

■ TITLE AND NUMBER OF ARTICLE: _____

■ BRIEFLY STATE THE MAIN IDEA OF THIS ARTICLE: _____

_____

■ LIST·THREE IMPORTANT FACTS THAT THE AUTHOR USES TO SUPPORT THE MAIN IDEA:

_____

_____

_____

_____

_____

■ WHAT INFORMATION OR IDEAS DISCUSSED IN THIS ARTICLE ARE ALSO DISCUSSED IN YOUR TEXTBOOK OR OTHER READINGS THAT YOU HAVE DONE? LIST THE TEXTBOOK CHAPTERS AND PAGE NUMBERS:

_____

_____

_____

_____

_____

■ LIST ANY EXAMPLES OF BIAS OR FAULTY REASONING THAT YOU FOUND IN THE ARTICLE:

_____

_____

_____

_____

_____

■ LIST ANY NEW TERMS/CONCEPTS THAT WERE DISCUSSED IN THE ARTICLE, AND WRITE A SHORT DEFINITION:

_____

_____

_____

_____

_____

We Want Your Advice

ANNUAL EDITIONS revisions depend on two major opinion sources: one is our Advisory Board, listed in the front of this volume, which works with us in scanning the thousands of articles published in the public press each year; the other is you—the person actually using the book. Please help us and the users of the next edition by completing the prepaid article rating form on this page and returning it to us. Thank you for your help!

ANNUAL EDITIONS: EARLY CHILDHOOD EDUCATION 97/98
Article Rating Form

Here is an opportunity for you to have direct input into the next revision of this volume. We would like you to rate each of the 44 articles listed below, using the following scale:

1. **Excellent: should definitely be retained**
2. **Above average: should probably be retained**
3. **Below average: should probably be deleted**
4. **Poor: should definitely be deleted**

Your ratings will play a vital part in the next revision. So please mail this prepaid form to us just as soon as you complete it.
Thanks for your help!

Rating	Article	Rating	Article
	1. Changing Demographics: Past and Future Demands for Early Childhood Programs		24. Breaking the Cycle of Violence
	2. The Next Baby Boom		25. Taking Positive Steps toward Classroom Management in Preschool: Loosening Up without Letting It All Fall Apart
	3. "Fly Till I Die"		
	4. The National Television Violence Study: Key Findings and Recommendations		26. The Caring Classroom's Academic Edge
			27. Misbehavior or Mistaken Behavior?
	5. It's Hard to Do Day Care Right—and Survive		28. Building Successful Home/School Partnerships
	6. NAEYC Position Statement: Technology and Young Children—Ages Three through Eight		29. Voice of Inquiry: Possibilities and Perspectives
			30. Project Work with Diverse Students: Adapting Curriculum Based on the Reggio Emilia Approach
	7. Educational Implications of Developmental Transitions: Revisiting the 5- to 7-Year Shift		
			31. To Build a House: Designing Curriculum for Primary-Grade Children
	8. Your Child's Brain		
	9. Labeled for Life?		32. Teachers and Children Together: Constructing New Learning
	10. Creativity and the Child's Social Development		
	11. Families and Schools: Building Multicultural Values Together		33. 10 Ways to Improve Your Theme Teaching
			34. The Worksheet Dilemma: Benefits of Play-Based Curricula
	12. Life without Father		
	13. Bridging Home and School through Multiple Intelligences		35. A Framework for Literacy
			36. Read Me a Story: 101 Good Books Kids Will Love
	14. Understanding through Play		37. Interactive Writing in a Primary Classroom
	15. Bringing the DAP Message to Kindergarten and Primary Teachers		38. How Good Is Your Early Childhood Science, Mathematics, and Technology Program? Strategies for Extending Your Curriculum
	16. Fourth-Grade Slump: The Cause and Cure		
	17. Strategies for Teaching Children in Multiage Classrooms		
	18. Preschool Integration: Strategies for Teachers		39. Where Are the Good Old Days?
	19. Nurturing Kids': Seven Ways of Being Smart		40. Sisterhood and Sentimentality—America's Earliest Preschool Centers
	20. A Profile of Every Child		
	21. Your Learning Environment: A Look Back at Your Year		41. The Movers and Shapers of Early Childhood Education
	22. Helping Children Become More Prosocial: Ideas for Classrooms, Families, Schools, and Communities		42. Child Advocacy Directory
			43. Mrs. Paley's Lessons
	23. Encouraging Positive Social Development in Young Children		44. It Takes a School

(Continued on next page)

ABOUT YOU

Name _____ Date _____

Are you a teacher? ❏ Or a student? ❏

Your school name _____

Department _____

Address _____

City _____ State _____ Zip _____

School telephone # _____

YOUR COMMENTS ARE IMPORTANT TO US!

Please fill in the following information:

For which course did you use this book? _____

Did you use a text with this *ANNUAL EDITION*? ❏ yes ❏ no

What was the title of the text? _____

What are your general reactions to the *Annual Editions* concept?

Have you read any particular articles recently that you think should be included in the next edition?

Are there any articles you feel should be replaced in the next edition? Why?

Are there any World Wide Web sites you feel should be included in the next edition? Please annotate.

May we contact you for editorial input?

May we quote your comments?

ANNUAL EDITIONS: EARLY CHILDHOOD EDUCATION 97/98